Critical Essays on
Jean-Paul Sartre

Critical Essays on
World Literature

Robert Lecker, General Editor
McGill University

Critical Essays on Jean-Paul Sartre

Robert Wilcocks

G. K. Hall & Co. • Boston, Massachusetts

Library of Congress Cataloging in Publication Data

(Critical essays on world literature)
"Selected bibliography of books in English on Jean-Paul Sartre": p.
Includes index.
1.Sartre, Jean Paul, 1905– —Criticism and interpretation. I.
Wilcocks, Robert. II. Series.
PQ2637.A82Z634   1988   848'.91409   87-24879
ISBN 0-8161-8839-4 (alk. paper)

This publication is printed on permanent/durable acid-free paper
MANUFACTURED IN THE UNITED STATES OF AMERICA

for Geneviève Idt

CONTENTS

INTRODUCTION

A Quasimodo of matter, with an enormous torso buckled into ropelike
muscles, I see his lantern jaw, his acrobat's arms, his terrifying agility, I
see him sliding from a skylight, hanging on to the gutter by his fingers,
pressing the flesh of his face against a sordid window-pane, I see him,
half-man, half-monster, all biceps and brain, sniffing everywhere the
strongest human odors and reigning over a world of dark shadows
peopled with shapeless masses, kneading with his hands the very paste
of things.[1]

Such was the bourgeois nightmare that Sartre had become for many
some forty years ago when Pierre Brisson, then director of *Le Figaro*,
crafted this bravura passage into an article ostensibly on Sartre's play
about the French Resistance, *Morts sans sépulture* (*Men without
Shadows*). Brisson's high-voltage gothic imagination certainly reflected a
popular response to Sartre in 1947 and one that, in many respects, he was
doomed to live with until his death in 1980.

The choice of Quasimodo, indicative of Brisson's reading habits and
of his sensitivity to those nineteenth-century literary figures who had
passed into the cultural myths of popular imagination, was also, of course,
determined by Sartre's dwarfish stature and his propensity for causing
discomfort to the various bourgeois hierarchies of his times. But the choice
also has a certain romantic accuracy to it. Quasimodo was not a villain,
after all — just a deformed monster. If the creature's heart contained
vitriol, it also contained gold or a memory of it.

I have not asked Michel Contat whether he discovered during his
many tête-à-têtes with Sartre what the latter thought of Brisson's article
which he had probably read. I suspect that Sartre's response to Brisson
may have been a wry appreciation tinged perhaps with that melancholy
which intrudes when one knows that another is right for the wrong
reasons. Monsters, in one form or another, were the leitmotiv of Sartre's
writings. Even without considering the film script, *Le scénario Freud*,
which John Huston had commissioned from him in 1958,[2] Sartre may well
be thought of as the Freud of the existentialist movement. The interests
and the influence of both men ranged far beyond the original narrow

confines of their early research disciplines (neuroanatomy and Husserlian phenomenology, respectively). Freud, it is true, generally abstained from the cut and thrust of politics, national or international; whereas Sartre (after, as he claimed, the experience of "radical conversion" in the prison camp Stalag XIID) entered this arena with gladiatorial zest, brandishing his polemical verve in the face of former friends and newly recognized enemies.

But it was not this aspect of Sartre's later notoriety (which gave rise to editorials like the one in *Paris-Match* with the headline: "Sartre: Une machine à guerre civile")[3] that disturbed the complacencies of Brisson and his contemporaries. It was precisely, as was the case with the furor that surrounded some of Freud's publications, the depth and the explicitness of his probings of the sexual and emotional entanglements of human beings often in a situation of perversion (or at least of perversity) and nearly always with a rhetorical force that was later to be directed toward political targets. Nor, again as with Freud, were the descriptions limited to those of physically expressed encounters with others. The imagination, which for Sartre was both a curse and the core of human possibilities, was ruthlessly examined for its production of sexual fantasies. The masturbatory hallucinations of Roquentin or Genet or, later, Flaubert are described with such literary persuasiveness that the reader is left in a state of vicarious arousal or vicarious disgust. Indifference before such passages, however desirable it may be felt to be, is virtually impossible. And such is the insidious strength of the writing that a desire to experience indifference becomes itself suspect and the reader is led to question, to challenge, those regions of the psyche normally left undisturbed, even by the self-reflecting consciousness. A monster looms on the periphery of the inner eye: ourselves. As Frantz declares posthumously on the tape recorder at the end of *Les Séquestrés d'Altona*: "One and one make one, that's our mystery." He continues: "The beast was hiding. All of a sudden we caught its glance in the intimate eyes of our fellow creatures; so we struck: legitimate self-defense. I surprised the beast. I struck. A man fell. In his dying eyes I saw the beast, still alive. Me." (Act 5, Sc. 3).

The confused, murderous intensity that Frantz experienced, and glimpsed, has nothing to do with sexual fantasy or what Freud would have called "displacement of libido."[4] And whatever monstrosities may occur in Frantz's experience, and expression, of his sexuality, they are not, for Sartre, the consequence of damage to his libidinal development; they are, rather, a "chosen" expression of his total being. In this respect, and unlike Freud, Sartre attempted to situate sexuality within a philosophical description of man (which is what phenomenology is); he refused to see philosophy as some sublimated manifestation of libido. Even toward the end of his life, as for example in the interview with Michel Sicard,[5] he was highly critical of what he saw as the simplifications inherent in the Freudian hypotheses on sexual sublimation. His studies as a young man of

Karl Jaspers's *Allgemeine Psychopathologie* (*General Psychopathology*) no doubt contributed to his skeptical attitude toward Freud's pansexualism. Furthermore, also in contradistinction to Freud, he never appears to have given some kind of moral "imprimatur" to procreative genital coupling. The strain of Judaeo-Catholic teleology that runs implicitly through the canon of Freud's writings is absent in Sartre. This made his own frank investigations of the world of fantasy and of sexuality the more outrageous.

He did not deny that sexual energies could be displaced — in sadism, in authoritarianism, in acts of judgment and condemnation[6] — indeed, much of his early explicit material is concerned precisely with this (in the philosophical writings as much as in the fiction). But what interested him was to discover the meaning such displacement had for the person within a specific situation. Jaspers distinguishes between *erklärende Psychologie* (broadly speaking, explanatory psychology going from necessary cause to necessary effect)[7] and *verstehende Psychologie* (a nondeterminist approach that tries to comprehend the meaningful unity of the individual). Sartre, who refers to this distinction in *Cahiers pour une morale*[8] opts for a *verstehende* approach that will grasp the individual discovering himself within a dialectical framework that includes his projects (and his understanding of them) as well as his formative past experiences. For Sartre, the formative past is not a block of repressed traumatic memories with a "once and for all" given significance; it is a constantly shifting set of values and lived or imagined experiences whose significance changes with the determining project in the present.

This leads me to one of the biggest confusions — one among many — perpetrated by Simone de Beauvoir. Her suggestion that Sartre's concept of "bad faith" was a kind of substitute-replacement for Freud's "unconscious" had led many people to "decode" *Being and Nothingness* in the light of this and to forget the crucial *philosophical* dimension of Sartre's description of human activities. Even the Jungian concepts of the "shadow" or the "anima" are not helpful here. To try to read Sartre through the veil of Freud or Jung is like trying to decipher a Braille text with a knowledge of the Morse Code. There are indeed dots in both systems; but they do not — they cannot — correspond.

One has to read Sartre's philosophy on its own terms. This means with an awareness of the German philosophers Kant, Hegel, Husserl, Jaspers, and Heidegger by whom he was undoubtedly influenced and with whom he engaged in a lifelong public philosophic debate. Heidegger's *Sein und Zeit* (*Being and Time*) was a crucial discovery for the Sartre who was to write *Being and Nothingness*, and his descriptions of modes of being owes much to his reading of Heidegger. There was, however, an important difference between the philosophies of the two men; where Heidegger was abstract and academic, Sartre, whatever abstractions he used, was determined to bring concrete (one might almost say clinical) human situations within the purview of philosophical speculation. As Gerald N. Izenberg points out in his admirable *The Existentialist Critique of Freud*: "Unlike Heidegger, however, Sartre was deeply interested in psychology from the beginning. He rejected Heidegger's absolute distinction between the empirical or 'ontic' realm and the ontological realm; it was *through* men's concrete interests, activities, perceptions, and passions that the quest for being took place. Thus for example, Sartre criticized Heidegger for paying no attention to human sexuality."[9] Such was this interest in psychology, especially that of extreme situations (what Jaspers had called *Grenzsituationen*), that the fiction published before *Being and Nothingness* — the five short stories collected in *Le Mur*, entitled *Intimacy* in English, and his first and greatest novel *La Nausée* (*Nausea*) — dealt almost exclusively with aspects of abnormal psychology.

The powerful descriptions of various states of madness and the attempts in *Being and Nothingness* to examine their structures and meanings (leading Hazel Barnes to write in her Translator's Introduction: "Sartre even speaks longingly of the need for an existential Freud")[10] may be read now, with our hindsight knowledge of *Les Mots* (*The Words*) and *L'Idiot de la famille* (*The Family Idiot*), in an enterprise of intertextuality that may allow us a better appreciation of the writings and of the man who wrote them than was available to his first readers. If, as I have said, monsters, in one form or another, were the leitmotiv of Sartre's writings, the first monster of them all, the theatrical and duplicitous Poulou, lurked knowingly and known within the consciousness of the craftsman lovingly (obsessively?) carving his image into the consciousness of the readers of fiction and philosophy.

Freud's crisis in his early years of maturity,[11] which was, significantly, the period chosen by Sartre to situate the Huston film script, led, as we know, to the painful exploratory descent into the inferno of those unconscious conflicts surviving from childhood which, according to his hypotheses, were liable to wreak havoc on the adult. The courage of Freud's self-analysis (however critically we assess the conclusions he drew from the experience) is not to be denied. In fact, his knowledge of that very courage may have given him the strength for the resilience he showed in later years when his theories were contested even by his followers. That Sartre was aware of this and responded positively to it should be evident to anyone who reads the film script. From his earliest writings there is every indication that Sartre felt and responded to the urgency of the autobiographical imperative. Even before his own circus animals were fully trained for public presentation he could have written, with Yeats, "I must go down to where all the ladders start / In the foul rag-and-bone shop of the heart." The nuance that distinguishes the Freudian descent from the Yeatsian one is important. In none of the Sartrean autobiographical writings (with the exception of the recently published correspondence with Simone de Beauvoir)[12] is there explicit reference to his sexual evolution;[13] there is, on the other hand, an overwhelming significance attached to his affective states, in relation to himself and to others, and to the theatricality of their expression and, frequently, of their composition. Where for Freud aspects of incestuous sexuality were the prime mover of the human condition, for Sartre it was the dramatization of the self in the presence of the Other (or in the interiorized and imagined presence of the Other).

Hence the fundamental theatricality of Sartre's human world: against this, against himself (one might almost say), the lifelong search for the twin virtues of lucidity and authenticity. The two did not necessarily go together. One has only to think of characters like the lesbian Inès of *Huis clos* (*No Exit*), by far the most frighteningly lucid of the infernal trio (Inès, Garcin, Estelle), or the post-hoc lucidity accorded by the autobiographic Sartre to the young Poulou, or Frantz, his last major stage representation of madness, to recognize that while various states of alienation may produced lucidity,[14] they rarely combine with that intransigent authenticity that Sartre claimed to pursue.

In the terms that he allowed himself the quest was tragically blocked. In relationships with the self or, on an intimate or social — but not yet political — level, with others, a growth in lucidity was accompanied by a corresponding awareness of the artifice at the heart of human existence. The play *Kean*, adapted in 1953 for the great French actor Pierre Brasseur from the romantic melodrama signed by Alexandre Dumas, père, provides perhaps the most accessible Sartrean text on this theme. In the opinions of C. R. Bukala and Catharine S. Brosman (writing from very different perspectives), the work is not merely an enjoyable theatrical tour de force, it is also a profound meditation on the dilemmas of selfhood, albeit in a comic vein. The fairground hall of distorting mirrors in which Jean Genet's accomplice Stilitano found himself trapped would be an appropriate allegory for Sartre's conception of the ego. In this respect one can understand Sartre's quasi-metaphysical need to insist — as he did even in old age — that the ego was exterior to pure consciousness. Jacques Lacan's much disputed theories about the realm of the Imaginary, which owe much (and the debt is frequently acknowledged by him) to his readings of Sartre, are more comprehensible when seen in the light of this philosophical source, though probably no more palatable.

In his program notes to the Paris premiere of *Kean*, Sartre, evoking the great actors of the past who had incarnated the leading role in the Dumas version, wrote, "they came to speak to the public about their art, about their private life, about their difficulties and their misfortunes, but according to the rules of their craft: with discretion and with delicacy, that is to say by slipping into the skin of another." When one looks at the corpus of descriptive analysis that Sartre devoted to the lives of others — Baudelaire, Genet, Flaubert (and even Mallarmé and Tintoretto) — one understands that he has applied this "rule of the craft" to himself. Even in

The Words it is a former, distant self—the self of the child who was still Poulou and not yet J.-P. Sartre—that is investigated. Through his studies "in the skin of another" one can begin to assemble a composite picture of Sartre himself. In a way he *was* Baudelaire or Genet or Flaubert, and in those passionate and analytical studies one can trace the outline and perceive some of the depth of the man who wrote them. Sartre himself was most explicit about the "magic" of what I would call this identificatory dialectic in his densely argued address to UNESCO in 1966 celebrating Soeren Kierkegaard.[15]

It is in *The Words*, the greatest of his "fictions" after *Nausea*, that Sartre comes closest to the contemporaneous writing self. It is significant that in this work there is little reference to the political commitment that was to mark so much of the last forty years of his life. Sartre's incursions into the polemics of politics were, in a sense, as much adventures as his inventions as a writer of fiction. They were "adventures" as Roquentin understood the term and, as such, were inauthentic except as Art.

In *L'Imaginaire*, written before World War II, Sartre had elaborated a theory of *analoga* wherein the imagined or aestheticized representation of a given reality would take the place in the imagining mind of the concrete situation experienced.[16] In politics these *analoga*, the imagined freedom of speech in Stalinist Russia, the imagined virtues of the proletariat, the imagined fraternity of the "Third World" (which phrase itself is a mischievous example of a journalistic *analogon*), inspired a veritable fireworks display of literary rhetoric. Was the writer deceived by his writing ("inebriated with the exuberance of his own verbosity," as Disraeli claimed of Gladstone), or the thinker by his ingenious thoughts? It is difficult now, with the substantial record of blindness recorded in carefully documented works like David Caute's *The Fellow-Travellers*,[17] to understand how an intellectual of Sartre's evident lucidity and commitment could so deceive himself and for so long, and—it must be said—so brilliantly. The "providential enemy," which was how the Catholic novelist François Mauriac once described Sartre, was, for the latter, the glib, capitalist bourgeoisie that appeared to rule France and the Western world. The "salauds" had already been denounced in *Nausea* and *The Roads to Freedom*; but they remained in Sartre's heated imagination the enemies of mankind. Their opponents, by a twist of logic that was neither necessary (in the Russellian sense) nor inevitable (in the Hegelian sense), became the implacable heroes whose cause was the future of mankind.

Michel-Antoine Burnier, in a cruel parody of the ironic persiflage of *The Words*, has written *Le Testament de Sartre*.[18] Inspired by an off-the-cuff conversational remark by Sartre—"One day I will write a kind of political testament. . . . I will reveal what I have really thought and what I think now, in retrospect. I know some who will grind their teeth: me, to begin with"[19]—Burnier has created a new kind of pastiche. Stylistically, it has the qualities of willful simplicity and balanced paradox of *The Words*;

at the same time, it is an accurate and amply documented account (frequently in Sartre's own words) of those postwar political peregrinations that were so often the despair of Sartre's more thoughtful admirers. In the introduction Burnier quotes one of Sartre's replies to him in the interview (reprinted here) on French Maoism that criticizes the "moderation" of the Terror of 1793: "The revolutionaries of 1793 probably did not kill enough and therefore unintentionally served the return to order and then the Restoration." Burnier, an enthusiast of Sartre's literary genius, was disturbed by the radical viciousness of the answers Sartre gave to him in the interview on Maoism. It is possible that *Le Testament de Sartre* was also conceived as an elegant revenge for this deception.

Sartre's Marxism, prior to the flirtation with the Maoists, shared, as Thomas R. Flynn suggests, the ethical concern that was implicit in *Being and Nothingness*. It had evolved during the years when he was compiling notes for the unfinished *Morale*. There seem to be three distinct tributaries that emerge into the stream of political thought from the late forties on. In the first instance, for all his blind spots, Sartre was capable of acute political analysis and, during the long Cold War period, focused his critical attention on the contradictions coming from the Left as much as from the Right (one tends to forget that he was for years vilified by various communist parties as a "capitalist hyena"). Second, his readings of Marx and Engels nourished an obscure desire to "philosophize" the political situations in which he found himself[20] and to analyze from this new perspective key moments of the French Revolution (it would make an instructive study to contrast Lefebvre, Camus — in *The Rebel* — and Sartre — in the *Critique* — on 1793). Third, the infusion of a kind of Marxism into the individualist revolt of the existentialist period helped to broaden, or legitimize, in a theoretical way, the visceral and, in effect romantic, revolt against his mother's, his stepfather's, his grandfather's, and, hence, his own class: the bourgeoisie. A psycho- and politico-analytical reading of *Les Mouches* (*The Flies*) would show that the germs of such reaction were already being cultivated by Sartre as early as 1943. It was probably this last factor more than anything that accounts for the glee with which he greeted May 1968 and for his later involvement with some of the Maoist groupuscules in France. Nonetheless, as important and headline-making as his political interventions were, Sartre remained deaf to the siren call to abandon the Flaubert and to write socialist realism (one of the rare moments in *On a raison de se révolter* where the mask of the bourgeois-intellectual scapegoat slips, and one sees the "real" Sartre). His fidelity to his craft and to the phenomenological investigation of the world of creation and imagination defeated in the long run the promiscuous temptations of suspect solidarity.

Freud once complained in a letter to Fliess that he was beginning to sound like Humboldt's parrot (unintelligible to any but himself). This was a risk that Sartre frequently ran, both in the broad sense of the intelligibility of his political actions and choices and, in the narrow sense, in his use of the French language—in particular, but not only, in *Being and Nothingness* and the *Critique of Dialectical Reason*. His efforts to forge the sinews of French grammar and syntax into the linguistic density of thoughts hammered out in the smithies of Jena and Freiburg led, not infrequently, to the Humboldt's parrot syndrome.

The ironic farewell to literature that *The Words* pretended to be marked a return to precision, clarity, and a dancing virtuosity with the French language and the classically ironic sense of self portrayed therein. This was, *mutatis mutandis*, to be the style largely chosen for the unfinished farewell of the three-volume *Idiot de la famille*. It was as if the exercise of *The Words* had refreshed his linguistic and imaginative powers and allowed him those wings of inspiration denied to Flaubert's parrot (which, one recalls, was stuffed) except in the hallucination of Félicité's dying vision. It is a return by a writer whose strength was the exploration and description of inner worlds to the compound enterprise of biography and displaced autobiography. Its very length has been seen as a lack of reciprocity toward the reader. Ronald Aronson concludes, "Jean-Paul Sartre has written a book nobody will read." My own feeling is that the Flaubert will be read with more pleasure, more passion, and more empathy (for Flaubert and for Sartre) than many of the far shorter political diatribes that so provoked Sartre's contemporaries and which nowadays are read—if they are read—as a grudging exercise in sociopolitical history. The Flaubert, on the other hand, has pleasures for the responsive reader on almost every page.

The solitary imaginary that was Gustave Flaubert, surely one of the greatest prose masters of the nineteenth century, was the perfect foil for the mature Sartre. The man who wanted to move the stars to pity but who recognized the limits of human art—"tunes for bears to dance to"—certainly had a sense of the tragic absolute that the artist in Sartre could appreciate. His rejection of his world and his brilliant creation through that rejection and through his genius of the imaginary worlds of *Salammbô*, *L'Éducation sentimentale*, and *Madame Bovary*, and even of the anguished comic elegance of *Bouvard et Pécuchet*, find an echo in the revealing narrative of Poulou's attempts with his mother to join the real world of other children in the Jardins du Luxembourg: "She would take my hand and we would go off again, we went from tree to tree and from group to group, always imploring, always excluded. At dusk I would be back on my perch on those high places where the spirit whispered, my dreams: I would take revenge for my mortifications by six childish words and the massacre of a hundred mercenaries."

The selection of the essays for this volume has been extraordinarily difficult. Four general considerations (apart from the evident one of space) have led to my choice of the material included here.

The most important task was to produce a volume that would possess, in spite of its anthological nature, its own inner coherence, a certain self-sufficiency, a certain structure that would give a sense of nonlinear progression to those aspects of Sartre's activities studied here. I wanted to achieve the effect of an "exploration en spirale" of Sartre. This is one reason for the inclusion of so many different approaches to his densest fiction *Nausea*, and for the inclusion, as a kind of coda or stretto to the fiction section, of Jane Tompkins's essay on *The Words*. It is also the guiding principle behind the unusual concentration on *Kean* in the theater section and for the decision to end that section, and the book, with an essay on what Jeremy Palmer calls "Sartre's least accessible play" where the themes of the self, of madness, of Sartre's politics, and of *our* politics come together.

The second consideration was both commercial and intellectual. There are two fine collections of critical essays on Sartre currently available: the Twentieth Century Views anthology edited by Edith Kern,[21] which has been on the market for a quarter of a century, and Mary Warnock's *Sartre*,[22] which first appeared in 1971. Their choice of material was sufficiently strong to make both these books still well worthwhile consulting. This volume should be seen not so much as a replacement of them, but rather as a valuable addition to them. With the exception of the late W. M. Frohock's interesting early (1946) response to *Nausea*, which now has its own historical significance as an indicator of early North American reaction to Sartre's fiction, most of the essays gathered here are the fruit of recent scholarship of the 1970s and 1980s.

The third consideration was just what to include and what to leave out from Sartre's enormously fertile career. As Michel Contat wrote to me shortly after Sartre's death, "I know of no life so full and, in spite of its errors, so fully successful as his." The sheer volume of major material from so many disparate fields — cinema, theater, philosophy, criticism, politics, psychology, fiction, autobiography, art criticism, to name but the most well known — points to the vibrant creativity that was Sartre's. Under the rubric of "cinema" alone one could produce a sizable volume of criticism whether on his own original screenplays (most of which were made into films) or on his adaptations, like *Les Sorcières de Salem*, starring Yves Montand and Simone Signoret, from Arthur Miller's play *The Crucible*. This third consideration caused this editor many sleepless nights! In the end, and I am sure that the decision will not be equally acceptable to all readers, I realized that I had to choose between a smattering of everything to demonstrate Sartre's polygraphic (the word is his) abilities, and between a highly limited selection that would correspond (within the limits imposed by the series) to the overall intention of the book.

The fourth consideration was the quality of the critical essays to be included within the chosen framework. While there are many excellent articles on Sartre in French, German, Italian, and Spanish, the exigencies of time and translation fees and the knowledge that this volume is destined for a largely anglophone market acted as a useful constraint. There are many fine articles that, for lack of space, I have had to omit. Having said that, there is, I believe, a uniform quality of freshness of perception and intellectual integrity in these collected essays. What is not uniform is the response to Sartre. This was intentional. This collection of essays does not represent a festschrift in honor of a colleague who can do no wrong, but the intelligent, sensitive response of different individuals to the intellectual, aesthetic, and moral dilemma that was Sartre.

Except where indicated in the notes, all translations of Sartre's texts into English are the responsibility of the editor. I should like to thank all the authors and publishers for their permission to reprint the material collected here. I have had many instances of scholarly cooperation for which I am most grateful. I should also like to record my heartfelt thanks to the staff of the Reference Department of the Rutherford Library of the University of Alberta for their unfailingly generous and courteous service.

ROBERT WILCOCKS

University of Alberta

Notes

1. Pierre Brisson, "Le cas Sartre et le théâtre," *Le Figaro littéraire*, 4 October 1947, 1, 3; my translation.

2. *Le scénario Freud* (Paris: Gallimard, 1984) was published posthumously with a preface by Sartre's analyst friend and colleague for many years, J.-B. Pontalis. The English translation is titled *The Freud Scenario* (Chicago: University of Chicago Press, 1986).

3. This was an anonymous editorial that appeared in *Paris-Match*, no. 599 (September 1960) condemning Sartre's letter of solidarity with the "réseau Jeanson," an ad hoc clandestine militant group headed by the philosopher Francis Jeanson to aid the F.L.N. in Algeria by the illegal transportation of arms and bombs in France.

4. This is certainly the case in the situation described in the play, but it is likely that Sartre recalled the powerful scene of the castration of Joe Christmas at the end of chapter 19 of William Faulkner's *Light in August*, which he quotes in section 2, "Second attitude toward others: indifference, desire, hate, sadism," of the chapter "Concrete Relations with Others," in *Being and Nothingness*, trans. Hazel E. Barnes (New York: Citadel Press, 1971), 382.

5. J.-P. Sartre and M. Sicard, "Penser l'art: entretien," *Obliques*, nos. 24–25 (1979):18.

6. This is most explicitly discussed in the extensive interview first published, in English, in *New Left Review*, no. 58 (November–December 1969), then, in French, in *Le Nouvel Observateur*, 26 January 1970, and collected as "Sartre par Sartre," in *Situations, IX* (Paris: Gallimard, 1972).

7. Jaspers does in fact also use this approach, but tends to limit it to the investigation of conditions such as organic brain syndrome. The distinction is more complex than I allow here. For discussion of these terms and Jaspers's use of them, see the valuable translators' preface to Karl Jaspers's *General Psychopathology*, trans. J. Hoenig and Marian Hamilton (Chicago: University of Chicago Press, 1963), ix.

8. Published posthumously by Gallimard in 1983 in an edition prepared by Arlette Elkaïm-Sartre. See, for example, p. 287.

9. Gerald N. Izenberg, *The Existentialist Critique of Freud* (Princeton: Princeton University Press, 1976), 233.

10. Barnes's modestly titled "Translator's Introduction" (viii–xliii) to *Being and Nothingness* is one of the best succinct commentaries on the book available in English. For book-length studies in English, see Wilfrid Desan, *The Tragic Finale: An Essay on the Philosophy of Jean-Paul Sartre* (New York: Harper Torchbooks, 1960) or Joseph S. Catalano, *A Commentary on Jean-Paul Sartre's Being and Nothingness* (Chicago: University of Chicago Press, 1980).

11. Our knowledge of this critical period has been considerably enhanced by the publication of *The Complete Letters of Sigmund Freud to Wilhelm Fliess 1887–1904*, trans. Jeffrey Moussaieff Masson (Cambridge, Mass.: Harvard University Press, Belknap Press, 1985).

12. *Lettres au Castor et à quelques autres*, 2 vols. (Paris: Gallimard, 1983). The first volume has been translated into English as *Thoughtful Passions: Jean-Paul Sartre's Intimate Letters to Simone de Beauvoir, 1926–1939* (New York: Macmillan, 1986).

13. This has encouraged some weaker mortals who have undergone Freudian psycho-analysis to claim that Sartre's discretion was the product of unconcious blocking rather than of philosophical consequence. See, for example, the question-begging Freudian psychoanaly-sis of Sartre by Josette Pacaly, *Sartre au miroir* (Paris: Klincksieck, 1980).

14. This point is raised by J.-B. Pontalis in his preface to *Le scénario Freud*, 16.

15. Reprinted in *Situations, IX* as "L'universel singulier," 152–190.

16. This theory is taken up again with much subtlety in *L'Idiot de la famille*. The concept is quite traditionally Platonist in origin and in its implications, but is employed by Sartre in a unique way. Jacques Lacan's reading of Freud's difficult concept of the *Vorstellungrepräsentanz* owes much to the Sartrean theory of the *analogon*.

17. David Caute, *The Fellow-Travellers* (London: Weidenfeld & Nicolson, 1973). One could also examine, and compare, from a leftist point of view, books like those of the Polish war correspondent Ryszard Kapuściński on the realities of the various "Third World" conflicts he has covered. See, for instance, his latest *Another Day of Life*, trans. William R. Brand and Katarzyna Mroczkowska-Brand (London: Picador, 1987).

18. Michel-Antoine Burnier, *Le Testament de Sartre* (Paris: Olivier Orban, 1982).

19. This is my translation of Burnier's reputed quotation in *Le Testament de Sartre*, 9. This seems, however, to be a reference to the end of the interview mentioned in note 6. If this is the case (and I can find no other reference in Sartre's published interviews), then Burnier appears to have added a personal flavor to this Proustian memory. While Sartre refers to a possible future "Testament" that he may write and in which he would include a record of his "errors," nowhere does he mention any grinding of teeth; he simply concludes (and these are the last two sentences of the whole interview): "I shall recount what I have done in this domain, what errors I have committed, and what the result was. By doing this, I shall try to define what constitutes politics to-day, in the historical phase in which we are living" (*Situations, IX*, 134).

20. His reading of Engels's *The Peasants' War in Germany* is a case in point. It is referred to in the *Critique* and, as I have argued elsewhere, the historical rebellious former pupil of Luther, Thomas Münzer (in Engels's interpretation of him), was the prototype for the character Nasty in *Le Diable et le Bon Dieu* (1951). See, Robert Wilcocks, "Thomas l'obscur: réflexions sur la praxis d'un personnage," *Obliques*, nos. 18–19 (1979):131–35.

21. Edith Kern, ed., *Sartre: A Collection of Critical Essays* (Englewood Cliffs: Prentice-Hall, 1962).

22. Mary Warnock, ed., *Sartre: A Collection of Critical Essays* (Garden City, N.Y.: Doubleday Anchor, 1971).

"On the Other Side of Despair": The Politics of a Philosopher

Sartre Remembered

Lionel Abel*

In the fall of 1948 Jean-Paul Sartre, lecturing at Carnegie Hall, made his second appearance before a general public in New York City. (On his first visit here, in 1944, he had spoken publicly, but he was not then widely known.) Prominent among his auditors in 1948, was Marcel Duchamp, who had told me he would not attend the lecture and urged me not to go either. In his most winning way of appearing—I think he really was— cynical, Marcel had this to say of Sartre: "One of those chaps the *école normale* turns out from time to time, who can write fifty pages for you on no-matter-what over the weekend." Then he amended the remark, "I mean *good* pages." But the effect was not a bit the less perjorative. All the time, when Sartre gave his talk at Carnegie, there was Marcel in a box seat. Taking his cue from Valéry's Monsieur Teste, he observed the audience more closely than the speaker on the stage, and then, with a gesture enveloping the others with him in one box, and the crowd below, too, exclaimed (in the tone of a tourist guide): "We are now before Sartre Cathedral!"

Chartres still stands, Sartre Cathedral is no more. But was the word *cathedral* ever appropriate to the expectations built by those who already knew something of Sartre in 1948? In point of fact, he had made no direct appeal to the religious feelings of those his works addressed; the interests to which he had spoken had been exclusively moral and intellectual, and he held this stand until late in his career when, in the middle fifties, he began to indicate that he had become somewhat less concerned about what was moral and what was not. (His moral indictment of the United States in the sixties for "genocide" in Vietnam was directed, he himself said, exclusively towards those of the petty bourgeoisie who were susceptible to "moral" forms of propaganda.) By then he had espoused Marxism and even denied many of the existentialist views he had himself advanced. He may in the end have wanted us to regard the ideas he expressed more than thirty years ago as among the follies of that time. Should we?

*From *The Intellectual Follies* (New York: Norton, 1984). © Lionel Abel. Reprinted with permission.

Sartre, of course, has a great many readers today. There are those who waited over these years for his latest pronouncements on philosophy, psychology, politics, and literature; on the other hand, nobody expects anything of promise or importance to result in philosophy from the ideas he set forth, and he himself claimed to have completely expressed his thought. But let me here give some indication of what was once expected of him. Claude-Edmonde Magny, writing on Sartre's *Being and Nothingness* in the late forties, judged that work to be the herald of many new developments in French philosophy, for no work of like scope had appeared since Bergson. Have her expectations been fulfilled? I think not. Sartre's phenomenological ontology, like the philosophical writings of his colleague and friend, Maurice Merleau-Ponty, have led to few significant discoveries in French thought, which is perhaps even more barren today than it was in the late twenties, when still dominated by the ideas of Bergson and Braunschwig. French philosophy has little to show today which can compare with the work now being done by our own American logicians and epistemologists, with the British followers of Wittgenstein and Austin, or with German social theorists like Habermas, who continues the work of the Frankfurt school. French structuralism is, of course, an important intellectual tendency, but it is not part of, nor does it have significant implications for, any of the traditional disciplines of philosophy. And it was inspired basically, not by Sartre's writings, but by those of his rival social theorist, the anthropologist Claude Lévi-Strauss.

What about the moral expectations of those who listened with admiration to Sartre in 1948 and found in his writing a stimulus to renew their own moral or political interests? Who were the supporters or followers of his existentialist ideas during the late forties and early fifties? I think they were in the main intellectuals who had been convinced, or at least partially convinced, by Marxist views, and then been disillusioned in these by the manner in which the Second World War had terminated. Many remembered Trotsky's pronouncement that if the war which began in 1939 did not end with the revolutionary overthrow of the capitalist system, then the Marxist outlook would be exposed as the very opposite of what it had taken itself to be. Its socialism would have to be called utopian, and *not* scientific at all. Other programs would be advanced and other ideals set up. And in the advancement of these other programs the individual would count for more than he had in the Marxist schema.

I had met Sartre before I heard his lecture at Carnegie Hall. *Partisan Review* had arranged a luncheon for him at a French restaurant on West Fifty-sixth Street, and I was invited to it along with Hannah Arendt. William Phillips and Philip Rahv came to welcome the visitor to New York, and to ask him to write for their review, but since neither of them spoke French they could only communicate with Sartre through Hannah or through me. But any difficulty in communication was due entirely to the language barrier, for we all saw at once that there was nothing whatever uncommunicative about Sartre. You wondered, once you heard him speak, whether there could be any kind of situation in which he might be at a loss for words.

The man I saw at that luncheon was short, stocky, thick-wristed and broad-chested. The thrust of his shoulders gave one a sense of physical power; his speech was sharp, crisp, virile, while his complexion was an unhealthy gray; even his sandy-colored, straight-falling hair seemed gray. In fact, his face was all grayness and animation, and you could not look him straight in the eyes, for each eye turned in a slightly different direction past a small, finely wrought nose in the center of a round face which, because of the nose's position on it, seemed all the rounder. Not at all handsome, he had what I judged to be one of the most interesting of modern faces (as one can see from the excellent photo of him in *Obliques*). I have often thought, after that first contact with Sartre, about the very special kind of virility evident in his style of speaking and in his attitude generally. One conclusion I have come to is purely speculative, but I shall set it down for whatever it may be worth. Sartre was haunted, I suggest, like most philosophers since Plato, by the idea of eternity. (I could document this judgment with quotes from *Being and Nothingness*.) Now what connection would there be between the idea of eternity and the attitude I have described as virile? I am reminded here of a gym instructor who used to say whenever some student hurt himself on the bars: "The pain won't last forever." His was a virile attitude towards pain, and I think Sartre took a like attitude towards most problems. But perhaps I would not have thought of him in just this way on the basis of his writings alone. His style of speaking, his physical forcefulness, even the set of his shoulders, conveyed the attitude.

As I remember, the editors of *Partisan Review* asked Sartre a great many questions and he answered all of them; his answers were never lacking in definiteness or detail. Philip Rahv wanted to know what he thought about Camus, who was already well known in the United States for his novel *The Stranger*. Sartre replied at once that Camus was a friend, a fine writer, a good stylist, and not a genius. This judgment, that Camus was no genius, simply delighted Rahv, and also Hannah Arendt, who, earlier in the conversation, had volunteered the view that in Camus' novel *The Stranger*, which we all admired, there was "a crack." But the reason Sartre had chosen to criticize Camus with such finality was in order to prepare us for his judgment of Jean Genet, the writer he said was the one real literary genius in contemporary French literature. And then he took my breath away, saying, "Genet has the style of Descartes."

What were our expectations of Sartre after that luncheon? I think Philip Rahv and William Phillips expected him to support in France the very positions, literary and political, which they themselves had advanced and defended in *Partisan Review*. But from what they said to him at lunch, I guessed then that they expected Sartre to attack Stalinist influence in Europe's intellectual circles. Hannah Arendt's expectations, as she expressed them to me, were quite similar. She expected him to do battle with the totalitarianism she herself was then engaged in defining and describing in her major work, *The Burden of Our Time*, which she was to publish a few years later. For my part, I don't know what I expected of him, except to be different from the French intellectuals and writers who had excited my interest before the War. And clearly Sartre was different from other French writers I had read or met. In 1948, I already knew something about his plays, and of his interest in the theatre, and I suppose I expected him to use the stage as a "factory of ideas," even as had Bernard Shaw. As it turned out, Sartre addressed none of these tasks, which, it must be granted, he may not have set himself. Back in Paris, he proceeded to attack, not totalitarian Russia, but the United States. He attacked the French workers, even, for not supporting the communist-led demonstrations against General Ridgeway's military operations in Korea. In 1954, when the Rosenbergs were executed, he called the American government which had executed them "Fascist." And then he abandoned the theatre and the novel almost entirely, to pursue the intellectual journalism which made his magazine, *Les Temps modernes*, the outstanding review in Europe.

I must note here that Sartre *did* satisfy the most contradictory expectations. For instance: During the thirties, in this country at any rate, but I think it was also true in England and in Germany (until Hitler came to power), there were serious prolonged intellectual efforts to bring Marxist ideas in line with an informed and nondogmatic discussion of literary works. The models for such efforts were the essays on literary topics by Lunacharsky, by Trotsky, and most especially by Georg Lukács. But I think nothing done in this way in the United States was equal to the analysis Sartre made in his brochure *What Is Literature?*, so that I remember thinking, as I read it, of how delighted Trotsky would have been to read literary judgments so subtly made which yet took into account the class influences on the writers treated. So if there were those, and there must have been such, who expected of Sartre a more subtle and more refined kind of literary analysis, this expectation he did fulfill, and I must add here that in the essay he gave us on Tintoretto, he made a similar kind of contribution to art history, once again taking his cue from Marxist notions.

But on the other hand, one of Sartre's important contributions to the political discussions of that period was to lay the theoretical groundwork for the assertion that it was possible to be a Communist *without being a Marxist*. This view was surely different from, if not exactly contrary to, the one advanced by Sidney Hook in this country during the early thirties, that one could be a Marxist without being a Communist. Hook was asserting that it was possible to think along Marxist lines without joining any particular group, or assuming responsibility for any group's actions. Sartre was asserting that revolutionary political action could be justified in other ways than those laid down in Marxist theory, and in taking this stand he can be said to have prophesied as early as 1949 the adventurous revolutionary perspectives and tactics of Castro, Guevara, Debray, and others. And he can be said to have achieved these contradictory results: to have upheld the Marxist view in literary criticism, where the relevance of such views is still questionable, and to have vindicated the abandonment of Marxist theory in revolutionary political action, the domain where it would seem to be pertinent. Sartre achieved all this, not in successive periods of his career, but from 1949 through the early fifties in the essays on literature and politics he published in *Les Temps modernes.*

But it was already clear in 1949, when Sartre began the publication of his essay "What Is Literature?" in *Les Temps modernes*, that the program he held out for other writers was in no sense a new one. He had already made a contribution to the criticism of literary works, but the only program he had to suggest for writers in *What Is Literature?* was the use of their literary skills to win a mass audience for radical ideas. In the theatre this meant the kind of left-wing Broadway attitude toward writing represented in the United States during the thirties by Harold Clurman and by Clifford Odets. And in the novel it meant the abandonment of the kind of writing which had won Sartre admirers for his novel *Nausea*; also it meant support for the kind of intellectualized soap opera he himself had given us in *The Age of Reason*, which so disappointed many of his readers that he did not even complete the novel. Here, I should say, Sartre made one of the worst mistakes of his career,[1] for which Adorno, comparing Sartre's plays unfavorably to those of Beckett, has already called him to account. A literature of commitment could not be promoted in the name of literature, it could only be justified politically; but Sartre's own political judgments were neither clear nor sure, as was to be revealed during the next two decades. Every man has a right to be mistaken in his political judgment, but then not every man can be the leader of other men, and Sartre made too many mistakes in politics to be a guide for others in determining a relation of literature to politics. All the same I think Sartre did manage in this period to write one fine political play, *Dirty Hands.* However, he himself did not take the play too seriously and, when in '49 I made some criticism of it to him (I had translated it for Knopf), he said to me, "Perhaps you're right, but the theatre is vulgar; if one wants to be subtle, one should write a novel." I remember I thought it strange at the time that a man who had called on writers to be responsible should blame the medium he had worked in for faults I found in his work. I said to him in reply, "Well I don't think the theatre *has* to be vulgar; I don't think Pirandello is, not to speak of Molière or Racine." As I remember, he did not argue this point, but went on to say that he thought plays were essentially myths constructed for *le grand public* (mass audiences), and not artistic works designed for the happy few; they, he thought, needed guilt feelings rather than additional happiness.

Here I want to add one further fact which is not directly pertinent. Merleau-Ponty and Hannah Arendt were very enthusiastic at that time about an essay on *Hamlet* by Harold Rosenberg which Merleau-Ponty planned to publish in *Les Temps modernes*, and which did appear there in 1951. Harold told me that his essay on *Hamlet* had been the inspiration for Sartre's political play. When I asked Sartre about this, he answered without hesitation and with his customary generosity, in the affirmative. Yes, he said, he had been influenced by Rosenberg's essay in the writing of *Dirty Hands.*

Suppose we turn aside now from what was expected of Sartre as a philosopher and try to respond directly to this question: What did he, as a philosopher, achieve? Here we will have to look at the situation of philosophy when Sartre appeared on the scene.

Modern philosophy, when Sartre produced his first philosophical work—I think it was his thesis, a phenomenological study of the imagination—had become extremely technical. What is now called philosophy of language had not yet done more than indicate a few of the alterations and revisions it has required of the language of philosophers. It seemed at the time impossible to treat any of the real problems of life as instanced in morals or in politics, or to describe the data necessary for treating such problems, in terms technical enough to satisfy the philosophically scrupulous. Perhaps the best way to grasp the language problem posed for philosophers before the fifties is to note its effects on Bertrand Russell, who had little in common with Sartre philosophically, but later joined with him in attacking American political action in Southeast Asia in the war crimes trial that was held in Stockholm. The noted British logician, mathematician, metaphysician, and publicist had, since the beginning of the century, produced philosophical writings of the most uneven character. On the one hand, he had come forward with works of logical analysis, like his essay "The Theory of Descriptions," now a classic; on the other hand he had turned out journalistic homilies on sex, education, manners, and morals which in their glibness, superficiality, and lack of rigor could not but shock any of his readers who were also familiar with his expert analyses in difficult areas of thought. Could it be that the serious questions of life were not to be examined with the same care as the technical questions of logic and theory of knowledge? Here Edmund Husserl had already, earlier in the century, suggested a solution—one, in fact, put forth by Aristotle. (But as Gide remarked, everything important that was once said has to be said again, otherwise it will be forgotten.) Husserl noted that not every discipline is capable of the same degree of precision. And to this idea he added another of his own: There *was* a definite way of being rigorous in investigating and conceptualizing any subject matter:

marriage, morals, and sex — just like space, time, and causality — could be studied phenomenologically. And to do this the philosopher would not have to exchange his own precise terms for the vaguer terms of journalists. Following this lead of Husserl's, Sartre, in *Being and Nothingness*, published in 1943, managed to bring off a philosophical treatise on the human condition in which the questions as to whether human action is free or determined, values are created by men or situated in some heaven of ideas, action is conscious or unconscious, were dealt with in a language aiming at psychological accuracy and logical refinement. One thing must be granted this work of Sartre's even today: it was an immense effort to give logical form to the treatment of problems which had been treated either without logic or against it, and to do this in terms of the most sophisticated concepts available to the theorist at that time. While the groundwork for such an effort had been laid by Edmund Husserl, and though Martin Heidegger, in *Being and Time*, published as early as 1927, had done something very similar, Sartre's *Being and Nothingness* is probably the most complete effort that has been made in modern times to deal in a philosophically precise manner with questions which, by their very nature, had seemed to condemn the theorist to inexactitude.

What can be said about *Being and Nothingness* in this regard today? Can it be said to have a rigor comparable to what we have come to expect in contemporary philosophy? Or does one indeed breathe in a purer intellectual atmosphere when reading Chisholm or Putnam or Kripke on the technical problems of theory of knowledge than when reading Sartre's analyses of the human condition in *Being and Nothingness*? I think it is clear that the language of philosophy has been altered during the last thirty-five or forty years in terms of rigor, for what was technically precise in 1943 would not pass muster for many American and English readers of philosophy in 1980.

When Professor Arthur Danto defends Sartre in a charming and eloquent little book devoted to the French philosopher,[2] he takes what is obviously a protective attitude toward Sartre's ideas, at times defending them with arguments Sartre might not have had the logical sophistication to call upon. And while Professor Danto is sympathetic to Sartre's work, one cannot help but feel there is something disparaging about his attitude toward it. Why should a philosopher need any other protection than that afforded by his own ideas and his own arguments for them? Surely something must have happened in the language of philosophy between 1943 and the present time which made Professor Danto feel that Sartre's ideas could no longer speak convincingly for themselves and now had to be spoken for more logically by him.

What happened in philosophy since 1943?

At about the time Sartre was writing his *Being and Nothingness*, another major effort was being made in philosophy of quite a different, though related, kind. If Sartre was trying to treat the problems of life —

matters of morals and politics—with a precision like that already achieved by philosophers in logic and theory of knowledge, Ludwig Wittgenstein in England was trying to do almost the exact opposite, that is, to treat the most complex problems of logic and theory of knowledge not in technical, but in natural, that is to say, in ordinary language. This development in modern thought, sometimes referred to as ordinary language analysis, also subjected to a very severe criticism the *theory* of language on which the better philosophical writings of Russell had been based.

Now, suppose we are asked to decide which was more interesting, more important, more valuable, the discussion of the problems of life in technical language, or the discussion of technical problems in ordinary language, what would our answer be? Here I do not feel required to give more than an indirect answer. In fact, the two efforts were in some sense parallel. Clearly, if one can talk about technical problems in ordinary language, then one can talk about morals or politics without having to mathematicize these disciplines. I must add here that when Sartre wrote his first great work, French philosophy, unlike Anglo-American, had resisted the effort to make it dependent on formal systems. So that a critical operation like Wittgenstein's was perhaps less needed in France than in England and the United States. I must add, too, that the yield of ordinary language philosophy has not been as great as was expected. "There's gold in them thar hills," announced John Austin. There was some gold, no doubt, but rather less than he thought.

I imagine some of my readers may be thinking that I have merely commented on Sartre's language and said practically nothing about what he employed that language to assert. Moreover, Sartre himself showed little interest in philosophy of language; this interest was, however, cultivated by his friend and colleague on *Les Temps modernes*, the philosopher, Maurice Merleau-Ponty. The latter made frequent trips to London, influenced some of the Oxford philosophers and, influenced in turn by them, made a major effort to connect phenomenology and existentialism with ordinary language analysis. During the late forties and early fifties I ran into Merleau-Ponty fairly regularly in Saint-Germain des-Prés. He was often accompanied by the beefy, though beautiful, Sonia Orwell, later Sonia Pitt-Rivers. Merleau-Ponty, with the pink cheeks of a provincial, was supremely sophisticated, and he tried to give you the impression when you got into an argument with him that he knew what you were going to say before you had actually said it. This is a very effective device. I remember once taxing Merleau-Ponty with not being able to use it against me. We were discussing an article of his which I believe Dwight Macdonald had republished in English in *Politics*. It was a defense of a sophisticated kind of Marxism and an attack on vulgarized Marxism. When Merleau asked me if the position he had taken appealed to me, I told him it did not. And then I asked, "Can you guess what I'm going to say against it?" "I suppose I can't," he replied, smiling. "Otherwise I would have taken it up in the article." My objection, which in fact he was not able to meet, is the following: I do not think one can defend the ideas of a mass movement by stressing a sophisticated version of them. For in a mass movement, ideas are necessarily going to be vulgarized. If you want to defend Marxism ideologically, then you must defend it *as vulgarized*, against the vulgarizations of rival movements. Incidentally, Sartre was much keener about matters of this kind than his friend, though he claimed to have been the pupil of Merleau-Ponty in politics.

But if Sartre was the keener here, this was — I would hazard the guess — not because he was the better, but because he was less purely the philosopher. For there was always a good deal of ideology in Sartre's philosophical writings and not a little of the psychologism which his teacher, Husserl, had condemned. Husserl was opposed to the use of philosophical concepts for the presentation of any *Weltanschauung*, or view of the world. Out of his very love of wisdom, he thought, the philosopher should not try to show us that he himself is wise, and this he could not avoid doing in trying to tell us what the actual world is like. Here, Jean-Paul Sartre did not follow his philosophical teacher. He tried, in *Being and Nothingness*, to combine both wisdom and rigor — philosophy as a precise science, and philosophy as a coherent picture of the world. Now I do not think this is the proper place to set forth and argue about the merits and demerits of Sartre's philosophical assertions. Moreover, there is a content to Sartre's philosophical writings which can be discussed without being over-technical. Sartre argued eloquently in *Being and Nothingness* for a very definite view of the world, and again for a very different view of it some twenty years later in his *Critique of Dialectical Reason*. These works are both highly ideological, and may be regarded as ideologies of and for modern man.

The denial of God's existence, a position one can hardly establish by rigorous argument, is very important in both these works of Sartre. Very much to the point here is a comment made about him by George Lichtheim some years ago when the political writer was editing *Commentary* in New York City. The value Lichtheim said he found in Sartre's existentialism was due to Sartre's peculiar kind of atheism. For the usual denial of God's existence tended to encourage people to expect a rationality in human affairs experience is likely to contradict. Religious belief, as Lichtheim saw it, had been a protection against a too-great expectation of reasonableness, a protection men in the past had benefited from, and which contemporary man, insofar as he has lost his traditional faith, has had to do without. Sartre's existentialism, said Lichtheim, was, of all the varieties of atheism which had been presented, the only one which prepared us to experience the irrationality of the world. It is interesting to note here that Sartre, an atheist, should in *No Exit* have written a play plotted about the punishment of sin after death. An atheist of the eighteenth or nineteenth centuries would have simply denied that life continues after death and denied, too, that there is any judgment of sin or wrongdoing after one's life is over. Of course, in his play Sartre is not saying the contrary. But he has no objection to *imagining* the contrary. An eighteenth- or nineteenth-century atheist would have had such objections.

Let me here try to indicate in what respect Sartre's *Being and Nothingness* and *Critique of Dialectical Reason* may be regarded as ideologies of modern man.

Modern man is, as Sartre has presented him to us, man torn from his traditional group, traditional religion, his traditional metaphysics or ethic. He is the spiritually unaccommodated man, and nothing is impermissible for him. He must decide himself just what it is he forbids himself to do. Modern man would, in fact, like to belong to some other time. He would like to be some other kind of being: a Christian, a heretic, a libertine, a sensualist. He would like to be unmodern, though modern he is, without knowing exactly what it means to be that. For being modern is precisely not having to be anything with true "resolute decision." He thinks of communism and at times would like to be a Communist, but not finally. He may try to be a Communist, but with results that he knows in advance. If he has children, he does not know what he wants them to become. To resolve the problem of generations he has to change into some other kind· of man than he is, send his children to a church he does not attend himself, to a synagogue of which he does not care to be a member. What kind of a man is this who has to be an entirely different kind of man just in order to have a family? It would be best of all, perhaps, not to have any children. But this would be to give up the only fundamental consolation men have found in growing old. Whatever else he is, modern man knows this: he is not pure. He knows he is impure of heart. "The pure of heart," said Kierkegaard, "think only one thought." This is the very kind of thought a modern man cannot think. Plato told us that musical purity required an instrument limited to only three strings. Modern man will not be so musically abstinent. He needs the fiddles, pianos, bassoons, and tympanum, and even these are not enough. He needs electronic wailings, the music of sounds that don't seem at all musical, and even then he isn't satisfied, nor can he be, for essentially he is dissatisfied with his mode of hearing, and not with the sounds he hears. What paintings please him? All sorts of paintings, but only to a limited extent. He looks at the golden forms of Tutankhamen's tomb on exhibition, admires them, but thinks, even as he admires, not merely how beautiful they are, but also this: "Why did I ever see anything else that diverted me from concentrating on beauty such as this? Why did I ever have to see Greek sculpture, Michelangelo, Donatello, Rodin, the Bodhisattvas, Brancusi, the sculptures of Ankhor Wat?" For every great form of art suggests to him a deliverance from his state as a modern man. It suggests such a deliverance, but the suggestion is never made good. Unstable, constantly facing the collapse of his most recent conclusions, modern man hopes to be supplanted by human beings more successfully adapted to the time, though he himself takes no little pride in his inadaptation to it.

As moderns, we are aware of the great difficulty — if one begins with the self — of proving the existence of other selves. And, swinging to the other side, the difficulty, if beginning with the others, of ever getting back to ourselves. So we no longer expect decisive arguments from philosophers on whether there are or are not other selves. But since we are moderns, we want to hear some argument, and an argument that appeals to us, that sympathizes with us, that tells us something of what the world is without denying what we ourselves are. And we want to hear an argument that even takes account of our social situation, for however well situated, we do not like to think of ourselves as members of a ruling class. The sweetness of life that ruling classes once knew, we ourselves shall never know. And we may even say that such sweetness of life belonged to a period when one could yield to an argument for the existence of others which was not a lower-class argument. But a lower-class argument is what we want to hear today, and that is what Sartre provided us with in *Being and Nothingness*. Certainly it does not persuade us that there are others (which we never really doubted anyway), but it does identify us, separating us from past generations who were interested in the problem and in other solutions to it. How does one know, according to Sartre, that there are others? When one is seen. The other's gaze freezes the movements of one's mind into a stillness like a stone's, and one's powers over words into silence. (One actually helps the other in this operation, for one has a secret wish to be a thing anyway, and escape from the pain of conscious life.) In any case, stared at, one becomes the object of the other's glance, and one knows one is not sovereign in this situation. One's *I* is deposed, and this can only be by an alien *I*. So the experience revealing that there are others is modeled on the kind of revolution in which a monarch is put down. It is also suggestive of the French Revolution to which, if we are moderns, we cannot but relate our feelings, our thoughts and all our hopes. And the gaze of the other has a keenness like that of the guillotine, lopping off one's self-awareness like the head of an aristocrat which, as Hegel has it, falls like a cabbage. It has been said that Sartre's real genius and originality is best instanced by his argument for the existence of others. And I think this is quite true though it would not convince any philosopher; it does not even convince us. But it does something else which is perhaps just as important. It tells us what we ourselves are, and this is certainly something both literature and philosophy are supposed to do.

Perhaps Sartre is not in the front rank of modern philosophers, who were his contemporaries, though there are some who still rank him with Wittgenstein and Heidegger. In any case, he is probably the best writer among contemporary philosophers, and certainly the best philosopher among contemporary writers.

In his various works, Sartre did try, I think, to keep philosophy and literature separate. They were, for him, quite different projects and he wanted to excel in each of them in terms he himself had set. Yet the effect of his success in both endeavors has been to create a confusion about the boundaries proper to philosophy, proper to literature. We have, for example, the lecture of Roland Barthes about how he would go about writing a novel were he indeed to write one, and the lecture is presented as the commencement of such a novel. And we have Jacques Derrida's philosophical writings which, as Richard Rorty rightly indicated, have more to do with *writing* philosophy than with philosophizing. We already distinguish between doing philosophy and talking about it, so Derrida may possibly have achieved something new: not the doing of philosophy *or* the talking about it, but the *writing* about the *writing* of it. Now Sartre, when he wrote *Being and Nothingness*, was doing philosophy, not talking about it, and not writing about the writing of it, if that is indeed something different.

All the same, Sartre's conversation was always that of the man of letters. I remember a lecture he gave on American literature in Paris under the auspices of UNESCO. As it happens, I did not greatly admire his talk. He described American literature as fundamentally optimistic, and how can one call men like Melville, Hawthorne, or Faulkner optimists? The lecture was given to a very small audience and I happened to be sitting in the front row. I mention this because the next time I ran into Sartre, I told him I was critical of his talk. In reply he said, "And I know what you were critical of." "How do you know?," I asked. He said, "I was watching you while I was talking." And then he proceeded to tell me exactly what my criticisms of his talk were, almost point by point.

Lunch with Sartre meant argument and still more argument. I remember one occasion especially. We had an appointment for lunch at noon, but just before noon Nicola Chiaromonte and Ann Matta dropped in on me at my hotel. At noon Sartre appeared with Simone de Beauvoir and at once invited Chiaromonte and Ann Matta to lunch, too. He brought us to Chez Lipp and we were taken upstairs to the room sacred to luncheon talks on the second floor.

We lingered over lunch for a long time and the conversation touched on many subjects. Sartre was interested at that moment in the suit for libel of Kravchenko, the Russian defector, against the French Communist party, and what amused him was that the Communist party lawyers accused Kravchenko of all kinds of things, including drunkenness, but did not accuse him of the one serious crime of which, in Sartre's eyes, he was obviously *guilty*, namely, treason. This drew very strong objections from Chiaromonte. Why was it treasonable to desert the Soviet bureaucracy and criticize the Soviet state? Sartre replied that Kravchenko had done more than that. He had also revealed information which had been entrusted to him by Soviet leaders who thought him loyal, and whom he had encouraged to think of him as loyal. Sartre's criticism of Kravchenko would not apply, of course, to the criticism of dissidents who had openly challenged the regime in Russia. And as a matter of fact I have myself heard very unsavory things about Kravchenko since. At a party in New York he said to a friend of mine who spoke Russian, pointing to the other guests, most of whom — it was a New York party — were Jews, "I don't consider the people here the real Americans. In fact I think there are very few real Americans in New York City." "And where are the real Americans to be found?," my friend asked. "In the South," said Kravchenko. "They're the people who once owned the big plantations." What he meant was, the people who had owned slaves.

Simone de Beauvoir said very little at our luncheon. She watched Sartre intently throughout the discussion like a spectator at a play or better still, like a substitute player on a football team, watching a star player and wondering whether an opportunity will arise to substitute for him. I do not mean to suggest by this that Simone de Beauvoir is lacking in conversation. On the contrary, in all my meetings with her I always found her lively and communicative. But with Sartre there, engaged in some argument that had meaning for him, she was without initiative and took her cue from him, entering the discussion only when he signalled her to do so. She certainly did not behave like an independent woman. The author of *The Second Sex* on this occasion, at least, was very much a feminine supporter of the male lead.

I said that Sartre was the best writer among philosophers, the best philosopher among writers, and if this is true, there should be some feature of his writing to which one could point which would illustrate a specific union or fusion of the literary and the philosophical. And in fact we can point to such a trait, illustrative of what Saint-Beuve might have called "a master faculty." As poets have shown their purely rhetorical or literary power by many discoveries in similes and metaphors, so philosophers have shown their peculiar insight into our use of words by turning up tautologies, our different ways of expressing a single meaning. Now Sartre, in his various literary biographies, but I am thinking most especially of his biographical work on Genet, *Saint Genet, Actor and Martyr*, is given to piling up tautologies in an ecstasy of analysis even as modern poets pile up images and metaphors. No doubt Sartre's famous prolixity is due to this aspect of his writing, but we should also note that through it his prose attains a great rhetorical value. When we have been told the same idea some twenty-five times in twenty-five different ways, we are clearer, first of all as to its meaning, and in addition we feel the intense interest in it of the writer, who has found so many different ways of communicating it. In piling up tautologies, Sartre has found a way of giving rhetorical force to the emotions he feels for the ideas he wants communicated. And the reader feels his emotion too. So we can say he has invented a rhetorical and literary use for a philosophical habit of mind.

Sartre has many talents, there are many sides to his personality. How is one to find an image of him that will do justice to all of them? Probably not by looking directly at the man, but at a particular problem of his, one that faces intellectuals generally, especially in this part of our century.

First of all, we must ask what is an intellectual? There are, of course, the positive definitions like, for instance, that he is someone for whom truth is always relevant, even when its practical importance is minimal, or someone who is interested in ideas as such, again without regard to what may result from holding them; there are also negative notions like, for instance, Heidegger's suggestion that the intellectual is the one in whom the primary experience of handling tools has become inauthentic and whose indirect inspection of objects lacks the genuineness of experience found in those who deal with objects directly, masterfully. Which of these judgments is correct? Incidentally, Sartre seems to have been inclined to the negative judgment, for he supported Heidegger's notion, for instance, that one uncovers or discloses the nature of a hammer not by inspecting it but by using it.

To such contemporary notions about the intellectual as such, I prefer the more concrete, dramatic terms suggested by Turgenev in his famous essay, "Hamlet and Don Quixote." These characters, Turgenev wrote, are the ". . . twin anti-types of human nature." He also thought Russia had too many Hamlets and was in need of more Don Quixotes. The Russian intelligentsia responded to the request for Don Quixotes in 1917, with the results we all know.

But to go back to Turgenev's distinction. Are Hamlet and Don Quixote really antitypes of human nature? Only of human nature insofar as it is reflective. In a way, Turgenev concedes this himself, for he notes the relation of Hamlet and Don Quixote with the "ordinary man," "the man in the street" and in this connection points up Hamlet's relationship with Polonius and the relationship of Don Quixote with Sancho Panza: the Danish prince ridicules the King's counselor even as the Spanish knight is ridiculed by his own squire. Now Polonius has nothing in him of Hamlet; Sancho Panza, nothing of the knight he serves. So Hamlet and Don Quixote are not antitypes of human nature, but antitypes of the intellectual.

So let us consider yet once again—the comparison has been made many times before this—what it means to be a Hamlet, and what to be a Don Quixote. Hamlet is the easier figure to describe, and by describing him, we can better understand the Spanish hero, his very opposite. Hamlet is that kind of intellectual who constantly sees the hiatus between the meaning of any of his actions at a particular moment and the meaning the same action will probably have on the final horizon of his days. The horizon of the moment and the horizon of the end are not at all the same.

He cannot ever bring them together. He begins to insist on their difference, and in this insistence lies the paralysis of his will to action. Don Quixote is the very opposite, though he begins with the same problem. He sees the difference between the meaning of a particular act on the horizon of its accomplishment, and the meaning of that act on the final horizon of his life, but his response to this perception is not paralysis of will, but resolution and decision. He will blot out the meaning of his act on the horizon of the moment and substitute for it the meaning he wants it to have on the final horizon of his life. Don Quixote, the intellectual, is not so different from Loyola and from Lenin. Whether they knew it or not, he was their model.

Let us note here too what is not Hamlet, what is not Don Quixote. That is to say, what is not the intellectual: the man of ordinary consciousness who lives by deliberately blurring the meaning of any act of his on the immediate horizon with its meaning on the ultimate horizon of his life. This, which the ordinary man does constantly, the intellectual must at all costs avoid ever doing.

Now what shall we say about Sartre in this regard? What dramatic model did he follow? During the Spanish civil war, according to all reports, he was paralyzed like Hamlet, while he saw the fellow intellectuals he most admired, like Malraux, for instance, go forth — what place was more appropriate than Spain? — to fight Franco, even as the mournful knight hurled himself against the windmill. By this I do not mean that the civil war in Spain was necessarily lost from the outset. If true, I do not know this to be true, and I do not think those intellectuals who went to fight in Spain, like Malraux and my old friend Nicola Chiaromonte, thought the war was lost. For Nicola it was the last good cause. But what I mean is that to go and fight in Spain one had to transform oneself into a fanatic. This Malraux was quite willing to do. Though not a member of the Communist party himself, he worked with the Communists, and refused to testify for Trotsky when the latter was charged in Moscow with collaborating with Hitler, and on a piece of evidence which Malraux personally knew to be false. But the Hamlet model had too great an attraction to Chiaromonte for him to sustain a fanatical pose in Spain. Chiaromonte was in the same air squadron as Malraux; in fact, he was the bombardier in the plane in which Malraux was the machine gunner. They were good friends and almost always saw each other at officer's mess. One day the French Communist party's contact with Malraux's squadron came for lunch. It was a melancholy day, as Chiaromonte told me about it, for him. There had been several casualties in their squadron just that morning. The Communist party man, Marcel Cachin, however, was full of self-satisfaction and optimism. He smacked his lips over lunch and when he was told of the losses that morning to the squadron said, "Oh, that's nothing, we can replace them." Chiaromonte, enraged, brought up the matter of the anarchists, like Durutti, whom the Spanish Communist party had had shot, and also the fate of Andreas Nin, the Trotskyist leader of the POUM. Cachin responded by calling Chiaromonte's political accusations "idle," and then said, "Let's be serious and have some more pork chops." Chiaromonte shouted at him, "To celebrate our fallen comrades?," and called Cachin a butcher and a blackguard. Afterwards, Malraux took Chiaromonte aside and said to him, "After your outburst, I don't think you can stay in our squadron. I suggest you shift to the Abraham Lincoln brigade." Chiaromonte knew that the Abraham Lincoln brigade was controlled by the Stalinists, from whom he could expect no mercy. He went back to Paris, but in Paris one could do little towards the victory of the Spanish Republic; one could only be ironical about its chances of success.

By remaining in Paris, Sartre escaped the exultations and ignominies of fanatical action in the Spanish civil war. But apparently he could not bear his isolation and inactivity, and after the defeat of France, having returned from a German prison camp, he commenced that furious and uninterrupted literary and intellectual activity which only came to a full pause recently after the publication of the third volume of his biography of Flaubert. After which Sartre's failing eyesight made it impossible for him to follow events as he once did. He announced that he would do no more writing and from then on would just give interviews. Let us now ask what dramatic model he followed in the period between the ending of the Spanish civil war and the late seventies, during which time he claimed to have said all he had to say.

In my judgment, Sartre was an intellectual through and through and he was always that. His hesitation never was between Hamletism and the consciousness of the ordinary man, or between that consciousness and quixotism. His hesitation was between Hamlet and Don Quixote, and he tried out the postures of both, the first during the Spanish civil war, and after World War II the second, when he tried to take communism away from the French Communist party in the radical grouping of *rassemblement* he started with David Rousset. And then when this venture failed and the *rassemblement* was dissolved, he took up the various extreme political positions, for the most part supportive of the USSR, which Merleau-Ponty characterized as "super-Bolshevik"; for instance, as I have already noted, in his essay entitled "The Communists and Peace," he denounced the French working class for not rallying to the Communist slogan that General Ridgway had used germ warfare in Korea, though he openly admitted the accusation against Ridgway was a false one. He broke with his former friend and comrade in the resistance, Albert Camus, in the main over the latter's pointing up of the Soviet concentration camp system, and he broke with his comrade in the *rassemblement*, David Rousset, on the same issue. All the same, he was continually attacked in the press of the French Communist party, so that even in this period of quixotic procommunism, he was occasionally forced to take refuge in an attitude of irony. In the early fifties, attending a public function called by the Communist party, he ran into a Party member who extended his hand in greeting. (The French always shake hands on meeting or on taking leave of one another; they also criticize Americans for not being sufficiently devoted to the custom.) Sartre looked at the hand extended toward him and asked the Party member, "Do you agree with everything in the editorial columns of *Humanité?*" "Yes," said the Communist. "Well, *Humanité* says that I'm a bastard," said Sartre, "so why do you want to shake my hand?"

Ever since the Russian Revolution and until recent years, quixoticism, the intellectual attitude based on Cervantes's hero, in its political and ideological form at least, has been procommunist. Not for nothing had the Russian Revolution declared war on Hamletism. What we must recognize, though, is that the Revolution supported and furthered an equally extreme intellectual posture and, in fact, for most of this century was able to recruit a goodly number of those ready to impose on the moment the meaning they hoped to give history at its close. There were exceptions, of course, and two immediately come to mind. There was T. E. Lawrence's effort to lead the Arab revolt during the First World War, and there was Malraux's support of General de Gaulle at the end of the Second. But these expressions of quixotism were in a way limited and parochial. The passion for some ideal political solution to all our problems carried most intellectuals into the Communist camp or to a position of favoring the Communists, or of favoring Russia against the United States. I believe all this came to an end with the publication of Solzhenitsyn's *Gulag Archipelago*, and the revelation of the struggle of the Soviet dissidents against the state, which Western intellectuals of first rank, like Sartre, had favored over American democracy. This much Solzhenitsyn and the other Russian dissidents, but he, most of all, achieved: they put an end to the long identification of communism as a political goal, and quixotism as an intellectual attitude. Even Sartre had to yield on this point, and after the publication of *Gulag Archipelago* attacked the Russian state and the Russian Communist party in no uncertain terms, though not with the violence he employed in Stockholm at the war crimes trial when he attacked the United States. When I read, in the last brilliant pages of his biography of Flaubert, Sartre's very finely drawn assessment of the relationship between Flaubert and Napoleon III during the war and after the defeat of 1870, in which Sartre shows how Flaubert tries to qualify, after the defeat, the regard he had had for Napoleon III before the catastrophe, I cannot but compare it with Sartre's own effort to substitute a certain lack of candor for the enthusiasm he had previously shown when commenting on the Communist world of eastern Europe. Surely he was finally as compromised by his political support of the USSR and of North Vietnam, by the way, as Flaubert was in his acceptance of the emperor and by being received by the princess at the Tuileries. And when one makes this comparison, the advantage is entirely with Flaubert, for we remember Flaubert not for his political attitudes but for the artistic purity of his work, which those attitudes did not invalidate. Sartre never placed his own art that high, nor can we. He placed politics above art, and his attacks on Flaubert's politics do not serve to justify his own.

I called Sartre's first major philosopical effort, *Being and Nothingness*, an ideology for contemporary man. Let me specify further: It is an ideology for contemporary man insofar as he wants to intellectualize his experience, and to reject the Communist faith. One can say of the Sartre who wrote *Being and Nothingness* exactly what he said of Flaubert in '48: "From the point of view he adopted—which is at once that of immediate lived experience and its metaphysical meaning, without regard to any social consideration—it is evident that his skepticism goes deep." But Sartre also wrote another philosophical work, *The Critique of Dialectical Reason*, and this, too, is an ideology for modern man, but from the very opposite standpoint. It is an ideology for the modern who wants to be a Communist. So we can say that Sartre created two distinct and different ideologies from opposite viewpoints and involving the very opposite goals. There are, of course, carry-overs from one ideology to the other, or thoughts, if you will, presented in the first which could appear in the second, and in the second which might have appeared in the first. But let us be clear about it. These two works are divergent. They are not like the two versions of *Sentimental Education*, which could both bear the same title. To make the parallel with Flaubert hold, we would have to change to title of his first version of *Sentimental Education* and call it *Unsentimental Education*, while leaving the title of his second version intact. But there are thoughts which would fit either text. For example, when Sartre, in *Being and Nothingness*, wants to prove the existence of others, he gives what I have called a lower class argument for this. *And this is the first time in the history of philosophy that something like the feeling of class inferiority was introduced as an argument at an epistemological level.* Now surely this argument would not have been inappropriate or out of place in *The Critique of Dialectical Reason*. In that work, Sartre describes the degeneration of the group once its moment of revolutionary activity is over, and along with this, the serialization[3] of the individual, something which occurs in any society—even one resulting from the overthrow of the capitalist state. Developing such ideas, Sartre thrusts us back into the atmosphere of *Being and Nothingness*, with its Flaubertian pessimism, which no more denies itself "the delights of irony" than did the Flaubert Sartre describes in his biography.

The very opposite values are set forth in, and very fundamental to, the two distant ideologies Sartre has created. In *Being and Nothingness*, the main value, I should say, is freedom and man as a moral agent, with the freedom to be a moral agent, the freedom also to construct the moral law which he himself decided will constrain him. In *The Critique of*

Dialectical Reason the main value is man, but not as the determinant of his own freedom, rather as a historical agency in historical situations he has not himself invented. In this second work, the emphasis is not on morality and not on freedom. It is on political action and the constraints within which this can operate. To give just one example: To act historically, according to Sartre's critique, the individual must yield up his liberties to what Sartre calls *the group in fusion*, to which the individual grants the power to take his life. As for morality, it is relegated to a general insignificance, after having been raised, in the previous work, to the highest point. What Sartre has to say about morality in the light of his announced conversion to Marxism was perhaps best and most clearly expressed in his biographical study of Genet, *Saint Genet, Actor and Martyr*, composed just before he set to work on the *Critique*. I quote from Bernard Frechtman's translation: "Either morality is stuff and nonsense or it is a concrete totality which achieves a synthesis of good and evil. . . . The abstract separation of these two concepts [good and evil] . . . expresses simply the alienation of man. The fact remains that, in the historical situation, this synthesis cannot be achieved. Thus, any ethic which does not explicitly profess that it is *impossible today* contributes to the . . . alienation of men."

This is from the same author who, in *Being and Nothingness*, conceived of the individual as free to act morally in any situation, even under torture.

As the creator of two distinct and quite different ideologies, full of insights into the complex mysteries of social and individual lived experience, Sartre has to be taken for what he has already been judged to be, one of the dominant figures of this age. That he constructed two ideological systems and not just one, is itself expressive of our age: Heidegger had two different periods in philosopy, though only the first of these is important, and Wittgenstein produced two different and distinct philosophies, though both are important and also deeply connected. To whom, besides these moderns, should we compare Sartre? I suggest to the other great ideological writers of this and past centuries. Sartre has already been compared to Voltaire (first of all, by Edmund Wilson), and I myself have compared the view in Sartre's *What is Literature?* to the position taken on literature by Bernard Shaw in his letter to A. J. Walkley. Moreover, both Shaw and Sartre had periods of political support for Stalinism. But I think I would prefer to compare Sartre as an ideological writer to Dostoevsky. Not that he is comparable to the Russian novelist as an artist or even as a dramatist; what makes a comparison of him to Dostoevsky possible and also right is that he made available to intellectuals of his period systematic ways of rationalizing their lives. The specifically religious value in literature has been its justification of life, and this kind of justification is made available to the individual in both of the ideologies Sartre set forth, so much so that despite the writer's avowed atheism, the mocking phrase of

Marcel Duchamp, "Sartre Cathedral," does not seem inappropriate after all when applied to either of his two systematic treatises. Perhaps instead of saying "Sartre Cathedral," we should speak of Sartre's cathedrals, for there were two of them, places of reverential yet modern decision, where, surrounded by emblems of the most refined intelligence, one could force one's spirit to sustain the stress of resolute ironic dubiety, or a fanatic faith.

Postscript

Sartre's last work, his biography of Flaubert, followed the novelist's life and career only through the first *Sentimental Education*, and stopped short of considering him during, or at work on, his two greatest productions, *Madame Bovary* and the second *Sentimental Education*, though Sartre did find occasion to comment on Flaubert's varying attitudes towards Louis Napoleon III during and after the defeat, and also towards the communards in Paris. But to treat Flaubert without discussing his two greatest novels, or showing him at work on them, would be like writing a biography of Hamlet (it will be remembered that Morgann, the eighteenth century wit, actually wrote a biography of Falstaff) and stopping short at the point where he sails for England, leaving out his return, his duel with Laertes, and his killing of Claudius. As a matter of fact, there are many things in Sartre's biography of Flaubert that could, with minor restatement, be utilized in an imaginary biography of Hamlet. Let us not forget that Kafka connected Flaubert with Kierkegaard (who connected himself with Hamlet) insofar as he felt he had to give up sentimental relations with women, for the sake of art. Sartre actually claims that Flaubert not only disliked mankind, but also his own characters, and he compares him unfavorably with Camus in this respect, who, he says, had a certain indulgence towards Caligula. But Camus' Caligula does not move us at all, and Flaubert's Emma does. Did Flaubert really despise humanity as Sartre claims he did? I will not try to answer this question directly, but instead call attention to Stephen Daedalus's remark about Shakespeare in the spirited analysis he makes of *Hamlet*. Daedalus, speaking here for Joyce, I believe, says of Shakespeare: "Man delights him not, nor woman neither." But Shakespeare's *characters* delight us. It is idle to inquire, since we can never find out, how he himself felt towards them. Let me indicate some of the common features of Shakespeare's Hamlet and of Sartre's Flaubert. Was Hamlet mad? Only by north-north-west, according to his own statement. And Flaubert? As Sartre has it, he was mad to the degree that an artist had to be mad according to the command of concrete reason between 1850 and 1900. (Sartre is never able to establish clearly what he means by concrete reason, and his whole notion of a binding prescription on artists of that period to be mad is absurd.)

All I want to show is that Sartre himself associates the kind of madness he finds in Flaubert with the kind of madness Shakespeare indicates in his hero. If Flaubert was mad, there was a kind of method to it, and certainly we can associate Hamlet's paralysis of will with Flaubert's passivity, which, Sartre says, Flaubert even "radicalized." And Sartre himself associates Flaubert with Hamlet in the mutism of his final days, which he also connects with the silence of the deposed emperor, relating "the provisional aphasia of the imperial Hamlet" to the remark to Horatio of Shakespeare's hero, "The rest is silence." A silence by Flaubert we must regret, for, as he told Maxime DuCamp, he had planned to write another novel, *Under Napoleon III*, which, Sartre says, in a passage of great brilliance, would be a study of "the vampirization of society by dreams." There is still another way Flaubert can be, in fact must be, associated with Hamlet; Flaubert's attitude toward the choice of words in writing must be associated with Hamlet's attitude toward possible action. As Hamlet notes the hiatus between the meaning of the deed it is possible for him to perform at the moment, and the meaning of that very deed on the horizon of his life, so Flaubert, working on his prose style, always sees the hiatus between the value of the word at hand which he can employ and the value of that very word in the prose style of which he has imagined himself the producer. As Hamlet is paralyzed in the choice of action, Flaubert feels paralyzed in the choice of words. The right word is always the word he has *not* chosen to use, and which haunts the word he has hit upon. From his position, no *mot* is *juste*. I think the demon of paralysis which fascinated Flaubert and tormented him in the choice of words was never exorcised until James Joyce did just the opposite from his literary forebear, and, in *Finnegans Wake*, wrote a book in the *wrong* words, chosen for being wrong, for being imposed by the physical movements of the user, by the language chances of the moment, and even by the sadism of the storyteller. The wrong words of James Joyce saved writers from *les mots justes* of Flaubert, and after *Finnegan*, William Faulkner could tell his Southern tales with an eloquence uninhibited by the notion of a perfected style.

Notes

1. Sartre's worst political mistake was his letter to Kosygin, published in 1966 in *Les Temps modernes*, urging the USSR to risk nuclear war with the U.S. to prevent an American victory in Vietnam.

2. Published by Viking in 1975.

3. An instance of serialization, according to Sartre, occurs when an individual has to queue up to get into a bus.

On Maoism: An Interview
with Jean-Paul Sartre
Michel-Antoine Burnier*

For more than two years you have been director of La Cause du peuple. *You have sold the paper on the streets, you write militant articles, you work on the new daily* Libération, *and you have participated in many of the Maoists' meetings and actions. You seem much closer to them and more engaged with them than you were previously with the Communist Party and with liberation movements such as the Algerian FLN. How do you explain this, and did you make this decision at the outset?*[1]

Sartre: I accepted the directorship of *La Cause du Peuple* after the arrest of the two preceding directors in the spring of 1970. The Maoists did not think they had a base of support broad enough to carry out the clandestine operation which the government tried to force them into. To meet both this process and repression, they came and asked me to help them. That represented, moreover, a new attitude on their part of interest in intellectuals and in finding out how intellectuals could be of service to them. They mistrusted "super-stars" but, at the same time, they appeal to well-known intellectuals who could avert Marcellin's attacks. They turned to the notion of "celebrity" back against the bourgeoisie — and they were right. I feel that the well-known writer has a double role: he is himself, and also the public thing called a celebrity over which he has no control unless he recovers it to serve in a completely different way. That is what I did with *La Cause du Peuple.*

At the beginning, it was clear that I was not in agreement with the Maoists, nor were they with me. I took a legal and not a political responsibility. I simply gave my name so the paper could continue and the militants could act and write as they intended to. In the same way, I accepted the directorship of *Tout Va Bien*; and under the same conditions I was a witness at the trial of militants from *Vive la Révolution* and of Roland Castro. Through a series of actions and struggles since then, I have been drawn progressively closer to the conceptions of *La Cause du Peuple.*

Then you disagreed with the strategy of the proletarian left in 1970, that a new resistance had to be launched against employers, considered as new Nazis, and against revisionists, considered as new collaborators. . . .

Sartre: I have never shared this analysis; and although traces of it remain, *La Cause du Peuple* itself has partially renounced it. For the last two years the problem for its militants has been to really adapt the Maoist strategy to France, not to transpose it lock, stock and barrel. The cultural revolution was unleashed in China well after the seizure of power. It is impossible to copy it or to be directly influenced by it in our situation. The French

*From *Telos*, no. 16 (Summer 1973):92–101. Reprinted with permission.

Maoists speak more willingly of an ideological revolution: liquidating the belief in capitalism among the workers, notably by kidnappings, by teaching resistance, braving repression, and rising above the deference inculcated by the dominant class. At the start, I agreed with the Maoists on almost nothing: not against them, but quite apart from them. But little by little, they have won more than legal protection from me. I met often with them and linked myself to them: little by little a convergence developed.

You have hardly explained the meaning of this action. In 1952, when you were reconciled with the Communist Party, you wrote three long articles "Les Communistes et la Paix." Separating yourself in 1956 from the French Communist Party which had supported the Soviet intervention in Hungary, you published the "Fantôme de Staline." Today, you stick to brief articles, an open letter to the President of the Republic, and interventions at meetings. You have definitely broken with the French Communist Party's system of thought — which in general you accepted, despite reservations, until about 1965–1966 — without clearly saying why and without giving reasons for your present close involvement with the Maoists.

Sartre: In 1952, American politics, the submission of the French government to imperialism, and above all, the repression of the demonstration against "Ridgway la peste" moved me quickly toward a position of solidarity with the Communists. It was very necessary that I explain my action. As I told you, I arrived at my present position much more gradually. First, in May '68, like most people I did not understand the significance or import of the movement. Neither did the Maoists, who immediately left the universities for the factories without evaluating a student revolt whose importance they now recognize. I felt estranged: one day a celebrity, the next day an old combatant. At the Sorbonne, to which I returned two or three times, my presence created some opposition and I was received a little coldly. I remember a meeting on the university situation at the end of 1968 or the beginning of 1969, at which students and professors had to decide their response to the Edgar Faure law. Mounting the rostrum, I found a note on the table: "Sartre, be brief!" I understood immediately that I was out of it. The other speaker's ideas were close to mine, but they had seen the struggle they were talking about and could advance concrete proposals. I had no proposals to offer, simply a general analysis — which had little significance. After the ebb in 1969, I felt farther away again. In 1970 everything changed. The government's persecution of *La Cause du Peuple* led me to take sides and go much further than I had originally imagined. A revolutionary movement has its requirements; you accept some and refuse others, but it draws you in. Especially when its leaders take into consideration outside critiques they regard as well founded. Here, theory is in gestation and the movement remains largely empirical, I would dare say, almost experimental.

On the contrary, it seems to me that the Maoist ideology is very rigid, with energetic sloganeering.

Sartre: When the question is a precise action at a given moment. But the militants of *La Cause du Peuple* do not constitute a party. It is a political group [*rassemblement*] which can always be dissolved. A strike committee with broad recruitment can absorb the committees for struggle organized by the Maoists in the factory. This procedure allows a way out of the rigidity in which the Communist Party has imprisoned itself.

Isn't there, paralleling this, another reality of Maoism, namely the first Maoists of 1965 at L'Ecole Normale Supérieure who formed a hard sectarian nucleus and survived the organizational changes? The real decisions were made secretly, apart from the mass of militants and allied organizations such as Secours Rouge or the Vérité-Justice committees with which the leadership maintained relations of subjugation and infiltration somewhat comparable to those that link the peace movement to the Communist Party.

Sartre: There has been that. But you cannot define the leaders as a sectarian group. They have nothing to do with the Politburo of a Communist Party. For a communist, a non-communist is a diminished individual whom one rejects or uses. Communists have relations of reciprocity only with Party members. Others are placed in negative or instrumental relationships. The Maoist leaders, on the other hand, state as a principle that non-Maoists can have a point of view as interesting as the Maoists' and that it must be listened to. If there is an authoritarian tendency, it is constantly questioned in any case by the Maoists' actions.

Then, how do you explain the disappearance of J'accuse? *That paper wanted to be democratic and open, and then one fine day it turns up integrated into* La Cause du Peuple *under the sole direction of Maoists.*

Sartre: *J'accuse* essentially failed for financial reasons. The paper did not sell enough, and it turned out that the more militant formula of *La Cause du Peuple* was better for circulation. In a certain way I regret this. Today, with *Libération*, we are trying out the experience of a democratic daily paper in which Maoists encounter each other, and in which we also pose a certain number of problems—sexuality, the condition of women, everyday life—including those which raise contradictions in the heart of the people.

It is clear, for example, that the majority of the working class, whatever the feelings or behavior of individuals, remains hostile to certain forms of sexual liberation and to homosexuality. You know this story about an event that occurred several months ago: using an air pump, some garage workers pumped up one of their comrades who was a homosexual and killed the fellow. *Libération* will also intervene in these questions to promote development. It accepts the risk of occasional unpopularity and of eliciting violent reactions or indifference.

All the anti-hierarchical and libertarian ideas must gain recognition in the paper through a confrontation in which the Maoists' experimental tendency prevails over the authoritarian side. Will *Libération* be a melting pot? Will it necessarily lead to a new synthesis? As yet I don't know. Take the example of women's liberation. Representatives of MLF [*Mouvement de la Libération des Femmes*] participated again yesterday at a meeting to prepare the paper. They think that there is a proper feminine dimension in the revolutionary struggle: otherwise people relapse into the traditional schemas that safeguard sexism even in victorious revolutions, such as 1789 and 1917. Now here is a group, composed of workers, but also bourgeoisie, who see themselves as revolutionary in referring first and foremost to the condition of women. On the contrary, the Maoists proceed from class struggle, and consider the proletarian revolution a priority which will eventually entail the liberation of women. Can these opposed views be reconciled? If the unification is made in favor of the Maoists, women will represent a minority tendency in a male party; if the women prevail, the idea of proletarian revolution will give way to a fermenting anti-authoritarianism. Will a new path be found to deal with both these demands?

You give the impression that the Maoist movement is composed essentially of males.

Sartre: There are women, but in my opinion they don't have equal status because they are too few and often timid. I remember a meeting last year when *La Cause du Peuple* was in pretty bad shape. The women present said nothing, except one who intervened on a minor point of women's demands. I insisted that the militants explain their position on women's liberation and that the women speak. Then an article appeared signed by a woman militant, repeating all the themes of the MLF with no reference to the Maoist ideas she usually developed. This revealed a double standard of consciousness: internally, the women sustained a feminine revolt which disappeared completely in their militant stance. The article was published; it elicited a lively reaction from workers who saw it as a symptom of agitation that was not very serious — and there the matter remains.

After two or three years of practice, how do you evaluate the strategic course of the Maoists? They placed in the foreground a certain number of essential ideas concerning the situation of immigrant workers and factory production rhythms. But it is also undeniable that their voluntarism and vanguardism [la fuite en avant] *lost for them, in the long run, many sympathizers and militants who were initially attracted by their brilliant actions. I am struck by the example at Toulouse. For two years,* La Cause du Peuple *had been able to count on a hundred solid militants and several hundred sympathizers — which is a lot. Last year, after the liberation of*

Geismar, there were only a dozen left, and the Communist League *had to come to build up attendance.*

Sartre: Up to 1970 the strong line rallied a membership chiefly composed of intellectuals and students—a group that the Maoists usually did not control. Except in specific cases, the popular center has not followed excessively abrupt calls to revolutionary violence. The Maoists had to proceed step by step to find popular sympathy. They immediately squandered their support by hurling themselves into a brutally repressed and misunderstood demonstration. Although they did carry along a fraction of the university and high school students.

The hard line lost some militants this way, and also because the organization let them go. Today, the Maoists criticize and break out of the notion of leftism: they want to be the left and to create a broad political organization [*rassemblement*]. They have attempted to do this around the Vérité-Justice committees in which little by little the notion of revolutionary justice clarifies the application of bourgeois justice, as in Bruay-en-Artois or at Saint-Laurent-du-Pont. . . . The factory committees for struggle no longer depend on Maoists alone: they reject politics—in the sense that groups and parties understand it—in order to root revolutionary action in the worker's demands and daily combat.

The Maoists do not want to deal with mere intellectuals; and for the most part it is intellectuals who have quit. Nonetheless, the line of political democracy they develop corresponds to their need to enlarge their field of action, in factories and with youth disgusted by the culture and labor imposed on them. This vast anti-hierarchic and libertarian movement, which must be taken into consideration, is developing without yet being very conscious of what it wants or what it is doing. This is true both in the high schools [*lycées*] and in the suburbs. In this regard, the increase of thefts in large department stores is significant. This is not habitual theft, which implies a reafirmation of property—"this object is his; I take it, it is mine"—but theft as a radical challenge to property.

Maoists have long neglected the youth revolt in all Western industrial countries: the underground, the counter-culture, the revolution in individual and collective behavior, communes, drugs, and rock music—which seems all the more important since it asserted itself as an international language common to university and high school students, and young workers in the U.S. and Europe. By preserving an exclusively political attitude, La Cause du Peuple *is left out.*

Sartre: This was the case up to 1970, when the Maoists conceived themselves as a strictly political *party.* They understood, however, that they were screwed if they did not reconsider their methods and their base of support. We just spoke about this: the committees of struggle, the Vérité-Justice committees, and *Libération* express this concern. The anti-hierarchic and libertarian movement goes beyond the Maoist circle, which nonetheless takes it into consideration. But although it begins near the Maoists, it ends up quite far away. We are in sympathy with the underground and the counter-culture — it remains to be seen if all their demonstrations can play a positive role in our direction. Certain tendencies refuse or discourage action, and then I no longer see their utility.

What do you think of the increasingly widespread use of marijuana?

Sartre: On the individual level it appears to me to have no great importance. I have smoked it: I got only a feeling of anesthesia and some curious and limited sensations. Each has the right to do what he wants; and the State must not object to this: Similarly, in the case of heroin — which, as opposed to hallucinogens, presents real dangers — in the name of what will the law prevent people from committing suicide? For me, the problem here is also to determine if their use of hallucinogens demobilizes militants. I know that the American Weathermen smoked marijuana between militant actions and it let them unwind. But when I see that some consider the recourse to hallucinogens a sufficient affirmation of their freedom, and then excuse themselves from action, I wonder.

Another tendency of counter-culture: ecology. . . .

Sartre: That is equally part of the project we wish to undertake with *Libération*. I don't think the society which will be born of a revolution can be a society of growth. To produce for people, of course, but no longer try to produce bigger and better markets. Without regressing, the nature of commodities and their mode of production will have to be profoundly transformed. Luxury objects or dangerous manufacturing will have to be eliminated, a human and ecological equilibrium will have to be recovered. In industrial countries production need not be increased to satisfy needs: it is sufficient to suppress profit and waste and to alter the needs of the economy and the distribution of wealth. Only socialism provides a solution if it doesn't end up in productivism and Soviet centralism.

China is not economizing. The Chinese magazines we receive in the West exalt the machine, growth and industrialization — which seems legitimate for a country just moving beyond the misery of poverty — but it doesn't define a radically different model of development.

Sartre: It isn't that simple. To me, the construction of small factories in the heart of rural communes is an interesting experience, and an original way to abolish the division of labor and limit the spread of cities and pollution.

Then how do you assess the political situation in China since the end of the cultural revolution and the disappearance of Lin Piao?

Sartre: China re-established order under the direction of the Party. That was predictable, since the cultural revolution was made by the base but under the authorization and control of a section of the ruling apparatus. Once the situation opened up and Mao's power was re-established, the movement was stopped by calling in the army and then reorganzing the Party. Externally, China has abandoned a strictly internationalist politics — aiding all revolutionaries wherever they are — preferring the power politics of a great nation. This was evident in Ceylon and Pakistan, when Chinese diplomacy relied on the governments in power rather than the popular insurrections.

Even during the cultural revolution, the leaders never publicly discussed the great questions on which they were in disagreement. Other than some late and fragmentary information, we are ignorant of the terms of the debate among Mao Tse-tung, Chou En-lai and Lin Piao. Do we even know whether Lin Piao was eliminated as an over-ambitious army chief or as a representative of the Left?

Sartre: Probably both. The disappearance of Lin Piao undeniably corresponds to a retreat. Yet, the cultural revolution was an intrusion of the masses into political life; and the past can never return. Some day the movement may reappear. The way they have abandoned it for hope in the slogans of the time necessitates a succession of cultural revolutions.

Do you think a revolution can take place in France in the near or not too distant future?

Sartre: Ten years ago I didn't believe so at all. Now I do: capitalism and its institutions have deteriorated so badly that a revolution appears probable. I am not sure at all if it could survive against the hostility of other countries. Despite famines and blockades, Soviet Russia succeeded and developed. But taking into account internal counter-revolution and foreign pressure I don't see how a country like France can be self-sufficient in the same way as an immense, mainly agricultural country. However that points to a more general problem. There is still no Marxist theory of revolution and the revolutionary State in developed countries. A long time ago — before the war — I had already seen proof that the Communist Party did not truly desire revolution since it had not engaged in any serious study of what would happen if it took power. For revolutionaries today, this ideological and scientific work seems to be a high priority even if it is still restricted to experts and intellectuals.

In the U.S., in Germany and Amsterdam, communes and groups of militants are trying on a small scale to create counter-institutions or alternative ways of life, an embryonic new society. Although this experience has sometimes fallen short, it has been very useful in helping form those who participated in it. In France, the Maoists hardly favor the developments of counter-institutions, except judiciaries with popular tribunals. At Bruay-en-Artois. . . .

Sartre: At Bruay, there never was a popular tribunal.

No, but the Vérité-Justice committees had finally taken that role in openly accusing, with circumstantial evidence, that the notary Leroy had murdered the young girl Brigitte. La Cause du Peuple *violently demanded the punishment of the supposed culprit. Was this a judicious battle? Don't you think the Maoists have taken risks and gone too far?*

Sartre: Probably. For me, the execution of Leroy without trial would be the same as a lynching, pure and simple; and at the time, I expressed my reservations in *La Cause du Peuple*. But even if the Maoists got carried away with polemics, they were fundamentally correct. The point was to denounce the scandal of class justice: the press demanded that the millionaire notary be released on bail, even though it never worries about the accused Algerians who rot for months in preventive detention. *La Cause du Peuple* especially wanted to expose the class struggle at Bruay-en-Artois: the opposition between this big bourgeois with his secrets and his power, and the life of the miners.

One can take that position — which is just — without the outrageous vocabulary which the Maoists used. For example, I was shocked by the headline of La Cause du Peuple *the day after the execution of Buffet and Bomtems: "The guillotine, but for Touvier!"*

Sartre: That headline was criticized in the next edition. The Maoists favor the execution of exploiters and enemies of the people. But it was an error to refer to the guillotine which, for the French, symbolizes bourgeois repression.

Without discussing street fighting or overt force, are you personally a partisan of political execution?

Sartre: Yes. In a revolutionary country, when the bourgeoisie has been driven from power, those who foment uprisings or conspiracies deserve the punishment of death. Not that I would feel the least anger toward them. Reactionaries naturally act in their own interest. But a revolutionary regime must eliminate a certain number of individuals who threaten it; and I see no means but death. One can always get out of prison. The revolutionaries of 1793 probably did not kill enough and therefore unintentionally served the return to order and then the Restoration.

I had the impression, instead, that they killed too many, and that above all they massacred each other. No revolution has succeeded in establishing a clear demarcation between the counter-revolution and the political opposition. That is the whole history of the French and Soviet revolutions: under the pretext of putting down reaction, they ended very quickly by killing those considered most dangerous in the heat of action and sectarianism: that is, the other revolutionaries who disagreed with them. This occurred in France in 1793, in Russia during the Moscow trials, and in the Spanish Civil War when the communists massacred the anarchists. Once unleashed, terror makes no distinctions. As the militants' terror turns closer on itself, they eliminate each other and democratic debate disappears. Finally, the revolution destroys itself, giving way to Thermidorian reaction, Stalinist repression, or fascism. . . .

Sartre: Of course, I oppose anything which could resemble the Moscow trials. But revolution implies both violence and the existence of a more radical party which imposes itself to the detriment of other, more conciliatory groups. Can one conceive of Algerian independence without the elimination of the MNA by the FLN? and how can the FLN be reproached for violence when for years it confronted daily repression, torture, and massacres by the French army? Inevitably, the revolutionary party ends up striking at some of its own members at the same time. I believe this is an historical necessity which we can do nothing about. Find me a way to avoid this and I'll subscribe to it at once. But I don't see it.

Is it necessary to take sides so simply? Can't the problem be posed before the revolution, in seeking to escape this necessity?

Sartre: That won't amount to much. During the revolution everyone is determined by the revolution itself. At most, one can find heroes capable of intervening to establish respect for democratic debate between the revolutionary forces and to maintain free discussion. One cannot say or desire more.

Now, we come to your activity as a writer. In less than five years, the old language of Marxist orthodoxy, which has stamped us all and in which you were debated during a good part of your life, has finally broken up. Revolutionary debate and analysis is being reborn after fifteen years of repetition and sclerosis. We witness the appearance of a new thought with Marcuse, Foucault and Deleuze, and also in millions of people—whether militant or not—who suddenly feel concerned with a theoretical debate which had been reserved to several hundred specialists. Here we find the best elements of Marxism, and also new ideas: anti-psychiatry and a reintegration of the data of ethnography and anthropology. Your 1952 work, Saint Genet, comédien et martyr *was ahead of its time: by way of social analysis and a certain conception of psychoanalysis you treated problems which have especially concerned us in the last two years: delinquency, prisons, homosexuality and the forging of morals and social values. Today, you have apparently removed yourself from this debate, torn between your appropriate militant actions and your work on Flaubert, a nineteenth century author, and whatever interest this study generates.*

Sartre: I don't believe I am absent from this debate, and my books on Flaubert claim to participate in it in their own way—first, by the basic question I intend to pose: in the present state of our knowledge, how can one know a man today? If I succeed, I will have clarified a method which goes far beyond the situation of a nineteenth century writer.

But, for example, the life of Nizan — who was your friend and whom you can speak about more easily than about Flaubert — also poses the question of the relations of man with history and of the writer with society. Nizan is still our problem: here is a revolutionary intellectual and writer who cried out his revolt and affirmed his freedom, who engaged in militant action and was destroyed by Communism. Through self-serving manipulation of his ideas and struggles, Stalinism installed its apparatus and its terror, and basically abandoned the revolutionary project. Generations of intellectuals and militants suffered this alienation: the worst there is. Probably it is not limited to Stalinism — we still see it at other levels. Isn't there an analysis to be done here as a preliminary to future action? Then why Flaubert rather than Nizan?

Sartre: What interests me about Flaubert is precisely that he refused to go to the limit. He supported the idea of an aristocratic bourgeoisie and rose up against the 1848 insurrection and democracy. I try to show why he acted that way, speaking of his childhood, his family, history, how he chose the imaginary, and his alienation. After this, the method will have to be able to serve for other analyses; and that seems as important as circumscribing the anti-hierarchic and libertarian movements.

You mention Nizan and seem to think I am in a privileged position because I knew him. That is false. Real relations between people certainly take place through communication, but never entirely: they are complicated by some magic. It is necessary to abstract oneself from this magic (man is a sorcerer for man, etc.) and to treat the subject under study through documents and witnesses, as if one had never known him. It can be said, moreover, that what we felt or guessed in our relations with one another must appear to us as one source of evidence among others, as ours. The problem remains of the intellectual as he can be considered today — and not by way of Nizan. For me, there are two sorts of intellectuals. The classic intellectual, who lives the contradiction between the universal and the particular, and the new intellectual, who is no longer content to sling his conscience over his shoulder but puts himself to the test by entering the factory. I will cite the case of a friend, an old electrician, who passed his *baccalauréat* by himself and is now an active degree candidate in philosophy. He no longer relates his knowledge to his own subjectivity but to his proletarian life and his craft instead. I think he represents a new kind of intellectual who tends to abolish — somewhat as in China — the division of labor imposed by capitalism. But I am 67 years old and can't go to work in a factory, so I remain a classic intellectual and write on Flaubert.

On the other hand, aware of the definite urgency of the present situation, I participate in a political movement and in *La Cause du Peuple*. There, I don't think I have to dispense counsel and truth *ex cathedra*. Today, that is no longer the intellectual's role. Maoists understand this and I agree with them. One doesn't have ideas all alone: truth comes from the people. It is no longer a question of giving ideas to the masses, but of following their movement, going to search them out at their source and expressing them more clearly, if they consent to it. In *Libération*, for example, I can present an idea which will be both a group's and mine. But I wouldn't dream of writing a book which will determine everything from beginning to end. As for theorizing and analyzing the present situation, as you ask me to do, I don't believe this period lends itself to such analysis. The movement is vast and contradictory — why Maoists, why MLF, and what can their relation be? You would have to devote years to it, which doesn't make sense in a moving situation.

What do you think of the elections? Will you vote?

Sartre: I will not vote. Universal suffrage is a way to separate the workers, to break class solidarity. The isolated individual abandons his voice with neither control nor a chance for opposition. Here is my sovereignty, do with it what you will, you can implement your program or not. I voted for Guy Mollet in 1956 thinking I would declare myself for peace in Algeria. I was very suprised at the result. I can conceive of direct democracy only: each assembly voting by a show of hands and delegating strictly limited powers to one of its members. Those elected do not represent their assembly but *are* their assembly in a certain sense. They simply present their assembly's demands to the employer, for example, because it isn't practical for 2,000 people to do it. But the elected member is always controllable and removable at any time. On the contrary, if you try to put Marchais in place of Messmer after a rivalry which can only pit two similar individuals against each other, you are just replacing Messmer with Messmer.

The Trotskyists are running candidates. They are going to vote for the unified left on the second ballot because they think a defeat of the UDR can precipitate a crisis.

Sartre: I call that the Machiavellian vote. It takes the vote for the opposite of what it is: voting for the Socialists and Communists becuse you hope that Pompidou will dissolve the Assembly and that, in deflecting these leftist parties, you will participate in the struggle which will have to follow. But that has every chance of working against you. The imponderables are such that you risk finding yourself with a government you don't want.

It is not necessary to enter the system. A vote, whatever the ballot, is a vote for the vote, an acceptance of the institutions. How can legal action — the Communist Party's, for example — overthrow the law? It will necessarily

destroy itself in contortions so absurd as to be improbable. This is one
reason I am drawn to the Maoists: I believe in illegality.

Notes

1. Originally published in Number 28 of *Actuel* and reprinted in *Tout Va Bien*, Number 4,
February 20–March 20, 1973, pp. 30–35. It was conducted by Michel-Antoine Burnier.
English translation is by Robert D'Amico.

L'Imagination au Pouvoir:
The Evolution of Sartre's Political
and Social Thought   Thomas R. Flynn*

> "What can I do? No more than I am doing. One must consider my age as
> well. A man of 68, if he were a political person all his life, could gain
> some supplementary knowledge at 69. But if he hasn't been politically
> active, if he has always been a sounding board for politics without
> directly engaging in it, what would you have him do at 69?"
> — Sartre to Maoist discussants (1973)[1]

The story of Sartre's leftists politics generally and his love-hate
relationship with the Communist Party in particular has been amply
documented.[2] But there is still need for an analysis of the intellectual
evolution which underlay these twistings and turnings in the public realm.
Want of such an account has led some critics to dismiss Sartre's political
pronouncements as the rantings of a knee-jerk radical, as ivory-tower
romanticism, or as sheer intellectual demagoguery.[3] What I propose,
within the limits of a journal article, is a brief analytical survey of the
growth and development of Sartre's political and social theory. Since this
involves his gradual politicization, the order will be broadly chronological. But the format I have chosen is primarily conceptual. I wish to
interpret Sartre's social awakening as the discovery of several basic
concepts and principles which serve as foundation stones for a theory
whose application has been recorded in the scholarly and popular press
over the last three decades. A concluding appraisal of the constants and
variables in his development will produce the following essays on specific
issues in Sartre's political and social thought.

Prepolitical Anarchism of The '30s

In his foreword to Paul Nizan's *Aden, Arabie*, Sartre recalls his
political indifference in the '30s: "I was apolitical and reluctant to make

*From *Political Theory* 7, no. 2 (May 1979): 157–80. © 1979 Sage Publications, Inc.

any commitment, but my heart was on the Left, of course, like everyone else's."[4] Elsewhere he describes his prewar anarchism: "To the bottom of my heart I was a belated anarchist. I put an abyss between vague dreams of collectivities and the precise ethnic of my private life."[5]

Yet Sartre displayed a theoretical interest in politics from the very start. One of his earliest publications, "The Theory of the State in Modern French Thought" (1927), surveyed then current theories of natural right and state sovereignty. Though of little more than biographical interest today, this essay reveals Sartre as an early foe of philosophical idealism, a battle he has waged (against himself as well as others) ever since.

But more importantly, Sartre was not blind to the political implications of his early work in phenomenology. At the conclusion of *The Transcendence of the Ego*, written in 1934, he voices approval of historical materialism while decrying the absurdity of "metaphysical materialism" — a position he maintains to this day — and suggests that his theory of ego and world as two objects for absolute, impersonal consciousness should suffice as "a philosophical foundation for an ethics and a politics which are absolutely positive."[6] This linking of ethics and politics is more than grammatical. Although the political falls victim to Sartre's benign neglect in the '30s, when it emerges it does so in a characteristically ethical context, the possibility of which is already evident to the early Sartre.

In the '30s and early '40s Sartre suffered from a weakness common to many "existentialists" in the political and social sphere: a rather narcissistic individualism and a preference for the oblique communication proper to imaginative literature and the fine arts — neither trait inclined to foster social theory or political action.[7] His philosophical apotheosis of the solitary individual (*l'homme seul*), which found literary expression in *Nausea* (1938), exhibited its social poverty in the famous epigram from *No Exit*: "Hell is other people."[8] By his own admission the prewar Sartre believed in literature as salvation and saw himself pursuing a quasi-religious vocation in the world of letters.[9] This accounts for the particularly moral flavor of such fictional analyses of the human condition as *Nausea, The Flies*, and *No Exit*.

His writings of the period manifest an almost congenital hatred of the bourgeoisie; but they do so in a style and for the sake of a personal freedom which, as Marxist critics would later point out, were themselves typically bourgeois.[10] There is something more than coincidental about Sartre's lifelong fascination with Gustave Flaubert, the quintessential bourgeois writer who so despised the bourgeoisie.

Vintage Existentialism (1938–1946)

Sartre has grown increasingly sensitive to the apparent conflict between ethics and politics or to what he terms "the means-end problem."[11] It is not surprising that his entree into political controversy should center on questions of *moral* responsibility for social injustice. The intellectual roots of his political and social theory at this stage are set in the concepts of *bad faith* and *being-in-situation*, developed in his masterwork *Being and Nothingness* (1943).[12] Like most Sartrean concepts, they have their imaginative analogues in his novels and plays of the period. But we shall examine their philosophical articulation in *Being and Nothingness* and their application to social issues in *Anti-Semite and Jew*, written in 1944.[13]

It is part of his Cartesian legacy and vital to his overall philosophic enterprise to insist that consciousness is fully self-transparent; it is without a shadowy side where responsibility would have to be shared with an id or even an ego.[14] Sartre concludes from this that we are completely responsible for the circle of meanings (the "world") which surrounds us and that we must acknowledge this responsibility by choosing to live the anguish it entails or by fleeing this dreadful condition through *bad faith*. These are the standard themes which established Sartre's reputation among café existentialists in the immediate postwar years. Their social and political potential rests in the "faith" aspect of "bad faith," for such a condition is inherently unstable. Like the created world of Descartes' God, faith faces the constant threat of instantaneous annihilation. The source of this instability is Sartrean consciousness itself, the famous *pour-soi*. It is characterized by a kind of inner distance, termed "presence-to-self," which renders it the sole exception to the metaphysical principle of identity and warrants the addition of the qualifier "in the manner of not-being it" to whatever predicate one might wish to ascribe to consciousness. So, to take a well-known example, a young man may wish to *be* the perfect waiter. But he will never achieve this identity the way a stone *is* a stone. Since he is conscious, he must ever be a waiter "in the manner of not-being it," i.e., as nonidentical with his image or ideal.[15]

This nonidentity of consciousness with itself is the ontological root of Sartrean freedom[16] just as self-transparency is the source of Sartrean responsibility: each one "knows" what he is doing.[17] Together they account for the "faith" of "bad faith." For every existential commitment, including the flight from commitment, establishes the meaning-direction (*sens*) of an agent's biography; and he is his biography "in the manner of not-being it," i.e., as sufficiently other to make radical conversion and/or betrayal a constant possibility. The persistence of this possibility of betrayal necessitates the later Sartre's theory of unity in the pledged group as *fraternity-terror*: each swears on his life not to use the power of betrayal which is ontologically his.

If the noncoincidence of consciousness with itself is a source of anguish, it also generates a muted optimism in Sartre. It serves as a premise for his object of unmasking the bad faith of individuals and classes. None has to be what he is; each could be/do otherwise; all are free-responsible for their situations in the ontological sense which enables one to urge them on to freedom in other senses. The initially negative character of this undertaking is gradually complemented by positive advocacy as Sartre becomes more actively associated with political movements on the left. Thus he argues in *Anti-Semite and Jew* that anti-Semitism as a "free and total choice of oneself" is a form of bad faith (pp. 17 and 20) based on a longing for the impenetrability of a stone (pp. 18 and 27). As we might expect, he considers anti-Semitism a distinctively bourgeois phenomenon. And he reveals his positive intent by describing in glowing contrast "the socialist revolution [which] is necessary to and sufficient for the suppression of the anti-Semite" (*Anti-Semite and Jew*, p. 151).[18]

Sartre introduces in this existentialist essay a distinction of major import for his subsequent social theory: that between the *analytic spirit* of the bourgeoisie along with the racist humanism it spawns and the *spirit of synthesis* which enables a person in the context of this essay to view someone as both Jew *and* man (*Anti-Semite and Jew*, p. 56). Now it is the liberal, democratic assimilationist who comes under fire: "He resolves all collectives into individual elements. To him a physical body is a collection of molecules; a social body a collection of individuals. And by individual he means the incarnation in a single example of the universal traits which make up human nature" (*Anti-Semite and Jew*, p. 55). In his subsequent essays against neo-colonialism and capitalism Sartre often underscores the normative status of (bourgeois) human nature as a pseudo justification for exploiting the natives or the proletariat. The frequency with which he employs this argument suggests the close link he forges between his epistemology and his abiding moral concerns.[19]

The spirit of synthesis, forerunner to his Dialectical Reason of the next decade, allows Sartre to understand individuals as being-in-a-situation, perhaps the most fruitful concept of this period for his social theory. As developed in *Being and Nothingness*, it is an admittedly ambiguous idea; the proportion of the given to the taken in any situation remains unclear.[20] Yet it is via this concept and the spirit of synthesis it evinces that a comprehensive social theory gains a footing in Sartrean existentialism. Sartre admits this a few years later in his important bridge essay, "Materialism and Revolution" (1946), when he characterizes the new, revolutionary social philosophy he is propounding: "It is the elucidation of the new ideas of 'situation' and of 'being-in-the-world' that revolutionary behavior specifically calls for."[21] But he begins this elucidation in "Anti-Semite and Jew" when he recommends that the Jew's situation, understood as the "perspective of choice," be radically changed if he would be free: "Thus we do not attack freedom, but bring it about that freedom decides on other bases and in terms of other structures." For Sartre claims that "political action can never be directed against the freedom of citizens; its very nature forbids it to be concerned with freedom except in a negative fashion, that is, in taking care not to infringe upon it. It only acts on situations" (*Anti-Semite and Jew*, pp. 148–149).

This directing of political action toward changing the bases and structures "on which freedom decides" constitutes an essential dimension of *political existentialism* and ushers in a new phase of Sartre's own public life. The spirit and ideal of this political philosophy are captured in the title "Socialism and Freedom [Liberté]" which he and Merleau-Ponty had given their short-lived Resistance group of intellectuals in 1941.[22] The year he writes *Anti-Semite and Jew*, he establishes the editorial board of *Les Temps modernes* as a vehicle for the "committed literature" whose basic principles he formulates in a series of articles entitled "What is Literature?" published in that journal three years later (1947). By the time he joins the Revolutionary People's Assembly (RDR) in 1948, his first attempt at direct political action and mass politics, he is solidly at another stage of his theoretical evolution.[23] But it should be clear from the foregoing that Sartre's politicization is not a *volte-face* nor political existentialism a mere juxtaposition of the incongruous.

Sartre's "Discovery of Society" and His Elaboration of a Political Existentialism (1946–1968)

"Every man is political," Sartre has told a recent interviewer. "But I did not discover that for myself until the war, and I did not truly understand it until 1945."[24] We have observed Sartre's political coming-of-age under the twin banners of socialism and libertarianism. Let us now follow his activist course from the mid '40s as a historical context for understanding those conceptual advances which mark his mature social and political thought.

It may seem ironic that a writer who places the individual above and fully responsible for the events which surround him should himself be submerged in the tides of war which brought him "the true experience, that of society."[25] Doubtless, the change was not as dramatic as Sartre implies. Still there is a definite shift of emphasis and tone in his writings of the postwar decade. They bespeak the committed intellectual who is beginning to suspect that if literature does not bring salvation, perhaps politics will.[26]

This surfaces first of all in Sartre's theory of literature as praxis or "committed literature." In his introduction to the charter issue of *Les Temps modernes*, he delivers a synopsis of the theory. Committed literature will "serve the collectivity by attempting to give it the literature suited for it." Indicative of Sartre's mistrust of party politics, the review will take a stand on political and social issues, but "it will not do so *politically*, i.e., it will serve no party. It will strive to extract the concept of man which underlies the opposing theses and will deliver its opinion according to the conception it supports."[27] The existential humanist inspiration of the enterprise is manifest: it is *opposing humanisms* which are at stake. And correlative to these conflicting value sets are *conflicting epistemologies:* the analytic spirit which led the assimilationist to tolerate all men—as long as they did not insist on being different—sustains the theory of uncommitted literature as an end in itself (*l'art pour l'art*). For the first time, Sartre associates his spirit of synthesis with a clear subscription to historical materialism. Indeed, he hopes that the review may contribute toward establishing a "synthetic anthropology."[28] And this is precisely what it undertakes twelve years later by publishing "Search for a Method" which, along with the *Critique of Dialectical Reason*, answers the question: "Do we have today the means to constitute a structural, historical anthropology?"[29]

It appears that at the very time he is elaborating a theory of committed literature in *What is Literature?* Sartre is himself losing confidence in the power of art to change men's situations. His intended tetralogy, *Roads to Freedom*, trickles off with two installments of Volume 4 in *Les Temps modernes* (1949). Less than ten years later he writes his last play, *The Condemned of Altona* (1959).[30]

But the intervening and subsequent years are rich with the fruit of Sartre's *political imagination.* His powerful vision of men disalienated and equal affords a vantage point from which he condemns exploitation and oppression of every form. Sartre often describes freedom as transcendence of the factical (*facticité*) in a given situation. As the factical assumes greater significance in the form of "structures" and "bases" of choice (what we shall soon term "objective possibility"), its transcendence requires more than aesthetic imagination.[31] Even literature-as-praxis proves a halfway house to direct social criticism and political polemic. Yet always Sartre working from an ideal which is egalitarian, socialist, libertarian, and profoundly moral in hue: he terms it the "reign of freedom" and the "City of ends" (*Situations*, Vol. 3, pp. 210 and 193).

Elsewhere I have argued that imaginative consciousness is paradigmatic of Sartrean consciousness *tout court*, for it is the locus of possibility, negativity, and lack.[32] That inner distance, presence-to-self, which grounds ontological freedom is best exhibited in imaging activities where "nihilating" consciousness holds the real at bay: anything is possible; nothing *has* to be the case. This realization which gave nausea to Roquentin should bring hope to the oppressed, Sartre believes. It is the dialectical materialists' substitution of causal law for imagination, of necessity for possibility, on the contrary, which renders their expressions of moral anguish so suspect (*Situations*, Vol. 3, p. 193, n.). And it is a failure of imagination, which is ultimately a failure of freedom, of which Sartre will accuse the Communists in '68.

If political imagination gradually subsumes aesthetic creativity for Sartre in the '50s and '60s, why his close association with the French

Communist Party in the early '50s, a group so notoriously lacking in both? Part of the answer lies in the failure of the RDR and Sartre's resultant political "realism," which led him to conclude: "Today, a worker in France can express and fulfill himself only in a class action directed by the Communist Party."[33] But, as we shall argue shortly, it would be wrong to view this as a tarnishing of his overall moral vision. Rather, Sartre's fellow-traveling should be read as an instance of his general thesis that one cannot do politics without dirtying one's hands.[34] Even his staunchest support of the party is qualified: "The purpose of this article ["The Communists and Peace"] is to declare my agreement with the Communists on precise and limited subjects, reasoning from *my* principles and not *theirs*" (p. 68; emphasis in the original). Not the words of an enthusiastic convert; but what else could one expect from a presence-to-self, not a self?

The history of Sartre's relations with the Communists can be summarized in five essays whose titles chart the parabola: "Materialism and Revolution" (1946), which considers true revolutionary thinking impossible from the standpoint of dialectical materialism; "The Communists and Peace" (1952–1954), the high point in Sartre's support of the party; "The Ghost of Stalin" (1956–1957), confirming Sartre's rejection of Stalinism and expressing his revulsion at the Soviet suppression of the Hungarian revolt; and finally "The Communists are Afraid of Revolution" (1968) and "The Socialism that Came in from the Cold" (1970), voicing respectively his reaction to the party's restraint during the events of May 1968 and to the Russian invasion of Czechoslovakia that same year. By the end of the '60s Sartre has come to regard the French party as amoral, authoritarian, and gradualist. He has cast his lot with *les Maos* and others who share his ethical and libertarian vision.[35]

The foregoing political itinerary marks the practical and public dimension of an evolution in Sartre's speculative thinking which can be understood as the discovery and development of four basic concepts and principles: (1) objective possibility, (2) the primacy of praxis, (3) the mediating third party, and (4) the ideal of positive, mediated reciprocity among members of a practical group.[36] Each articulates his ongoing reflection on his "experience of society"; together they constitute the essence of Marxist existentialism as formulated by Sartre over the last quarter century.

(1) *Objective possibility.* Formulated by Weber and interpreted by Lukàcs in light of the Hegelian-Marxist concept of objective contradiction, this concept figures prominently in the social theory of the later Sartre, even if he uses the expression sparingly.[37] As he systematizes his conception of History (with a Hegelian "H"), the importance of objective forces and limits grows apace. As we have observed, the concept of being-in-a-situation is the forerunner of objective possibility in Sartre's earlier, Promethean existentialism. But the absence there of any systematic account of objective limits fosters the impression that the individual agent

can set whatever course he chooses by a mere change of existential project or gestalt-shift.[38]

We noted Sartre's growing awareness of the problem of objective limits in *Anti-Semite and Jew*: the need to change the *bases* and *structures* of the Jew's choice. In *What is Literature?* he claims that the "City of ends" cannot be realized "without an objective modification of the historical situation." He adds that the Kantian maxim of treating all agents as ends is futile as long as "the fundamental structures of our society are still oppressive."[39] Describing French social and economic Malthusianism a few years later, he writes: "The meanness is in the system; one must not see a national characteristic in it, but the collective situation which our lords have made for us" ("The Communists and Peace," p. 183); and "[Malthusianism and the discouragement of the workers] subjectively express the objective limits which the structure of the economy imposes on praxis" ("The Communists and Peace," p. 186).

In the *Critique* Sartre provides the ontological footing for objective possibility in the concept of the *practico-inert*. The latter denotes recalcitrant matter (the facticity of *Being and Nothingness*) as formed by and deforming human praxes. It emerges as the objective bearer of such praxes as the racist idea, economic "laws," and class-being;[40] in sum, of the *structures* which limit and alienate praxes.

If the twin values, socialism and freedom, form the dominant motif of Sartre's social thought, he recognizes an inevitable *tension* between the objective demands for a socialist revolution (structural change) based on objective possibility and the absolute worth of the individual as an end in himself — the recurrent problem of means and end, of ethics and politics. In the late '40s, at least, he is rather sanguine about their complementarity: committed literature, for example, will "fight for the freedom of the person *and* for the socialist revolution."[41] But after a decade of attempting such a conjunction, he refers in somewhat chastened fashion to "the strange circular conflict, where all synthesis is impossible, which is the untranscendable contradiction of History: the opposition and identity of the individual and the common" (*Critique of Dialectical Reason*, p. 559).

(2) *The Primacy of Praxis.* "Praxis," for Sartre, signifies purposive human activity in its historical, material environment.[42] It is the vehicle for introducing the existentialist values of individual freedom and personal responsibility into the Marxian realm of impersonal forces, dialectical necessities, and objective contradictions. It preserves a place in methodological Marxism for such existential psychoanalyses as Sartre's brilliant studies of Genet and Flaubert and his own autobiography. For the principle of the primacy of praxis grounds the claim, essential to Sartrean humanism, that "a man can always make something out of what is made of him" (*Between Existentialism and Marxism*, p. 35). And the point of such analyses is to determine just what these men have in fact made of

what society and especially early childhood experience have made of them. What at an earlier stage of his career resulted in literary biography, e.g., his rather unsuccessful study of Baudelaire (1946), emerges in these later works as full-fledged social criticism effected with the aid of that amalgam of existential psychoanalysis and historical materialism which he calls the "progressive-regressive method."[43]

This principle serves several other functions in Sartre's social theory. It justifies his search for oppressive praxis and hence for individual, moral responsibility at the base of "impersonal" social and economic phenomena: "In short, it is men whom we judge and not physical forces."[44] This is the presupposition behind his polemical essays of the '50s and '60s, castigating those responsible for the exploitative systems of capitalism, neocolonialism, and imperialism.

Moreover, it grounds his understanding of sovereign praxis which renders "state sovereignty" an alienating idea. "Sovereignty" is a descriptive and original term for Sartre; he writes: "Sovereignty is simply the unilateral (*univoque*) relation of interiority between the individual as praxis and the objective field which he organizes and transcends towards his own end." It is not bestowed on men or institutions from above. "Man *is* sovereign" just as man *is* freedom in *Being and Nothingness*. "The only limitation on man's sovereignty over all Others is simple reciprocity, that is to say, the total sovereignty of each and all over him" (*Critique of Dialectical Reason*, p. 610). It follows that the sovereignty of the group leader can only be *quasi*-sovereignty, and that *nonreciprocal sovereignty*, which is the essence of authority for Sartre, is necessarily alienating (see *Critique of Dialectical Reason*, pp. 607ff.). But the proper locus of authority is the institution and, above all, the state. So the primacy of praxis supports Sartre's political anarchism as well.

Finally, praxis is dialectical and totalizing. As dialectical, it proceeds reciprocally and via the negation of negative situations, e.g., the overcoming of scarcity and the meeting of needs. As totalizing, praxis synthesizes a multiplicity of parts, both historical and structural, into a *practical* whole. Sartre underscores its telic aspect when he writes that "to totalize is to grasp the world from the front in a practical unveiling" (*Situations*, Vol. 8, p. 441). The notion of totalizing praxis is an application of his spirit of synthesis and, along with the practico-inert as the locus of objective possibility, provides the key to Sartre's structural, historical anthropology. Because of the primacy of dialectical, totalizing praxis, this anthropology must ultimately rely upon Dialectical, not Analytical, Reason.

(3) *The Mediating Third*. The development of this concept is perhaps Sartre's most significant advance over the socially impoverished categories of *Being and Nothingness*. We noted the basically dyadic character of interpersonal relations in it; they are all forms of the self / other dichotomy epitomized by the famous Sartrean "look" (*le regard*). The closest he comes

to constructing a social theory on that basis is his discussion of the "we" and the "us." But the "we" is dismissed as a "subjective *Erlebnis*" whereas the "us" merely extends the status of being-for-others to a plurality. The third party whose look constitutes the "us" is but a form of the Other. It should be designated the "objectifying" or "alienating" third.[45]

The mediating third, introduced in the *Critique*, differs from the alienating third in that it unifies *without objectifying* the other praxes so united. It is now conceptually possible for Sartre to talk of fused and pledged *groups* where each agent is *the same* as (though not identical, much less interchangeable with) the other members. These are united not only by the external "look" of the Other but also by the internalization of their multiplicity as a means to a common project. Whereas some form of otherness is inevitable among individuals who are presences-to-self, what Sartre calls the "serial alterity" of the impotent mob or the faceless crowd is exchanged for "free alterity" of the group member, thanks to the role of each as mediating third.

Thus, internalized multiplicity and interest create the "common individual," Sartre's equivalent of Rousseau's citizen who thinks in terms of "us" and not of "me." But, unlike Rousseau, Sartre's mediating third precludes the totalitarian threat by remaining a *revolving relation of individual praxes*. Although he allows that group praxis is a "synthetic enrichment" of individual praxis and thereby warrants ascriptions of social predicates such as power, pledge and function, Sartre denies that the group is a superorganism or a product of collective consciousness. The mediating third is pivotal to this "dialectical nominalism,"[46] Sartre's via media between methodological holism and individualism. And, of course, the mediating third preserves the identity and responsibility of the individual agent even within the white heat of group activity.[47]

(4) *Mediated Reciprocity.* As praxis replaces consciousness at the focal point of Sartre's theory of man, the dialectic subsumes the descriptive and phenomenological, and the triad sublates the dyadic either/or in his social thought: "The *real* relation between men is necessarily ternary" (*Critique of Dialectical Reason*, p. 109; emphasis in the original). Binary relations such as those traced with scientific rigor by Lévi-Strauss are taken to be abstract in the Hegelian sense of "not fully determined." The real is dialectical, and who says "dialectic" says "mediation." So the major problem for the Sartre of the *Critique* (1960) and *The Family Idiot* (1971–) is to discover those *mediating factors* which forge individual and society (both abstractions) into concrete, historical reality. As a Marxist, he believes that economics is decisive;[49] but as an existentialist, he maintains the primacy of free, responsible praxis: one can always make something of what others have made of him.

The "others" have always constituted a problem for Sartre. In the mid '40s we saw them characterized as hellish. The success of a Sartrean social theory depends on his finding a more adequate solution to this question. In the *Critique* he approaches its resolution. There he claims that *all* human relations are fundamentally reciprocal and that their positive or negative character (cooperation or struggle) depends entirely on what *mediates* these reciprocities.[50] If the practico-inert mediates human action, as occurs in situations of material scarcity where one class owns the instruments of labor while another uses them to produce commodities for a wage (*Critique of Dialectical Reason*, p. 789), then man is a product of his own product and social struggle is the order of the day. But if "the inhuman power of mediation" can be taken from the practico-inert and be returned to each and to all in the community (i.e., as mediating thirds), man can be transformed into "a *product of the group*, that is to say — as long as the group is freedom — *into his own product*" (*Critique of Dialectical Reason*, pp. 672–673, emphasis in the original).

Sartre sees the deep origin of the group in this liberating project. When the group begins to fuse, as in his example of the Parisians storming the Bastille, its members experience "the brusk resurrection of freedom" — the kind of spontaneous action community that Sartre experienced, at least imaginatively, during the Resistance.[51] The fused group offers a taste of utopia. Except for the "derealizing" activity of the imaginative artist, now admitted to be socially impotent, nowhere else in contemporary society does Sartre find this victory over alienation, separation, and conflict, transient though it be.

Sartre joins Rousseau and Marx in constructing what Sheldon Wolin terms as "regenerative" political philosophy.[52] With an end to material scarcity and to the authority structures proper to institutions will come "a new society in which all powers will have been done away with because each individual [will have] full possession of himself. [For] revolution . . . is a long movement in which power is dismantled" (*Life/Situations*, p. 84). The nature of the new "socialist man" to emerge from this revolution or of the "philosophy of freedom" which alone will be adequate for him can scarcely be conjectured in our present, alienated state.[53] Still, Sartre expects that life in a "socialism of abundance" will entail the end to politics as a profession, "for each one will become mediator of the whole (*ensemble*)."[54]

Recently Sartre has warned: "Either man is finished . . . or else he will adapt by bringing about some form of libertarian socialism" (*Life/Situations*, p. 83). His anarchist vision of the new society is a theoretically sophisticated and politically tempered expression of those vague ideals which inspired him and Simone de Beauvoir in the '30s. Too much has transpired in the intervening decades to warrant talk of having come full circle. Nonetheless, there is a singleness of purpose connecting the strands of his philosophic and literary career that invites a comparison of the constants and variables in his thought as a whole. Let this reflection constitute our final attempt at a survey of his work.

Beyond Marxism: Plus ça change . . .
(1968 to the Present)

I have indicated various paths by which one might go beyond Marxism
(*Life/Situations*, p. 61).

Although their political and social implications are only gradually
worked out, one can find at least five constants in Sartre's thought,
orchestrating his public philosophy in a particular key: (1) the ultimacy of
individual freedom-responsibility; (2) the obligation of the intellectual,
especially the writer, to give bourgeois society a bad conscience; (3) the
persistent problem of means-ends, i.e., of ethics and politics; (4) the
lasting relevance of the analytic-synthetic distinction; and (5) an abiding
commitment to the anarchist idea of an end to authority in a society where
all relations are eye level and all associations voluntary. Together these
form the existentialist core of political existentialism as championed by the
later Sartre.

(1) Individual freedom-responsibility, taken under different but related descriptions as both fact and value, is a nonnegotiable for Sartre. We
have witnessed its expression in his later works as the principle of the
primacy of praxis and the functional concept of the mediating third. It
entitles us to describe his philosophy as a humanism from beginning to end
and explains his sharp opposition to unqualified structuralist claims.
Moreover, it adds a sense of seriousness absent from orthodox Marxism to
both conjuncts of Marx's claim that "men make their own history . . . but
under circumstances . . . given and transmitted from the past."[55]

(2) Describing his appraisal of the writer's vocation in the '30s, Sartre
notes: "To tell the truth about existence and to strip the pretenses from
bourgeois lies was one and the same thing, and that was what I had to do
in order to fulfill my destiny as a man, because I had been created in order
to write" (*Life/Situations*, p. 45). We have witnessed his disillusionment
with the artist's power to alter people's situations. Indeed, he has characterized *The Words* as his "adieu to literature" (*Life/Situations*, p. 111). But
he continues to view the committed writer's mission as one of unmasking
bourgeois bad faith. If the writer in a starving world would not join the
exploiters by his lack of commitment, Sartre leaves him but two choices:
renounce literature in order to educate the people (as Sartre claims to have
done) "or pose problems in the most radical and intransigent manner,"
i.e., in a way applicable to our nonrevolutionary societies. "What I ask of
the writer," he challenges, "is not to ignore the reality and the fundamental problems which exist. The world's hunger, the atomic threat, the
alienation of men — I am astonished that these do not color all our
literature."[56]

(3) We remarked Sartre's early and continued interest in the means-
end problem. In this we agree with Francis Jeanson that Sartre never

abandoned his ethical concerns *überhaupt*, even though he has consistently condemned bourgeois moralizing and sharply criticized its ethical superstructure during his years of sympathy with the Communist Party.[57] The reason for insisting on this permanent feature of Sartre's thought is his own recent assessment of his ethical development. After describing the moral concerns of his youth, he continues: "I passed from an idealist realism when I was eighteen to an amoralist realism when I was forty-five, and thence I recovered morality as the basis of realism, but this time materially or, if you will, as a materialistic and ethical realism" (*On a raison de se révolter*, p. 78). While it is true that his remarks of the '50s and early '60s are in the "realist" vein of cracking-eggs-to-make-omelets, he continues to ascribe moral responsibility to oppressors and exploiters throughout the period on the basis of the principle of the primacy of praxis, and he is obviously appealing to his readers' sense of moral indignation — a method he has employed from the very start. Perhaps Sartre best summarized his attitude toward the means-end problem at that time when he reflected apropos of his differences with the then recently deceased Albert Camus: "Ethics (*la morale*) taken by itself both demands revolt and condemns it" (*Situations*, Vol. 4, p. 127).

(4) "At a certain level of abstraction" Sartre writes in the *Critique*, "class conflict expresses itself as a conflict of rationalities" (*Critique of Dialectical Reason*, p. 802). Sartre has been operating at that level of abstraction at least since distinguishing the analytic and the synthetic spirits in *Anti-Semite and Jew*. In "Materialism and Revolution" he contrasts the bourgeois and proletarian methods of thinking as analytic and synthetic respectively (see *Situations*, Vol. 3, p. 154). His identification of this analytic spirit with a bourgeois humanism based on an unchangeable human nature serving as a moral norm is another constant in Sartre's political and social theory. It links this distinction with the ethical humanist implications of his famous existentialist maxim "existence precedes essence," for this saying is a scandal to the analytical spirit.

(5) Sartre has claimed that both their libertarian beliefs and their ethical stance attracted him to les Maos (*On a raison de se révolter*, p. 78). He admits to having been antiauthoritarian ever since he came to know his stepfather (*On a raison de se révolter*, p. 172). His early disgust at the "natural right" of the bourgeoisie to govern was powerfully expressed in *Nausea* and in the short story "The Childhood of a Leader" (1939). This egalitarianism motivates the true revolutionary's opposition to the bourgeois system of rights-duties, described in "Materialism and Revolution" as a cry from the oppressed that "we too are men" (*Situations*, Vol. 3, p. 188). One senses here the anticipated sound of the citizens in the City of ends, "a system of the world which does not yet exist and which will exclude all privileges de facto and de jure" (*Situations*, Vol. 3, p. 192). For Sartre considers revolution an attempt "to bring it about by violence that society move from a state where freedoms are alienated to another founded on

their reciprocal recognition" (*Situations*, Vol. 3, p. 218). We have noted that authority, for Sartre, is nonreciprocal sovereignty and that the practico-inert mediates by alienating. The category of mediated reciprocity merely lends theoretical support to Sartre's lifelong commitment to eye-level relations. Coupled with the overriding values of socialism and freedom, this justifies our locating Sartre's social thought in the tradition of French anarchism extending back to Proudhon.

These several constants by no means exhaust the features of Sartre's social thought which have withstood his shifts and reassessments. They should, however, suffice to confirm our suspicion that, despite his talk of an existentialist "ideology" adjective to Marxist "knowledge" (Savoir),[58] *Sartre remains an existentialist.*[59] Still, his existentialism should now be qualified as Marxian. Since the latter exploits the variables in Sartre's political and social evolution, we shall conclude by considering briefly three of these vehicles for accommodating his "experience of society" as conceptualized in Part III.

The first and most fundamental variable in Sartre's thought is his concept of freedom itself. His initial essays in phenomenological psychology evidence a concern to bring to light that "dreadful freedom" which each of us *is* by virtue of consciousness. But this "noetic" freedom to give meaning-direction (*sens*) to our world proved to be politically ineffective and, save for the Other's "look," solipsistic as well. With Sartre's growing awareness of the objective limits to one's existential situation we observed his broadening of the meaning of "freedom" No longer is it only an ontological structure (the *pour-soi* as presence-to-self) or merely a function of meaning-giving (the noetic freedom to "choose" our world), though both senses of the term are retained. Since objective structures can limit choice and thus condemn some individuals to the nonreciprocal service of others, it is these structures and bases of choice which must be altered. In an interview given to *Comoedia* in 1943, Sartre distinguishes freedom in-consciousness and in-situation. The latter requires others' freedom.[60] This subsequently becomes the "concrete freedom" of "Materialism and Revolution," which Sartre distinguishes from mere "stoic" freedom, a concept suspiciously resembling the noetic freedom of his earlier works ("Materialism and Revolution, pp. 235–239). And concrete freedom later emerges as the political and social freedom of the *Critique*, now possible only in the reciprocity and mutuality of the group. The logical consistency of this broadening of Sartre's concept remains a matter of dispute.[61]

As his concept of freedom has broadened, Sartre's understanding of "responsibility" has grown as well. In the halcyon days of existentialism, he urged his dramatic heroes, e.g., Roquentin and Orestes, to accept full responsibility for the consequence of their choice in an absurd world. Like the Kierkegaardian choice on which it was modeled, responsibility was an individuating phenomenon. But in a raft of polemical essays penned since the war, he has ascribed responsibility to collectives, e.g., the French middle class, and to individuals by virtue of their membership in collectives, e.g., the industrial capitalist. No doubt, the concepts of praxis and mediating third prevent these ascriptions from devolving into impersonal casual attributions.[62] But clearly it is no longer individual responsibility *simpliciter* which is being employed in these articles or analyzed in the *Critique*. And this raises an unresolved ethical implication of Sartre's middle way between holism and individualism. Can there be *moral* responsibility which is collective without positing an ontologically collective subject?

Finally, the concept of being-in-situation has changed qualitatively to the point of requiring a new term, "objective possibility," for its denomination. This evolution occurs in tandem with that of the two preceding variables, as the analysis in Part III has indicated. However, the existentialist antecedents of objective possibility are sufficiently clear to warrant talk of change, not substitution.[63]

Sartre encourages us to adopt the synthetic viewpoint in his own life when he remarks: "We know that this distinction between private and public life does not really exist, that it is pure illusion, a mystification. . . . One's existence forms a whole which cannot be split up. Our lives inside and outside, subjective and objective, personal and political — all necessarily awake echoes in one another because they are aspects of one and the same whole, and one can only understand an individual, whoever he may be, by seeing him as a social being" (*Life/Situations*, p. 44).

Sartre's own being-in-situation is that of a gifted writer, endowed with formidable powers of imagination and insight into the human condition and committed to individual freedom from alienation under every guise. Once he "experiences society," he enlists the conceptual resources of Marxism and the political muscle of the Communist Party in the cause of social and political freedom. But if the means shift according to Sartre's changing perception of the kinds of alienation, the end remains ever the same: the full freedom of the individual to enter voluntarily into reciprocal, eye-level relations with his comrades in the City of ends.

We should not let this sustaining vision, his ethical ideal, blind us to the significant theoretical advances in social and political theory made by the later Sartre. His concepts of the practico-inert and the mediating third party, his employment of the progressive-regressive method, and his general project of laying the foundations for a structural and historical anthropology, deserve the attention of every serious student of social and political thought. But notwithstanding its solid conceptual skeleton, which we laid bare in Part III, Sartre's theory remains primarily a product of political imagination by one of the greatest philosophers of the imagination of all time. This assessment gains historical confirmation from the decisive effect on Sartre's life of the events of May 1968. His resonance with them was total, for they carried a peculiarly Sartrean tone:[64] the moral indignation, the spontaneity, the comraderie (reciprocity), the heightened sense of disalienation, the practical unity in opposition to authority — and the ultimate failure of it all; in sum, *"l'imagination au pouvoir."*[65]

Notes

1. Philippe Gavi, Jean-Paul Sartre, and Pierre Victor, *On a raison de se révolter* (Paris: Gallimard, 1974), p. 274.

2. The best account in English is Michel-Antoine Burnier's *Choice of Action*, Bernard Murchland [trans.] (New York: Random House, 1968), even though it limits itself to the perspective of *Les Temps modernes*. For a step-by-step analysis of Sartre's relations with the communist movement over the past 30 years see Franco Fé, *Sartre e il Communismo* (Firenze: La Nuova Italia, 1970). Helpful because of his personal involvement in the story is Francis Jeanson's *Sartre dans sa vie* (Paris: Seuil, 1974). A valuable study in the history of ideas is Mark Poster's *Existential Marxism in Postwar France* (Princeton, NJ: Princeton University Press, 1975).

3. See, for example, Thomas Molnar, *Sartre: Ideologue of Our Time* (New York: Funk & Wagnalls, 1968), pp. 98ff.; or Georges Lukács, *Existentialisme ou Marxisme?* (Paris: Nagel, 1961), p. 136.

4. Joan Pinkham [trans.] (Boston: Beacon Press, 1970), p. 51. Simone De Beauvoir echoes this judgment in her autobiography: "Sartre built his theories, fundamentally, upon certain positions which we both adhered to with some passion. Our love of freedom, our opposition to the established order of things, our individualism, and our respect for the working class — all these brought us close to the anarchist position. But to be quite frank, our inchorence defied any sort of label. We were anticapitalists, yet not Marxists." *The Prime of Life*, trans. Peter Green (New York: Lancer Books, 1966) p. 46. Later in the same work she describes "our anarchism" as being "as deep-dyed and aggressive as that of the old libertarians" (p. 88).

5. *Situations*, 10 vols. to date (Paris: Gallimard, 1947–), Vol. 4, p. 217.

6. Forrest Williams and Robert Kirkpatrick [trans.] (New York: Noonday, 1957), p. 106.

7. This is doubtless why, once he formulates the theory of committed literature in the mid '40s, he must devote so much effort to convincing critics that the adjective in that phrase does not devour the noun. See "What is Literature?" *Situations*, Vol. 2, pp. 55ff.

8. *No Exit and Three Other Plays*, Stuart Gilbert and Lionel Abel [trans.] (New York: Vintage Books, 1955), p. 47.

9. See Jean-Paul Sartre, *The Words*, trans. Bernard Frechtman (New York: Fawcett Crest Books, 1964), pp. 111–12.

10. See, for example, Lukács, *Existentialisme*, pp. 108ff.

11. In a lecture delivered at the opening session of UNESCO at the Sorbonne, November 1, 1946, Sartre delineated the responsibility of the writer in our time: "He must . . . give his thoughts without respite, day in, day out, to the problem of the end and the means; or, alternatively, the problem of the relation between ethics and politics." As translated by Betty Askwith, this address was published as "The Responsibility of the Writer" in *Reflections on Our Age* (New York: Columbia University Press, 1949), p. 83.

12. Hazel E. Barnes [trans.] (New York: Philosophical Library, 1956).

13. George J. Becker [trans.] (New York: Schocken Books, 1956).

14. This was already a consequence of his *The Transcendence of the Ego*, the title of which denotes both an objective and a subjective genitive. Husserl's transcendental ego has

been superseded, and the empirical ego of introspective psychology has been assigned a place in the world of things: the ego is an object *for* consciousness.

15. This accounts for Sartre's fascination with role-playing, our appearance before the Other. This inner distance makes actors of us all. Bad faith seeks to abolish the distance between consciousness and role. This problem becomes the theme of his adaptation of the elder Dumas' comedy *Kean* (1954).

16. "Man is free because he is no self but self-presence," *Being and Nothingness*, p. 440 (trans. emended).

17. Sartre distinguishes "knowledge," which is reflective and dichotomized into subject and object poles, from direct, nonreflective awareness, which he will later term "comprehension" (*Verstehen*) or the self-awareness of praxis. It is the latter which justifies his ascriptions of far-reaching responsibility to agents who always understand where their interests lie. See, e.g., his account of the provincial bourgeois' reaction to news of the Paris massacres of 1848 in *Critique of Dialectical Reason*, Jonathan Rée [ed.] and Alan Sheridan-Smith [trans.] (London: New Left Books, 1976), pp. 74–76 and 754–770.

18. Anticipating his later remarks about group praxis and life in a "socialism of abundance," Sartre adds: "In a society where members feel mutual bonds of solidarity because they are engaged in the same enterprise, there would be no place for [anti-Semitism]" (*Anti-Semite and Jew*, pp. 149–150).

For Sartre's response to François Mauriac's subsequent challenge to comment on anti-Semitism in socialist states, see Burnier, *Choice*, p. 88.

19. I develop this point in my "Praxis and Vision: Elements of a Sartrean Epistemology," *Philosophical Forum* 8 (1976), pp. 21–43.

20. In analyzing any situation, "the for-itself cannot distinguish the contribution of freedom from that of the brute existent" (*Being and Nothingness*, p. 488).

21. *Literary and Philosophical Essays*, Annette Michelson [trans.] (New York: Collier Books, 1962), p. 253. "Materialism and Revolution"— along with "Présentation" of *Les Temps modernes* (1945), "Existentialism is a Humanism" (1946), and "What is Literature?" (1947) — is a bridge essay, revealing the shift and sometimes the inconsistencies of a philosophical individualist incorporating the newly discovered social realm into his systematic thought.

22. The enterprise did not last nine months, and Sartre returned to his own form of resistance, the unmasking of bad faith, by finishing *The Flies*; see Jeanson, *Sartre*, pp. 133–134.

23. The RDR was a short-lived nonparty formed by David Rousset and others to reconcile Socialists and Communists into a common front against capitalism at home and colonialism and superpower politics abroad. In formulating the rationale for this *rassemblement*, Sartre appeals to "situation" as "an idea capable of uniting the Marxists and non-Marxists among us." He adds what is by then a well established theme for him, viz., that "the only way to liberate men is to act on their situation" (Jean-Paul Sartre, David Rousset, and Gerard Rosenthal, *Entretiens sur la politique* [Paris: Gallimard, 1949], pp. 38 and 39).

24. Jean-Paul Sartre, "Self-Portrait at Seventy," in *Life/Situations. Essays Written and Spoken*, Paul Auster and Lydia Davis [trans.] (New York: Pantheon Books, 1977), pp. 44–45.

25. Jean-Paul Sartre, "The Itinerary of a Thought," in *Between Existentialism and Marxism*, John Mathews [trans.] (New York: William Morrow, 1976), p. 34.

26. See his interview "A Long, Bitter, Sweet Madness," *Encounter* 22 (June, 1964), pp. 61–63.

27. "Présentation des Temps modernes," *Situations*, Vol. 2, p. 30.

28. *Situations*, Vol. 2, pp. 22–23.

29. Jean-Paul Sartre, *Search for a Method*, Hazel E. Barnes [trans.] (New York: Vintage Books, 1968), p. xxxiv. Originally published in two issues of *Les Temps modernes* (1957), it later appeared as a quasi-preface to the *Critique*.

30. I am discounting his adaptation of Euripides' *The Trojan Women* (1965).

31. His study of Jean Genet, *Saint Genet, Actor and Martyr* (1952), is understood by one of Sartre's most perceptive critic as implying that "the most radical and strenuous work of liberation may only be able to be carried out in imagination because it cannot suppress the original condition of total alienation" (André Gorz, *Le Socialisme difficile* [Paris: Seuil, 1967], p. 209.

32. "The Role of the Image in Sartre's Aesthetic," *The Journal of Aesthetics and Art Criticism* 33 (Summer 1975), pp. 431–442.

33. *The Communists and Peace*, with *A Reply to Claude Lefort*, Martha H. Fletcher and Philip R. Berk [trans.] (New York: George Braziller, 1968), p. 131.

34. Commenting on his play *Dirty Hands* (1948), which takes this as its theme, Sartre identifies himself with its pragmatic protagonist, Hoederer, who is willing to make short-term compromises for the sake of substantial long-term gains; see Michel Contat and Michel Rybalka (comps.) *The Writings of Jean-Paul Sartre*, vol. 1, *A Bibliographical Life*, Richard C. McCleary [trans.] (Evanston: Northwestern University Press, 1974), p. 192.

35. See *On a raison de se révolter*, pp. 75–77.

36. Other concepts might have been chosen; in a system which purports to be dialectical, one must always begin *in medias res*. But no other concepts seem more far-reaching in explanatory significance for the later Sartre than these, and other leading candidates for these positions are intelligible precisely in relation to them. Thus, for example, scarcity (*la rareté*) is a characteristic of objective possibility and of the mediation of the practico-inert; violence is interiorized scarcity; need is a qualification of the relation between practical organism and environment or world (cf. definition of praxis); and dialectic itself is intelligible to Sartre only as the "logic of praxis," the reason for his continued opposition to DIAMAT.

37. The term is most clearly developed by George Lukács in *History and Class Consciousness*, Rodney Livingston [trans.] (Cambridge, Mass: MIT Press, 1971), pp. 46–81. On the divergent uses of "objective possibility" by Weber and Lukács, see Maurice Weyembergh, "M. Weber et G. Lukács," and Iring Fetscher, "Zum Begriff der 'Objektiven Möglichkeit' bei Max Weber und George Lukács," *Revue Internationale de Philosophie*, no. 106 (1973), pp. 474–500 and 501–515, respectively.

38. Sartre realized this himself when he remarked: "The other day I reread a prefatory note of mine to a collection of these plays — *Les Mouches*, *Huis Clos*, and others — and was truly scandalized. I had written: 'Whatever the circumstances, and wherever the site, a man is always free to choose to a be a traitor or not. . . .' When I read this, I said to myself: it's incredible, I actually believed that!" *Between Existentialism and Marxism*, pp. 33–34.

39. *Situations*, Vol. 2, p. 296. For an example of Sartre's application of this concept, see *Search for a Method*, pp. 93ff.

40. See *Critique of Dialectical Reason*, pp. 300–303, 747–749, and 250–251, respectively.

41. He expected the RDR to reconcile the conflict between individualism and society; see Sartre, *Entretiens*, p. 40.

42. Sartre defines praxis rather ponderously as "an organizing project which transcends material conditions towards an end and inscribes itself, through labor, in inorganic matter as a rearrangement for the practical field and a reunification of means in the light of the end" (*Critique of Dialectical Reason*, p. 734).

43. The regressive phase of this method, developed in *Search for a Method*, requires a detailed analysis of major features of the subject's biography, e.g., Flaubert's passiveness, in order to establish the "objective conditions" for their possibility, e.g., the state of family life among the French upper middle class under Louis Philippe. The progressive phase then pushes forward from these conditions in a spiral movement toward a totalizing synthesis of

the agent, his motives, and products (objectifications) in order to account for that unique phenomenon which is the agent himself as "singular universal," e.g., Flaubert as the author of Madame Bovary. In effect, this is the dialectic of totalizing praxis and objective possibility translated into a general methodology.

44. *Search for a Method*, p. 47; in other words, the "meanness" is not entirely in the system.

45. "Thus there are two radically different forms of the experience of the we, and the two forms correspond exactly to the being-in-the-act-of-looking and the being-looked-at which constitute the fundamental relations of the For-itself with the Other" (*Being and Nothingness*, p. 415).

The relation between objectification and alienation in the later Sartre is disputed. The gamut of opinions as to their practical identification runs as follows: clearly yes (Pietro Chiodi, *Sartre and Marxism*, Kate Soper, trans. [Hassocks, Sussex: Harvester Press, 1976], pp. 21 and 93, and appx. 2); more yes than no (Raymond Aron, *History and the Dialectic of Violence*, Barry Cooper, trans. [Oxford: Basil Blackwell, 1975], pp. 42, 101, and 232); and emphatically no (André Gorz, *Socialism and Revolution*, Norman Denny, trans. [Garden City, NY: Anchor Books, 1973], pp. 253–256). This last is a translation of Gorz, *Le Socialisme*, with significant omissions and additions.

46. See *Critique of Dialectical Reason*, p. 37.

47. Failure to appreciate the role of the mediating Third in the *Critique* has led a commentator such as Mary Warnock to speak of Sartre's having "allowed the individual to be swallowed up in the group"; see her *The Philosophy of Sartre* (London: Hutchinson University Library, 1965), p. 134. At the other extreme, it has permitted Lucien Goldman to judge the *Critique* incurably individualistic. He claims that the affirmation of a collective subject "constitutes the principal opposition between dialectics and Sartrean though"; see *Marxisme et sciences humaines* (Paris: Gallimard, 1970), p. 249, n. But it is precisely the genius of this concept to preserve individual identity while allowing the ascription of collective predicates as befits a Marxist theory; see my "Mediated Reciprocity and the Genius of the Third" soon to appear in the *Sartre* volume of P. A. Schlipp's *Library of Living Philosophers*.

48. On Sartre's controversy with the structuralists—Althusser, Lévi-Strauss, and others—see "Jean-Paul Sartre Répond," *L'Arc*, 30 (October, 1966), pp. 86–87; and Claude Lévi-Strauss, *The Savage Mind* (Chicago: University of Chicago Press, 1966), pp. 245–269.

49. Affirming "full agreement" with Engels' claim that economic conditions are in the final analysis "the determining conditions," he cautions that it is the *contradictions* within these conditions which he considers to form "the driving force of history" (*Search for a Method*, p. 31).

50. See *Critique of Dialectical Reason*, pp. 113, 374–376, and 735. The post-*Critique* Sartre, commenting on the remark which has hounded him for years, "Hell is other people," observes: "I mean that *if* relations with the Other are contorted, corrupt, then the Other can only be hell" (as quoted in Jeanson, *Sartre*, p. 114; emphasis added).

51. Though his own role in the movement was modest, he writes glowingly of the "Republic of Silence": "We have never been freer than under the German occupation." *Situations*, Vol. 3, p. 11.

52. *Politics and Vision* (Boston: Little, Brown, 1960), p. 274.

53. For "socialist man," see *On a raison de se révolter*, pp. 337 and 340; for the "philosophy of freedom," see *Search for a Method*, p. 34.

54. *On a raison de se révolter*, p. 188. I have developed the anarchist implications of this claim in my "An End to Authority: Epistemology and Politics in the Later Sartre," *Man and World* 10, 4 (1977), pp. 448–465.

55. Quoted by Sartre, *Critique of Dialectical Reason*, p. 35. See "The Eighteenth

Brumaire of Louis Bonaparte," in Karl Marx, *Political Writings*, Vol. 2, *Surveys from Exile*, David Fernback [ed.] (New York: Vintage Books, 174), p. 146.

56. Sartre, "A Long, Bitter, Sweet Madness," p. 62.

57. Referring to Sartre's apparent abandonment of the ethical viewpoint, e.g., in his 1964 interview, "A Long, Bitter, Sweet Madness," Jeanson counters: "In reality, no preoccupation has been more constant with him than that of posing the moral problem." And in support of this, he quotes Sartre's admission two years later that "history and ethics intermingle. . . . Ethics is everywhere." Jeanson, *Sartre*, p. 230 n.

58. See *Search for a Method*, pp. 84 and 170.

59. Asked recently, "As far as labels go, do you prefer 'existentialist' to 'Marxist'?" Sartre replied: "If a label is absolutely necessary, I would like 'existentialist' better." *Life/Situations*, p. 60.

60. For a thorough account of the evolution of Sartre's concept of freedom, see Jeanson, *Sartre*, pp. 264ff.

61. Michel Contat is one of the latest to raise the issue when he asks Sartre whether the best known elements of his thinking, viz., freedom and individual responsibility, do not constitute the very *obstacle* to true political awareness as Sartre has come to understand it. Sartre replies that this is a danger only for "a theory of freedom which does not explain what the forms of alienation are." He insists that a careful reading of his own writings will absolve him of that failing (*Life/Situations*, p. 89).

62. I have treated at length Sartre's various uses of "responsibility" in my " 'We are All Assassins': Jean-Paul Sartre and the Problem of Collective Responsibility" (Ph.D. dissertation, Columbia University, 1970). One can gain a better appreciation of Sartre's changing understanding of responsibility by contrasting his two protagonists, Orestes of *The Flies* (1943) and Franz of *The Condemned of Altona* (1958), a play which numbers among its themes that of collective responsibility.

63. What I have termed "objective possibility" in order to emphasize its antecedents in Marx, Weber, and Lukács, Francis Jeanson designates by another term; but his point is basically the same. Discussing Sartre's evolution from *Being and Nothingness* to *Critique of Dialectical Reason*, he observes: "What has changed for Sartre in the interval is not the perspective of freedom; it is the perspective of contingency. The former hasn't become less radical, less demanding, less 'idealist'; it is the latter which has become more *realist*" (Jeanson, *Sartre*, p. 266; emphasis in the original).

64. A pseudonymous professor at the University of Paris (Nanterre) had characterized the May events as a "Sartrean" revolution; see Epistémon, *Ces idées qui ont ébranlé la France* (Paris: Fayard, 1968), pp. 78–87.

65. A graffito on a Left Bank wall during the events of May, 1968. It furnished the title for a Sartrean essay and, I believe, if fortified with the necessary ethical component, captures the spirit of Sartre's life project, from his first thesis on the imagination for the diploma in advanced studies (1926) to his exchange of literary for political imagination in the '50s.

This Place of Violence, Obscurity and Witchcraft

Robert Denoon Cumming*

Dialectical Intelligibility

A striking intellectual feature of our time is that its most influential philosophers have been bifurcated: we allude to the "later Wittgenstein" and the "later Heidegger" — even to "Heidegger I" and "Heidegger II." Admittedly there was also a precritical and a critical Kant, but our entire philosophical interest is taken up with how he became the critical Kant, whereas the *Tractatus* and *Being and Time* still retain a philosophical interest of their own. What this apparently unprecedented state of affairs illustrates about the stresses or distresses of our time I leave to others to decide.

A third very influential philosopher has suffered the misfortune of not having been allowed to bifurcate into his own earlier and later self. The already well-worn label "existentialist" was promptly affixed to Sartre's *Being and Nothingness* (1943) and the threadbare label "Marxist" to his later *Critique of Dialectical Reason*. The problems of interpreting Sartre then became largely problems of determining whether or not the "Marxist" was still an "existentialist." Nowadays Sartre's influence may have waned; in fact he has himself acknowledged (in English) that he is a "has been."[1] But he has become a "has been" without its having become clear what he has been. One reason is that Sartre, in contrast with Wittgenstein and Heidegger, has always seemed a derivative and eclectic philosopher. Interpreters who had stressed the influences of Husserl, Heidegger, and Hegel on *Being and Nothingness* were well prepared to dismiss the *Critique* as the accretion of still another influence, Marxism.

I do not believe anyone interested in social philosophy in the grand manner can afford to be quite so dismissive these days. There is little that is explicit in Wittgenstein or Heidegger which can be labeled social philosophy, even though extrapolators of implications have produced such philosophy. We are left with Sartre: whether we search the recent past or look toward the horizon, there is no other comparably influential contemporary who started out with a philosophy and who tried on his own to make it over into a social philosophy. Moreover I deny that Sartre's social philosophy is eclectic in the sense that it is seriously incoherent. I claim that it can be credited with that sustained effort at coherence which we acknowledge as the application of a method.

However in pushing this claim, I concede what may be a worse sin than eclecticism. The social structure that comes to the fore in Sartre's philosophy and determines the character of other social structures is the "practico-inert." Such barbaric jargon is of course entirely acceptable

*From *Political Theory* 7, no. 2 (May 1979):181-200. © 1979 Sage Publications, Inc.

sociology, but Sartre goes on to describe the "practico-inert" as "this place of violence, obscurity and witchcraft."[2] Such vivid descriptions have earned for the *Critique* the slur "literary sociology." Rather than just discount Sartre as incurably a man of letters by temperament or vocation, I shall try to explain how and why his philosophy gets methodologically contaminated by literature.

Sartre's own methodological claim regarding "this place" is that it exhibits "dialectical intelligibility" in spite of its "violence, obscurity and witchcraft." I shall sort out some of the basic traits of the dialectic whose application renders such structures intelligible. It is impossible to reproduce Sartre's actual dialectic in the *Critique*, for the *first* basic trait which has to be stressed is that a dialectical development conforms to the transformation of a *content*. Hence Hegel warns against "impatience," explaining: "The length of the way must be endured, since each phase is necessary, and besides, we must linger at each phase."[3] Judging by the unresponsive reception accorded Sartre's *Critique*, such endurance cannot be counted on. His expositor can only cope by oversimplifying. Thus I shall linger at the single phase of the "practico-inert," and shall rely on illustrations which are relatively simple. In particular, I shall exploit an early and quite literary illustration of what is in effect the "practico-inert," although Sartre had not yet coined the expression. But the illustration will be sufficient to demonstrate the primarily dialectical character of his method, notwithstanding the fact that at this early period he preferred to characterize his method as phenomenological. Later, in his "Marxist" *Critique*, he does characterize his method as dialectical, but my illustrations from the *Critique* will demonstrate that his earlier method has undergone adjustment rather than drastic revision, that it still retains a secondary component which is phenomenological, and that it still remains "literary."

Redefinition

In 1945 Sartre made his first trip to the United States on a journalistic assignment arranged by Albert Camus. In his report, Sartre presents his experience as an attempt to determine "what America is."[4] Such an attempt illustrates a *second* trait of his dialectic. It is a method of sustained *definition*. Thus Plato's *Republic* is a sustained attempt to define justice; *Das Kapital*, a sustained attempt to define capitalism. Those who employ undialectical methods usually get their definitions out of the way promptly and then settle down to what they regard as the real business of dealing with objective facts.

A dialectician is skeptical of this procedure. "Yesterday," Sartre reports, "it was Baltimore, today it is Knoxville, the day after tomorrow it will be New Orleans, and after admiring the biggest factory or the biggest bridge or the biggest dam in the world, we fly away with our heads full of figures and statistics." A dialectical method does not proceed inductively by accumulating objective facts or figures. This inductive scientific procedure Sartre identifies in the *Critique* as "analytic reasoning" to which he opposes his "dialectical reasoning." Why is analytic reasoning inadequate? The objective facts Sartre has listed are random and unrelated; their range of implication is indefinite, so that they cannot settle the problem of definition. The biggest dam? So what! The biggest bridge? So what! A dialectical method cannot operate on facts that remain isolated; instead its process of definition continues by correlating *relations* (its *third* trait).

As we all know, the most dialectically significant of these relations is often that between *opposites* (a *contradiction*), and this relation can be distinguished as a *fourth* trait. An illustration is the way Sartre's method of "dialectical reasoning" is itself defined by its opposition to the scientific method of "analytic reasoning."

A dialectical attempt to define "what America is" may hardly seem to be the "simple" example promised, at least not to the social scientist who would reason analytically. But a *fifth* trait of Sartre's dialectical method is that it is applied to states of affairs with which we are already familiar but do not examine until they are brought to our attention by some contradiction. The examination then deals with the preconceptions and presuppositions that constitute this familiarity rather than with an array of facts that have never been tampered with. In other words, Sartre's dialectic is less a process of definition than of redefinition, and we find Sartre making use of definitions already available—"the two contradictory slogans that are current in Paris—'Americans are conformists' and 'Americans are individualists.' " These are not facts he has encountered in America; they are definitions which he has brought with him.

It is by virtue of this process of redefinition, which subsumes as a *sixth* trait the preceding traits, that Sartre's dialectic is a "critique," but since this label has too specifically Kantian associations, I shall characterize the resulting dialectic as *reflexive*. The contradictory definitions of justice that Socrates deals with in the first book of the *Republic* are also current slogans. Whether it is Athens or Paris, dialectic dislodges familiar preconceptions from the back of men's minds, by forcing them into relation with each other and displaying some implicit contradiction between them.

Social Transformation

The contradiction triggers *movement*, which is a *seventh* trait of dialectic. The first trait, I have indicated, is that this movement is a development in which the dialectic conforms to the transformation of a content. This dynamic conformity displaces the inert conformity that is being subverted by the movement. In other words, the process of redefinition takes hold of something whose inertness was the familiarity it enjoyed from our previously having taken it for granted. The process of redefinition is the recovery of the process of transformation to which we have become insensitive. (Thus the "practico-inert" will be rendered intelligible by Sartre's exposing the practical activities that originally produced the inert state of affairs which now seems imposed on us as the way things are.) At the beginning of Plato's *Republic*, conformity is exhibited by the slogans offered as definitions of justice. These having been subverted by contradictions in the first book, the dialectic develops by tracing the process by which the unjust society these definitions manifest might be transformed into a just society. The process is reflexive, involving a critical redefinition of the participants' preconceptions.

Sartre's definition of America as conformist is an attempt to recover the dynamic process by which an individual is transformed into an inert, conforming American. In fact, the original title of Sartre's report was "How a Good American is Made." Sartre starts out with a familiar preconception: "Like everybody else, I had heard of the famous American 'melting-pot" that transforms, at different temperatures, Poles, Italians, and Finns into American citizens. But I did not know what the term 'melting-pot' actually meant." He soon finds out:

> The day after my arrival I met a European who was in the process of being melted down. I was introduced, in the big lobby of the Plaza Hotel, to a dark man of rather medium height, who, like everyone else here, talked with a somewhat nasal twang, without seeming to move his lips or cheeks, who laughed with his mouth but not with his eyes, and whose laughter came in sudden bursts, and who expressed himself in good French, with a heavy accent, though his speech was sprinkled with vulgar errors and Americanisms.
>
> When I congratulated him on his knowledge of our language, he replied with astonishment, "But I'm a Frenchman." He had been born in Paris, had been living in America for only fifteen years, and before the war had returned to France every six months. Nevertheless America already possessed him half-way. . . . He felt obliged every now and then to throw me a roguish wink and exclaim: "Ah, New Orleans, pretty girls." But what he was really doing was conforming to the American image of the Frenchman rather than trying to be congenial to a fellow-countryman. "Pretty girls," he said with a laugh that was forced. I felt puritanism just around the corner, and a chill ran through me.
>
> I had the impression I was witnessing an Ovidian metamorphosis. The man's face was still too expressive. It had retained the rather irritating mimicry of intelligence which makes a French face recognizable anywhere. But he will soon be a tree or a rock. I speculated curiously as to the powerful forces that had to be brought into play in order to actualize these disintegrations and reintegrations so reliably and rapidly.

We saw that Sartre started out with opposed preconceptions regarding America—the one defining Americans as "conformists," the other defining Americans as "individualists." We now see that he next defines the way conformity is secured by redefining the preconception of America as a melting-pot. His redefinition is dialectical: a Frenchman is transformed into his opposite — an American. This Franco-American is an *ex-sistential* phenomenon:[5] as a French expatriate he is "outside" himself, violently dislocated from his proper place. The process of his transformation is itself composed of opposing movements — his disintegration as a Frenchman and his reintegration as an American. The contradiction is carefully balanced: the Frenchman is visualized as having reached the "half-way" point in the process of transformation.[6] The climactic opposition between French and American culture in 1945 was in the attitude toward sex. (The only area where Sartre could have found Frenchmen and Americans so diametrically opposed today would have been in their attitudes toward philosophy.) The American attitude towards sex is in turn contradictory — at once prurient and puritanical.[7] Observe, too, how even Sartre's detailed touches are dislocating contradictions: the Franco-American talked "without seeming to move his lips or cheeks"; he "laughed with his mouth but not with his eyes," and "sudden bursts."

The Affective Reaction

"What America is" is defined in terms of the process of transformation that makes a Frenchman over into an American, but a dialectical process of definition cannot be reduced to this sort of process of transformation. The *definiendum* is only the objective pole of the dialectic, which sets up a *bilateral* relation between a subjective pole and this objective pole. This is an *eighth* trait of dialectic. Here we can see how misleading it is to regard Sartre's method as strictly phenomenological. In Husserl, consciousness as "consciousness of something" is a unilateral reference to the object "intended" (e.g., a cube, a tree). But the object in Sartre's dialectic is characteristically another subject. This bilateral relation provides a terrain for a dialectical shift, such as the dueling between self and other in *Being and Nothingness*.[8]

A social scientist might ask why Sartre selected as the object of his consciousness an ex-Frenchman, instead of an ex-Italian or an ex-Pole. As a matter of statistics, the number of Frenchmen that have been melted down into Americans is not comparably significant. Sartre's warrant is identical to my own. It is not a matter just of literary flair, but illustrates a further accentuation of what I have called the reflexive character of Sartre's dialectic. He himself is a Frenchman or rather a stand-in for his French reader. As Sartre will later explain, "The truth of a dialectical movement can only be demonstrated . . . if one is drawn into the movement."[9] In the present episode it is not just an ex-Frenchman who is undergoing a dislocating transformation but an actual Frenchman, Sartre, who is in the process of defining him. Sartre's initial impression that he is talking to an American is dislocated and transformed into the realization that he is talking to a Frenchman who is being transformed into an American. Such a *reversal* is an *eighth* trait of dialectical method. It is part of the subversion of preconceptions indispensable to their redefinition.

In Sartre the process of redefinition is designed less to delineate objectively the way the melting pot operates as a process of transformation than to elicit reflexively an *affective* reaction (a ninth trait). The subject is not just disconcerted and disoriented by the discovery that the apparent American was once a Frenchman like himself. He is disgusted. Reactions of revulsion such as this frequently impel Sartre's dialectic, and Sartre can elicit it even to the extent of nausea.

We recall that Sartre began by admitting that he did not know before this episode "what the term 'melting-pot' actually meant." He only knows when he is exposed to his own affective reaction. This reflexivity also holds for the other subject. Sartre initially becomes conscious of someone who appears to him to be an American; the appearance is then contradicted with the claim, "But I'm a Frenchman." This is not, however, what he really is objectively; it is only what he still appears to himself to be. And Sartre's own feeling of disgust reaches its climax when he discovers that the Frenchman is no longer a Frenchman and not quite yet an American, but is instead "conforming" to the requirements of "an American's image of a Frenchman."

Finally, since the entire dialectical process of redefinition turns reflexively on Sartre and his reader being French, it cannot remain objectively and straightforwardly anti-American in what it is opposed to, but is complicated by the reflection: "The man's face was still too expressive. It had retained that somewhat irritating mimicry of intelligence which makes a French face recognizable anywhere." Thus if the Frenchman at the Plaza has been disparaged as only a subjective appearance (not a real Frenchman but only "the American image of a Frenchman"), a real Frenchman enjoys no real superiority, since he is only apparently intelligent.

Self-Reference

Caught up in the reflexivity that is pivotal to Sartre's dialectic are traits which I have already sorted out. Self-definition is at stake, but the self is a "contradictory composite," since I become "conscious of" it as "something" which is like an object in that I attribute to it certain properties (e.g., bravery or cowardice), and yet it cannot be detached (as a real object can) from its dependency on the subjective act of consciousness by which I produce it (or its properties) by becoming self-conscious.[10] This self is not brave or cowardly in the same sense that grass is green or ink is black.

At the lower level of the particular self-images that Sartre selects we also encounter contradictory composites: not only the Franco-American but also the protagonists of *The Respectful Prostitute* and of *Saint Genet, Actor and Martyr*.[11] In each of these cases, what preoccupies Sartre is the violence the individual does to himself in perpetrating the contradictions—not physical violence but reflexive psychological violence, which further requires for its implementation his self-deception; for the individual must bewitch himself in order to obscure from himself the contradictory character of what he is perpetrating.[12] Thus the prostitute can define or identify herself as a victim of her society by identifying herself with another victim, the black who is about to be lynched; but she also becomes "respectful" when she is instead duped into identifying with their persecutors and into conforming with mores in terms of which she is herself beneath respect.

Sartre's other title I have cited also embodies contradictions. *Saint Genet* confers sanctity on a criminal. The rest of the title introduces a secondary dialectic with an additional contradiction: if the original Genet (the victim of Diocletian) was a saint (the patron saint of actors), our contemporary Jean Genet acts the female role of a passive homosexual. Sartre equips him for the martryrdom of the female role with a pun, *saint/ seins*.[13]

The reflexive and affective character of Sartre's existential dialectic is one of the differences between it and a Marxist dialectic. Even when Sartre felt politically close to the French Communist Party, his summons to collaboration included a reflexive twist: "One cannot struggle against the working-class without becoming an enemy of mankind and of oneself."[14] Such twists, often propelled by some affective reaction or larger-scale reflexive maneuver, are designed to dislodge familiar, ostensibly objective preconceptions (e.g., with respect to "what America is" or to how the bourgeoisie maintains its domination) so that the individual "finds himself there" by having to consult his own reaction to what is transpiring.[15] At this juncture Sartre is able to incorporate some characteristics of the phenomenological reflexive appeal to immediate experience. When Sartre admitted that he had "like everybody else . . . heard of the famous American 'melting-pot' " but "did not know what the term . . . actually meant," he had not yet had the immediate experience the encounter with the ex-Frenchman provided.

Closely associated with this reflexive and affective emphasis on immediacy of experience are other differences between an existential and a Marxist dialectic. Marx's *Das Kapital*, as a dialectical attempt to define what capital is, is broadly similar to Sartre's definition of the melting-pot: it is an analysis of the contradictions operating in the process of transformation whereby a capitalistic society must disintegrate in order to be integrated into its opposite—a socialist society. In the case of Sartre's encounter with the Franco–American, the movements of disintegration and reintegration are accelerated, as if they were taking place right there in front of Sartre in the lobby of the Plaza, rather than proceeding at what would be the historical pace of a melting-pot—the historical pace a Marxist analysis would respect. Their acceleration accentuates the sense of dislocation associated with the transformation of Sartre's initial impression, and thus seems to have more to do with the rapidity with which Sartre reacts reflexively (or would have his reader react) to the Franco-American than with any actions on the part of the Franco-American as they might be appraised objectively.

Other examples can be cited where scope is rapidly sought reflexively. When Sartre suggests the reflexive reference required to analyze anti-Semitism by citing Richard Wright—"There is no black problem in the United States, only a white problem"[16]—it is clear from the brusque shift that Wright was addressing himself to white readers in the hope of eliciting their reflexive recognition of the truth of his pronouncement. When Sartre similarly defines the Jew as "a man whom other men treat as a Jew,"[17] it is clear that he is peremptorily circumventing a considerable accumulation of specific sociohistorical evidence, and addressing these other men directly in the hope of eliciting their reflexive recognition of the truth of his definition.

Mechanistic Explanation

In his later so-called "Marxist" writings, Sartre elaborates his reflexive dialectic in opposition to what he calls Marxist "objectivism," which makes "subjectivity an absolute effect—i.e., an effect which never transforms itself into a cause."[18] The individual becomes the predetermined product of social history; he is not the voluntary agent who can carry out the reflexive accomplishment of remaking himself by making history. Sartre criticizes Marx himself for writing, "The materialist conception of the world simply refers to the conception of nature as it is in itself, without an extraneous addition." A reference simply to objective nature is undialectical, and Sartre interprets Marx as "stripping himself of all subjectivity" and adopting an ostensibly objective point of view.[19] But the notion of an objective point of view conceals a contradiction: a point of view is always the point of view of a subject. Granted the sequence of levels Marx distinguished as constituting "the objective hierarchy of social structures," this "dialectical sequence does not determine by itself the way which it is experienced."[20]

Here Sartre finds Marxism guilty of a "reversion" to bourgeois analytic reasoning—that is, to a mechanistic explanation which is only applicable where analysis can cleanly separate effects from their causes. Where the reflexive dimension of our experience intrudes, this separation cannot ultimately be maintained: an effect on us enters inextricably into a process of transformation by our agency. Thus a mechanistic explanation does violence to the structure of our experience. This opposition that Sartre sets up between a dialectic adapted to the structure of our experience and analytic reasoning is itself a dialectical version of the opposition by which Husserl distinguished his reflexive phenomenological descriptions from the causal explanations of natural science.

At a lower level the reflexive character of Sartre's dialectic renders him alert not only to circumstances under which our behavior does in fact tend to become mechanical but also to the concomitant reflexive tendency to become bewitched in order to obscure from ourselves what is happening to us. Thus the Puritanical depravity of the Franco-American is exposed by applying to his experiences both the mechanistic metaphor of the "melting-pot," which derives from metallurgy, and an "Ovidian metamorphosis," which is magical and mythical.

The Machine

An obvious next step from here to Sartre's "Marxism" is to consider the way behavior tends to become mechanical when involved in the operation of a machine. In Sartre, this becomes an encounter with the "practico-inert." Where the starting point in a Marxist analysis would be some technological development, the invention of some tool (the lever, the wheel, the stirrup, the pulley, the steam engine), Sartre starts out phenomenologically with the immediate experience of the individual, with the way he has this experience, and hence with the reflexive movement through which the individual makes himself his own tool.[21] When the individual leans on a lever, or pushes a wheelbarrow, or pulls a rope over a pulley, he is using his own body as a subjective tool for using the objective tool. Thus his immediate experience is the reflexive experience of his own instrumentality, and the transformation of the structure of his experience has to be taken into account in dealing with his becoming a worker, or a different kind of worker from the type that prevailed at a previous stage of social history. In other words, technological development is more than man's causal transformation of his external environment; man's reflexive self-transformation is involved. When the tool that is introduced is the machine, we are dealing with a technological development which can be visualized by Sartre, not as lying at the basis of the substructure and generating a sequence of effects which extend into the superstructure, but as "interposed between men" as their dialectical antagonist—"the inhuman" which "disrupts [déchire] human relations."

Of course, Marx also deals with such disruptions. But what is striking in Sartre is the way the machine is interposed between the individual and himself where it tends to disrupt the reflexive relation by instituting a mechanical relation. It is here that Sartre's emphasis passes from the violence inherent in the capitalistic system to the violence the individual does to himself. For example, "girls working in a factory are ruminating a vague dream," but they are "at the same time traversed by a rhythm external to them" so that "it can be said that it is the semi-automatic machine which is dreaming through them." The rhythm of the machine was "so alien to a girl's vital personal rhythm that during the first few days it seemed more than she could endure." But "she wanted to adapt herself to it, she made an effort." So she "gave herself to the machine," which takes possession of her work, until finally "she discovers herself as the object of the machine."[22] A dislocating reversal has taken place: the machine is no longer her tool; she has become its tool. But the machine cannot qualify as a subject; we are left with the contradiction that she is no longer the subject of her own experiences.

Being and Nothingness Sartre characterizes as an "eidetic analysis of self-deception" — that is, as an analysis of its essential structure.[23] The example from the *Critique* of the girl tending a semi-automatic machine illustrates a certain adjustment in this analysis, since the structure of her experience has been violated by the machine in a fashion which contributes to her deception. The ensuing rumination is an obscure and bewitched effort to regain her own subjectivity:

> In vain would she take refuge in her most intimate "privacy"; this attempt would betray her at once, and would be transformed into what is simply a mode of subjective actualization of objectivity. When semi-automatic machines were first introduced, investigations showed that women workers who were trained to use them surrendered to their sexual fantasies as they worked; they recalled their bedrooms, their beds, the previous night — everything that specifically concerns a person in the isolation of the couple closed with each other. But it was the machine in them that was dreaming of caresses: the kind of attention demanded by their work allowed them neither distraction (thinking of something else) nor total mental application (thinking would slow down their movement). The machine demands and creates in the worker an inverted semi-automatism which complements its operation — an explosive mixture of unconsciousness and vigilance. The mind is absorbed but not used. . . . It is accordingly appropriate for her to let herself go to passivity.[24]

The "essential discovery" of Marx, Sartre announces, "is that work, as an historical reality and as the utilization of specific tools in an already determined social and material situation, is the real foundation of the organization of social relations."[25] Having seen that a "tool" undergoes subjective, metaphorical extension in Sartre, when we make ourselves our own tools in order to employ tools in a literal sense, we can anticipate that work will undergo a similar extension. In Sartre, work involves not only transformation of the external environment but also reflexive self-transformation — "the work of our inner life — resistances conquered and perpetually reborn, efforts perpetually renewed, despairs surmounted, provisional setbacks and precarious victories." Sartre cites psychoanalysts who "consider certain developments of our inward life to be the result of a work which it performs upon itself."[26] The addition of this reflexive dimension to "work" in the literal Marxist sense suggests how Sartre feels he is able to combine psychoanalysis with Marxism.

Conflict

We can move now from the level of production to the level of social relations. Although Sartre repeatedly endorses the Marxist conception of class-conflict, it is treated in his reflexive dialectic by reference to the "practico-inert" as the "practice which actualizes in urgency everyone's relation to his being as an object."[27] (The same description would hold for the activity of the girl tending the semi-automatic machine.) Sartre's simplest model for this process of actualization is boxing: my antagonist makes a feint to my head, I cover, and this action enables him to hit me in the stomach. Thus I can be deceived into performing an action that enables my antagonist to employ my own action against me.[28] This reflexive dimension of an action still intrudes when Sartre offers an explicitly social example of conflict, that of two armies opposed. This example is another rather different reflexive and metaphorical extension of the Marxist conception of work, for Sartre defines war as "the work of man on man."[29] As with the example of boxing, a feature of the "urgency" involved is a demand that one's "consciousness must be as lucid as that of the enemy."[30] For "one not only has to actualize one's own objectivity, starting out from a particular action by the enemy," but one also has to carry out reassessments. Thus it is known that the enemy is "going to advance to a particular place to attain a specific objective." But for us this objective can be assessed as a "trap," an "ambush." Yet in assessing the prospect, we have to recognize that "the enemy has his own game to play; he foresees the trap, and we foresee his foresight."[31]

To recognize this reflexive dimension is to recognize, according to Sartre, that contemporary Marxism lacks a lucidity and flexibility of application which have become urgent. In short, "the origin of critical investigation is itself dialectical" — "the divorce between *blind* unprincipled praxis and *paralyzed* thought." From this "contradiction, lived in malaise and at times in agony," emerges a "reflexive and critical consciousness." Each of us is prompted "to reexamine his intellectual tools."[32] This is metaphorically speaking what Sartre is up to in the *Critique*.

The Individual

The reflexive dimension of Sartre's social philosophy that I have been examining as a methodological trait is usually referred to as his individualism, and a more adequate exposition would take into account the individualistic character of his phenomenology of experience. But the individual himself is dialectically reconstructed in Sartre. Take his comments on the stylistic change which supervenes in the course of his trilogy of sociohistorical novels, *Roads to Freedom:*

> During the deceptive calm of 1937–38, there were people who could still maintain the illusion of having their impenetrable individual histories. [So far Sartre is dealing with the familiar, solid, individual who is susceptible of bourgeois, analytic reasoning.] But when September 1938 arrived [in *The Reprieve*, the second novel which deals with the Munich crisis as a social experience] . . . the individual, without ceasing to be a monad, feels that he is playing in a game that transcends him. He is still a point of view on the world [the subjective point of view which is sacrificed in Marxism], but he is surprised to find himself in a process of generalization. . . . He is a monad which has sprung a leak and which will go on leaking without ever sinking.[33]

We are already aware that the individual is a "contradictory composite" by virtue of the reflexive dimension of his experience. Here he becomes a "contradictory composite" by virtue of the social dimension of his experience: monads do not leak; what does leak eventually sinks. We are confronted with an individual whose experience, although social, remains his own experience.

Sartre upholds this reflexive dimension by repudiating the discounting of the individual and of the particularity of the individual's experience: "That such a man," Engels argued, "precisely that particular individual, emerges at this particular epoque and in this particular country is naturally a matter of pure chance. If Napoleon had not turned up, someone else would have taken his place."[34]

But who are the particular individuals whom Sartre reinstates when he undertakes "to reexamine his intellectual tools"? Not Napoleon, whom Engels perhaps used as an example because he had been a "world-historical" individual in Hegel. In reexamining psychoanalysis in order to develop the reflexive dimension he would add to Marxism, Sartre selects Baudelaire, Jean Genet, Flaubert, as well as himself. The "rumination" of the working girl may have its place in the *Critique*, but all these individuals are engaged in literary activity. This hardly startles us, since we have just watched Sartre state the problem of the individual involved in a social transformation in terms of a shift in style (in his *Roads to Freedom*). We have also watched him extend metaphorically the meanings of "tool" and of "work" in Marx. Not only does Sartre "reexamine" his "intellectual tools" in the *Critique*, but he introduces language as the first social institution that comes up for appraisal as a specimen of the "practico-inert" — what the writer comes up against in its inertness and would make over into his own set of tools.[35]

Metaphors

Where Marx provides us with facts and figures regarding social transformations, Sartre also provides us with metaphors: "Like everyone else, I had heard of the famous American 'melting-pot' that transforms, at different temperatures, Poles, Italians and Finns into United States citizens." Like an American, a metaphor is the outcome of a process of social transformation. "Melting-pot" has been transformed from its literal meaning in metallurgy into a term depicting the social transformation of aliens into Americans. Of course, this metaphor has long since become a familiar commonplace, as Sartre reminds us when he admits, "Like everyone else, I had heard." A dead metaphor is thus the outcome of the process of transformation that produced it, for it has been detached from its relation to this process. When we refer familiarly to America as a "melting-pot" we do not usually think of the metallurgical derivation. In its detachment and rigidity the outcome is a challenge to Sartre as a dialectician committed to the relational and the dynamic, even though his more fundamental concern in reviving the metaphor is to bring out the violent character of the process of social transformation. Observe how Sartre revives the metaphor. Just as he puts the social process of producing an American into motion again by introducing the contradiction of the man protesting "But I'm a Frenchman" when Sartre takes him for an American, so he puts the social process that produces the metaphor into motion again by contradicting the metaphorical character of the dead metaphor: "Like everybody else, I had heard of the famous American 'melting-pot' that transforms, at different temperatures, Poles, Italians and Finns into American citizens." Sartre's interlarding "at different temperatures" construes the metaphor literally, so that the reader is half prompted to ask: "How hot for a Pole? Hotter for an Italian? Must be very hot for a Finn?" This recapturing of the literal meaning dislocates the inert metaphor and renews our awareness of the process of transformation that has gone into the making of the metaphor, at the same time that our awareness is renewed of the process of transformation that has gone into the making of a "good American."

To characterize the renewal as a recapturing of the literal meaning is inaccurate. When Sartre takes the metaphor literally, he is reversing the sequence (from the literal to the metaphorical) by which it was originally produced. Similarly, he is reversing the sequence in the process of transformation that a melting-pot familiarly involves. In a literal melting-pot a solid metal which is rigid is melted into fluidity; in America as a metaphorical melting-pot someone whose native culture gave him definite shape becomes malleable. But the Franco-American is instead losing his French fluidity and becoming rigidly American. Recall how "like everyone else here, he talked . . . without seeming to move his lips or cheeks; how he laughed with his mouth but not with his eyes"; how his laugh was "forced" when he insinuated "New Orleans, pretty girls," and "a chill" ran through Sartre. We are to assume (by dialectical contrast) that the lips and cheeks of a real Frenchman move when he speaks, that he laughs with his eyes as well as with his mouth, and that he is equally flexible in his relations with girls. But the Franco-American, Sartre anticipates, "will soon be a tree or a rock." Contradicting the familiar rigid-becoming-fluid by recognizing that the fluid must become rigid helps release the metaphor "melting-pot" itself from its moribund rigidity, as well as plays up the metallurgical rigidity of American conformity.

Literal Sociology

I have tried to demonstrate that Sartre's sociology does indeed deserve the epithet "literary," if only by virtue of his small-scale reliance on metaphors and his large-scale reliance on literary works in delineating social processes. But I have also suggested that this reliance is not the sort of haphazard incompetence that is to be expected when someone with imagination stumbles into an area where stubborn facts and figures should prevail. Throughout his career, and before his dialectic ever became "Marxist," Sartre employed a dialectical method. He revives "Marxism" in much the same way he revives a dead metaphor: Marxism is (in its own terms) the outcome of a process of social transformation. The Marxism that Sartre copes with, Stalinism, is more specifically the outcome of a phase in this process during which it has become detached from the process. Its application to succeeding phases has become merely "ceremo-nial," like the application of a dead metaphor.[36]

However, Sartre does not revive Marx's original Marxism any more than he revives the original metaphor "melting-pot." Marx himself was sensitive to the difference between his dialectical materialism and the mechanistic materialism of the French enlightenment, and Sartre likes to graft his own dialectical materialism on this distinction, in order to consign to the eighteenth century the ceremoniously mechanical ideo-logues of the French Communist Party. But Sartre in fact incorporates in his opposition to mechanistic materialism a reflexive phenomenological appeal to immediate experience. Thus when we revived the dead meta-phor, he started out by conceding that he "did not know what the term 'melting-pot' actually meant" until he was confront by the Frenchman being melted down.

Sartre can incorporate this phenomenological appeal to immediate experience because he disavows Husserl's conception of phenomenology as "rigorous science."[37] With this disavowal Sartre's method can become primarily dialectical and literature can inherit the reflexive function of reliving the immediate experiences of a social history which in the Marxist interpretation has become "ossified."[38] Thus Sartre's first effort to deal with social history was an answer to the question *What is Literature?* whereas his most persistent and final effort, for which the *Critique* itself prepared the way, is his three-volume interpretation of the transformation of French society as the experience which lies behind Flaubert's literary works and Flaubert's own transformation from "the family idiot" into "the creator of the 'modern' novel."[39]

Notes

1. *Life/Situations* (New York, 1977), p. 22. I cite from, but frequently revise, the available translations of Sartre in English.

2. *Critique of Dialectical Reason* (London, 1976), p. 318.

3. *The Phenomenology of Spirit* (Oxford, 1977), p. 17.

4. *Literary and Philosophical Essays* (New York, 1955). The portions of the report I cite is found on pp. 97–98.

5. *Ex* ("outside") derives its metaphorical force in Sartre from Heidegger's etymologizing use of *ex-sistere* and *ekstasis* ("dislocation") in *Being and Time*. The prefix undergoes further manipulation in Sartre's transition to a dialectic of *Being and Nothingness:* "Heidegger's philosophy characteristically describes *Dasein* by using positive terms which conceal implicit negations. *Desein* is 'outside of itself, in the world'; it is 'a being of distances.' All this amounts to saying that *Dasein* 'is not' in itself" (*Being and Nothingness* [New York, 1966], p. 52).

6. Similarly when Sartre analyzes Flaubert's family, he finds that it suffered from "an internal disequilibrium" because it was "half-way bourgeois, half-way rural [sc., feudal] in its structures" (*L'idiot de la famille* Paris, 1972], Vol. 3, p. 34). This balanced lack of balance is clearly a demand of the dialectic rather than the result of sociological computation.

7. Sartre has continued to equate Americanism with Puritanism, which is one of his favorite social phenomena. In denouncing, on behalf of the Russell Tribunal, American genocide in Vietnam, Sartre faced the question of whether its perpetrators "were clearly aware of their intent," and one feature of his reply was to reply was to refer to the "miracles that Puritan self-deception [*mauvaise foi*] can pull off" (*Between Existentialism and Marxism* [New York, 1975], p. 80).

8. For a brief exegesis of Husserl's "consciousness of something," see my *The Philosophy of Jean-Paul Sartre* (New York, 1965), pp. 10–11. Although *Being and Nothingness* starts off phenomenologically with an analysis of "consciousness of something," it becomes fully dialectical with the introduction of the other into the analysis: "While I attempt to free myself from the hold of the Other, the Other is trying to free himself from mine, while I seek to enslave the Other, the Other seeks to enslave me. We are by no means dealing with unilateral relations with an object-in-itself, but with reciprocal and moving relation" [ibid., p. 209].

9. *Situations* (Paris, 1965), Vol. 7, p. 21.

10. For the self as a "contradictory composite," see *The Transcendence of the Ego* (New York, 1957), p. 84. Not just a self-image but any image is inherently contradictory according to Sartre (see *The Philosophy of Jean-Paul Sartre*, p. 88).

11. How the relations between levels are handled dialectically will be discussed in considerable detail in my *Starting Point* (Chicago, 1979).

12. Such reflexive psychological violence is at the focus of Sartre's interest in Flaubert. Where a Marxist would be interested in praxis, Flaubert, Sartre notes, "from his earliest childhood . . . cannot make contact with human praxis," for "his realm . . . is *pathos* — that is, affectively insofar as it is pure violence, succumbed to without his accepting it" (*L'idiot*, Vol. 3, p. 48).

13. Of course, the original Saint Genet is merely a pious legend, but Sartre's point regarding Jean Genet's affectivity is that he would confer legendary status on himself.

14. *Situations*, Vol. 6, pp. 86–87. The comparison with Marxism is feasible because it is also a dialectical relational analysis. Thus Marx argues, "The antithesis between propertylessness and property . . . remains indifferent, not grasped as a dynamic connection in its internal relation as contradiction, so long as it is not understood as the antithesis of labor and capital" (*Writings of young Marx on Philosophy and Society*) [Garden City, 1967], p. 301). In

this present essay there is no intent on my part to do justice to Marxism or any other dialectical philosophy besides Sartre's. I am only trying to clarify certain features of Sartre's "Marxism."

15. For Heidegger's analysis of *Befindlichkeit*, see section 29 of *Being and Time*.

16. *Anti-Semite and Jew* (New York, 1948), p. 52.

17. Cited by Michel Contat and Michel Rybalka in *The Writings of Jean-Paul Sartre* (Evanston, 1974), Vol. 1, p. 145.

18. *Situations*, (Paris, 1964), Vol. 6, p. 27.

19. *Search for a Method*. p. 32. The first quotation is actually from Engels, and its attribution to Marx is a curious mistake on Sartre's part, since he is eager to saddle Engels with as much of the blame as possible for rendering Marxism undialectical.

20. *L'idiot*, Vol. 1, p. 686. Sartre would impose a reflexive interpretation on "the reaction," which Marx concedes, "of the superstructures on the substructures from which they derive" (ibid.).

21. The original phenomenological analysis, which I am oversimplifying, is found in *Being and Nothingness*, pp. 422–429. I am also neglecting Sartre's debt to Heidegger's analysis of the relation to the tool as something "available" (*zuhanden*) rather than as something "confronting" us as an object (*vorhanden*).

22. *The Philosophy of Jean-Paul Sartre*, pp. 462–463. Political theorists have usually been tantalized by Sartre's activism. But my examples are selected to suggest that he is more adept at delineating its dialectical opposite, "pathos," and the ruminations that take place in its "realm" (see n. 12 above), by virtue of the reflexive and affective character of the phenomenological component of his dialectic.

23. *Situations* (Greenwich, 1965), p. 161.

24. *Critique*, p. 233. Sartre is trying to avoid the simplistic notion of "reification" as the "metamorphosis of the individual into a thing" (ibid., p. 176). I cite a phase of the dialectic where Sartre's *ex-sistentialist* metaphor becomes materialistic: "man, defined by his being-outside-himself . . . is defined as *bewitched matter*—that is, specifically as an inorganic, worked materiality which develops a non-human activity because its passivity synthesizes the serial infinity of human acts which sustain it" (ibid., p. 219).

25. Ibid., p. 152.

26. *Search for a Method*, p. 12. Sartre cites "mourning" as an example of "work" in this reflexive sense and refers us to Daniel Lagache's *Le travail du deuil*.

27. *Critique*, pp. 808–809.

28. *Search for a Method*, p. 157. Sartre admits that the example of boxing represents an abstraction from the complexity of social relations since the individuals involved are "of the same profession, the same age, in a closed-off sector" (*Critique*, p. 806).

29. *The Philosophy of Jean-Paul Sartre*, p. 444.

30. *Critique*, p. 809. Sartre's concept of "urgency," like most of his concepts, is not natively social psychology but derives from his psychology of the individual. Husserl carefully distinguishes between an "intentional" act of consciousness and "attention," but Sartre obtains from Heidegger's analysis of affectivity a conception of consciousness as appetitive, which he consolidates with *in-tentio* so that consciousness becomes "*ad-petitio*" (*The Philosophy of Jean-Paul Sartre*, p. 264). Thus the intentional act of consciousness becomes dialectically an *attente*—an expectant "waiting upon" what it is a "seeking toward." Hence "urgency" becomes a pivotal phenomenon, as in the famous episode of the woman about to be seduced: "She knows . . . that it will be necessary sooner or later for her to make a decision. But she does not want to feel the urgency of it" (ibid., p. 147). Sartre's contempt for the woman about to be seduced, for the Frenchman being melted down into an American, for Flaubert, for our time, is obvious; but in each instance it is contempt for passivity that is dictated by his dialectical version of phenomenology.

31. *Critique*, pp. 807–809.

32. Ibid., p. 50; emphasis added.

33. Contat, p. 113.

34. *Search for a Method*, p. 56.

35. I can only suggest the character and scope of Sartre's analysis of language as an example of the "practico-inert" by sampling some of his generalizations: "A good example is language. . . . There can be no doubt that language is in one sense an inert totality. But this materiality is also a constantly developing organic totalization. . . . Every word is . . . external to everyone; it lives outside, as a public institution; and speaking does not consist in inserting a vocable into a brain through an ear, but in using sounds to direct the interlocutor's attention to this vocable as public exterior property. . . . Language as the practical relation of one man to another is praxis, and praxis is always language" (*Critique*, pp. 98–99).

36. Contemporary Marxism, according to Sartre, has "reduced" its "analysis . . . to a simple ceremony." It "consists solely in getting rid of detail, in forcing the meaning of certain events" (*Search for a Method*, p. 27). It has thereby become "frozen" (ibid., p. 28). In the *Critique* Sartre's recurrent description is "sclerotic." In reaching the linguistic and ideological levels, I have skipped over the political level where the same development takes place. Here institutions constitute a detached, rigid outcome of a process which had been fluid in its earlier revolutionary phase.

37. *Situations*, (Paris, 1972), Vol. 9, p. 70.

38. The inheritance is not acknowledged by Sartre who comments instead that "in the book I am writing on Flaubert [sc. *L'idiot*] I have replaced my old notion of consciousness . . . by what I call *le vécu*" (ibid., p. 108). But *le vécu* or *l'expérience vécu* had been his old translation for *Erlebnis* (usually translated into English as "lived experience"), which was Husserl's term for experience as it is immediately given to consciousness, and thus exhibits the reflexive character that enables a phenomenological analysis to take hold. In *What is Literature?* (1947) Sartre had already credited novels with enabling us to "live our experiences" (p. 217). This can be true for the writer himself: "Fiction enabled Flaubert to say what he feels" (*L'idiot*, Vol. 1, p. 195) but would otherwise have remained "unsayable" (*Situations*, Vol. 9, p. 111).

39. On the one hand, Sartre finds "Flaubert's "existence an excellent resumé of a century of vicissitudes in French society (*L'idiot*, Vol. 2, p. 1199); on the other hand, "Flaubert as the creator of the 'modern novel'" is at the crossroads of all our literary problems today" (*L'idiot*, Vol. 1, p. 8).

Sartre's *L'Existentialisme est un humanisme*

Terry Keefe*

It is a quarter of a century since the original publication of Jean-Paul Sartre's *L'Existentialisme est un humanisme (Existentialism and Humanism),*[1] and we are now far enough away from what Jacques Guicharnaud has called "those years" to see post-war French Existentialist philosophy in some kind of perspective. Yet in spite of the commonly acknowledged fact that *L'Existentialisme* . . . has been the most widely read of all Sartre's

*From *Philosophical Journal*, 9, no. 1 (January 1972):43–60. © T. Keefe. Reprinted with permission.

philosophical works, especially in English-speaking countries, no very serious or systematic attempt seems yet to have been made to evaluate this text in the light of the appropriate standards and terms of reference. Finding the right yardsticks and criteria is a matter of some importance here, for this is a rather special piece among Sartre's published works and, for reasons that need to be examined, it has received somewhat peculiar treatment at the hands of many of his commentators. I should like, in this article, to do two things: firstly, to re-examine briefly the vexed question of the *status* of the book; and secondly, to make a tentative start — though no more than a start — towards a just appreciation of its general merits and defects. The two tasks hang together, in so far as I believe that the work has often been misjudged precisely on the basis of certain loose, largely unfounded assumptions about its status.

I

A glance at a number of critical works on Existentialism in general or on Sartre in particular is sufficient to bring to light a puzzling range of attitudes towards *L'Existentialisme*. It is not altogether surprising, considering its brevity, that some commentators should fail to refer to it at all and confine themselves to Sartre's more substantial philosophical works, but it is strange to find that while others refer to the book constantly and quote quite extensively from it, a fairly considerable number of critics claim quite explicitly and dogmatically that the text cannot be taken as a serious statement of, or source for, Sartre's philosophical views.[2] If this last judgement were visibly based on internal evidence, on a careful scrutiny of the text itself, there might be nothing particularly disturbing or unusual about the general state of affairs. This, however, is apparently not the case, for when the refusal to take any account of *L'Existentialisme* is explained at all, it is almost invariably justified by reference to a passage in a book by Sartre's friend, Francis Jeanson. In *Le Problème moral et la pensée de Sartre*, Jeanson states that: "all those who . . . base their views on this text alone, will be inclined to take him to task for its completely hollow pseudo-morality. And this is indeed the view of Sartre himself who, in this respect, considers his own lecture a 'mistake.' "[3] This comment, taken together with the fact that Sartre wrote a very favourable letter-preface to Jeanson's book, seems to constitute the only firm "evidence" on the basis of which *L'Existentialisme* is sometimes dismissed out of hand.

Admittedly, it is possible that there is other evidence that Sartre came to feel seriously dissatisfied with his own text — there may, for example, be comments buried somewhere in one of the dozens of published interviews that he has given. But none of the critics who give the book such short shrift either quotes or even mentions any such evidence, and a recently published and very thoroughly documented account of all of Sartre's publications, interviews included, up to 1969 fails to cast any further light on this matter.[4] Furthermore, there is definitely *some* evidence to the contrary, or at least, evidence that in 1949 (Jeanson's book was published in 1947) Sartre was still very far indeed from a wholesale repudiation of *L'Existentialisme*. In a newspaper interview in which he tried to answer some objections raised against Existentialism by George Lukács, although Sartre acknowledges that *L'Existentialisme* 'n'est qu'une oeuvre de passage," he explicitly denies having changed his philosophical views between *L'Etre et le Néant* (*Being and Nothingness*) of 1943 and this text of 1946: "Lukács claims that you have changed your philosophical views in passing from *Being and Nothingness* to *Existentialism and Humanism?*" "That's completely wrong. It goes to show that Lukács has scarcely read *Being and Nothingness*, for all the allegedly new aspects of my philosophy that he claims to discover in my lecture have already been expounded in *Being and Nothingness*. . . ."[5]

However little importance one may attach to this particular exchange, it seems to run counter to any suggestion that Sartre rapidly came to regret all, or even most of what he had written in *L'Existentialisme*. In other words, until such time as texts are produced to substantiate this suggestion, we have some definite reason to be sceptical about it and only Jeanson's comment, quoted above, to support it. And with regard to the latter, at least two important observations need to be made. Firstly, in the brief chapter containing the passage in question Jeanson is centrally concerned to expose the inadequacies of another critic, Luc-J. Lefèvre, who, he claims, has taken *L'Existentialisme* as his *only* source for Sartre's views on morality—a procedure which, we may admit, certainly needs to be criticised. Secondly, it has to be noted that Jeanson's reference to Sartre's own views is rather vague: to put "erreur" in quotation marks suggests that this was Sartre's own word in this connection, but what *exactly* did he say? When? And about precisely what? Without in the least calling into question Jeanson's good faith in reporting a remark by Sartre, one might surely be forgiven for believing that on a matter such as this, a single word in quotation marks is scarcely a very solid reason for completely ignoring *L'Existentialisme*.[6] Moreover, it is not at all clear that Jeanson himself wished to draw any conclusion as strong as this: his main purpose in his book is to argue only that nothing that Sartre has published up to that time (including *L'Etre et le Néant*) constitutes a *fully worked-out* Existentialist or Sartrean morality.

In any case, there is a great deal to be said for stopping to ask, at this stage of the argument, whether we are not in danger of attaching rather too much importance to a philosopher's (reported) comments on his own published works. There are general theoretical grounds, as well as some more particular exegetical ones, for letting *L'Existentialisme* stand on its own feet, for simply judging it on its merits. It is hard to believe that, on reflection, anyone would seriously wish to suggest that even if it could be demonstrated beyond question that Sartre now thinks (or came to think in

1947) that *L'Existentialisme* contains mistakes, or that it was a mistake to publish the text, this would, in itself, be a sufficient reason for neglecting the book altogether, or for not taking it as an accurate expression of his views in 1946. In addition to relying on some notion of Sartre's infallibility which, *ex hypothesi*, Sartre himself would have shattered, such an argument would have worrying implications. Sartre has recently called his study, *Baudelaire*, "A very inadequate, an extremely bad one"[7] — presumably we must now take this off our bookshelves too. Again, he has said of *Réflexions sur la question juive*: "Les insuffisances me sautent aux yeux . . ." (Its deficiencies are very obvious to me),[8] so that this text must also go. And as for the film-script, *Les Jeux sont faits* (another extremely popular text, incidentally), it is difficult to think of a sufficiently thorough way of disposing of copies of this, since it is "tout le contraire d'une pièce existentialiste" (the very opposite of an Existentialist work): "Mon scénario baigne dans le déterminisme, parce que j'ai pensé qu'il m'était, moi aussi, permis de jouer" (My film-script is steeped in determinism, because I thought that I, too, was allowed to play games)[9]. . . . Where would this process ever end, and would it leave us with any texts by Sartre to read and discuss? It seems that, in the end, we *have* to examine *L'Existentialisme* as it stands and judge it by the quality of the thoughts it contains — whatever Sartre may think, or have thought about the book.

To be absolutely fair to Jeanson and certain other commentators, however, one has to admit that they sometimes appear to have been troubled by something in the text itself, as well as by the circumstances of its composition and Sartre's own attitude. Sartre's claim that everything in *L'Existentialisme* was already in *L'Etre et le Néant* could, after all, simply be wrong, and in fact it has been implied, not infrequently, that there is at least one major philosophical position defended in the former of which there is little if any trace in the latter: namely, the Kantian point that, crudely put — as Sartre himself puts it early on — in choosing for ourselves morally, we choose for all men (p. 25/29). It is perhaps preferable to say something about this point before proceeding to an evaluation of *L'Existentialisme*, since it has been seen as relevant to the question of the status of the text. The view concerned is stated in a number of ways by Sartre. He claims, for example, that I fashion an image for the whole of mankind in choosing for myself (p. 27/30); that one has always to ask oneself what would happen if everyone did the same (p. 28-9/30-1); that it is as if the whole human race were watching what a man does and regulating its conduct accordingly (p. 31/32); that every man realises himself in realising a type of humanity (p. 71/47); that in committing myself I commit all mankind (p. 74/48); and that since only the attitude of strict consistency is that of good faith, I am obliged to will the freedom of others at the same time as my own (p. 82-3/51-2). One could certainly distinguish between these different formulations, but for present purposes it is reasonable as well as convenient to group them together and refer to them as the thesis of the "universalisability" of moral judgements.

Although, naturally, opinions regarding its general validity vary considerably, I doubt that any critic would wish to deny that the thesis of universalisability is a philosophically respectable one: it goes back at least as far as Kant and is still vigorously defended today by English-speaking philosophers like R. M. Hare.[10] What has been questioned, rather, is whether universalisability in ethics is a concept that arises as a logical consequence out of the metaphysical or ontological foundations of Sartre's Existentialism. It has been implied that, on the contrary, universalisability is to be seen as a kind of expedient in the text of *L'Existentialisme*, as an unfounded, almost arbitrary attempt to avoid some of the obviously unpalatable moral consequences of Sartre's emphasis on the individual's freedom — and moreover, an expedient which is inconsistent with the views expressed in *L'Etre et le Néant*.[11] At a certain level of generality, the weight of evidence might well be thought to favour this view, but I believe that a far more thorough and penetrating examination of the whole question is needed: not only are there passages in *L'Etre et le Néant* which, at least, propound a view *similar* to that of universalisability,[12] but above all, in other texts dating from the same period as *L'Existentialisme* Sartre is to be seen explicitly appealing to universalisability in one form or another.[13] What can be said with some certainty is that whether or not universalisability in ethics has a logical basis in Sartre's more fundamental philosophical positions, the use to which he puts the idea in *L'Existentialisme* is by no means unique in his writings: there is no justification whatever for taking his advocacy of this idea in *L'Existentialisme* as some kind of aberration, much less for dismissing the whole text on this ground. Indeed, the writer of one of the most thoughtful books on Existentialist morality has acknowledged the differences in this respect between *L'Existentialisme* and *L'Etre et le Néant*, but claimed that it is the views contained in the latter that have subsequently been abandoned![14] If one were examining in general the question of universalisability in Sartre's Existentialism, it would, of course, be of considerable interest to know that there may be major texts where he does not use the idea at all, but any suggestion that *L'Existentialisme* is not worthy of serious philosophical attention just because it contains that idea would be utterly indefensible.

We have, therefore, to return to our earlier point that there appears to be nothing seriously wrong with the credentials of *L'Existentialisme* as a source for Sartre's philosophical views at a particular point in time. There is room for further information about, and investigation into, certain aspects of the "history" of the text and its place in Sartre's writings, but this involves material external to the work itself and should not be allowed to prejudge in any way our critical assessment of what it actually contains. If *L'Existentialisme* is a poor book, as is so commonly claimed or implied, this can only be because what Sartre says in it is in some respects inadequate or unsatisfactory: the way is now clear for us to look into this matter, albeit briefly and generally.

II

L'Existentialisme is so much shorter and so much less technical than *L'Etre et le Néant* that this in itself seems to have been enough to cause some serious-minded critics to treat it with relative contempt. This is a very unfortunate mistake, which involves ignoring the obvious truth that certain kinds of texts need to be judged by certain standards and others by entirely different ones. It is inherently unlikely that the criteria appropriate to the evaluation of a monumental, technical "Essay in phenomenological ontology" will be very useful when it comes to judging the text of a public lecture in which the speaker was deliberately attempting to popularise his philosophical views. For popularisation *L'Existentialisme* unmistakably is. It is the text of a lecture delivered (on 28th October 1945 at the Club Maintenant in Paris) at the very height of the vogue for Existentialism, as certain rueful references in it suggest.[15] In the discussion following the lecture, Sartre quite explicitly defends the "vulgarisation" of philosophical theories and claims that there is a need for this that it is peculiarly incumbent upon Existentialism to meet (p. 101–3/57–8). Although some might possibly deplore this view, it is not easy to see any good reason why we should despise popularisation as such, even of the most technical philosophical views. What matters, surely, is to distinguish between good popularisation and bad, and one of the reasons why critics' assessments of *L'Existentialisme* have been so dogmatic and unsubstantiated may be that they have been unwilling to face up to the problem of deciding what are the relevant criteria for evaluating a work of popularisation. There seems to have been little more than a widespread, rather vague assumption that what *L'Existentialisme* ought to do is to encapsulate accurately the views expressed in *L'Etre et le Néant*, and while there is manifestly *some* validity in this expectation, a careful look at the text itself shows that other important factors are involved.

It is quite crucial to see the significance of the fact that *L'Existentialisme* is the record of an essentially *polemical* lecture. Either because he believed that this made for the best kind of popularisation, or because the occasion demanded something rather special, Sartre chose to cast his talk in the form of an intellectual offensive or counter-offensive. Some of the adverse comments on *L'Existentialisme* might lead one to suppose that it is a loose, shapeless work, hastily or shoddily put together,[16] but as soon as one registers its polemical nature, it becomes clear that the text has, in fact, a strong and fairly carefully worked-out structure. The four groups of objections raised against Existentialism that Sartre is setting out to refute are enumerated right at the beginning (p. 9–11/23–4) and might be labelled as charges of (i) quietism, (ii) pessimism, (iii) (epistemological) subjectivism, and (iv) moral subjectivism. Once Sartre has outlined the basic theoretical tenets of his brand of Existentialism and explained the meaning of the three central concepts of anguish, abandonment and despair (p. 16–54/26–41), he proceeds to take up and answer these charges one by one, and in order: quietism (p. 55–8/41–2), pessimism (p. 58–63/ 42–4), subjectivism (p. 63–72/44–7), and finally moral subjectivism (p. 72–89/47–54), which he divides up under three sub-headings and devotes as much space to as to the other three objections put together. He concludes with a few paragraphs explaining the relationship between Existentialism and humanism (p. 90–5/54–6), which he has announced as his topic near the beginning.

It is well worth dwelling for a moment on this question of the general nature and structure of *L'Existentialisme*, for we sometimes tend to take the form of a published work for granted, and it would be easy to miss the point that one of the most distinctive and perhaps meritorious features of this text is the way in which it blends exposition and polemic. The attempt to fend off certain objections may more or less have imposed itself in 1945–6, and the criticisms that Sartre answers are manifestly ones that were in the air at the time, but it is possible to argue, without reference to the particular circumstances, that Sartre's decision to cast the lecture in its present form was, in any case, an intrinsically interesting and sound one. Certainly, almost all of the people attending this lecture in 1945 would already know, or think they knew, something about Existentialism, but is there not something important and perfectly generalisable in this fact that sheds light on our reactions to any philosophical doctrines in popularised form? The layman does seem to have a strong tendency to raise, at a very early stage, fairly obvious, perhaps "commonsensical" objections against any wide-ranging philosophical theory. One of the dangers, therefore, of popularising such a theory by straightforward, direct (albeit simplified) exposition must surely be that the audience (perhaps taking this as a *substitute* for more detailed study) will go away convinced that there are certain equally simple but decisive objections to what the philosopher has argued, but which he has somehow failed to take into account. Now, Sartre's approach to his subject-matter in *L'Existentialisme* provides against this kind of danger in a rather neat, if obvious, way. Having spelt out the particular reproaches to his philosophy that he intends to answer, Sartre explains what that philosophy is, so that any trivial or unworthy objections arising out of ignorance or misunderstanding will automatically be rebutted, and he is then in a position to explain in detail precisely why the possibly weightier, but certainly more popular criticisms mentioned at the beginning are misguided. The whole conception of the lecture is a tight, functional one and the text has the characteristic of the best-planned of pieces that, given exactly what the author wishes to do, his plan seems so natural that we can scarcely see how it could reasonably have been different. Moreover, the execution of Sartre's project is not without a certain elegance: he skilfully rounds off his counter-attack, for instance, by looking at his own views in a slightly wider perspective, and contrives to show — with just an appropriate touch of paradox — that Existentialism is exactly the opposite of what it has commonly been taken to be, that it is a particular sort of humanism.

One further point arises out of a simple account of the structure and content of *L'Existentialisme* and a clear understanding of the polemical nature of the work. It is not in the least surprising in the light of what has been said that it fails to cover, even in a popularised, summarised form, all of the major views that Sartre expressed in *L'Etre et le Néant*. For the whole orientation and aim of his lecture is quite different. Whereas *L'Etre et le Néant* is primarily, as its sub-title suggests, a work of ontology, Sartre has quite deliberately given *L'Existentialisme* a predominantly *moral* flavor. It is revealing in this respect that in the course of discussing popularisation he should imply that this activity may well involve coming down from loftier theoretical planes into the moral or political arena (p. 101–2/58). His application of Existentialism to politics is to be found in other writings, but a distinctive feature of *L'Existentialisme* is that it is most centrally concerned with the moral implications of Existentalism. And granted that this is so, it is *bound* to be the case that certain points — even crucial ones — expounded in *L'Etre et le Néant* will not be covered in this text. This can best be brought out by reference to one major example, and one that takes us some way into the substantive process of evaluating *L'Existentialisme* philosophically.

Presumably, if anything is basic to the (essentially ontological) argument of *L'Etre et le Néant*, it is the distinction between being *en-soi* (in-itself) and being *pour-soi* (for itself). But not only do these terms not appear at all in *L'Existentialisme*, the distinction that they embody is not really called upon to play a prominent role in the argument. In effect, what replaces this distinction in Sartre's popularised account of Existentialism is the fundamental tenet (which he claims to be common to Christian and atheist Existentialists) that, in the case of man, existence comes before essence (p. 17/26). And the first thing that we can now say about this is that it is perfectly legitimate to effect such a substitution in a popularised as opposed to a technical description of Existentialism, and one that is designed to bring out its moral rather than its ontological aspect. The terms of this particular formula are less strikingly technical ones and at least apparently clearer in meaning, and they lead on more directly or more naturally to moral matters — to Sartre's claim that since Man has no pre-existing essence, he is no more and no less than what he makes of himself, he is responsible for what he is (p. 22/28).

To suggest, however, that in the context of *L'Existentialisme* it is permissible (probably even desirable) to highlight some formula such as this in place of the *en-soi/pour-soi* distinction is not necessarily to say that

the particular formula that Sartre chose is a good one: we may well want
to go on to ask separately whether the statement that "l'existence précède
l'essence, ou, si vous voulez, qu'il faut partir de la subjectivité ("*existence
comes before essence*—or, if you will, that we must begin from the
subjective"), does or does not constitute a satisfactory, brief, non-technical
formulation of the core of Existentialism. The question is much more
complicated than it looks, but we should not be over-impressed by the
fact—for it is a fact—that many philosophers would want to raise all kinds
of objections to the statement. There *are* serious problems attached to each
of the key concepts, "existence," "comes before" and "essence," and Mary
Warnock is perhaps right to say that the statement is not "readily
intelligible" as it stands and has little point except in the context of the
complete system of Sartre's philosophy. Nevertheless, in *L'Existentialisme*
Sartre is trying to go some of the way at least towards outlining that
system, and the statement itself does not stand in isolation but is further
elucidated in the text. As the very label for the philosophy concerned
might suggest, Sartre did not, as a matter of fact, do at all badly in his
attempt to sum up the point of Existentialism in a single sentence. This
may or may not be a wise thing to attempt in the first place (although it
seems to be the ultimate consequence of popularisation and, indeed, of
any talk about "-isms" in philosophy), but granted that this is the task in
hand, Sartre clearly acquitted himself rather well. To justify this judgement would be a major operation involving the sort of summary account
of Existentialist thought as a whole provided by so many general works:
suffice it to say that no single alternative formula appears to have
particularly strong claims as a rival to Sartre's, and that one has only to
read a number of these critical works to appreciate both its sharpness and
its influence.

Yet whilst one is examining the statement that existence comes before
essence, it has to be said, on the debit side, that the use to which Sartre
puts this formula in *L'Existentialisme* and the immediate context of points
and arguments in which he sets it—these offer serious causes for philosophical complaint, even—or especially—at the level of popularisation.
Firstly, problems associated with the term "essence" are allowed to raise
themselves particularly acutely in this lecture. While Sartre explicitly
asserts that there is a universal human condition (p. 67/46), he equally
explicitly denies that there is a human nature (p. 22/28). Yet the proposition that existence comes before essence in the case of man logically
presupposes that there *is* a human essence in some sense or other of the
term—otherwise it is difficult to see what existence is being said to
precede. It may well be possible to reconcile these three different assertions and indeed I believe that one has an idea of how Sartre would
propose to do so, but whatever truth there may be in his views, there are
unquestionably deficiencies or gaps in his attempt to express them in
L'Existentialisme: he needed to be a good deal clearer about the relation-

ship between the three concepts of essence, nature and condition, or perhaps more careful in his use of the terms.

Another important weakness in *L'Existentialisme* that is closely bound up with the statement that existence comes before essence concerns the way in which this view is related to the idea of God. Perhaps one can understand that Sartre should not include in this work the technical arguments against the existence of God that he deployed in *L'Etre et le Néant*, but simply *state* near the beginning that there is no God. Furthermore, there are considerable advantages in terms of comprehensibility, pointedness and force that Sartre reaps as a result of taking the absence of God as the starting-point for his exposition. But there are also corresponding losses. If Sartre's statement near the end that Existentialism is no more than an endeavour to draw all the logical consequences from a consistently atheistic position (p. 94/56) seems plausible, it is rather less so a few lines further on when he says that it would make no difference if God did exist. Again, there may well be no formal contradiction between these claims, but at the very least their juxtaposition reminds us of one clear-cut disadvantage of Sartre's starting his account of Existentialism from the non-existence of God: it makes it very difficult indeed to see how there can possibly be Christian Existentialists, as Sartre has freely acknowledged there are. Of course, he was under no obligation to explain Christian Existentialism and might be defended on the grounds that he is elucidating only his own brand of atheist Existentialism. Yet this is not quite satisfactory, since the title of his lecture, his reference to what Christian and atheist Existentialists have in common and so on give us the right to expect an account which, at least, does not appear to preclude the possibility of a Christian Existentialism in the way that the present one does. And this leads on to the related but slightly more general point that Sartre's conception of God and the Creation in *L'Existentialisme* is a peculiarly narrow, even caricatural one. This comes out in his statements that, for the most part, we think of God the Creator as a kind of superior artisan, and that we compare God's concept of Man with the manufacturer's concept of the paper-knife (p. 19/27). Basically, what seems to be wrong with these comments is that they make no allowance for the fact that a Christian may well believe that God created Man with free will. In general, it can be objected that the freedom on which Sartre lays so much emphasis in the book is freedom from human nature (whatever that amounts to) rather than freedom from determinism, which he makes no attempt here to rebut. But more specifically, one does not have to be religious to see how ill-founded is his implication that belief in the existence of God is incompatible with the belief that Man is what he makes of himself. It is no surprise that Christian critics have sometimes argued that the God that Sartre rejects in *L'Existentialisme* bears little resemblance to the God of Christianity.[17]

We passed on to make a number of judgements on the philosophical content of *L'Existentialisme* in the course of trying to establish that it is perfectly reasonable for that work to diverge—perhaps even substantially—from *L'Etre et le Néant*. While leaving to others the task of drawing up a list of such deviations, perhaps we should note that there is one much less direct, and indeed purely negative way in which reference to that major philosophical work can sometimes serve as a kind of check. It is quite clear that *L'Existentialisme* ought to be more or less self-contained, that it ought, given its aims and nature, to be comprehensible to someone having no knowledge of *L'Etre et le Néant*. If we have to be familiar with the detailed argument of the latter in order to understand certain sequences or points in the popularised work, then it is, to that extent, poor, unsatisfactory popularisation. Now, there clearly *are* such passages in the text of Sartre's lecture, although I believe they are few. One, for instance, is to be found near the end, at a fairly important stage in the lecture, when Sartre is trying to explain what Existentialist humanism is, and is led to talk of transcendence ("dépassement"—p. 92–3/55). It is hard to believe that this sequence is readily comprehensible to anyone who is not already acquainted with Sartre's account of the nature of the *pour-soi* or consciousness in *L'Etre et le Néant* (part II). Here is a case where the omission of a section of the argument contained in the latter makes something in *L'Existentialisme* obscure or problematic. Another such case comes in the middle of the text where Sartre is referring to the Cartesian *cogito* and makes the mysterious statement that "l'homme qui s'atteint directement par le *cogito* découvre aussi tous les autres" ("the man who discovers himself directly in the *cogito* also discovers all the others"—p. 66/45)—mysterious, that is, if one does not know and remember Sartre's explanation of our being-for-others through the concepts of shame and "le regard" in *L'Etre et le Néant* (part III, ch. 1). Admittedly, in this particular case Sartre does imply that his explanation or demonstration of the point is to be found elsewhere, but this scarcely helps the reader of *L'Existentialisme* and the point concerned is so crucial to Sartre's argument that, again, one might justifiably charge him with inadequate or unclear popularisation. However, if in both cases the text simply does not seem full or explicit enough, we do well to remember that part of the *point* about popularisation will usually be to express something less lengthily. This in no way excuses Sartre over the sequences in question, but although this would be a difficult point to establish even if one had the space, I believe that these two examples and perhaps one or two others are very much the exception rather than the rule. For the most part, it just is *not* the case that one has to be familiar with *L'Etre et le Néant* in order to understand what Sartre is saying in *L'Existentialisme*: on the whole, he succeeds in making his popularised account of his philosophy self-contained and clear as it stands, and the few really obscure passages stand out all the more strongly as a result.

If one were to pursue this sort of line of inquiry, a great deal more could be done towards a full evaluation of *L'Existentialisme*, but perhaps because of the very angle of attack, an unduly negative and carping balance-sheet would be likely to result. In parallel with the kind of questions already asked, we need to ask a separate set designed to bring out the positive merits of Sartre's text. This side of the enterprise might well prove more difficult than the first: if there is likely to be fairly widespread agreement concerning certain faults in the lecture, the question of its strengths and merits may be more intimately bound up with one's own attitude towards Existentialism as a philosophy. Nevertheless, the task is far from an impossible one. Some general points strongly in Sartre's favour have already been touched upon, and could easily be pulled together and filled out: we have praised the conception and structure of the text, suggested that Sartre did rather well in finding a brief formula to sum up the foundations of Existentialism, and claimed that in general his treatment of difficult and complex philosophical topics is clear and self-contained. However, since all of these virtues came to the fore in the course of our answering adverse criticisms, it remains to draw attention, very briefly indeed, to certain characteristic qualities in Sartre's text which deserve to be weighed in the balance against any weaknesses, general or particular, that are noticeable in the work.

Even when all criticisms have been voiced, *L'Existentialisme* remains a highly stimulating and therefore valuable text, one whose subject-matter is deserving of the closest examination. Firstly, it raises and discusses — or at least adopts a specific position on — philosophical issues of the utmost intrinsic importance. For all kinds of reasons, it really matters, philosophically speaking, whether there is a human essence and whether, if there is, this has anything to do with God, if there be a God; whether there is a universal human condition; whether Man is free, etc. In however popularised a form Sartre raises these questions, and whatever the nature of the views he himself expresses on them, we should be thankful to him for providing a public forum, or using a public occasion, for their airing. Secondly, and more specifically, *L'Existentialisme* is a particularly fertile text on the subject of ethics or morality — perhaps, incidentally, more so than any other single text of Sartre's. This is not, by any means, necessarily to say that the ethical or "meta-ethical" views outlined there contain no mistakes, but Sartre's errors — if errors they be — are not stupid, careless ones, as has perhaps been implied, but genuine philosophical mistakes of the kind that all philosophers make. Every major point that Sartre makes about morality in *L'Existentialisme* is interesting, thought-provoking and important. We may, in the end, wish to disagree with what he has to say about universalisability, about the lack of *a priori* values, freedom, and so on, but we should be exceedingly foolhardy simply to *ignore* his arguments on these matters. Slightly more positively still, the work draws our attention to a number of the more characteristic and distinctive contributions that Sartre and other Existentialists have made to ethical thought in the twentieth century: the emphasis on abandonment and Man's consequent responsibility for what he is, the idea that to refrain from choosing is itself a choice, and the rich notions of bad faith and authenticity. When Sartre talks about the importance of creation and invention in morality (p. 77/49), he reminds us of whole areas in the moral sphere that have recently been largely neglected by philosophers working within the Anglo-American, "Analytical" tradition — areas that he himself has explored with considerable penetration in other works.

Finally, on the general stylistic level, another merit of *L'Existentialisme* that is rather easy to take for granted, but which should not be underestimated, since it is of peculiar importance in popularisation, is Sartre's power of concrete illustration. In spite of the fairly highly theoretical nature of what Sartre has to say (He claims early on that Existentialism is "intended strictly for technicians and philosophers"), we do not remember *L'Existentialisme* as a dry, abstract work, largely because he sprinkles his text with references, analogies, examples and illustrations which enliven it considerably as well as appositely crystallising some of the points he is making. Occasionally, as when near the beginning he is inveighing against certain petty or contradictory reactions to Existentialism, such elements are markedly personal and could be omitted without loss to the main philosophical argument. But much more often, when Sartre dwells at greater or lesser length on particular cases or analogies (the illustration of the paper-knife, the "anguish of Abraham," the man who joins the Jesuit order, characters in *The Mill on the Floss* and *La Chartreuse de Parme*, and countless additional major and minor examples), he does so to sharpen and clarify his argument. There can be little doubt that he is remarkably successful in this, and that very few of his images and comparisons miss the mark or obscure the issue. Furthermore, there is one outstanding case in the text of an example of a moral dilemma — that of Sartre's pupil who has to decide between staying with his mother and leaving her to join the Free French Forces — that seems peculiarly memorable and significant from a number of different points of view; it is interesting to note that this very case has been discussed recently by a number of English philosophers.[18] In general, then, it is well worth recording as a major quality of *L'Existentialisme* as a work of popularisation Sartre's highly successful use of concrete illustrations. This gift quite naturally calls to mind Sartre the creative writer rather than Sartre the formal philosopher, and serves as a timely reminder of the fact that there are important senses in which a very great deal of Sartre's literary output proper can be seen as popularisation of his philosophical views; there is perhaps something rather implausible in any suggestion that *L'Existentialisme* is bound to be of little value *qua* popularisation, when we think of the esteem so widely accorded to Sartre's novels and plays.

The incompleteness and inadequacy of this general evaluation of *L'Existentialisme* need no underlining: if the work really is worth more attention than has often been paid to it by critics, then it is worth a far more rigorous and detailed examination than I have had space to make. Having tried to establish that, on the present state of the evidence, reasons for ignoring this text as one (although not a privileged) source for Sartre's views at a particular moment are immeasurably weaker than they have very frequently been taken to be, I have done little more than seek major landmarks, in the largely unmapped territory of evaluating a work of philosophical popularisation as such. Certain standards and criteria emerged from a very general look at the text: it seemed that some of the appropriate questions to ask were whether the book was clear and self-consistent; whether it had structural strength and was self-contained; whether it was stimulating and reasonably concrete. A number of things had to be said against *L'Existentialisme* in these and other respects, but it was always clear that there would be such things, and what was more important was that so many favourable judgements could be made. There is ample room, however, and perhaps a definite need, for a more detailed and penetrative attempt to find the right balance between praise and criticism, and, at best, we have done no more than lay down some suggested guide-lines and make a few substantive points. Evaluating a philosophical work of any kind is, at least in part, to *do* some philosophy, and that is likely to mean that no evaluation, in any case, will be definitive, but this is no more a reason for not undertaking the task than are some of the external "reasons" previously adduced for not bothering to look carefully at *L'Existentialisme est un humanisme* at all.

Notes

1. Paris, Nagel, 1946 ("Pensées"); English translation by Philip Mairet, Methuen, 1948. In this article the work will usually be referred to as simply *L'Existentialisme*. Page references will be given first for the French and then, after the stroke, for the English edition, as follows (p. 9–10/23).

2. Among the critics who use *L'Existentialisme* as a source for Sartre's ideas are: Wahl, J. (*Les Philosophies de l'existence*, Armand Colin, 1959); Olafson, F. A. (*Principles and Persons*, Johns Hopkins Press, Baltimore, 1967); Kingston, F. T. (*French Existentialism. A Christian Critique*, Univ. of Toronto Press, 1961); Coffy, R. (*Dieu des athées; Marx, Sartre, Camus*, Chronique Sociale de France, Lyon, 1963); Pilkington, A. ('Sartre's Existentialist Ethic," *French Studies* XXIII, No. 1, Jan. 1969: pp. 38–47); Plantinga, A. ("An Existentialist's Ethics," *Review of Metaphysics* 12, 1958–9: pp. 235–256).

Those who have explicitly rejected it as such a source are mostly English-speaking critics: Warnock, M. (*Existentialist Ethics*, Macmillan, 1967, and *The Philosophy of Sartre*, Hutchinson, 1965); Manser, A. R. (*Sartre, A Philosophic Study*, Athlone Press, 1966); Cranston, M. (*Sartre*, Oliver & Boyd, 1962). But see also Alberes, R-M. (*Jean-Paul Sartre*, Classiques du XXs siècle, 8th ed. 1964).

Greene, N. N. (*Jean-Paul Sartre: The Existentialist Ethic*, Ann Arbor, Univ. of Michigan Press, 1961) seems to want to do both of these things at the same time!

3. Paris, Editions du Seuil, 2nd ed. 1965: p. 36 (English translations in brackets following the French are my own, except where they are enclosed in quotation marks to indicate that they are taken directly from Mairet's translation of the text.)

4. Contat, M. & Rybalka, M.: *Les Ecrits de Sartre*. Chronologie, bibliographie commentée, Gallimard, 1970. This is an excellent work and an indispensable tool for the detailed study of Sartre (I am indebted to it for a number of references subsequently given in this article), but the main entry for *L'Existentialisme* (pp. 131–2) simply says baldly (and, I believe, mistakenly on at least two counts) that "c'est d'ailleurs le seul volume que Sartre ait en grande partie renié," without substantiating the point there or, as far as I have been able to see, elsewhere in the book.

5. "Jean-Paul Sartre reproche à Georges Lukács de n'être pas marxiste," *Combat*, 20th Jan. 1949.

6. It is rather interesting to note what may be signs of unease over Jeanson's comment: Warnock: "it *seems* that Sartre himself regretted its publication" (*Existentialist Ethics*, p. 39); Manser: "as he himself has admited, the lecture was *probably* a mistake" (op.cit. p. 137); Albérès: "et *je crois que* M. Sartre en a très humblement fait l'aveu" (op.cit. p. 64n – my own italics in this and the previous cases).

7. "Itinerary of a thought. Interview with Jean-Paul Sartre," *New Left Review*, no. 58, Nov–Dec. 1969: p. 50.

8. "Jean-Paul Sartre et les problèmes de notre temps," *Cahiers Bernard Lazare*, no. 4, Apr. 1966: pp. 4–9.

9. Interview with Paul Carrière: *Le Figaro*, 29th Apr. 1947.

10. Particularly in *Freedom and Reason* (Clarendon Press, 1963), and "Universalisability," *Proceedings of the Aristotelian Society* 55, 1955: pp. 295–312.

11. Paris, Gallimard, 1943 ("Bibliothèque des Idées"); translation by Hazel E. Barnes: *Being and Nothingness*, Methuen, 1957. On this point see, for instance, Manswer: op cit. p. 137; Cranston: op. cit. p. 79ff; Warnock: *The Philosophy of Sartre*, pp. 131–2.

12. For instance, pp. 601–2 and 641–2.

13. In: another popularised account of Existentialism in *Action* (no. 17, 29th Dec. 1944); *Réflexions sur la question juive* (1946), Gallimard's "Idées," p. 72; *Qu'est-ce que la littérature?* (1948), Gallimard "Idées," pp. 30–1 and 265–6; an interview in *Combat*, 3rd Feb. 1949 etc.

14. Olafson: op. cit. p. 194n.

15. p. 12–13/24 and 16/25–6. Simone de Beauvoir relates (*La Force des choses* pp. 50–1) how she herself delivered a lecture at the same club, and how the place was so crowded for Sartre's talk that a number of women fainted from the heat and crush.

16. The presentation of the only French edition of the book has perhaps contributed to this impression, with its text in newspaper-like columns and (unhelpful) side-headings that one suspects are not Sartre's own.

17. Coffy: op. cit. ch. III.

18. See, for example, MacIntyre, A.: "What morality is not" (*Philosophy* 32, 1957: pp. 325–35); Bamborough, J. R.: "Unanswerable questions" (*Proceedings of the Aristotelian Society*, Supplementary Vol. XL, 1966: pp. 151–72).

The Selves in the Texts: Sartre and Literary Criticism

Three Methods in Sartre's Literary Criticism

Fredric Jameson*

It is safe to say that Sartre's work as a whole has left its mark on every French intellectual experience of the last twenty-five years; its enormous ideological impact may be measured by the position of Sartre in French intellectual and literary life today, a position that has no equivalent in any other recent national experience.

Yet it would be wrong to assume that this personal authority is at one with the influence of Sartrean existentialism. Indeed, the purely existential strain in Sartre's thought, which finds its most intense expression in *Nausea*, has always been limited by the presence of other modes of thinking and may be most clearly observed at work in what we may call works of *applied* existentialism, such as the book on anti-Semitism or Simone de Beauvoir's *Second Sex*. For in these works the principal instrument of analysis (or *method*, as it will be called here) remains the notion of anxiety in the face of freedom, of a flight into the reassuring conducts of bad faith, whether in woman's submission to the comfortable and secondary role of an object for a masculine freedom, or in the justification by the anti-Semite of his own unjustifiable existence through the "thingification" of Jews. Yet even here, the concept of objectification, from which the concrete character of these analyses derives, is not really existential in origin. From this point of view, Sartre's literary criticism offers a privileged and relatively closed realm within which to identify the other strands in his thinking, and it will be our thesis in the present essay that these are not so much existential as dialectical in character. The intellectual coherence which will be demonstrated here is less that of a unified theory than one of a basic attitude toward literary material; Sartre is the meeting place between a linguistic optimism, a conviction as to the unlimited expressive possibilities of language, and a formal pessimism, a feeling that literary forms, insofar as they always stylize lived experience, are always distortions of it.

*From *Modern French Literary Criticism*, ed. John K. Simon (Chicago: University of Chicago Press, 1972), 193–227. Reprinted with permission.

Sartre's originality, among contemporary critics of styles, lies in his treatment of literary style as an objective rather than a subjective phenomenon. As against those for whom the work of art is the privileged occasion of contact with some deeper force, with the unconscious, with the personality, with Being, or with language, Sartre takes his place among the rhetoricians. The work of art is a construct designed to produce a certain effect; the style of the work of art is the instrument with which a certain illusion of time is conveyed. The objectivity of style in the work of art shows up most clearly in its accessibility to pastiche and imitation, for pastiche remains the best way of trying on the lens of a strange new style, of seeing what the world looks like through it.[1]

But this objectivity brings in turn another form of objectivity with it; if style is a model of time, a certain kind of optical illusion of temporality, then the number of possible styles must be in some sense limited by the number of ways time itself can be deformed or projected. And in this light Sartre's early essays on style in modern writers[2] turn out to be, not principally reviews or occasional articles, but rather chapters of a phenomenology of different attitudes toward, different models of, narrative time.

The basic problem of narrative time is that of the event and the way the novelist disposes his raw material into events, preparation for events, consequences leading from them. At this point the nature of the raw material, of the content of the novel, is of less importance, although ultimately that content—the legendary gestures of Faulkner, the social ambitions in Dos Passos, the sexual guilt of Mauriac—comes to seem symbolic of the way the story is told, emblematic of the kind of time registered in its style.

But initially style is felt as being a structure imposed on a relatively formless raw material; it is somehow an addition to it, a rearranging or reordering of it. If, in the existential formula, existence precedes essence, style, or a certain temporal structure, functions precisely as an essence with respect to the directionless unformed lived existence of the story material. For real time is, according to Sartre, a synthesis of all three temporal dimensions at once; and memories, remembered moments, carry their dead future with them, just as anticipated moments in the future are projected, not in a void, but as the future of somebody with a clearly defined past. But when we try to narrate our experiences, to put time into words, inevitably we do violence to this temporal synthesis, and we lay stress on one dimension of time to the exclusion of the others.[3] Stylistic innovation implies precisely this new way of telling events, or rather the invention of a new illusion of the passage of time, a new projection of the temporal synthesis.

Faulkner's world, for example, is a world without a future; in it, events do not happen, they *have* happened already, they are already legendary, frozen, immobilized. Everyone recognizes the distinctive quality of those stunned and breathless evocations of suspended gestures, the way the Faulknerian sentence rises toward the Event and hangs in midair as though mesmerized by it, in a stillness in which only the words, adjectives and present participles, continue to pile up vainly, in their very obstinacy conveying something of the irrevocability of the act itself. For where the future as a temporal dimension does not exist, the present also loses its force, becomes an already-past; and the Faulknerian present, amputated of its future, resembles nothing quite so much as those images of space that the idiot Benjy watches unwinding on either side of him as he rides along backwards in the carriage. The characteristic of this present is a repetition, an *enfoncement*, a succession like the ticking of a clock, in which events move into the past, growing tinier and tinier in the distance like objects receding. And from this primary apprehension of time, a Faulknerian grammar can be constructed, in the light of which his other stylistic peculiarities find their place and perspective (the fresh starts, the "becauses" and "so's," dangling "and's" and "or's," the use of negation to reinforce the single isolated gesture, the attempt to conjure up a fresh present with the repeated sound of the word "now").

The temporal progression in Dos Passos presents certain affinities with that of Faulkner. Here also events have been transformed into things; here also a storytelling voice has warped experience from the very start, converting it into anecdotes and stories, lending it solidity, objectivity, the appearance of a kind of destiny. But where the narrative voice of Faulkner was an epic one, finding its source in the very point at which gestures are turned into legends, the voice of Dos Passos is that of gossip, and for it all events are to be retailed like so many items in a social column, with the same breathless enthusiasm, the same vacuity and distraction. The style of Dos Passos is therefore the very embodiment of the "objective spirit" of our society, of inauthenticity become public opinion. The narrator of the novels of Dos Passos is the "everybody" of Heidegger, the German "man" or French "on," the anonymous degraded consciousness of mass man; and there is in his narration a radical discrepancy between the stylization of events, the impersonal accounts of anonymous destinies, and the lived events themselves.

But in Dos Passos the narrating voice does not fully identify itself with any one of the temporal dimensions as Faulkner's did with the past. Rather, the time of Dos Passos is the time of History in which the present dominates — not our lived present, but a present already past, a succession of events which have solidified and taken on permanency without quite becoming incorporated into a massive official past, which remain somehow halfway between living events and stale, finished ones, which we surprise in the moment of turning past. The peculiar pathos of Dos Passos is that in his optic we can see events from two different temporal perspectives at once: both in the naive excitement and freshness they have for those living them in the moment, and, over a great distance, in that dreary statistical objectivity that the youthful experiences of old people take on for later generations.

At this point in Sartre's analyses two different types of value judgment intervene. First, what might be described as a purely aesthetic one: both of these styles are *invented* and not premeditated, they don't describe a new way of looking at things, they produce it as a kind of optical illusion in the reader's mind. This is the meaning of the judgment on François Mauriac: in Mauriac's novels also, as in Faulkner and Dos Passos, the freshness of lived experience was converted into a kind of destiny, was seen from the outside like a thing. In Mauriac also we are unable to live a genuine present of events on account of the intervention of a view of them from above, from outside the action itself, on account of the superposition of another perspective. Mauriac, says Sartre, takes the point of view of God on his characters; hence his well-known conclusion: "God isn't an artist; neither is M. Mauriac."[4]

But the difference between Mauriac on the one hand, and Faulkner and Dos Passos on the other, is precisely that Mauriac has not invented a new stylization of time. He does not embody his contradictory vision of the world in a new formal principle, a new method of storytelling. Instead, he simply intervenes in his own narration; interrupts the thoughts of his characters to place an author's appreciation; into their subjective reality drops the "fateful" hint as to their predestined fates.[5] It is not the ideology of Mauriac which Sartre objects to; the worlds, the world views, of Faulkner and Dos Passos were equally contradictory, represented analogous distortions of lived experience. Faced with this contradiction, however, Mauriac does not attempt to overcome the contradiction in his material by stylistic means: he merely alternates his two methods of looking at his characters instead of imposing a new illusion of time through his language. He does not invent; he merely cheats.

There is a second type of value judgment implicit in these early essays, one which will become more pronounced later on. This kind of judgment is precisely an ideological one, a way of evaluating the various kinds of effects resulting from the different modern stylistic innovations. In a general way, one can say that these effects are right-wing or left-wing, tend to give revolutionary or conservative views of the world. But it is not so much the view of the world which counts in this judgment (both Dos Passos and Faulkner present basically *false* pictures of time), but rather the effect this world view has on the reader, the way it makes him think of himself and his life, and of the society around him. Faulkner's time is inhuman because it perpetuates a view of the world in which the future is dead, in which action is impossible. And no doubt such a picture has profound symptomatic value. Faulkner's integrity as an artist reveals a genuine dimension of things, lives without futures, change without hope: "We're living in a time of impossible revolutions, and Faulkner uses his extraordinary art to describe this world dying of old age and our own suffocation."[6] Yet Faulkner's art tends to mesmerize us, to cause us to be fascinated with our own impotence and with the immobility of the world. His legendary gestus invites us to become fixated on the past, his dreamy, urgent, and hypnotic sentences encourage us to dwell in the intolerable.

The stylization of Dos Passos on the other hand has the immediate effect of disgusting us with ourselves, of making self-complacency impossible. The rather obvious and awkward intrusions of history into *U.S.A.* in the form of the biographies and the Camera Eye are only the most external symptoms of a reality in the very texture of the style. In the movement of the narrative sentences we are able to watch our subjective experience transformed into the substance of history itself, into inauthentic collective representation; we watch our own private feelings turn into those of anybody at all, and the process has something of the horror of the absorption by viscosity described in *L'Etre et le néant*.[7] Thus the reader of Dos Passos through the process of reading discovers his own inauthenticity, his own inextricable involvement in history. His reaction is evidently not a political one; yet it touches that vision of ourselves and the world which is the very source of political action.

What we have said about the distortion of narrative time in favor of the past could be shown equally with respect to the present as well. The world of Giraudoux, for example, this world of Aristotelian essences, is a perpetual present, a present of fresh beginnings, a morning world without any genuine past or future, in which change takes the form of a replacement of one image by another, like leafing through the pages of a family album. Its optimism is no doubt as false as Faulkner's pessimism; yet it is a genuine stylization and represents one of the extreme possibilities of that deformation which narration brings to lived time.

The events of *L'Etranger* seem at a far remove from this fairy-tale universe; yet it also is a succession of pure presents, and in it the *passé composé* has the effect of camouflaging the passage of time, the Hemingway-like succession of bald sentences making each present seem a complete unit in itself, a self-sufficient moment that needs links with neither past nor future. It is in this way, through the movement of the style, that Camus's notion of the absurdity of abstraction and of hope, of any kind of existence beyond the bounds of the present instant, is demonstrated, not as an abstract idea, but as an experience lived by the reader sentence by sentence.

It is significant that the essay on Camus should close with a question of terminology. Sartre is reluctant to describe *L'Etranger* as a novel; he would rather see it in the tradition of the *conte philosophique* that goes back to Voltaire. Indeed, the principal tendency of everything that has preceded may be described as a defense of the *novel* against that rival form which the French call the *récit* ("narrative" or "tale" are not altogether satisfactory English equivalents). The genuine novel is for Sartre that form of narration which emphasizes, in its temporal stylization, neither the past nor the present, but rather the future. The novel exists as a form when we are thrown into the minds and experiences of characters for whom the future, for whom destiny, has not yet taken shape, who grope and invent their own destinies, living blindly within the entanglement of one another's unforeseeable actions and under the menace of history's unforeseeable development. In this perspective, the future is that which is sought passionately through the present, that which will ultimately return upon the events narrated to give them their meaning. Such a form requires an absolute nonintervention on the part of the novelist; but its open perspective, the blankness stretching before reader and character, can paradoxically be conveyed either through a completely objective or a completely subjective mode, as long as either is applied systematically throughout the work. The novelist can show us the entire stream of events through his characters' eyes, making us share their limits of vision, the imperfection of their points of view, as is the case in Joyce or Henry James; or he can withhold this subjective, psychological reality entirely and give us nothing but the external actions, the words and gestures, of his characters, in the manner of the American "behavioristic" novel of the thirties, the novel of Hemingway or Dashiell Hammett.

It is evidently difficult to draw a clear line between this genuine novel and the mixed practice of the *récit*. But it seems clear that if for Sartre the modern American novel stands as a kind of privileged model for what the open form ought to be, it is the French realistic tradition of the nineteenth century which furnishes the classic illustration of the motivation behind the *récit*.

Beneath the objective surface of the nineteenth-century novel the old-fashioned storyteller lies hidden. This is the secret truth of the form, the key to its distance from experience and to the deformation it imposes on lived events. In order to grasp the significance of the techniques of the *récit*, we must first understand the experience of storytelling itself, its meaning as a social phenomenon in its own right. Here is a description of the most typical storytelling situation, the framework of a Maupassant novella:

> First the listeners are presented to us, generally some brilliant and socially distinguished group which has come together in the salon at the conclusion of a dinner. It's night, and night cancels everything out, weariness as well as passions. The oppressed sleep, the rebels sleep also; the world is shrouded, history catches its breath. All that remains, a globe of light within the surrounding nothingness, is this watchful élite absorbed in its ceremonies. If intrigues are going on between its members, loves, hatreds, we don't know about it, and in any case desires and rages have been stilled for the moment; these men and women are absorbed by the task of *preserving* their culture, their customs, and of exchanging ritual *recognition* with each other according to the forms. They stand for order at its most refined: the stillness of the night, the

silence of passions, everything in this scene bears witness to the stabilized bourgeoisie of the late nineteenth century, which thinks that nothing further will ever take place, which believes in the permanence of capitalist organization. Hereupon the narrator is brought forward: an older man, somebody who "knows life" and has a thing or two to say about it, a doctor, a military man, an artist or a Don Juan. He has reached that point in life when, according to a respectful and convenient myth, man is freed from his passions and looks back on those he has known with indulgent lucidity. His heart is as calm as the night; he is utterly detached from the story he is about to tell; if once he suffered from it, now that suffering is sweet, he looks back on it and contemplates it in its truth, that is to say *sub specie aeternitatis*. It's true that once upon a time something painful took place, but all that has long since been over and done with; the people involved are all dead or married or consoled. Thus the adventure is a brief disorder which has been repealed. It's told from the point of view of experience and wisdom, listened to from the point of view of order. Order triumphs, order is everywhere, and contemplates an ancient and abolished disorder much as the peaceful water of a summer day might preserve the memory of the ripples that had once passed over it.[8]

It is in the light of this basic situation that the principal techniques of the nineteenth-century novel are to be understood: the recapitulation of the past history of the characters or the place of the action; the omniscient narrator; the secondary narrative figure who, drawn by rumor and legend, approaches closer and closer to the truth of the story; the use of social values (sentiment, judgment on adultery) as channels of conventional expectation; and so forth. The living voice is the source of these later, more sophisticated formal developments and remains imminent in them, like the *gestus* of the Roman orator in later rhetoric, or the traditional gestures and mimicry of the Russian *skaz* which Eichenbaum found preserved and transformed in *The Overcoat* of Gogol.[9] It represents a choice of the past, or of the timeless, as against the uncomfortable present; but unlike the innovations of the modern writers we have examined, this choice is not an individual one, but one inscribed in the very values of society itself, and of the middle class which dominates it. This narrative style is therefore the appropriate reflection of the historical moment in which it originated, and becomes problematical, in the twentieth century, when that moment is itself at an end.

In the early 1950s a new motif makes its appearance in Sartre's work: the distinction between an *act* and a *gesture*, between the *real* and an attitude toward it which seems to drain it of its reality, transform it into mere appearance, *irrealize* it, to use Sartre's term.

The groundwork for this theme had already been laid in one of Sartre's most technical and impersonal writings, *L'Imaginaire* (1940), which demonstrated the basic incompatibility between the act of perceiving and the act of imagining. Both are ways of relating to external objects, but in the second mode the object is apprehended as being *absent*, and my relationship to it is precisely a kind of absence. The implication of this thesis is that, contrary to popular belief, I am never in any danger of mistaking imaginary phenomena (hallucinations, obsessions, dream-images) for real ones. There is a radical difference in quality between the two experiences, the imaginary one is always known to be unreal. I therefore dispose of two possible ways of living the real world: in the first I stand in an active, practical relationship to its objects; in the second I put their reality between parentheses and live with their absence, with their idea or image. These two modes of existence point to two fundamentally opposed passions; for there can be a passion for the unreal, for the imaginary, which leads its subject to prefer imaginary feelings to real ones, psychological satisfactions to genuine ones, gestures to acts. It is in this sense that Sartre can say of a writer like Mallarmé[10] that his literary creation is the equivalent of a destruction of the world; such a passion for the imaginary has as its motivation a kind of resentment against the real, and finds its satisfaction in a symbolic revenge upon it.

The starting point of this theory of the imaginary is, however, a theory of the real, which can be briefly summed up as follows: consciousness is basically activity; our primary relationship to the world is not a contemplative or static one, not one of knowledge but one of action and work; the "world" in the phenomenological sense is not motionless space spread out before me, but rather time, "hodological" space, a network of paths and roads, a complex organization of means and ends and projects, unveiled through the movement of my own adventures and desires. This notion, with its emphasis on the primacy of work over mere abstract knowledge, may seem Marxist in origin, indeed provides the connecting link between existentialism and Marxism in Sartre's later works; but in fact it originates directly in Heidegger.[11] For the latter we apprehend objects first as tools and only later on as things-in-themselves, as static substances. For human reality, involved in its projects, each object is primarily a frozen project, an immobile imperative, a thing-to-be-used-in-a-certain-way — *zuhanden*, available, lying to hand in case of need. And just as scientific objectivity is a later, more sophisticated development among human attitudes toward the world, so also is the apprehension of the thing or object as *vorhanden*, as simply being there, as an entity with no evident relationship to myself.

Heidegger's theory of art is based on these two dimensions of the object itself;[12] for him the work of art causes us to suspend our preoccupation with things as tools, to step back from our immediate involvement in them, and to grow aware of them as vessels of Being. But his illustrations are mainly poetry (Hölderlin, Trakl) and painting (Van Gogh), and his theory lays stress primarily on the content of literature (objects as revelatory of Being itself) rather than on its forms. In this respect Sartre's theory of literature is more exhaustive.

For Sartre the principal distinction between poetry and prose is that the reader take a utilitarian attitude toward the latter. In it language functions as a system of signs, and the reader's mind is primarily involved, not with the signs themselves, but beyond them, with the things signified. The relationship of the reader to prose language is therefore an active, practical, transcendent one; he uses it, and like all tools it dictates by its own structure the operations necessary to use it properly. For the prose writer also language is the instrument of an act, a secondary or indirect mode of action which Sartre calls action by revelation (*dévoilement*). By naming things, by constructing verbal models for experiences which until then had remained formless and inchoate, the writer acts on his readers, makes it impossible for them to live as they had before (if they wish to continue to be unaware of a given feeling, for example, they must now, after it has been named, *deliberately* avoid thinking about it; they can no longer enjoy the uncompromised innocence of the ignorant).

Poetry on the other hand is distinguished from prose in that in it language intervenes between the reader and the abstract meanings; in poetry it is the words which are primarily apprehended, the meanings in turn become mere pretexts for an awareness of language in its materiality. Thus in poetry a practical, utilitarian attitude toward language is replaced by a contemplative one, for a doing is substituted a being. This is why for Sartre the history of modern poetry is, in terms of the lives of the poets and of their relationship to society, not one of accomplishment but one of failure:[13] When I succeed, I pass from one practical goal to another, the means go unnoticed in the effortless progress from end to end. But when I fail, when my racket misses the ball suddenly, then the means stand out in all their materiality; I become conscious of my own body in its awkwardness, of the racket, of the disposition of space around me. So with the poet: he is able to apprehend the materiality, the being, of language with intensity only against the background of the collapse of his own real projects and of the failure of language as an instrumental means toward an end.

The distinction between an object taken as a means and one taken as an end in itself can be prolonged into the very structure of the poetic image. In the beginning Sartre tends to consider the poetic image in a relatively static fashion, as the symbol and reflection of the consciousness which conceives it. Following Bachelard, he sees the sensation, or the poetic image, as an "objective symbol of being and of the relationship of human reality to that being."[14] Thus the images of Baudelaire are characterized by a certain *spiritualized* quality: objects "which can be apprehended by the senses and yet resemble consciousness. The entire effort of Baudelaire was to recuperate his consciousness, to possess it and hold it like a thing in the palm of his hands, and this is why he seizes on anything that has the look of consciousness objectified: perfumes, muffled lights, distant music, so many little closed mute consciousnesses, so many images of his unattainable existence at once taken into himself, consumed like hosts."[15]

But here the relationship between consciousness and its product (the image, the poem, the sensation) remains one of mere reflection; later on, Sartre will conceive of it as a more dynamic interaction, particularly in those suggestive pages of *Saint Genet* (1952) in which he distinguishes two basic types of modern images, the expansive and the retractile.[16] In the first a single object ("l'aube") is felt to be an expanding multiplicity ("comme un peuple de colombes"). In such an image, basically inanimate space or externality has been apprehended as an arrested glimpse of an explosion in progress; what is lifeless and measurable has been suddenly endowed with energy and movement, felt to be a moment of a universal and dynamic progress.

The other type of image is one in which existing multiplicities are reduced to unity, in which a movement which was outward-exploding becomes circular, cyclical, in which the chaos of external objects are subordinated to the hierarchical order of the closed image. (Sartre's examples are the restaurant scene in *A l'Ombre des jeunes filles en fleur*, where the tables and the people at them, the waiters and the entire surroundings, are transformed into a single unified planetary system; as well as certain hermetic images of Mallarmé and of Genet himself.)

These two poles of spatial configuration, which are not unlike Jakobson's opposition between metaphor and metonymy, reintroduce into the heart of the poetic image the distinction already described above between the practical/transcendent, the vision of the thing as a frozen use or potential project, and the irrealizing/contemplative, the category of the self-sufficient thing-in-itself. In the first kind of image the reader feels reflected back to him his own energy and generosity, his own transcendent power, "the unity which human work imposes by force on the disparate"; in the second the "whole world is represented according to the model of a hierarchical society."[17] It is characteristic of Sartre that he sees in these two kinds of imagination a fundamental opposition between left-wing and right-wing thinking, between an open revolutionary type of thought and a closed one which wishes to contemplate permanence or eternity in the flux of things themselves. But it is no less characteristic that he furnishes a psychological explanation as well. The first, exploding type of imagery is a figure of freedom itself, of the projection of consciousness out into the world of things, of the transcending of anxiety through choice and activity; the second attempts to conjure anxiety away by suggesting perfect order, by situating consciousness, not in a dangerous indeterminacy, but in the midst of a world in which everything has its appointed place, in which values are inscribed in things themselves.

In the novel, where the attitude toward language is a relatively straightforward, practical one, the distinction we have been developing finds its application in content, in the treatment of the objects of the novel's world, in their relative distance from characters and novelist. Static description, for example, that characteristic of the nineteenth-century novel, is to be understood in the light of this opposition between the practical/transcendent and the contemplative:

> Since Schopenhauer it's an accepted fact that objects stand forth in their fullest dignity when man silences the will to power in his own heart: their secrets are disclosed only to those who consume them at their leisure; you're supposed to *write* about them only at those moments when there's nothing to *do* with them. The fastidious descriptions of the last century are a rejection of practical use: you don't touch the universe, you swallow it raw, through the eyes; the writer, in opposition to bourgeois ideology, chooses that privileged instant to tell us about things when all the concrete relationships that linked him to them are broken save for the tenuous thread of vision itself, when they separate beneath his look, sheaves of exquisite sensations come apart.[18]

But this technique, in which a whole life style is inculcated through an apparently natural and harmless description of surroundings, is only one distortion among the many possible when the object of the practical world passes through into the mirror world of art.

The unique optical illusion of Kafka's world, for example, is created by the emphasis on means at the expense of ends, on a monstrous instrumentality of things which points everywhere and leads nowhere: "The means soaks up the end like a blotter soaking up ink."[19] Purpose is implicit in every manufactured thing, in every item of the city's inventory; but normally, absorbed in the passage from one end to another, from one project to another, we fail to notice this structure of the objects around us. Kafka makes us intensely aware of it by suddenly concealing the second term, masking the teleological purposes which would make the objects around us comprehensible and natural to us; and at once they stand out starkly in their instrumentality, with astonishment we see for the first time that dimension of human reality which is activity, which brings tools into being around it. Sartre is careful to distinguish this unique vision from the apprehension of the absurd, as it takes place in Camus for instance; for the absurd is the awareness of a world in which ends simply do not exist and never have, in which there are no tools, no point to any activity, in which it is not teleology that surprises us but precisely the opposite of it.

Yet it should be noted that Kafka's world is not a lived experience but an artistic projection, a technical feat made possible by a rearrangement of the structure of his raw material. For if in real life such a substitution of means for ends was possible in some of the inventions of the surrealists (Duchamp's sugar cubes suddenly turning out to be heavy bits of marble), such moments, being contradictions in terms, rapidly disintegrate, and the stable world of cause and effect quickly takes shape around us once again.

Hence the great interest of the experiment of Genet, who by his position as an outsider *within* our practical world succeeds in undermining its objects, in *irrealizing* them and substituting for our practical attitude toward them a demoralizing aesthetic and contemplative one, replacing action with the aesthete's values, with Beauty or the Imaginary.

For an object can be neutralized with respect to its practical functions and transformed into something magical, into an image, by the rearrangement of the time scheme in which it is perceived. Genet is struck by red velvet armchairs, gilt mirrors, abandoned in a field.[20] For the utilitarian mind these objects are understood as moments in a process, their position can be deciphered by consulting the future: housecleaning is a project, the preservation of the empty lot for its investment value is also a project, the image itself is nothing but a momentary juxtaposition of prosaic, wholly unmysterious activities. But for Genet the visual intensity of the juxtaposition is everything, the present takes precedence over past history or future destinations, and indeed the latter become mere pretexts for the former; whatever the mysterious sign which these abandoned armchairs are trying to convey to him, the woman of the house picked that day to move them out *in order for* Genet to witness it. In this reversal of the real and the imaginary it is the practical project which is appearance, illusion, and the visual image which is reality.

And as it is in the world of material objects, so also with those objects which are words: the latter shed their practical uses, drift up into Genet's mind like strange and fascinating fragments of an exotic reality, a single odd-sounding term or expression becomes a poem in itself. So also with human behavior: the vision obsessed with the imaginary rather than the real tends to retain isolated gestures for their own sake rather than operations comprehensible only in the light of some larger practical purpose, to see the human world as a discontinuous series of instants (the "Divinarianes" of *Notre-Dame des Fleurs*), of striking or characteristic remarks or anecdotes. And evidently in a kind of "motivation of the device" this stylistic predilection ends up producing the kind of content which can best satisfy it; seen principally through the lens of isolated gestures, the characters of Genet turn out to be people whose lives are led *in order to* make gestures, whose principal value is the acting out of their creator's aesthetic, who are themselves aesthetes, transvestites, exhibitionists, criminals.[21]

To this characteristic selection of content corresponds a peculiar quality of the typical Genet image; its essence is "toc," the sham, the fake, that which shows garish bad taste. The older literary criticism analyzed function, structure, and tone and had as its basic presupposition that the image *worked* in some way (otherwise the work in question was faulty or not worth analyzing). Here the point is that Genet does not want his images to work; the solid coherent image is taken as a reality by the reader, what was imaginary in the writer's mind becomes a feature or component of a world which enjoys a certain objective existence outside him. But since Genet's passion aims at the symbolic destruction of the world, at an undermining of its solidity, he cannot afford to tolerate this paradox or dialectic of the literary process, this density or materiality which is the end-product of his unreal daydreaming. So he sabotages his own art, he short-circuits his material so that it will remain purely imaginary for the reader as well, he creates images which are visual in appearance but which the reader is at a loss to visualize. (The flower images come to mind — "There exists," decrees Genet, "a close relationship between flowers and convicts: the fragility, the delicacy of the former are of the same nature as the brutal insensitivity of the latter.")[22] Such images call for the performing of mental operations which are contradictory, which the reader cannot complete.

This prolongation of the unreal to the very heart of the literary image itself is repeated on the level of the plot as a whole. Genet's characters and story do not have the objective self-sufficiency of the conventional work of fiction. They are instead quite clearly products of his desire, wish-fulfillments, fantasies, and at every moment they threaten to vanish away and leave us face to face with the lonely dreaming consciousness from which they sprang. Genet alone is the hero of all his books, his novels are books about novel-writing, about the imagining of characters and stories, and in them we watch desire trying out its voice and inventing the forms in which it is symbolically to satisfy itself: first images, faces, phrases, anecdotes; then the willful setting in motion of the wish-fulfilment itself; finally those moments when the dream seems to *take*, and scenes unfold which are somehow external to the dreamer, have their own terrible autonomy and logic (as in the murder and trial scenes of *Notre-Dame des Fleurs*). Thus the entire work remains profoundly imaginary in its very core, is not drawn by the reader out into a kind of objectivity but instead draws him into its irreality, contaminates his mind with the imaginary. Genet's revenge against the real world thus falls on the reader as well.

This peculiar relationship to the object and to its image is not an exclusively literary invention on Genet's part. Just as Kafka's objective situation as a government functionary put him in a position to explore the predominance and proliferation of means over ends, and to do so objectively, without any personal intervention, so the very situation of Genet as orphan and thief, as social outcast, places him at distance from ordinary utilitarian objects and activities, causes him to stare at them from the outside and to invent a whole system of values (beauty, the importance of the gesture) and a whole rearrangement of time (the hallucinatory present) in order to live them in a contemplative mode, all practical, transcendent relationships to them being closed to him.

Both Kafka and Genet represent artistic deformations of our lived experience of the world. Their value is first of all artistic, in the invention of new techniques through which to project their contradictory vision of things, and secondly ethical, in the way the former brings us to a heightened awareness of the practical structure of our world, in the way the latter forces us to look at ourselves and our society through the eyes of its outcasts, its functional rejects. But it is characteristic of Sartre that he should feel, along with these value judgments, a certain impatience with the artifices and detours, with the formal untruths, which art entails; and that he should at the same time sketch out a program for an art in which this deformation of lived reality would be overcome.

Such an art was to have been the "literature of *praxis*" or of *production* described at the end of *Qu'est-ce que la littérature?*[23] The model for such a literature was the novel of aviation developed by Saint-Exupéry, work centering on the technical relationship of men to things, in which objects are neither described in an objective, contemplative way nor irrealized, but transcended toward their use, revealed by their position in the human project itself. And the aesthetic formula behind such a work is neither that of static description nor of poetic irrealization but rather that expressed as an artistic law by Valéry, namely, that the density of a literary object is in direct proportion to the multiplicity of relationships it entertains with the other elements of the work. But this literature, which presents striking similarities with the theory of socialist realism (and with works such as the early films of Eisenstein), was never brought into being by Sartre and his generation.[24] It was a utopian ideal, one dependent in the long run on the nature of the writer's society, on the possibility in it of experiencing objects, not as alienated commercial wares, but rather as tools or as the products of human work; on the possibility of addressing readers who feel themselves engaged in activity, rather than those passively enmeshed in routines and systems that are beyond their control. In this sense, the idea of a literature of praxis remains a negative, a critical one: one which reminds us of the ultimate and authentic relationship to objects within the free project, as tools to be transcended toward a future, as crystallized human activity.

The dynamic element in Sartre's existentialism is a Hegelian graft, the idea of the Other and of Otherness. It is this concept which completes the idea of freedom with a description of the way freedom objectifies and alienates itself in its objects. (Flaubert's *Madame Bovary* is for example misappropriated by his contemporaries, and transformed into an object unrecognizable to him.) It is this notion which permits the free consciousness of *L'Etre et le néant* to escape from its isolation in the monad, to discover its dimension of Being-for-other-people and its inextricable involvement in an intersubjective world. Later on, the notion of Otherness serves as a means of accounting for the relationship between the self and the institutions around it with which it must come to terms; in particular, it accounts for the paradoxical phenomenon of the divided self, the Hegelian unhappy consciousness, in which people are obliged to choose themselves as Other for Other people, to feel their center of gravity outside the self.[25] Finally, Otherness is the source of the optical illusion of Good and Evil, of the ethical manichaeanism which results in justification for the Self and condemnation of the Other (anti-Semitism, anti-communism, racism, social stereotypes of the insane and the criminal, and so forth).

But dialectical thinking involves the setting into relationship with each other of two incommensurable realities, two phenomena which cannot be thought in the same conceptual framework. The scandal of Otherness is precisely this revelation of an underside of existence, a dimension which is out of reach, which cannot be dissolved by ordinary analytical thought, and which always *turns* it, reckons it into the account beforehand. (Imagine someone with a horror of other people's judgments; to escape them he always does the opposite of what people expect; at length a superior judgment falls, imprisoning him this time in a larger perspective: he is simply *capricious*.) The scandal of literary Otherness for literary critics is this obligation to go outside the neat world of the single conceptual framework, to make a dialectical leap from the comfortable, imminent system of forms and purely formal analysis to an unpleasantly external reality. For Marxism this external reality is the economic and social situation, the historical form which material conditions take; and the Marxist literary dialectic involves the disagreeable reminder that the major part of writers' and readers' lives is spent in the preoccupation with material questions, that the work of art, in appearance self-sufficient and above history, is conditioned (even more radically than by the purely literary history of its form and content) by such external and absolutely nonliterary phenomena as the state of book publishing in the period, the increasing enrichment and leisure of certain classes of the society, and so forth.

Merleau-Ponty has pointed out[26] that the originality of Sartre's view of literature with respect to this materialistic dialectic is that for him the work of art is not felt to be retrospective, a product of a certain social background, but rather prospective, itself a way of choosing the social group to which it speaks and of which it will eventually become emblematic. The Otherness of the work of art for Sartre is constituted not so much by the *milieu* in which it originates as by the *public* which it calls forth for itself.

For the theory of prose was based on the idea that an appeal to the reader was built into the very structure of prose language: the words of the novel are signs rather than material objects; they require certain mental operations in order to be completed, to be endowed with signification. The writer cannot himself complete the signs which he prepares for the reader; he knows their meaning too well already, he cannot approach them with uncertainty and groping experimentation, against an open future; he can never see his own work with the eyes of an outsider; as operations to perform, his own words remain for him a dead letter.

Thus on the most basic level all prose requires the cooperation of a reader to come into being, does not exist until a reader has somehow re-created it and brought it to being with his own freedom (by living *through* the characters, by agreeing momentarily to lend the novel's signs his own personal experience, his own memories, his own expectations and solidity). But the reader is implied on a more specific level as well; the kinds of signs chosen by the writer tend to limit his readers to a certain group or class, to imply a certain kind of background knowledge in them which limits the availability of the work to initiates only. An American writer would for example feel he had to explain to a European audience allusions which Americans would grasp without comment on his part. But literature is primarily allusion; a work in which everything is explained, justified intellectually, accounted for, is quite inconceivable, so that all works of literature in one way or another speak to a closed group of people at the expense of others.

Beside the formalist or the social and biographical methods, there is thus a place for a new type of examination which would describe the work of art in terms of the public which it implies; and it is this new type of literary history which Sartre writes in *Qu'est-ce que la littérature?* (1948). The logic of his position distinguishes two kinds of public, the *real* (that group implied by the background required to read the work), and the *virtual* (those groups deliberately or implicitly shut off from access to it). The various possible relationships of literature to its public will therefore tend to be governed by two kinds of possible opposition: one between real and virtual publics, the other between two different possible real publics, both of which may happen to be available to the writer at that moment of history. Sartre's history of literature amounts to a working out of the various possible combinations and permutations of these terms.

His central distinction corresponds to the more fundamental Hegelian one between abstract and concrete;[27] for Sartre the work of art becomes concrete only to the degree that it approaches an ever widening public, one which tends toward universal readership as an outside limit. For the writer who must limit his readership severely must also limit the range of experiences treated; must translate them into the terms understood by the group; must therefore practice symbolism and abstraction as a habit of mind developed and imposed by his confining situation as a writer in a certain society. The archetype of this abstract literature is that of the Middle Ages, in which the reading of literature was limited primarily to the writers themselves, to the clerical caste which possessed the specialized technique of the written word. In such a situation, where the virtual public extends for all practical purposes to the whole of society at large, the subject matter of literature shrinks to an almost modern purity; the only available content is the literary activity itself in the form of pure spirituality, at its most abstract, in other words, religion, a symbolic apparatus in which the entirety of the concrete world is present in inverted reflection, transformed into abstraction or pure idea.

The ideal counterpart to this moment in which the virtual public eclipses the real public is of course one in which the two are identical, in which the real public includes all of humanity. This utopia of literature is difficult to imagine, but clearly presupposes a literature from which all abstraction has been eliminated, in which ideas as separate entities no longer exist, and in which every kind of subject matter possesses its intrinsic importance and meaning. The history of modern philosophy offers perhaps the most convenient analogy, where little by little, and through its own self-criticism, philosophy as system, as an independent structure of abstractions, has been replaced by the various sciences (logic and linguistics, history and economics, sociology, psychology) into which its own concrete content evolved. The movement in literature would be the reverse of that described in medieval times, where writing was a technique like any other, and for that very reason separated off from all the others into its own closed guild or caste. Here writing as an action becomes in a world of unalienated work the symbol of any other kind of human energy or transcendence, serves as a relationship of analogy and similarity rather than the sign of inequality and unlikeness which it had been in the earlier period.

Between these two extreme moments, all the other forms which a literature can take, which French literature has taken: the property of a ruling class which was its real reading public (during the seventeenth century), a mediation between two different real publics, the nobility and the bourgeoisie (in the eighteenth century), the possibility of an appeal to the oppressed class (during the nineteenth century), the possibility once again of a mediation between two classes, the workers and the bourgeoisie (in the twentieth century), and finally, a refusal of any public, the reduction to the public of the clericature of the Middle Ages, to a public of other writers, posterity and the great literary dead (our own literature, modernism, the religion of art from its beginnings in the nineteenth century). It is clear from this scheme that the dialectic of literary development is not always a logical or predictable one; the privileged position of the eighteenth-century writer, for instance, who could speak to two classes and be imprisoned by neither, should in the nature of things present itself again in our time, except that the influence of the Communist party over the workers makes it impossible to address them directly. The literature of the nineteenth century ought to have been once again a literature designed for a ruling class, as in the seventeenth century, except that the best writers refused this kind of service and took refuge in dandyism, hatred of the bourgeois, and art for art's sake. To explain why this was so would involve an analysis of the specific nature of bourgeois, as opposed to earlier feudal, values. Indeed, it has not been sufficiently noticed how significant a part of Sartre's life work has been given over to a portrait and an analysis of the French middle class;[28] this is perhaps his most important contribution to the history of ideas behind literature, as opposed to the purely literary examination of forms, and there is implicit in his work as radical a revision of modern French social and intellectual history as that which Lukács undertook for modern Germany.

It is characteristic that with the possibility of disengaging himself from his own class (as in the eighteenth century) ruled out, Sartre should turn to the kind of "internal emigration" represented by the example of Genet. The appeal to the reader was built into the very linguistic structure of Genet's work; Sartre shows in concrete detail how his poetry (pure materiality of language) is infected and undermined by an instinctive prose (a system of signs, organization by paraphrasable significations).[29] For the appeal to the Other was at the very source of Genet's creative impulse; victim of an initially verbal trauma (accusation, being *named* a thief), he first experiences words as impenetrable objects, as Otherness, and his attempt as a writer is to recapture this dimension of language for himself, either to see himself from the outside as others see him, or to make them go through the same strange contradictory experience themselves, that of being looked at from the outside, of being unable to seize from the inside the language of their writer-accuser. The favorable judgment on Genet is therefore similar to that passed on Dos Passos; such literature has a value of contestation, reflects back to the middle classes their own truth in all its ugliness as seen, not from the vantage point of another class, but from a point on the very margin of their own, in Genet's case through the eyes of a criminal and outcast.

It should be added that besides this "prospective" criticism, there is also in Sartre, particularly in the existential biographies, a "retrospective" criticism as well, one which evaluates the effect of his background, his *situation*, on the writer. Thus both Genet and Giraudoux present medieval characteristics, have basically medieval imaginations,[30] but this is not to be attributed to their sharing in one of those Platonic abstractions such as the medieval world view which German idealistic literary criticism used to favor. Rather, the medieval world view was itself the expression of an agricultural society, and it is to the degree that Genet's background, his life situation, was by accident agricultural in a predominantly industrial society, that certain objective similarities appear between his way of thinking and those of medieval times.

It is in the light of this reduction to the lived situation of the writer that the much discussed notion of *engagement* (commitment) is to be understood. The emotional logic of this idea is characteristic of Sartre: if in fact we *are* our situation, it seems to run, then we ought to *choose* to be it, with all its limitations, we should prefer a lucid awareness of it to imaginary evasions and the mystification with abstract or unreal issues. Indeed, the whole bias of Sartre's philosophy is against placelessness and against the kind of introspection in which I lose my own limits, in which I forget my observer's position in the universe and come to identify myself with privilege, absolute spirit, or whatever justification subjectivity invents in order to persuade itself of its isolation from other people, its implied superiority over other people. In literary history the form that this passion for privilege has taken is the religion of art, the attempt to escape one's own historical moment by associating one's self mentally with eternity in the form of the confraternity of art, the great tradition, or posterity. *Engagement* is therefore not a political notion, or a call to propaganda, but serves a primarily negative function: that of cutting away all the imaginary dimensions we give ourselves in an effort to avoid awareness of our concrete historical condition.

From a positive point of view, the idea of engagement can be seen as a theory of living literature. Already the notion of a public and the mechanism of alienation had seriously restricted the immediacy of the literature of the past; if Flaubert's *Madame Bovary* is not one but a whole series of different literary phenomena nesting inside one another (the book Flaubert wrote, the one his contemporaries read, that of the naturalists, of the subsequent generations, etc.), then we cannot so much read it directly as decipher it, separating the various historical objects of our attention. Perhaps one might express this death of past literature in a different way by saying that it is for the modern reader exotic, just as foreign works are exotic. For implicit in the idea of *engagement* is a limitation to the given national society itself, inasmuch as the various nations of the world have developed at unequal rates, have different social structures and face dissimilar problems, in short present different kinds of content to the writers who must work in them. *Engagement* thus involves a reduction to the present, both in space and time, and the advantage it holds forth is that of an immediate contact with the problems and lives of its readers in the present. The ideal is political only insofar as any really complete picture of the present in all its contradictions would ultimately have to emerge into a political dimension of things; and the criticism of engaged literature as occasional literature and mere propaganda is only a caricature of a more accurate criticism that might be made of it, namely, that it imprisons the writer perhaps too dramatically in the present, neglects the passage of time required between conception and execution as well as the lag between generations, and ultimately that it tends to reduce art to a relationship between two people of common background and situation, that is, to return the work of art to that direct interpersonal relationship which was its origin.

There is no doubt that Sartre's attitude toward literature is an ambiguous one, full of suspicion of its duplicities and illusions, its necessary indirection. Yet at the same time literature is a crucial form of self-consciousness, one which we do without only at the risk of sinking back into the animal kingdom: "Through literature the collectivity turns to reflection and mediation, it acquires an unhappy consciousness of itself, an unstable reflection which it perpetually attempts to modify and to ameliorate."[31]

The source of this ambiguity can be found in Sartre's idea of consciousness in general. Consciousness is a not-being, a nothingness, a withdrawal from the solid world of things and Being and a distance from it; here the value of consciousness is negative, and all our acts of consciousness in their various ways (desire, work, knowledge, imagination) constitute a negation of the given object and a heroic activity with respect to the latter's mindless passivity. But at the same time, as we have already seen in connection with the idea of engagement, Sartre is passionately unwilling to preach withdrawal from the world or refuge in the purely subjective, the mystical, the imaginary. Thus slowly the value judgment shifts around to the other side and comes to adhere to that consciousness which chooses, not negation of the world in general, but negation of that *particular* given object; in other words, which chooses not so much withdrawal as attachment to the immediate world around it and to its immediate objective situation.

This double movement is visible in his literary criticism as well. He visibly prefers an art which challenges society, which shows it a hostile portrait of itself, to an art at one with its public, sharing its values implicitly, serving as apologia for them. Yet in a larger sense all art is contestation in its very structure; the basest flattery forces its subject to see himself, to take the first step on the road to reflection and self-consciousness, so that the first internal judgment on various works of art as compared with one another seems to fall before this second, more global one as to the structure of art in general. In the same way, he clearly prefers an art which insists on human activity and on the practical structure of things, rather than one in which a contemplative, poetic, irrealizing relationship to them is encouraged; yet it is obvious in a larger perspective that all art is imaginary, and that even the literature of praxis represents a momentary withdrawal from the real world of means and ends. Finally, a model of the world in which the future is alive is to be preferred to one in which an exaggerated attachment to the present or past seems to shut off human possibilities. On the other hand, if all language is essentially a deformation of experience, an essence imposed on existence, then even the future-oriented style is an optical illusion, does not genuinely reflect the world but merely conveys a striking and persuasive caricature of it, in its way defends a kind of thesis. Perhaps the most fundamental example of this antinomy is to be found in the idea of freedom itself, in the apparent opposition between the structural fact that all consciousnesses *are* free and the moral imperative to them to *become* free, the implication that only some of them have done so.

The attitude that we have just described probably accounts for the gradual retirement of Sartre from the writing of novels and plays.[32] Even the interest in Genet is characteristic in this respect, if we compare it with the earlier interest in Dos Passos: the latter was thought of as an artist and praised for his art. The former can be considered an autobiographical writer, both in the content he uses, and in the form, which as we have seen takes the shape of the satisfaction of personal desires on the writer's part. Genet's works, therefore, if they show great artistry, can also be felt to have the solidity of documents, of fact.[33]

In his own work it is increasingly clear that for Sartre the novel is simply not capable of doing justice to the complexities of lived experience; hence the existential biography as a more adequate form, one which is able better to unify the various isolated and interconnecting dimensions of a given life (childhood, death, the body, social class, etc.):

> The novelist shows us now one, now another of these dimensions in the form of "thoughts" which alternate in the hero's mind. But he's lying to us: these dimensions don't (or don't necessarily) have anything to do with "thoughts" as such, and they all coexist together, man is imprisoned *inside* them, at every moment he stands in relationship to *all* the walls that surround him at once, he doesn't cease for a moment to *know* that he's imprisoned. All these walls make a single prison, and this prison is a single life, a single act; the significance of each wall changes, changes all the time, and its transformation in turn has repercussions on all the others. What a totalization therefore must reveal is the multidimensional unity of the act; this unity is the basic condition for the reciprocal interpenetration as well as the relative autonomy of the various dimensions, and our old habits of thought tend to oversimplify it; language in its present state is ill-equipped to perform such a unification.[34]

It is well that these absolute demands should be made on art, that this ultimate challenge be addressed to the novel as a form. It is well that Sartre should force us to pass an absolute judgment on literature as a whole, as well as relative ones. But at the same time we should not forget the earlier Sartre, the one who evaluated literature not in terms of an impossible totality but in the light of what it could best do, how it could best be used, the philosopher of freedom who only recently described again the kind of liberation which the ordinary man owes to literature: "If once he has lived this instant of freedom, if for an instant in other words he has managed to escape—by means of the book—from the forces of alienation or oppression all around him, you can be sure that he won't forget it. And I think that literature can have that effect, or at least that a certain kind of literature can."[35]

Notes

1. See the pastiches of Dos Passos, *Situations I* (Paris: Gallimard, 1947), p. 23, and of Genet, *Saint Genet, comédien et martyr* (Paris: Gallimard, 1952), p. 472; and see also

Simone de Beauvoir's discussion of the use of Dos Passos's style as a critical instrument, *La Force de l'âge* (Paris: Gallimard, 1960), pp. 143–44.

2. Written for the *Nouvelle Revue Française* and for *Cahiers du Sud* from 1938 to 1944, they are collected in *Situations I*, to which all references are made.

3. The most revealing discussion of this incommensurability of words to lived time is to be found in the chapter on adventures in *La Nausée* (Paris: Gallimard, 1938), pp. 57–59.

4. "Dieu n'est pas un artiste; M. Mauriac non plus." *Situations I*, p. 57 (All translations are mine.)

5. This point is related to the ideological criticism elsewhere in *Situations I* of Bataille, Ponge, and Renard, all of whom introduce the external and objective categories of scientism into their subjective experience and thereby deform it.

6. *Situations I*, p. 80.

7. See *L'Etre et le néant* (Paris: Gallimard, 1943), pp. 695–704.

8. *Situations II* (Paris: Gallimard, 1948), pp. 180–81.

9. *Théorie de la littérature*, ed. T. Todorov (Paris: Seuil, 1965), pp. 212–33.

10. Preface to *Poésies* of Mallarmé, Poésie (Paris: Gallimard, 1966).

11. *Sein und Zeit* (Tübingen: Niemeyer Verlag, 1957), pp. 66–88. And see the discussion of Marxism as an ontology in *Über den Humanismus* (Frankfurt am Main: V. Klostermann, 1947).

12. *Der Ursprung des Kunstwerkes*, Universal-Bibliotheck (Stuttgart: Reclam, 1960).

13. *Situations II*, pp. 85–88, n. 4.

14. "Le symbole *objectif* de l'être et du rapport de la réalité humaine à cet être." *L'Etre et le néant*, p. 693.

15. *Baudelaire* (Paris: Gallimard, 1947), p. 203.

16. *Saint Genet*, pp. 429 ff.

17. Ibid., p. 430, n. 1.

18. *Situations II*, p. 263.

19. *Situations I*, the essay on Maurice Blanchot's *Aminadab*, p. 131.

20. *Saint Genet*, p. 256.

21. Criminality, the choice of evil, involves for Sartre an analogous withdrawal from Being and from the real, a similar and equally contradictory attempt to destroy what is at the same time affirmed (theft is inconceivable without the institution of private property against which it is directed); evil, like Beauty, is *parasitic*.

22. *Journal du voleur* (Paris: Gallimard, 1949), p. 9.

23. *Situations II*, pp. 264–66.

24. A few of the works of this period give an idea what such a literature might have been like, in particular those whose characters are working-class people, as in the two movie scenarios, *Les Jeux sont faits* and *L'Engrenage*, and in Simone de Beauvoir's *Le Sang des autres*.

25. See in particular *Saint Genet*, *Réflexions sur la question juive* (Paris: Morihien, 1946), and Beauvoir, *Le Deuxième Sexe* (Paris: Gallimard, 1949).

26. *Les Aventures de la dialectique* (Paris: Gallimard, 1955), pp. 209 ff.

27. It is this insistence on the primacy of the concrete, its relationship to the historical development of society at a given moment, rather than their actual estimates of past literary history, which Sartre shares with the Lukács of the *Théorie des romans*; see Beauvoir, *La Force des choses* (Paris: Gallimard, 1963), p. 130, n. 1.

28. From the "salauds" of *La Nausée* to the analysis of the generations of the bourgeoisie in *Critique de la raison dialectique* (Paris: Gallimard, 1960), pp. 687–734, and to the recent biography of Flaubert.

29. *Saint Genet*, pp. 402–11.

30. *Saint Genet*, pp. 435–42; and the essay on Giraudoux in *Situations I*, esp. pp. 96–98.

31. *Situations II*, p. 316.

32. This process of disintoxication with literature is of course the explicit subject of Sartre's autobiography, *Les Mots* (Paris: Gallimard, 1964).

33. Other indications of this increasing refusal of the artistic and predilection for the real, the document, can be found in the remark on the *anti-novel* in the Preface to Nathalie Sarraute's *Portrait d'un inconnu* (*Situations IV* [Paris: Gallimard, 1964]) and in the Preface to André Gorz's autobiography *Le Traître* ("Des rats et des hommes," *Situations IV*).

34. "Question de méthode," *Critique de la raison dialectique*, p. 74.

35. *Que peut la littérature?* edited by Yves Buin (Paris: L'Herne, 1965), p. 127.

L'Idiot de la famille:
The Ultimate Sartre?

Ronald Aronson*

For virtually his entire career Jean-Paul Sartre has been an activist writer. His very first book, *Imagination* (1936), has a tone of aggressive combat as Sartre attacks past theorists for their faulty views of imagination. Throughout his early writings Sartre passionately opposes false claimants to the truth — such as Freud in *The Emotions*, or Husserl in *The Transcendence of the Ego* — and "at long last" sets forth the correct approach. His little essay "Une Idée" presents Sartre's discovery of intentionality in a spirit of exultation.[1] Even Sartre's early literary criticism — I am thinking of his affirmative articles on Dos Passos and Faulkner and his criticism of Mauriac — has a driving, impassioned quality. Sartre's tone makes sense to us when we see that what is at stake in each case according to him is no less than human nature itself. Are humans passive, externally conditioned things or are we free and self-determining? Sartre's intellectual mission in these early writings cannot be separated from a moral mission: to make people aware of their freedom. *Nausea*, most of the stories collected in *Intimacy*, the novels of *Roads to Freedom*, *No Exit*, *The Flies*, even *Being and Nothingness*, all express Sartre's moral mission. These words want to reveal to us both our freedom and the ways in which we evade it. They exhort us to throw aside our illusions and dodges and face squarely our "monstrous spontaneity."

In all of these works Sartre writes with grand and noble purposes: to find and make us see the truth, in order to affect how we act. Words for him are not neutral, are not merely academic, but are rather tools. Writing is a form of action. When he declares this as he discovers Marxism he is merely imparting a political tinge to his long-established practice. Sartre's writing remains a moral undertaking. Whether directed at Mos-

*From *Telos*, no. 20 (Summer 1974):90–107. Reprinted with permission.

cow, the French Communist Party, the French bourgeoisie, leftist intellectuals, or people in general, Sartre's political writings seek to create self-awareness and provoke change.

In all this Sartre overvalues the power of words. His overvaluing of words, his overemphasis on subjective freedom and spontaneity comes from Sartre's sense of being overwhelmed by the world, his urge to find a secure refuge and field of action.[2] In his thought, I have argued, the opposing terms structurally entail each other—be it passive perception and self-determining imagination, an overwhelming world and the free individual, absurd reality and rigorous art, man the "useless passion" and art the successful passion, "hell is other people" and writing-reading seen as the City of Ends, the practico-inert and individual *praxis*.[3]

From the very beginning Sartre fought against the dualism implied by his conceptual structure and rejected the implications of his own thought. In *Nausea*, for example, he attacks the "stupid jerks" who promote art as a realm of consolation, and yet there is precisely where his own thought leads. Separating the individual from the world he creates in common with others, Sartre engenders an overwhelming world which must be fled and a menaced, isolated individual whose freedom must be defended at all costs. What keeps this from becoming a full-blown dualism? The answer is Sartre's activist impulse, his sense of intellectual and ethical mission, his determination to overcome the separation his thought creates by insisting that the individual become active in the world. Individuals are free, yes, but they are *situated* freedoms. And they should become *engaged*.[4]

Sartre's extreme optimism about writing overlies, therefore, an extreme pessimism about the reality he would change. This contradiction has been the key to that combination of missionary zeal, commitment to freedom and deep-seated negativism which we know as existentialism. It has also been the key to Sartre's failure as an activist writer. In *The Words* (1964) he admits his failure, however. And following on that admission he begins to give up that activism of words, separating writing from political action. By the 1970's the intellectual activist has become intellectual *and* activist. Whatever he does in his study high above Paris, the political tasks take place below, on the streets, such as hawking *La Cause du Peuple* and helping the masses to express themselves.

The separation of moral-political action from writing is a major event in Sartre's career: for the first time he writes without a worldly, practical mission. Remove this activist impulse and what happens to Sartre's thought? *L'Idiot de la famille* gives us the answer. Sartre's *Flaubert* reflects his thought freed from responsibilities, relieved of missionary duties, purged of its activism. It is, in short, Sartre's first wholly *scholarly* work. Scholarly: Sartre does not try to bring us to act or think differently, to expose us to ourselves or to convince us of a vital truth. Not since the descriptive sections of *Psychology of Imagination* has Sartre been so immersed in studies without immediate life-relevance. Indeed, he is willing to stop imposing on us and to leave us to follow his pursuit of his subject. In this very healthy sense Sartre's readers count for less in *L'Idiot de la famille* than in virtually any of his writings and his subject matter counts for more. He is interested in Gustave Flaubert as an example of what we can know about a person and for his own sake—not for any warnings we may draw from his failures, as with Baudelaire, and not for any paths to liberation he may open up for us, as with Genet.

The work does have global importance for him, however, but it is of a scholarly sort. "Its subject: what can we know about a man these days? It seemed to me that the only way to answer this question was to study a specific case: what do we know about Gustave Flaubert, for instance."[5] Transforming his audience has ceased to matter, but this shift has simply intensified Sartre's urge to grasp the world in words: "The underlying plan in my Flaubert is to show that, eventually, everything can be communicated and that—without being God, being a man like any other—one can arrive at a perfect understanding of another man as long as one has all the information necessary."[6]

Thus does Sartre's energy, freed from its activism, turn into one of the most incredible intellectual encounters in history. To communicate everything, to understand Flaubert completely—this, and no less, is Sartre's goal. And to do so he writes a study which, when completed, will contain roughly as many words as Gustave Flaubert's entire collected works! I have suggested that Sartre ceases to oppress his readers when he gives up on changing us. But if he leaves us in peace in one way Sartre certainly oppresses us even more in another. 2800 pages so far, Sartre's *Flaubert* is absolutely overwhelming. Freed from the usual restraints imposed by his past political and moral purposes, Sartre seems now able to indulge himself and write as much as he likes. *L'Idiot de la famille* makes the enormities of *Being and Nothingness* (722 pages), *Saint Genet* (578 pages) and *Critique de la raison dialectique* (755 pages) appear modest and self-disciplined by comparison.

Freed from responsibilities, Sartre's thought returns to one of its basic and original impulses: concern with the imaginary. Sartre's starting point of the 1930's led from and to the imaginary as the unreal realm where real life's basic contradictions and problems would be temporarily resolved. In his turn towards political activism after World War II Sartre suggested that political action might overcome some of these problems, and argued forcefully that imaginary work, particularly writing, had a real political function. And some of his best political plays showed his characters trapped in the imaginary, unable to act in, or even face, the real world. But by never abandoning and going beyond the basic terms of his thought, Sartre doomed from the outset his radical intellectual project.

His plays were too absorbed by the *problem* of relating to reality and the temptation to escape into imagination; his political essays had too much of the unreal, the imaginary, the arbitrary construct in them.

Sartre's *littérature engagée* never became *real*. His Marxist philosophy was contradicted by his fight to establish a preserve of individual freedom and this became merely academic. It was doomed by its inability to cast off the imaginary pole and fully accept and plunge itself into the real, social, historical world. Relating to the real world, then, Sartre's thought was vitiated by the imaginary. And so his return to Flaubert has the earmarks of a *re-turn*: locked into his conceptual structure, Sartre simply throws overboard the impulse to activism and returns, in a far more sophisticated way, to explore his basic theme of withdrawal into the imaginary. This Sartre is right to speak of his *Flaubert* as a sequel both to his early *Psychology of Imagination* and his later *Search for a Method*.[7] To continue his studies of how the imaginary is created, to understand a man fully: both scholarly impulses get completed in his Flaubert.

A study of a person who lived out his life in the imaginary, *L'Idiot* is also an imaginary work in itself. Much of it is an elaborate construct built from relatively little evidence. Here it is useful to compare Sartre's *Flaubert* with a more conventional biography, such as Enid Starkie's *Flaubert: The Making of the Master*.[8] Of Gustave's mother, Starkie tells us only that she was "of a gloomy disposition" plus the few available facts of her life. Starkie's implied methodological premise is to stick as closely as possible to the facts, to venture hypotheses rarely and only when she explicitly indicates their hypothetical character. Her goal is less to explain Gustave than to describe him. Sartre, on the other hand, begins with the facts as sighting-points for his project of understanding. And since explanations on one level entail yet other levels, Sartre moves further and further from the facts in building the terms of Gustave's character structure. Thus, from the available evidence he builds an entire chapter on Caroline Flaubert, explaining how she *must have* felt and what her needs *must have* been. Orphan of a physician, foster child of another, she became the devoted wife of yet another. Her obedience, together with Achille-Cléophas' rural petty-bourgeois background and domination of the family, made his wife into his "incestuous daughter," and "eternal minor." Thus Gustave's mother *must have* wanted to furnish Achille-Cléophas with an heir and welcomed Achille's birth. Thus she *must have* wanted a daughter in whom she could relive, with parental care and love, her own childhood. Thus she *must not have* wanted Gustave, and in consequence *must have* cared for him meticulously without loving him. Thus Gustave *must have* been cared for yet deprived, and out of this combination developed his passive way of relating to reality.

In moving so quickly, of course, I fail to do justice to Sartre's analysis. My point is, rather, to demonstrate what Sartre himself emphasizes, namely that hard evidence is unavailable at the level on which he tries to understand Flaubert, that to *explain* him Sartre can write only about "Flaubert as I imagine him."[9] This odd formula indicates that Sartre is writing what he calls a "true novel." "I would want my study read as a novel since it is history, indeed, of an apprenticeship which leads to the failure of a whole life. I would want at the same time for you to read it while thinking that it is the truth, that it is a *true* novel." By this Sartre means a study which is rigorous and yet, when necessary, he will construct its own materials. "It is Flaubert such as I imagine him; but, having methods which appear to me to be rigorous, I think it is Flaubert such as he is, such as he has been. In this study, I have need of imagination at each instant."

This is remarkable: *the* definitive study of Flaubert is at the same time a literary construct of who he must have been, a biographical novel. Sartre is self-consciously creating a new genre. Does this reliance on imaginary constructs in the midst of a rigorous and systematic study indicate that, finally, Sartre's thought is giving in and becoming consumed by its imaginary pole? The point is that Sartre is returning to that original pole of his thought in form as well as content: an imaginary study of an imaginary person. And if this doesn't convey the sense of withdrawal strongly enough, we should be clear that this is an *interior* study. Sartre traces the formation of Gustave's subjectivity, his intentional structure, and not any worldly action or pattern of actions. Once again Sartre's Flaubert is the opposite of Starkie's: she is above all concerned with what Gustave *does*, and so observes him from the outside. However Sartre's approach may be dictated by his goal of understanding Gustave, the book's pervading impression of withdrawal *vis-à-vis* Sartre's earlier worldly projects is too strong to shake off: an imaginary study of the interior development of an imaginary person. A work of escape about an escapist?

All this has been to view *The Family Idiot* from the outside, in the context of Sartre's entire *corpus*. Read for itself, both these hints of brilliance and of defeat get borne out, and Sartre's Flaubert assumes an amazing dual spectre. It is a magnificent book and a terrible one, the one alongside the other, one inside the other, in the same pages, the same paragraphs, the same words. It is a gamble, the most extreme effort in a corpus of extreme efforts. I shall get to how it fails soon enough, but first I must pay my respects.

The reviews, as I will show, have not criticized *L'Idiot* enough, but neither have they praised it enough. In it Sartre once again scandalizes most academics by trying to grasp the whole, by refusing to accept limits in trying to discover and communicate everything one can know about a person today. With unequalled energy Sartre sets himself against all intellectual cynicism. I marvel at his optimism and his effort.

How do we go about understanding anyone? Most biographies embody an unholy mélange of the most contradictory approaches, remaining tentative and unsure of their goals and methodological principles beginning to end. Thus Starkie, while refusing to speculate about Gustave's deeper motivations or his emotional conflicts, assumes that the city of Rouen must have affected Gustave's character and so devotes more space to discussing it than to discussing his mother. Thus she confirms Gustave's homosexuality but refuses to speculate about his hostility to his brother Achille. Thus she refuses to explore the possible autobiographical meaning of Gustave's early writings while acutely considering and resolving many disputed problems of Flaubert scholarship. Starkie accepts her methods as ready-made and is above all concerned to give us a *picture* of Gustave. And she does so: his actions, the main events of his life, his development as a writer, his friendships and love affairs, the structure and meaning of *Madame Bovary*, Flaubert's aesthetic doctrine. All this is taken up through 1857 in only 400 pages of text, with a second volume given over to the rest of Flaubert's life.

Compare this very successful conventional work with Sartre's *Flaubert*. Its subject, we heard Sartre say, is to find out what we can know about a man today. One can answer this general question only by studying a specific case: "what do we know — for example — about Gustave Flaubert?"[10] *Par exemple!* Critics of *L'Idiot* are irritated by the apparently ancillary role given to Flaubert himself. But Sartre is after all developing a method in this study. Whether or not we are interested in Flaubert, he wants to leave us with a systematic and self-conscious biography which we can apply elsewhere. Compared with Starkie's relatively unselfconscious, eclectic, and even contradictory method, Sartre is concerned to know exactly where he is going at every moment and why. It is not enough, then, to simply say that Gustave's mother didn't love him, or that he had difficulty grasping the meaning of language, or that he gave himself over to play-acting. In each case Sartre must set out the general framework within which such analyses take place: how love is connected with self-valuation with an active approach to the world; what language means as one of the child's first encounters with the world; the meaning of acting. This constructing of frameworks continues throughout the book, time and again taking us away from Gustave in order to develop the tools for understanding him. Thus the biography becomes philosophy, becomes psychological theory, becomes the biography of Alfred Le Poittevin, the study of laughter as a social fact, the history of Rouen College during the 1830's, the explanation of how pet dogs relate to human language.

No stone is left unturned in this model biography, but this is only one reason why it is so much longer than Starkie's *Flaubert*. By page 2136 Sartre has gotten through Flaubert's seizure of early 1844, a point which Starkie reaches by page 120 of her account. Gustave is 22, and will now abandon the law for a semi-invalid state and a writing career. But while for Starkie the major events are yet to come, Sartre regards the decisive steps as having already been taken. Starkie's brevity and Sartre's verbosity, then, are also due to the very different ways Starkie and Sartre see Flaubert.

What does it mean to understand someone completely? Starkie's very conventional and not at all unworthy solution is to describe him as fully as possible. Certain areas yield no conclusive answers; they will be left out. For the rest she assembles all the available facts in an interesting and swiftly-moving account. We see Gustave, from the outside, and quite well. In reading Gertrude Collier's *Memoir*, for example, Starkie observes "the extraordinary beauty and charm of Flaubert at twenty, and the originality and naturalness of his bearing. As we have already seen, he was tall, slight and graceful in all his full movements, he had the most faultless limbs and the great charm of utter unselfconsciousness in his own physical and mental beauty."[11]

Nothing could interest Sartre less than such details. *L'Idiot* seeks to explain Gustave Flaubert, not to describe him. Sartre assumes that we have much information at our finger-tips—that we have read Flaubert's major works, that we already know the details of his biography. *L'Idiot* is an *interior* biography: to explain Gustave, to understand why he wrote *Madame Bovary* and what he meant by it, we must go beneath the available information and grasp his underlying character structure. Who was Gustave Flaubert? On one level, everything he did and said; but on a far more important level, Gustave was a particular project flowing from his particular way of experiencing and pursuing his needs in all their contradiction and complexity.

Sartre's approach allows for no pluralism or drift either within or without. Set at a very early age, Gustave's life is his project, unfolding itself across time: the interior exteriorized. To be ambivalent or lackadaisical would itself be a project, as would merely flowing with events. These are various ways of being oneself: of organizing one's needs and purposes and projecting them outward coherently. All this is to say that humans are *intentional*. We act in order to achieve purposes; our life is that coherent set of actions.

Thus the need for an *interior* study, which tries to get to the project behind Gustave's actions, which tries to reconstruct Gustave's underlying character structure. Sartre's first goal is to locate the main elements of Gustave's constitution and then he will go on to show them unfold themselves in time.

These elements have a very definite source: early childhood. Sartre's bitter book on Baudelaire pays no attention to the poet's childhood, but rather assumes a kind of freedom to change in terms of which Baudelaire must be judged as escapist. His Genet dwells briefly on the child and discovers there the problem which must be overcome later, but not the project to overcome it which is Genet's liberation. His short study of Tintoretto begins when the painter is already a young man of thirty, passionately trying to win a master's reputation. *The Words*, on the other hand, focusses on early childhood, but not at all with an analytical eye. Sartre locates there only a general sense of his schooling in the imaginary as a way of avoiding reality; no problems or contradictions, no project which his life will carry out. *L'Idiot*, then, is his first effort to root the adult so wholly in the infant. Little Gustave, he tells us, will be born into a feudal family ruled by a *pater familias* who also happens to be a self-made man of science. This bourgeois family bearing a deep trace of his father's rural origins will produce an heir, Achille, destined to succeed his father as Master of the Hôtel-Dieu of Rouen. And it will produce a second son, Gustave, destined to be inferior to the firstborn, and a girl, longed for by his mother as a way of reliving more happily her own sad early years. The other children died at or near birth, so that from the beginning Gustave was handled and cared for as someone bound to die. Destined for inferiority, lacking any avenue of revolt in this semi-feudal family, cared for meticulously but never loved, Gustave early developed his main character traits: passivity, a sense of destiny, an inability to relate to the real world.[12] He did indeed have a "Golden Age" after about three or four, when his father loved him and took him around the countryside on his house calls. But lacking the early reciprocity of mother-love, Gustave developed no sense of the reciprocity of language: his father cast him out of grace when, at seven, he could not yet read. This child will become imaginary; he will become actor, then author, then poet, then artist. The artist will write *Madame Bovary*.

Is this a Freudian account? Only generally. Sartre makes no use of Freudian concepts, such as repression, the unconscious, the tripartite personality structure, or the stages of sexual development. He insists on the primacy of early childhood, of family structure, of relations between infant and parents. But his is a rather unusual determinism: "There is spontaneity but starting from a prefabricated essence."[13] Meaning that, indeed, Gustave does develop his own "free singular project," but only on the basis of the given internal and external conditions and only along the route made necessary by that network of conditions. Accepting all these qualifications does not lead Sartre to any behaviorist determinism or mechanistic causality. People are still people and they behave dialectically: creating themselves on the basis of, but by going beyond, the given conditions. Thus Gustave Flaubert—or any of us—is above all a project, a center of intentionality.

More Freudian than his earlier Genet, *L'Idiot* is also more Marxist. Gustave's character structure takes shape within the contradictions of the Flaubert family. And the family—parvenu but patriarchal, resting on individual ability but seeking to found a dynasty—localizes its socio-historical reality and intimately conveys it to Gustave. Furthermore, for orientation and self-clarification the growing child was forced to choose between or somehow combine not an infinite variety of attitudes, but his father's bourgeois atomistic rationalism and his mother's deism. Family structure and parent's ideologies did not merely *influence* Gustave: his project took shape *through* them, so that he constituted himself *in terms of* them. Thus, for example, the mature Gustave's reactionary political attitudes are prefigured in his early relationship of vassalage towards his father, in his rejection of bourgeois values of self-sufficiency and independence, in his desire to live as a rentier.

Gustave Flaubert is above all a socio-historical being, a *singular universal*. At college at Rouen from 1831–38 he experienced, with the other schoolboys, the collapse of bourgeois universalism, the realization of how narrow were the bourgeois claims to freedom and democracy, the capitulation of the bourgeoisie to the church. Time for activism and politics were over: together, at night, they retreated into the imaginary, living out their fantasies in romantic novels, plays and poetry. For some of the schoolboys this was necessary preparation, for after 1830 the demands on literature were such that the writer had to be a neurotic. Caught between its eighteenth-century demand for autonomy as a political force and the nineteenth-century fact that the bourgeoisie were in power and wanted it to sing their praises, literature asserted its autonomy in an aestheticist, abstract way. Thus did it preserve itself and avoid having to serve unappreciative masters; but thus did it also stake out an increasingly self-enclosed and unreal world. Those most capable of flourishing in this world of withdrawal were those, like Gustave, who wrote as an expression-solution of their neurosis.

Here, it should be obvious, is a marked shift from every one of Sartre's other writings. In *L'idiot* we see him acknowledge the priority in human development of *a mandate to live* over the feeling of being *de trop*, which *Nausea* and *Being and Nothingness* made so much of. We see him now say that "pure lived life, the simple 'being-there,' in short incarnating in itself, in succession, every form of our *savored* (*dégustée*) facticity are convenient abstractions which we never encounter without being affected by them ourselves — in oscillating between certain elements of interior experience, in passing deliberately over others in silence."[14] If pure life itself is not primary, then what is? Not individual *praxis*, because, we are now told, it emerges only in and through a social world. *L'Idiot* differs from every one of Sartre's early biographical and autobiographical ventures in that it situates Gustave's development squarely in a socio-historical world and finds him developing *in terms of* that world. On a theoretical level we can see this striking shift expressed in his comment on the theme of "sense and non-sense": "In truth sense and non-sense in a human life are human in principle and are transmitted to man in the earliest stages of his life by man himself. Thus we must dismiss those absurd formulas: 'life has sense'; 'it has none'; 'it has one that we give to it' — and understand that we discover our goals, the nonsense or the sense of our lives as realities prior to this coming to consciousness, prior perhaps to our birth and prefabricated in the human universe. The sense of a life comes to the living man through the human society which sustains him and through the parents who engender him: for this reason it is also *always* a non-sense. But inversely the discovery of a life as non-sense (that of children who are supernumeraries, undernourished, consumed by parasites and fever in an underdeveloped society) reveals just as clearly the real sense of this society and, through this reversal, it is life—as organic need—which becomes, in its pure animal necessity, *human sense* and it is the society of men which, by the sentence of unsatisfied need, becomes *pure human non-sense*."[15]

This approach is, of course, no more strictly Marxist than Sartre's approach to Flaubert's infancy is strictly Freudian. Sartre, for example, pays no attention to the concrete social relations or material conditions of the Flaubert family's life, or of the Rouen schoolboys, or of the nineteenth-century French writer. His Marxism is more general: a sense that Gustave is a historical individual, a singular universal, and that he can be understood only in terms of social realities; a sense that those realities, such as the family, have structures which pre-form the experiences in and through which individuals become individuals. History and society precede Gustave and make him what he is. And this happens through the family, society's primary shaping institution. Sartre's Marxian line thus joins his Freudian one as he argues that adequate love leads to self-worth which alone enables us to relate to the world reciprocally, from strength. Gustave's early inability to accept words as designating objects shows that he has been cut off from *praxis*, the cardinal society category, by his earliest contract with his mother. "In this first moment acculturation without love reduces Gustave to the condition of a domestic animal."[16]

Gustave Flaubert, then, is the person produced in and by this set of conditions. He has no unique instinctual drives, no special talents, no inherited traits, no essence of his own which meets and is affected by these conditions. Rather, he *is* that set of conditions, as interiorized, lived, totalized, formed into a project, and re-exteriorized. Any male child, we might assume, born into that family on that date would have made himself to be Gustave Flaubert, author of *Madame Bovary*.

This brief description of Sartre's purposes has included a good deal of appreciation. Every aspect I pointed to contains serious faults, and beyond these many individual shortcomings are simply fundamental problems about the project itself. But whatever its weaknesses this book remains admirable, this interior biography and methodological study using generally Freudian and Marxist methods to completely explain Gustave Flaubert. Towards the end of his article on *L'Idiot*, the *Times Literary Supplement* reviewer asks why Sartre wrote the book in the first place. In probing for the book's deepest purposes he suggests that Sartre may have a parodistic intention at heart: "It seeks out the heart of the whole suspect enterprise of literature, of literary scholarship, of criticism. It would subvert no less than the whole, perhaps inhuman, perhaps lunatic, world of words about words, of language parasitic of language, in which Sartre grew up and which he has been troubled, increasingly self-contemptuous master."[17] Burying himself—and us—in words to destroy them: it is an interesting idea, but it lacks appreciation. The reviewer can approach the strengths of Sartre's project only ironically. He regards Sartre with the overly-sophisticated contempt of someone who will never be caught attempting too much or building too grandly, who will never make the mistake of saying too much based on too few facts. David Caute's review begins with a similar tone, wittily scoring points against the man who would make such foolish mistakes, who would return, after all these years, to "the old bedevilled theory of infrastructure and superstructure, of the determining material factor and the determined intellectual reflection. This monist system of explanation is just as lethal when it sings 'family' as when it sings 'means of production.' "[18] These reviews are bad not because their authors' criticism is wrong, but because of their tone of superiority. They can regard Sartre's new effort at understanding *only* with annoyance, poking fun at his task (Caute: "Try this for size: 'What can one know of woman today? For example, Joan of Arc' ")[19] when they are not trying to fathom why on earth he undertakes it. Whatever else it is, *L'Idiot* is a colossal undertaking, a remarkable effort by one human being to understand another down to his most subtle and contradictory intentions. For this, and from its many promising directions it deserves more appreciation than condescension.

Still, it is a terrible book, the kind of book that makes you want to throw it down and shout: "Won't he ever shut up?" If, as Joseph H. McMahon points out, the *Critique* merely "comes close" to cancelling itself out because of its many faults, then *L'Idiot* succeeds completely. It should not be read, and, except for Sartre's friends, a few Sartre or Flaubert scholars, or Ph.D. candidates in search for a new field to explore, it won't be. Why? Because it can't be. *L'Idiot de la famille* violates elementary rules of human communication which the political Sartre expressed so well in *What Is Literature?* It has no respect for the reader and makes impossible demands on him; it is undisciplined, self-indulgent, boring and unreal.

Its actual physical length alone is oppressive. My comparison with Flaubert's collected works should give us some sense of scale: is there really that much of importance to say about Gustave Flaubert's first thirty-six years? *L'Idiot* forces us to raise the question of *book* length. What does it mean, after all, to say that a book is too long.

Certainly appropriate book length depends to some extent on the book's content. But such relativism can be deceptive, as you can see by thumbing through the books on any shelf of your own library. The overwhelming majority of book-length writings fall between two and four hundred pages, with decreasing numbers in each additional hundred pages up to, say eight hundred. The point is that book length is determined not by the requirements of the subject alone, but by the requirements of the subject *comprehended* and *communicated*. And it seems that there is fairly limited range within which most full-length studies fall. Below a certain length it seems that the subject is not being treated adequately, and beyond that it seems that comprehension gets distorted by excessive length. The human mind will only hold so much of a subject at one time, be it a scientific study, or a story, or a biography. Between such upper limits of ordinary book length and Sartre's 2800 pages lies a no man's land which staggers the imagination, let alone the possibilities of understanding. All of that psychic information and speculation about Flaubert simply cannot be kept in any one mind long enough to form a coherent picture.

Thus a book which is supposed to communicate to us a profound understanding of Gustave Flaubert itself demands to first be mastered — to be studied over a period of months and even years, again and again to be synthesized and boiled down in our mind and on paper. It is not just an impossibly long but interesting, coherent story. It *feels* long from the very beginning. What makes *L'Idiot* too long? For one thing, Sartre makes no distinction between his activity of study and its socially meaningful results. He insists that we accompany his exploration, rather than being willing to give us its conclusions. It is up to us to distill its meaning, after following him through thick and thin, through feast and famine, down each and every byway he chooses to explore. He is verbose, of course, but that is not the problem. The problem is that communicating a total understanding for Sartre means taking us on his rounds and exploring every conceivable source of insight rather, say than establishing a basic pattern and indicating, using summaries and footnotes, that the analysis is thus corroborated or thus extended by the subsequent sources. I think of our wearisome journey through Flaubert's juvenilia which establishes the elements of his attitude towards his father. In one exhausting section Sartre forces us to follow him through *Passion et Vertu, Quidquid volueris, Rêve d'enfer, Bibliomanie, La Peste à Florence, Un Parfum à sentir*, and Gustave's literary journal of age thirteen. 130 pages devoted to roughly an equal number in Flaubert! Certainly we should note that Sartre doesn't analyze every one of Flaubert's early writings: he has enough sense to select the most relevant ones. But he plunges into them with a total disregard for proportion, for the reader's staying power, and for good scholarship. It seems that he is proving, proving, proving his analysis at every point. And to prove it he must reconstruct the meaning at every point. And to do this he must write on and on. Frankly, I trust conventional scholarly methods: It would have been enough for him to briefly outline each work, to speak of their decisive elements, and then to add them together in a total picture of the child's basic attitudes.

No discrimination or pruning in *L'Idiot*: each and every detail, each moment of Gustave's shaping process, calls out to us with equal urgency. And so we scarcely ever know if we are in the main stream or in the backwaters.

This is bad scholarship. No distinction here between investigation and its intelligible, communicable results; no sense of proportion about what is and isn't important; no sense of what constitutes adequate proof. Thus he drones on, hammers home the same points again and again, rebuilds his basic analysis over and over. The subject seems always about to get out of hand, and Sartre seems always to be grasping after it, to be laboring frantically to reproduce it. And so in addition to its sheer length the book takes on a slipshod, chaotic, overstuffed quality. Whatever became of the mutual respect between readers and writer, to the pact between freedoms? Instead of meeting us as equals in the social world of scholarly communication, Sartre imposes on us his more private and subjective world and forces us to accompany *his* journey through each and every turning. The book's every aspect only strengthens our sense of its involuted, inward, unreal quality. Unreal: as if in writing it Sartre has left the social world and withdrawn into an inner world wholly of his own making. Unreal: it takes place wholly inside a person, this side of his worldly action, and develops mostly by means of Sartre's imaginary constructs.

L'Idiot contains nearly no action. The extended textual analysis of Flaubert's juvenilia, for example, occurs as part of one of two chapters which together take up 468 pages. In these pages Gustave commits not a single act! Their entire space is given over to a study from several directions of his intentional structure. First the basic elements are isolated, using his early writings; then Sartre reconstructs the relationship between each developing layer of Gustave's character structure, showing how one passes into and produces the next; finally they are cast in terms of how Gustave lived them in relation to his parents' ideologies. But perhaps Sartre is simply isolating elements here in his regressive analysis of Gustave's constitution. Perhaps the book's second part, on "personalization," will tell us how he acted to make himself from these elements. Will we then see him in action, at play, with family and friends?

Hardly. Sartre merely touches on him performing his first plays in the billiard room of the Hôtel-Dieu's master's lodgings, then entering college, then clowning around with his schoolmates, reading at night, rebelling and getting expelled. The only action he focusses on is internal: Gustave's slow transformation from imaginary child into artist. This process of self-creation is, after all, what *L'Idiot de la famille* is all about. It is not the story of an adventurer or politician, but of a writer—and one whose inner life was primary. In part, then, the book's inwardness stems from its choice of subject. But only in part: Starkie's *Flaubert* is a lively and interesting story. The events which matter little to Sartre interest her and us. What Sartre gives us, on the other hand, is a detailed analysis of their *structure* and *meaning*. Thus 250 pages near the end of the second volume dwell on the extended implications of Gustave's fainting fit at *Pont l'Evêque*, which led to his semi-invalid life, and to which Starkie gives three pages.

But, after all, I lauded *L'Idiot* for being an interior study. By definition Sartre is interested not in the things Gustave did but in the ways he felt which *led to* the central things he did. The book is trying not to describe Gustave Flaubert but to explain him. This requires a constant looking beneath the surface for structures and meanings. A *flesh-and-blood* picture of the Rouen schoolboys is not what counts but rather exploring their passivity before their fathers' domination, their withdrawal into literature. To account for these things we must get to essentials, to history, to motivation. Beneath the surface: such explanations have none of the drama of descriptions. They leave the events behind us trying to get to their causes, and so reducing their contingency and tension to a comprehensible set of links. If the study seeks reasons and causes and structures perhaps it cannot help but be a bad story. Is *L'Idiot*'s suffocating quality thus a pardonable consequence of its fruitful and new direction?

Or is something wrong when we turn page after page, confront layer after layer of exploration of intention and meaning, without seeing Gustave *do* anything? Is this "true novel" good psychology but terrible reading?

Our boredom guides us to the central question about the book: does this interior study manage to grasp the real Gustave Flaubert? I think not. By focussing entirely on Gustave's interior it gives us a false picture of him, and so fails to redeem its promise to "arrive at a perfect understanding of another man." Such understanding would include, among other things, a sense of how the person lived his life: what he did, how he earned his living, how he explained himself to himself, how the socio-historical structures imposed themselves on him. Yes, I agree with Sartre: Gustave's intentional structure is decisive and that roots itself in earliest childhood. But *what* he does is decisive as well. Sartre has not claimed to explore *an* essential but neglected dimension of Gustave which, later, must be placed alongside other dimensions for a complete understanding; rather, in exploring Gustave's interior he claims to be rendering the whole person. No, he is wrong — *the* biography of Flaubert will give us the whole person by showing what he does as well as why.

It may well be that Sartre has saved the objective, active side for his study of *Madame Bovary*. That book, after all, is a magnificent social act committed by its author. But what is to keep Sartre's explication from being merely an equally subjective analysis of the meaning to Flaubert of Flaubert's masterpiece? He has promised to show in it Flaubert's defeat and triumph, which suggests that he may turn to the novel's obvious greatness. But nothing in his first three volumes has prepared us for this: Sartre, unlike Starkie, conveys no sense of Gustave's developing literary talent, no sense of his ability to express and capture experience in socially communicable ways. Gustave dissolves, again and again, into his neurosis. Sartre builds no sense, in short, of him being able to cope, to grasp, to act. So far we know only of his defeat, his escape, his weakness.

Perhaps the most outrageous and bizarre quality of *L'Idiot de la famille* is that it is a series of elaborate constructs. Sartre calls it a "true novel," because it is "Flaubert such as I imagine him":

I imagine that Madame Flaubert, a wife by vocation, was a mother from duty. An excellent mother, but not a charming one: punctual, assiduous, skillful. Nothing more. The younger son was cautiously handled: his swaddling clothes were changed in an instant; he didn't have to cry, he was always fed in the nick of time. Gustave's aggressiveness did not have the opportunity to develop. But he was frustrated: well before weaning but without crying or rebellion; lack of tenderness is scarcely to the pain of love as undernourishment is to hunger. Later, the *ill-loved* child will consume himself; for the moment he does not really suffer: the need to be loved appeared from birth, before the infant would even be able to recognize the Other, but it does not yet express itself by precise desires. Frustration does *not affect* him — or scarcely does so — it *makes* him: I mean that this objective negation penetrates him and that it becomes in him an impoverishment of life: an organic poverty and some ingratitude or other at the heart of life-experience. No anguish, he never has occasion to feel himself abandoned. Nor alone. The moment a desire awakens, it is immediately filled; if a pin pricks him and he cries, a quick hand will remove the pain. But these precise operations are also parsimonious: everything is economized at the Flauberts, even time, which is money. Therefore he is washed, fed, cared for without haste but without useless complaisance. Particularly his mother, timid and cold smiles hardly if at all, and doesn't chatter: why trouble to speak to this child who cannot understand? Gustave has much pain grasping this sparce character of the objective world, of otherness; when he becomes conscious of it, when he recognizes the faces leaning over his cradle, a first chance of love has already escaped him. He does not find himself, on the occasion of a caress, to be flesh and supreme end. It is now too late, for him to be, in his own eyes, the *destination* of maternal acts: he is their object, that is all. Why? He doesn't know it: A long time will not be required for him to feel obscurely that he is a means. For Madame Flaubert, indeed, this child is the means for accomplishing her duties of motherhood; for the doctor-philosopher from whom the young woman is completely alienated — he is first a means for perpetuating the family. These discoveries will come later. For now, he has bypassed valorization: he has never felt his needs as sovereign necessities, the outer world has never been his jewel-box, his larder, the environment reveals itself to him gradually, as to others, but he has only known it first in this cold and dismal consistency that Heidegger has named "*nur-vorbeillagen.*" The happy necessity of the loved child compensates and transcends his docility as an object to be manipulated; there are in his desires an intangible imperiousness which can appear as the rudimentary form of the project and, in consequence, of action. . . .[20]

This paragraph, which continues for another page and a half, is typical. In it Sartre builds from the slightest information and imagines what little Gustave must have felt, based on what his mother must have done given how she must have felt, given a few scanty facts about her: her childhood as orphan, her apparent devotion to Achille-Cléophas, her sombre bearing, as reported by her niece. From those few facts at the base Sartre's account spirals upward, producing its own facts as it goes, according to his understanding of basic structures of childhood — until it sights the basic passive and imaginary postures of the mature man, Gustave Flaubert. The book's bulk consists of such inventions, reconstructing Gustave's "personalizations" — the process whereby he shapes his basic project from such elements as these — every step of the way. This particular paragraph, however, is unusual because Sartre follows it with a frank discussion of his way of proceeding:

> I confess: this is a fable. Nothing proves that it was like this. And, worse yet, the absence of these proofs — which would necessarily be of singular facts — returns us, even when we create fables, to schematism, to generality: my account fits sucklings *in general*, not Gustave in particular. No matter, I wanted to carry it to its conclusion for this reason alone: the *real* explanation, I can conjecture without the least resentment, could be exactly the opposite of the one that I invent; *in any event* it would have to pass on the ground that I have defined: the body, love. I have spoken of maternal love: This is what fixes the objective category of otherness for the newborn, it is this which in the first weeks permits the infant to feel as *other* — from the moment he is able to recognize it — the satiny flesh of the breast. It goes without saying that filial love — the oral phase of sexuality — goes from birth to the encounter with the Other — it is the conduct of the mother which fixes its limits and intensity, which determines its internal structure. Gustave is immediately conditioned by his mother's indifference; he desires *alone*; his first sexual and alimentary impulse towards a "flesh-nourishment" is not *reflected* for him by a caress. . . .[21]

Sartre's methodological pause is important. It tells us that he must construct, as any explanation must, that he does so from a firm basis which he is willing to defend. *All* children are shaped, from the outset by the presence or lack of physical mother-love. And, I suppose, by its quality: anxious, intense, calm, contradictory or whatever. Given this woman, given who Gustave became, what *must have been* their initial relation? The imaginary construct proceeds along rigorously defined channels.

Sartre may be right and it is certainly interesting to entertain such brilliant speculations on occasion. The problem, however, is that a book built on a chain of such speculations is unreadable. On occasion Sartre returns to real life and to facts and observable events: it is a breath of fresh air. But for most of the time we are absorbed in such patently unreal constructions. We can be away from the facts for a while, but we demand the study to be grounded there. A fine balance between the hypothetical and the real asserts itself in judging any work of the mind claiming to represent reality. Certainly all thought, all writing "leaves" reality in some sense, and all thought and writing is a construct. But such constructs claim to be the *concept* of reality: reality rendered, captured, expressed, understood in thought. Extended constructs may thus be useful, but Sartre loses contact with the reality to be described. Not because Sartre isn't trying to *explain* a real person's inner workings, but because in doing so he is forced to construct *too much*. He does not merely fill in a few blanks but rather erects entire chains of experience — such as the Rouen schoolboys' relations to their fathers. There is not enough grounding in reality, not enough rooting in facts and evidence. Gustave Flaubert — and Sartre may indeed understand him — becomes too much a construct of Jean-Paul Sartre's imagination.

Sartre's "imaginary" study, his "true novel" thus contains the worst of both possible worlds. On the one hand, all the staggering interiority of an extended subjective case study; on the other hand, all the unreality of an extended construct. A novel may be unreal, but at least it is *concrete*: it deals with living, breathing people and their *actions*. A case study may occasionally be so interior as *L'Idiot* — but at least it is *factual*: it bases itself on and constantly returns to the factual evidence. Sartre's "true novel" is thus twice removed from reality. Each indulgence Sartre grants himself — the book's length, its lack of proportion and discipline, its total inwardness, and its systematic fable-construction — takes him further from his readers. Each successive demand on us to follow him is overwhelming: taken together, they give us the sense, in the end, that in *L'Idiot de la famille* Sartre has retreated from communication completely. Can, "eventually everything . . . be communicated"? Eventually, I rather think all Sartre's readers will be gone, and he'll be speaking only to himself.

Sartre at his best and worst: *L'Idiot* is the ultimate Sartre. It should be obvious that his entire career has led to this imaginary study of the interior of an imaginary person. Sartre's thought originally opposed a free person to an unbearable world and gave him no satisfying out but the imaginary. At the same time it rebelled against this conclusion and, until *What Is Literature?* articulated their real uses, looked down on the substitute world of imagination and art. Refusing to accept its own conclusion, Sartre's thought pointed towards the real world. He even spelled out a radical intellectual project which was, however, built on the sandy basis of his conceptual structure. That project's failure began to disturb Sartre, but he chose to criticize his own character in *The Words* rather than tackling the substance of what he was doing wrong. His initial mistake was not in seeing his writing as politically important, but rather in trying to make writing, defined as a refuge and escape, into a political weapon. Thus Sartre's writing never completely enters the social and historical world and at the same time claims too much of a role in that world. No wonder that, after 1968, Sartre begins to abandon an unrealistic and overly demanding intellectual activism.

And so his writing returns to the imaginary. Not to his original terms, but to the pole that he attacked so sharply. Not to *Nausea* but to the route condemned there: to Antoine Roquentin's escape into biography. He goes even further, into the portrayal of a writer, someone whose self-transformation into an imaginary person was the key fact of his life. Sartre clearly and decisively takes the retreat that has been such an issue throughout his career. And with his Flaubert he turns it into a brilliant and triumphal return, creating a monument of human understanding and energy. But it is a sad and shabby return as well. The rich tension between reality and the *irréel* is gone from Sartre's thought, as is the worldly pull, the moralism. In following Gustave Flaubert his thought now leaves the world. It takes up residence outside any realm of human communication. He has taken the ultimate step, for which he so sharply attacked French writers from 1850 to 1900: Jean-Paul Sartre has written a book that nobody will read.

Notes

1. "Une Idée Fondamentale de la 'Phénomenologie' de Husserl: L'intentionalité," *La Nouvelle Revue Française* (1939), p. 1.

2. See my essay, "Interpreting Husserl and Heidegger: The Root of Sartre's Thought," *Telos* Number 13, Fall, 1972.

3. See my essay, "Interpreting Husserl and Heidegger: The Root of Sartre's Thought," *Telos* Number 16, Summer, 1973.

4. See, for example, *What Is Literature?*, written in 1947.

5. *L'Idiot de la famille* (Paris, 1971), Vol. 1, p. I, tr. in *Le Monde Weekly*, May 20–26, 1971, p. 6.

6. "Interview with Jean-Paul Sartre" by Michael Contat and Michel Rybalka, *Le Monde Weekly*, June 17–23, 1971, p. 6.

7. See "Questioning Jean-Paul Sartre," *New Left Review* Number 58, p. 53, and *L'Idiot*, Vol. I, p. 7.

8. London, 1967; Paperback ed., 1971.

9. "Entretien Avec Jean-Paul Sartre," by Michel Contat and Michel Rybalka, *Le Monde*, May 14, 1971, p. 20.

10. *L'Idiot de la famille, op. cit.*, vol. 1, p. 7.

11. Enid Starkie, *Flaubert: The Making of the Master, op. cit.*, p. 88.

12. For a good, if ironic, summary of this analysis see the review in *The Times Literary Supplement*, September 24, 1971, p. 1133.

13. *L'Idiot, op. cit.*, Vol. 1, p. 351, n. 1.

14. *Ibid.*, p. 141.

15. *Ibid.*

16. *Ibid.*, p. 147.

17. *Times Literary Supplement, op. cit.*, p. 1135.

18. "The Refusal to be Good," *Modern Occasions*, Winter, 1972, p. 311.

19. *Ibid.*, p. 309.

20. *L'Idiot, op. cit.*, pp. 136–137.

21. *Ibid.*, pp. 139–140.

Sartre's Concept of the Self   Hazel E. Barnes*

The word "self" appears to mean all things to all people; it is often used in the vaguest possible way by psychotherapists who should know better. For some it is the hard kernel of unchangeability in the person, and for others it is an ideal to be realized. If Sartre's concept of the self has often been misunderstood, this is largely because he uses the same term to refer to different things in distinct contexts, which he himself keeps clear but his readers do not. Also, his emphasis on one rather than the other of these has changed as his interest and thought have developed. I should like here to do three things. First, I want to differentiate among various ideas of self as Sartre has defined them in his early theoretical work and see how they stand in relation to his overall view of what the individual is. Second, I will consider what became of these theoretical formulations when Sartre, much later, set out to study the case of Flaubert. Third, by way of conclusion, I want to point up a paradox. At either end of Sartre's career readers have complained that somehow Sartre lost the living person. In *Being and Nothingness* (1943) the radically free and isolated individual seemed to be too little in touch with the everyday world to be real. All that remained was an abstract, impersonal consciousness. In *L'Idiot de la famille* (1971–72), by contrast, some readers were disturbed by Sartre's claim that every person is "a singular universal" (*un universel singulier*). Gustave Flaubert appeared to be only the *product* of his familial and societal conditioning. History demanded and in effect wrote the novels signed by his name. Suppose that we ask: Who *was* Flaubert? What would we mean if we were to answer, "He was himself"?

I

There are three sharply defined usages of "self" by Sartre: first, the self of prereflective consciousness; second, the self as ego or as personality; third, the self as value. To these I am adding a fourth category of the self as embodied consciousness. Sartre himself is not inclined to use the word "self" to represent the total person as embodied consciousness, but clearly that is his goal when he wants to discover "what we can know of a man today . . . Flaubert, for example."[1] The "person" includes all of the first three notions of self, none of which can be wholly dissociated from the body. In *Being and Nothingness* he was concerned primarily with defining the ontological status of consciousness, ego, the body, their differentiation and their interdependency; the stress was always on consciousness. In *L'Idiot de la famille* ego and the body received far more attention.

*From *Review of Existential Psychology and Psychiatry* 17, no. 1 (1980–81): 41–65. Reprinted with permission.

The Self of Prereflective Consciousness

Every consciousness is a self-consciousness, Sartre declares, for consciousness is always aware of itself as consciousness. The self of prereflective consciousness derives from the fact that in being aware of an object, consciousness is aware of not being the object. To be conscious of a thing is to be aware that the awareness and the thing are not the same. For example, if there is suddenly a bright light, the immediate reaction is not that *I* am seeing a bright light; consciousness of the light implies that the light is somehow *there*, in front of consciousness, but not consciousness itself. I am referring, of course, to the famous "nihilation," of which Sartre makes so much. The human individual, whom he calls being-for-itself, is that part of being which effects a psychic withdrawal from the rest of being (being-in-itself). To nihilate is to be conscious *of* something as an object not identical with consciousness.

Thus there are two inextricable ingredients in any act of consciousness: consciousness *of* the object and a self-consciousness which Sartre indicates by putting the "of" in parentheses: *conscience (de) soi*. The latter is consciousness' awareness of itself as being aware. Sartre says that prereflective consciousness is personal in that there is a return to self, a slight displacement such as is indicated by some of the French reflexive verbs—for example, *il s'intéresse à* . . . (he interests himself in . . .).[2] The adjective "personal," while it may be correct grammatically, is misleading here. The awareness of being aware is totally void of individualizing psychic qualities. It is the condition of all consciousness rather than the differentiating "selfness" of a particular consciousness. If by "personal" we refer to the traits of a personality, I should say that this self-consciousness is individual but nonpersonal. It need not be empty of emotion. It may be a pain or a pleasure consciousness, for instance, but it is not accompanied by any sense of "I" or "me." It is pure intentionality, directed toward an object. One might be tempted to call it instaneous, but that is not quite correct. All consciousness involves temporality for Sartre, for it is always directed toward a future and posited against the background of a past.

His insistence that the prereflective consciousness is egoless is heavily consequential for Sartre. By separating it from what is normally thought of as the personality, he postulates a radical freedom from psychological determinism as traditionally conceived. It is the prereflective consciousness which makes the original "choice of being," or fundamental project, by which we relate ourselves to the world. In *Being and Nothingness* Sartre argued that it is this nonpersonal self-consciousness that gives me my uneasy, usually unacknowledged realization that there is nothing absolutely fixed or necessary in this choice, that it might have been entirely different, and that it could—at least in theory—be replaced by another choice and consequently a different personality structure.

The Self as Ego

Another way to express this idea is to say that the familiar personal self is not part of the structure of a consciousness but its product. As a consciousness reflects back upon earlier acts of consciousness, it begins to impose a unity upon those experiences. The result is a network of interlocking responses in which the activity of an agent must always be assumed. The true agent, of course, has been the original prereflective consciousness, but as it is objectified by the reflective consciousness, it seems to take on qualities inseparable from the accumulation of particular interactions with the world. Here we have the emergence of the ego. We must not confuse this with the Freudian ego, which comprises only a part of the psychic structure. The Sartrean ego is coexistive with all of one's psyche; but note that psyche, for Sartre, refers to all of the mental and emotional *objects* of the reflective consciousness, not to the original prereflective consciousness. The ego, including both the "I" and the "me," is what most people mean by self in popular usage. In what we may call the natural attitude, it is made up of a bundle of character traits and a structured personality. It is what I *am*, manifested in a thousand external acts and reactions. The *I* both creates the *me* and springs forth from it so that, at least theoretically, I can study it in its now quiet past and therefore know the form it will take and how it will appear in the future. The ego is my permanent, enduring self, which distinguishes me forever from all other selves. Nevertheless, Sartre insists that the existence of the ego is purely ideal. It is the purely formal unity that a present consciousness perpetually imposes on its past and future intentional acts.

There is a difference according to whether it is the past or the future that we are considering. The essence of what I have been in the past is a part of my being—that being-in-itself which I (as being-for-itself) drag along behind my present existence—like a mermaid with her tail.[3] Thus it is correct, if rather pointless, to say that I have a self in the past, but the statement is true only from the point of view of the present. It is this self— the essential core of one's personal biography—which is the object of what Sartre calls "impure reflection." This last is ordinary introspection such as we frequently indulge in when we are recalling past happenings, trying to evaluate and to understand ourselves, to pin down our half-formed hopes and vague unhappiness. It is closely associated with the psychological analyses by novelists who seek to reveal to readers the complexity of emotional states. (Sartre alludes especially to Proust.) Impure reflection is a process of isolating and categorizing emotions, for example, as though they were things in themselves, and the whole procedure is carried out well within the framework of our fundamental project. Our psychic life, the object of our introspection, can indeed be grasped by a consciousness, however inadequately, either my own or that of therapist or biographer.

Yet despite our familiarity with our autobiography, we recognize the sense of frustration that accompanies our attempt to pin down the real me or true self. The explanation lies in the fact that I apprehend an object where I sought to lay hands on a subjectivity. What is original about Sartre's rediscovery that the subject who thinks is not the subject thought of is precisely the fact that the original self-consciousness is not the personalized self. To ask what kind of self I am is to formulate the question improperly. Instead, I should ask what kind of self "my" consciousness has created.[4] This is indeed to raise more than a psychological question. Sartre has noted that it is on the level of *pure reflection* that morality is posited.[5] For a consciousness to look at its own product and to pass judgment on it is the original ethical act. But what is pure reflection? Is it an attainable goal or an illusion?

Sartre acknowledged that he had never adequately clarified his intention with regard to pure reflection. I think I know why. There is a troublesome ambiguity in the term itself. It hints at an ethics, and it suggests a form of self-knowledge. But Sartre states explicitly that consciousness cannot know itself knowing. If taken as a self-knowing, the ideal of reflection is impossible to achieve. For Sartre knowledge is consciousness' direct presence to an object in-itself. The self of prereflective consciousness cannot become the object of knowing at the same time that this consciousness is the reflecting agent. Perhaps it is easier to represent this in French than in English. We have seen that in every conscious act there are two things:

1. *conscience de l'objet*
2. *conscience (de) soi*

In reflective consciousness (assuming it to be a form of knowing) we would have the same situation.

1. *conscience de soi (= l'objet)*
2. *conscience (de) soi*

There is no way to suppress the second line. We attempt simply to combine these in a single line

conscience de conscience (de) soi

But this would be to suppress the self-awareness of the reflecting consciousness. It is equally impossible to perform the act which might be expressed as

conscience (de) soi de conscience (de) soi.

That is, we cannot do it if we intend that the second *conscience (de) soi* is the same as the first one. The intermediate *de*, which is the verbal equivalent of the act of nihilation that accompanies every intentional consciousness, separates them as surely as they are separated in their position on the page. We may say either that there is not enough separation between the two: the reflecting, since it *is* the reflected-on, cannot get outside it. Or we may say that there is too much separation: the object of consciousness is no longer the present consciousness but a past consciousness. The reflecting is no longer the same as the reflected. Sartre expresses the dilemma in a homely image. A donkey tries to reach a carrot attached to a stick fastened to the shaft of the cart he is pulling. Every movement to touch the carrot pushes it out of reach.[6] We cannot make of our consciousness an object without falling to the level of impure reflection.

Pure reflection, Sartre says, is not a full knowledge but rather a *recognition*; it is not a new consciousness but an internal modification of the prereflective consciousness. Sartre compares it to the situation of a person writing while aware that someone else is watching him. Indeed, pure reflection is the first faint hint of my having, factually, an outside, of my being-for-others. Even if alone, a consciousness can be, as it were, its own witness, but it can be so only if an external object is retained. In the midst of an activity I may suddenly reflect on myself as performing it without ceasing to keep the job to be done as the object of my consciousness. As I reflect, I am aware also that I am *not* the activity any more than I would be a tree that I observed. Joseph Catalano gives a particularly clear example taken from sport.

> If I am now reflecting on my playing tennis, I am aware of myself as playing tennis; I am certain that the self-that-is-playing tennis is the self reflecting on my tennis playing. . . . When I reflect on my tennis, I am aware that I can never perfectly *be* the self that is playing tennis. But this very nihilation (which is reflection), namely, that I can not-be a self that is identified with my tennis playing has its origin within the act of tennis playing, within the *being* of the original pre-reflective awareness that the being of consciousness is not identified with the being of tennis playing.[7]

Sartre himself chooses for illustration of the difference between prereflection and reflection Descartes' enterprise of doubting and points out that in "Cogito, ergo sum," the cogito is already on the reflective level.

Whether we consider the reflecting tennis player or the French philosopher seeking to prove his existence by trying to doubt it, we are immediately aware that reflection involves temporality. To be aware of myself doing something is to be aware of myself relating what has just been to what is to come. Pure reflection reveals to consciousness that as a nihilating intention, it is a pursuit of self, not a self that *is*.

It is easy to grasp that this over-the-shoulder glimpse of consciousness is possible, but why does Sartre assign to it so much importance? How can it possibly serve, as Sartre at the end of *Being and Nothingness* suggests that it might, as a basis for a new ethics?[8]

Where Sartre has not spoken, we cannot make assertions for him with any confidence, but I believe that he has given us a slight hint. Sartre recognized that it is possible to reflect on the memory of a nonreflective experience. I think we can see here the germ of one form of pure reflection — the attempt to hold up to consideration the elements and intrinsic qualities of the spontaneous conscious act, stripped of the overlay of associations after-the-event; the intent would be to examine a choice or an act as it was in itself at the time of its making. Precisely this is the aim of Hugo in *Dirty Hands*; but Hugo fails. Forced to rely on memory, he is unable to establish with certainty the reasons why he shot Hoederer in the past; he can only determine now the meaning he would like the act to have for the future. Granted that years had elapsed and Hugo had changed. But his failure perhaps explains why Sartre never developed the concept of pure reflection. Is it ever possible to be sure that one has isolated a former act of consciousness from its later overlay? Perhaps Sartre believed that we might train ourselves to look at our only-just-past reactions and to isolate what was genuinely spontaneous from what was influenced by individual and social presumptions. But this is to state a truism, or else Sartre envisioned some technique which he lacked the capacity, ability, or will to spell out. Sometimes I wonder if pure reflection is anything different from Sartre's habit of thinking against himself, of being willing to throw everything into question — both the existing structures of society and the furniture of one's psychic habitation. Sartre seemed to say as much in a late interview: "You know, I have never described [pure reflection]. I said that it could exist, but I showed only the facts of accessory reflection. Subsequently I discovered that the non-accessory reflection was not a way of looking that was different from the immediate, accessory way of looking but was the critical work you can perform on yourself during a whole lifetime, through praxis."[9]

Sartre certainly suggests elsewhere, and perhaps implies even here, that the self which is the goal of pure reflection is indeed the original *conscience (de) soi*, but the purpose of reflection would not be to discover that self as object but to liberate it from the incrustations of ego. This view would fit in with a remark by Sartre in *The Transcendence of the Ego*. There he says that in pure reflection the ego may be present but only "on the horizon" and as something which consciousness overflows and maintains by a continuous creation. He adds, "Perhaps the essential role of the ego is to hide from consciousness its own spontaneity."[10] The reason, of course, would be fear of what the full realization of our freedom would entail. Paradoxically, the revelation of the selfness of prereflective consciousness brings the realization that there is no self as substance, that a free consciousness has never been identical with the self it has made in the past or with the self that it projects toward the future.

The Self as Value

So far we have not discussed the future dimension. Sartre, we recall, claims that the ego is the ideal unity imposed by consciousness on all its psychic activity, future as well as past. Unlike the past, the future does not belong to being-in-itself. As the not yet, it depends on the nihilating action of the for-itself, which transcends what exists here and now. The future, so far as particular futures are concerned, has a purely virtual existence. There is no way to predict the dispositions and reactions of that "I" who will keep the rendezvous with the future that I presently project — not even if the world and other persons should perform their parts perfectly. The ego here is called on to unify acts still wholly imaginary. To speak of a future self is to postulate that a consciousness will continue to create a self that can be grasped only retrospectively. But Sartre now introduces an entirely different concept of self, one which does not belong to the ego and which is by definition never realized. Under the heading "The Self and the Circuit of Selfness," he discusses a self that is purely ideal, a value that we try to realize. It is metaphysical (or ontological) rather than psychological. We might think of our pursuit of this self as a corollary to the curtailed project of pure reflection.

Sartre argues that the for-itself is a lack of being which seeks to achieve being. Several other ways in which he expresses this idea might be formulated as follows: Consciousness is process, not substantial entity. It exists only as directed toward something other than itself. Consciousness is consciousness *of* something (Husserl). It is born, supported by a being which it is not (Sartre). Human reality is not what it is in the way that natural or manufactured things are. Human reality is what it is not and is not what it is. As a lack of being, the for-itself reaches out toward being. Consciousness is not a self and does not have a self; but as a self-making process, it pursues a self. Or, as Sartre says, it seeks to come to itself.

This future self Sartre links with desire and equates with value. He calls it a value because it is always the still unattained object of my desire. If I am thirsty, he says, what I desire is not just a glass of water but a thirst satisfied. I want to be simultaneously a desire as lack and a desire fulfilled, to be conscious of myself as a lack that is filled.[11] Thus the ultimate desire or value, of which all other desires are tributary expressions, is that I should *be* the self I have to make. This ideal is, of course, the desire to be in-itself-for-itself, which Sartre describes as the self-contradictory passion to be the Self-cause, or God.

Clearly one cannot have both unrestricted freedom to grow and a built-in program. If each consciousness is a continuous self-projection, we cannot say that the future self exists or will be grasped in the way that for the traveler the city of his destination exists and will eventually be reached by him. Yet we may raise the question as to whether pure reflection, in the extended sense in which we interpreted it with respect to the past, is relevant as regards our future consciousness. Obviously there can be no reflexive reaction on the future, but I think there is one way in which pure reflection can function so as to keep the future open to a free consciousness. The pure reflection which reveals to me that my spontaneous prereflective consciousness is not imprisoned within an ego can act to prevent me from preparing to make the future a repetition of the past, out of anxiety or insecurity. Frequently one rehearses so thoroughly the part one will play in a future event that one blinds oneself to unexpected possibilities and blocks off in advance any chance of spontaneous choice. A pure reflection not only would open up the past to new meaning but would regard the future as provisional.

At this stage we can see the wide variations in Sartre's use of the term "self," and we can recognize how distinctively and how precisely "self" must be employed in a Sartrean oriented psychotherapy. Obviously any notion of self as a two- or three-tiered structured psyche, such as Freud or Jung conceived, is out of the question. So is the humanistic concept of self-actualization if it is attached to a coherent pattern of inborn potentialities—what I like to call the "acorn theory" as presented, for example, in the work of Fromm and Maslow. The primary task for the person who would live in good faith (in Sartrean terms) is to keep the various categories of self clear in one's attitude toward one's life. This means, as Sartre puts it, that I should live with the realization that my nature is a demand but not a recourse. The ego is neither the cause of my actions nor a pattern to guide them; it is not a fixed self though it may be thought of as the self to which my consciousness has become accustomed. My spontaneous self-consciousness (the prereflective consciousness) is responsible for each new choice just as it has been the author of what I have made myself in the past.

The Self as Embodied Consciousness

Up until now I have been considering consciousness and psyche almost as if they were unembodied, but such was never Sartre's intention. In everyday experience my sense of my own self and of the Other's self is inextricably linked with the body even if, on some occasions, I may feel that there is a certain incongruity between external appearance and the inward life. It is natural for us to want to use the word "self" to refer to the total person even though Sartre tends to avoid this usage. In any case we cannot adequately grasp the sense in which Sartre's three kinds of "self" come into play unless we include the body. For a philosopher who has sometimes been mistaken for an idealist, the early Sartre assigned considerable importance to the body. In *The Emotions*, while he rejected the James-Lange theory which claimed that bodily reactions *caused* the emotions, Sartre nevertheless kept body on the active side; it is not a mere passive receptor or register of psychic reactions. Speaking of emotional behavior rather than of purely internal states (if indeed we may claim that these exist), Sartre claims that my consciousness assumes the emotional mode as a magical way of altering a lived situation in which I cannot modify the world itself. By effecting bodily changes, I alter my relation to the world. For example, I faint in the path of a menacing monster, thus "annihilating" myself since I cannot annihilate the beast. Or a woman patient is racked with uncontrollable sobbing *in order that* she may be unable to articulate a painful confession to the therapist.[12] In short, emotional behavior is purposeful and seeks to effect its purpose by means of the body. In *The Transcendence of the Ego* the body stands for "the illusory fulfillment of the I-concept" on the nonreflective level. It supports the empty, purely formal "I-concept" which allows me to answer, without intermediate mental process, the question, "What are you doing?" when my action has been nonreflective. If I am breaking up sticks, I say, 'I' am breaking up sticks, and I see and feel the object 'body' engaged in breaking the sticks. The body thus serves as a visible and tangible symbol for the *I*."[13]

Being and Nothingness has a long chapter devoted to the body. Sartre claims that we must recognize that it has three ontological dimensions: First, there is the Other's body — or the body for the Other. Here Sartre stresses the fact that I always consider the Other's body as the expression of a consciousness, not as an inert object in the world. Second, there is my-body-as-known-by-the-Other. At times the body (whether my own or the Other's) is pure object, as when I probe for a sliver or diagnose the extent of an injury. Of more concern to us here is the third dimension — the body-as-for-itself. This is the lived body or — as Sartre phrases it — the body I exist. Sartre denies any dualism. Sensations are not a hybrid something — not quite subjective, not quite objective — which are sent to consciousness by the body. The body *is* conscious. It is in and through the body that consciousness is present to the world, that it is individualized, that it has facticity, that it has a past. But consciousness does not use the body as an instrument for its separate needs. The relation is not that of agent and tool. A non-thetic awareness of body is inseparable from consciousness: "The body is what this consciousness *is*; it is not even anything except body. The rest is nothingness and silence."[14]

The last half of the quotation reminds us that we cannot reduce consciousness to body. It is nothing except body, but we must read this in the sense that consciousness is no thing, that it is a nihilating process. As for-itself, the body is not the object *of* consciousness as it is in the other two dimensions. Consciousness does indeed nihilate the body in the way that Being-for-itself nihilates all Being-in-itself. But its nihilation of its own body is different from its nihilation of perceived objects in the world. The relation is closer to the bond that links present to past acts of consciousness. Mentally, as physically, the point of view of consciousness has the body as center of reference. If my eyes pain me as I read, my reading consciousness is also a pain-consciousness, and I do not separate the two, except in reflection, any more than I separate my view of a landscape from the conditions of light and air that enfold and reveal it.

The purely physiological aspects of body are virtually ignored in

Being and Nothingness. When Sartre does mention them, he always adds that a free consciousness determines one's reactions. It is my basic choice of being that decides whether my fatigue enhances the pleasure of a hike or serves as an excuse for resting or turning back. Even under the sadist's knife, my consciousness decides when and whether I can no longer endure the torture. In the caress and embrace of sexual desire, the lover seeks to *incarnate* his own and the beloved's consciousness, in the vain hope of grasping the Other's entrapped consciousness as one skims the cream off milk. Moments of ultimate physical closeness (not the completion of orgasm) are supremely satisfying in realizing symbolically the impossible union in oneness of consciousnesses. What normally passes for a psychosomatic phenomenon was of no interest to Sartre at this date. It becomes of major importance in his study of Flaubert.

Let us turn now to *L'Idiot de la famille* and observe how Sartre uses the different notions of self when he attempts to understand the concrete reality of a once living person.

II

L'Idiot de la famille, a three-volume study of Flaubert which attempts to combine the approach of existential psychoanalysis with that of Marxist sociology, offers a final synthesis of Sartre's thought. As compared with his earlier books, the work shows no glaring theoretical inconsistency in its analysis of areas where Sartre or we would use the term "self," but the difference in emphasis and the added significance that are assigned to ego and body give us a much different picture of the interplay of subjective consciousness and conditioning and of how personality is developed. These nearly three thousand pages do not lend themselves to an easy summary of what Sartre believes to be "the truth of Flaubert." I will limit myself to a few observations which are especially relevant to the various uses of "self" by Sartre as I have outlined them.[15]

The Self of Prereflective Consciousness

In the Flaubert study we find virtually no discussion of the free prereflective consciousness as such, but existence is everywhere implied. We see this partly by what is omitted. There is a total absence of any mention of genetic or endocrinological determinism. Sartre explicitly rejects the existence of innate genius or talent, and the idea of intelligence as something biologically given and measurable. Far from positing that Gustave Flaubert had any natural facility with words, Sartre argues that it was Gustave's difficulty with language which led him eventually to literature. He gives considerable weight to the psychosomatic, but the emphasis is always on the underlying intention. He insists that Flaubert's famous nervous crisis in 1844, which all biographers recognize as a turning point in his life, was due to hysteria, not epilepsy. Where Benjamin Bart, for example, sees Flaubert as a novelist whose will to succeed triumphed over the ravages of a disease which impaired his powers,[16] Sartre views the crisis as the neurotic but successful solution of an otherwise insoluble conflict. To Flaubert himself it seemed like a death and rebirth. It was in fact a self-effected liberation, won at great psychic cost.

Freedom has not been lost in *L'Idiot de la famille*, but it appears chiefly in the paradoxical form in which Sartre presented it in an interview at the time of the first publication of the work. "A man can always make something out of what is made of him. This is the limit I would today accord to freedom: the small movement which makes of a totally conditioned social being someone who does not render back completely what his conditioning has given him."[17]

Sartre periodically directs our attention to the indispensable "small movement" amidst what would otherwise pass for a classic study of psychological determinism and unconscious conditioning. He does this partly by relying on his early concept of bad faith as a lie to oneself, in which the subject is never wholly ignorant of what he refuses to reflect or acknowledge. But now he attaches less of moral condemnation and speaks rather of the opaqueness of the lived experience (*le vécu*). A distinction between knowledge and comprehension, mentioned in *Being and Nothingness* but not fully developed, becomes crucial in the Flaubert study. A person may be wholly aware of an impulse, a wish, may vaguely sense its connection with an underlying structure of personal significances, without holding it up to a purifying reflection that would result in the kind of knowledge demanding deliberation and decision. What happens is something like what occurs more overtly when one looks at a set of papers piled helter skelter on the desk. One feels, "I ought to look over those. Some of those things certainly need attention. But I won't get into it now." Sartre claims that behavior such as "failure conduct" or the will to fail (*conduite d'échec*), is intentional (i.e., purposeful) but not deliberate. He notes that Flaubert himself referred to the "fulgurations" or sudden revelations of the stageset of his life world. One of these was expressed in the adolescent Gustave's unexpected realization that he envied, in a person he despised, the man's capacity for immense and genuine feeling. In later life a moment of retrospective self-understanding effected the confession to George Sand, "I was a coward in my youth."

Pervading the pages of *Being and Nothingness* was the presence of an anxious consciousness seeking in vain for meaningful structure outside itself and forced to recognize that rational order and purpose were only the thin human overlay imposed upon an incomprehensible world of matter. Flaubert himself was not disposed to recognize the terrifying responsibilities of this lonely freedom though he did in fact seek refuge in art from what he conceived to be the futility of existence in a world that failed to meet our high aspirations. We find a truly Sartrean echo of our despair in the face of an alien world, in one of his important digressions; somewhat surprisingly, the context is a discussion of practical jokes.

Sartre observes that it is through the world that I come to know myself. (Recall that all consciousness is consciousness *of* something other than itself.) "The world is what separates me from myself and announces me to myself" (II. 1312). Most of the time I exist with the assumption that things are indeed roughly what they seem. Despite my knowledge that my senses have on occasion deceived me, I cannot live without assuming that there is a broad area of daily life in which they can be trusted. Yet I retain a slight awareness of the ultimate unknowability in the things of which I am conscious. While the anguished awareness of this uncertainty is not present in every act, it exists as part of our "global feeling of our insertion in the world." What Sartre is speaking of is not just my realistic fear of accidents but a fundamental sense of estrangement. The practical joke is an attempt to evoke deliberately a rupture in the normal world of the person who is duped. Suppose that I, the victim, am offered what looks like a sugar cube for my tea but is actually a piece of celluloid. When it floats, I have a momentary but total feeling of disorientation. "I appear as a stranger to myself, my customs are disqualified, my past abolished, I am naked in a new present which is lost in an unknown future." Suddenly my secret suspicion is confirmed: "My relation with being, with *my* being, was only an appearance; the *true* relation is discovered. It is horrible; I come to myself, a terrifying monster through a monstrous world" (II. 1313).

To be the dupe of one practical joke is unlikely to be fatal; it may even be salutary. A prolonged series of practical jokes perpetrated on the same victim, especially if it is a child, might well induce, Sartre suggests, "an artificial psychosis by forcing him to live his normal adaptation to the real as a permanent disadaptation"[18] (II. 1314).

The Self as Ego

This last statement by Sartre takes us away from the abstract, isolated consciousness confronting the world and others as objects and reminds us of the way that the Other as subject may intrude into the most private recesses of my relations with myself; that is, with my self in the sense of ego. In *L'Idiot de la famille* there are at least three important contexts in which Sartre uses his own distinctive concept of ego as the product of consciousness, not as the subject synonymous with consciousness. The first concerns what Sartre believes to be Gustave's nonverbalized belief with regard to his own ego and its formation. For reasons which we will note shortly, the child Gustave, Sartre claims, failed to develop as an active agent. Instead, he conceived of himself as being made by the Other. By means of other people's acts and words, he hoped to learn what he was. In short, his ego was an alter ego, both in his own mind and, to a degree, in reality. In Sartrean terms we may say that Gustave widened the breach between basic consciousness and the ego, feeling that his ego was the product not of his own consciousness but of others' and that there was no escape from it. Sartre finds evidence in Flaubert's adolescent writing that he felt other people (his father especially) had made him what he was. At the same time he retained obscurely a resentful consciousness of being a free impulse which did not want to be limited to this nature that had been bestowed upon him.

Sartre appears to share this view. In his discussion of the gradual development of Flaubert's adult personality, he brings to bear all of the familiar elements of family conditioning—my second point. Gustave's "prehistory" includes the background and character of his parents, his relation to siblings (not only the older brother and younger sister who lived, but also the two brothers who died before he was born and the expected sister whose place he usurped). "Protohistory" is Sartre's term for the early years of childhood. We may subdivide it into what he calls "constitution" and "personalization." Constitution refers to the fundamental patterns of affectivity which Sartre believes are set by the infant's relations with its mother. Personalization, beginning in protohistory but extending beyond it, refers to the way that the child internalizes and unifies its lived situation in the family. Although the mother's role is still important in personalization, Sartre gives primary emphasis, in the case of Gustave, to the influence of the father and less directly of the brother. We will look more specifically at the parental influences when we consider Sartre's treatment of psychosomatic factors in the fully embodied consciousness we know as Gustave Flaubert. For the moment I will simply point out that the discussion of Gustave's psychic formation, although it is superficially closer to a traditional psychoanalytical approach than one might have expected, remains distinctively Sartrean. Parental influences are fully as significant in Sartre's analysis as in Freud's, but they are handled differently. Though Sartre may refer to the Oedipus complex, for example, his discussion of the child's psychological development bears no relation to the patterned stages of sexual and personal evolvement as outlined for males and females respectively in psychoanalytical texts.

A third illustration of Sartre's use of his concept of the ego occurs when he is discussing reading. As one would expect in a work by Sartre on Flaubert, considerable weight is given to the effect on Gustave of the books he read. Sartre is interested in the nature of the literature itself, both as an expression of the social factors which produced it and as a molding influence on a new generation of writers. What is more relevant to us here is his discussion of just how we as readers emphathize with an imaginary character and why fiction is so effective in helping to form a personality and even on occasion to alter our points of view. Sartre's explanation works only if we accept his basic position on consciousness and the psyche. Since the basic consciousness which I am is not structured, there is always implicit in me the awareness that my ego stands apart, at the horizon, as it were, of my consciousness, as the result of my structuring of experience. Therefore, since the ego is a quasi-object in the field of the reading consciousness, I as reader am free to project my ego into the ego of the character. As I identify my self with his, suddenly the reactions of the hero become part of my own past. As Sartre reminds us, our memory often confuses real events with imaginary ones. (We recall the way in which one's dream of a person may color one's attitude toward him or her in waking life.) I cannot move into the fictional world of another being without modifying the color of the world in which I live when I am not reading.

Something else happens, too, Sartre says, while I read empathetically. Although the "I" of my ego and the "I" of the hero are merged, I retain the feeling that each is inextricably linked with a transparent consciousness. Since the hero has been objectified by the author, I seem to grasp the hero's free consciousness — and my own — as objects even while I remain subject. Suppose that I am reading the tale of a Castilian nobleman. Sartre writes, "The Castilian is [the reader] himself appearing to himself at last as the object which he is in the world, and at the same time the Castillian is his [the reader's] own subjectivity as it appears in *itself* to an impartial all-knowing observer. In short, it is the in-itself-for-itself finally achieved (II. 1376).

The illusion depends in part also on the particular relation that exists between me and the author. It seems that out of the black marks on the page I freely create the fictional character and his world. But my creation is a re-creation in so far as it is guided by the inscribed intention of the author. One is inevitably reminded of Augustine's declaration — that our freedom consists in voluntarily doing God's will.

The Self as Value

Unexpectedly, we have moved from ego to the self as in-itself-for-itself, or value. It should not surprise us that this impossible goal is achieved only in an act of imagination. With respect to Flaubert and the ideal of self-coincidence, Sartre makes two important points. First, even as a child Flaubert thought of himself as living out a preordained destiny. As an adult he liked to think that he was incapable of change and inwardly impervious to anything which might touch him externally. He was what he was, once and for all. He refused, insofar as it was possible, to live with a future dimension. His life was a cyclic repetition. When political events transformed his society, he felt that he had outlived himself. And in fact critics have remarked that despite innovations in plot and setting, his last books have the same themes and attitudes as the early ones. Flaubert tried to defy time, not by remaining youthful in spirit but by considering himself already an old man when he was in his early twenties. Second, he chose art over life. Rather than to live as a man in time, he wanted to *be* the artist who creates imaginary eternities. He tried to make himself a work of art, partly by role playing, partly by casting himself in a form that excluded the transient and the spontaneous.

The Self as Embodied Consciousness

The somatic plays a major role in Sartre's analysis of Flaubert, both in the initial conditioning of his "constitution" or basic affectivity and in the climactic nervous crisis which established once and for all his "fundamental project"; that is, his way of being in the world. We observed earlier that Sartre attributes to the mother the primary responsibility for the baby's constitution. While denying that he himself has been influenced by Lacan, Sartre is like Lacan in stressing the symbiotic relation of the baby to its mother in infancy. Psychic and somatic are inextricably intertwined. Sartre claims that Madame Flaubert was overprotective but unloving in her treatment of the son who came when she wanted a daughter and whom in any case she did not expect to live very long.[19] Maternal love, Sartre declares, is not an emotion but a relation. The underloved child's first experience of himself as body is that of being a thing, dependent on another, but with no sense of reciprocity. The result in Gustave's case was a basic passivity fundamental to all of his reactions in later life.

On the sexual level, passivity and not a latent homosexuality or unresolved Oedipus complex was at the root of a certain femininity in Flaubert's character which his contemporaries noted. This hypothesis explains his intense, somewhat dependent relations with Louis Bouilhet and Maxime du Camp and his uneasy liaison with Louise Colet. Letters show that Flaubert was not impotent, but he appears to have feared Louise's strong sexuality as much as he longed for it. He saw her as seldom as he could manage, even at the height of his professed ardor. Like Léon in *Madame Bovary*, he seemed in some ways to be her mistress more than she was his. He expressed the wish that Louise could be man to the waist and woman below, that the two together might form, as it were, an hermaphroditic couple. What he really wanted, Sartre claims, was to be roused to virility by the caresses of the hands of the strong woman — in other words, the phallic mother.

Psychological consequents outside the sexual context were even more important. Nonvalorization was one of them, and Sartre claims that Flaubert never did develop the self-esteem that is requisite for being at ease with oneself. Sartre argues that the underloved child develops no sense of being an active agent in control of his destiny. To make the child feel that he is a sovereign around whom the world revolves, that it is he who decides what will happen, that the world awaits his striding down the path he will choose — all this is not to be regarded as the temptation of an overfond mother but rather the duty of an intelligent one. When we recall Sartre's view of the human being as a "useless passion," inhabiting a universe without support for human values, where nobody is privileged, we must conclude that Sartre is advising now the deliberate inculcation of a falsehood. But its intent is to instill in the child the true notion that he is an active agent who will make his own destiny (I. 143).

Sartre claims that the unloving overprotectiveness of Gustave's mother imprinted on the child's "constitution" (perhaps we would more naturally speak of "psychic disposition") a dependent passivity. There are still other consequences which Sartre obviously would expect to find in any child in a similar situation. First is a certain aboulia, a lack of capacity for true desire, which manifested itself even in Gustave's childhood as ennui or distaste for life. Sartre believes that if a baby is fed and cared for strictly by an adult's schedule with no concern for his specific hungers, thirsts, and discomforts, he fails to make the natural association between desiring and satisfaction and may never learn the pleasure of being satisfied. Then, too, helplessness creates a feeling of unreality. Sartre cites an episode from his own life and one from Gide's *Journal* to illustrate the way that one's sense of being totally out of control and at the mercy of external forces can leave one with the feeling that what goes on is not really happening, is like something in a dream (in dreams as we remember them, of course, not as we are immersed in them). Finally, Sartre adds, Flaubert's inability to feel clearly the distinction between real and unreal resulted in his confusing truth and belief — or better, in not recognizing the existence of truth as an absolute criterion. So strong was this feeling in Gustave that Sartre associates it with Flaubert's later decision to become a "worker in the imaginary," a creator of fiction. The mother's influence came first and laid the foundation for Gustave's passive constitution. Sartre speaks of this as "the first castration."[20]

The father not only reinforced the damage the mother had done, but exerted the decisive influence on Gustave's "personalization." Sartre dwells at length on the difficulties of a second son in the kind of patriarchal family in which the first boy plays the role of heir apparent. We have evidence for Gustave's jealousy of his older brother Achille. But Sartre goes far beyond the simple postulation of sibling rivalry. To be the younger son was to be marked as inferior, a pale copy or replica, at best a standby. Sartre thinks that there was a fatal interplay between Gustave's gradual realization of what it meant to be a second son and the natural difficulties inherent in moving from childhood to boyhood. Sartre speaks of the crisis of the "second weaning," which takes place when the child reaches the age of six or seven. This is the time when the engaging helplessness of the toddler is seen as clumsiness; the prattling cherub is suddenly a chattering nuisance. It marked the abrupt end of the "golden age" when Dr. Flaubert took Gustave along with him on his house calls. Gustave now is left at home, and his mother tells him that he must learn to read. Family documents record that Gustave had great difficulty in grasping the skill of reading, whereas Achille had mastered it easily. Sartre makes a great deal of this incident. He gives three reasons for Gustave's troubles. (We may observe once again the absence of physical explanations such as dyslexia or other natural disability.) First, he was suddenly called upon to act, but his constitutional passivity had not prepared him for the role of active agent. Second, he had regarded words as things which came from the Other. He had not learned reciprocity. It was not natural for him to reconstruct their meaning for himself. Finally, his presentiment of what would be demanded of him made him reluctant to leave the golden age of childhood. Gustave did indeed finally learn to read, but the crisis was catastrophic. Dr. Flaubert concluded that his son was retarded. Gustave accepted the pronouncement of his inferiority. It is from this episode that Sartre gets his title: *The Family Idiot*.

In the literary pieces which Flaubert wrote in his early and mid-adolescence, Sartre finds documents to support his picture of Gustave's life-world. The boy lived in an environment both theological and feudal. God the Father had justly condemned his evil son, but the prodigal longed and secretly hoped for forgiveness. The Father was a feudal suzerain who had no use for the homage of the vassal who loved him. The son exiled from Paradise simultaneously accepted the malediction and resented it. He loved his father and wished for his death. He resolved to live out his unhappy fate to its extreme in the hope that at last the cruel father would pity the son he had destroyed.

When Gustave went to school, his pride in being a Flaubert and his shame at being the rejected, inferior cadet resulted in two modes of behavior: compensating daydreams and aggressiveness. These were two sides of a coin. The fantasies were sado-masochistic. Sometimes Gustave imagined himself to be a Giant looking with scorn on the stupidity and baseness of the human ants below; often he identified himself with a cruel, destructive, powerful figure like Nero. In the schoolyard he was bitingly sarcastic in his taunts and not above joining with others in verbally tormenting the weak. He seems also to have been the leader in creating an imaginary character, the Garçon. Taking turns at the role, the boys used this fictional being as a mouthpiece by which to mock both bourgeois values and the dreams of the Romantics. Sartre claims that this spontaneous social psychodrama was therapeutic for the group and for Gustave but in quite different ways. For most of the boys it was effective in ridding them of the temporary aberrations induced by empathy with Romantic heroes — metaphysical despair and temptations to suicide. They became, like the Garçon, reconciled to enjoying the benefits of being bourgeois, even as they scoffed at its refined pretensions. Gustave enjoyed the double reward of being loved as one of the group and yet believing that he had demoralized his companions. To demoralize, Sartre insisted, remained Flaubert's chosen mission as a writer. *Madame Bovary*, for example, shows us that, except in art, there is no alternative to the foolish, self-defeating dreams of Emma and the gross materialism of the successful Homais.

In describing how Gustave finally came to grips with his family situation and by the same stroke launched himself on his career as an artist, Sartre ties together the constitutional passivity, paternal conditioning, and the psychosomatic. At the lycée Gustave's record was respectable but not brilliant. When he excelled, it was in those fields least propitious for a prospective medical student — in history and literature. Rather than explaining this record as the result of natural interests or talents, Sartre sees it resulting from Gustave's resolve not to imitate Achille but to demonstrate the inferiority to which his father had condemned him. This was the first manifestation of what Sartre calls "failure conduct" or, to use the more familiar term, the will to fail. It is an obvious strategy to be employed by a "passive agent." The latter is Sartre's term for one whose constitution is marked by passivity. When he acts, as all of us must do, willy-nilly, he tries to convince himself that he is coasting with the current, giving in to circumstances beyond his control, refusing to acknowledge his own part in shaping the circumstances.

A bourgeois son was expected to work at some sort of profession. Since Gustave showed no talent for medicine, the obvious alternative was law. He hated the very thought of it, but he was duly enrolled and even made a show of studying. Sartre describes him caught between two impossible demands: His passivity makes him incapable of defying his father, but he is equally unable to obey his father. To do so would be to sentence himself to a life in which he must not only acknowledge his mediocrity but seem to be contented with it. The sole solution is to show that he *cannot* obey. This means that he must accept total disgrace. He does in fact fail his first set of exams. But this is not enough. He will be expected to repeat them. Somehow he must demonstrate his inability to hold any kind of job. Now the negative strategy becomes a positive calculation. If he can stay at home, like an unmarried daughter, supported by his father until eventually he inherits his share of the estate, then he will have everything he requires. The dependent, feminine aspect of his personality will be fostered. He, and not the brilliant Achille, will live in the bosom of the family, who will be forced to pity him, to care for him, hence to love him. And he will be free to write. Radical failure will be a form of salvation. Loser will win.

It would have been easy for Sartre to defend such a hypothesis if he had been willing to resort to the concept of an unconscious. Sartre tries to work without it. The will to fail, he says, can be sustained only as a project in bad faith. But a divided intention, auto-suggestion, and somatic reactions are essential accompanying elements. The conflict was genuine and manifested itself on at least three levels. First, Gustave's fear of public failure and parental displeasure was acute, as painful in immediate anticipation as was the more remote hated career. Either outcome was intolerable. Second, Gustave at times tried to assume the role of active agent. He declared to a friend his resolve to work disdainfully until he had won his law degree and then refuse to practice. But the habit of passive obedience was so strong in him that he must have known that this was sheer bravado. If defiance were to be his solution, now was the time to announce it. Finally, two attitudes, deriving respectively from the family's attitude and from his reading in Romantic literature, were mutually contradictory: the Flaubert pride demanded that the greatest must show himself able to do the least. But opposed to this was the ideal of the Romantic hero whose greater vision prevented him from seeing how to perform the lowly task at his feet — the eagle that loses the footrace, or Plato's philosopher newly descended into the cave. Each set of attitudes poisoned the other. Gustave would in all sincerity force himself to study and try to succeed — as indeed he did on his retake of the first examinations. But most of the time his efforts were self-defeating. He would postpone study until the last moment; then in a sudden panic he would try to do too much in too short a time. Having decided in advance that the legal code was meaningless jargon, he attempted to master it by sheer memorization, refusing to take the intellectual steps which, by viewing law as the evolutionary accretion of historical development or as logical construction, might have made it interesting and easier to retain. He neglected his physical well-being so that ill health by itself might render him incapable. Finally, as it became obvious that only a desperate solution would save him, he called on his body for more decisive intervention.

Sartre cites several pieces of evidence to show that Flaubert, however confusedly and inaccurately, was aware of the interaction of psychic and bodily reactions. Gustave applied to himself the theory that in some persons agitations of the senses, instead of stimulating intellectual or artistic creativity, passed into the nervous system, causing physiological disturbances. This is what happens, he said, in the case of those musically talented children who will never be Mozarts. A second indication that Sartre finds is Flaubert's reference to a prolonged period of sexual abstinence at just this date. Combined with his confession to a sudden impulse toward self-castration which came over him one day, Sartre argues that probably Gustave found himself impotent in this time of pressure, not an unlikely thing to have happened. But Sartre goes on to hypothesize that Gustave associated the wish and the reality. Had a momentary, rejected impulse been accepted and acted on by the body? A third point refers to earlier days at home. Gustave had amused himself and the family by doing imitations of an epileptic, a former journalist who had been reduced to beggary by his affliction. Gustave recorded that he threw himself into this performance to the point of almost being in the other man's skin and added that his father, fearing it might have some harmful effect on his son, forbade any repetition of the act. Sartre claims that Flaubert was afraid lest his imitations of madness and his habit of imagining abnormal mental states might, through the power of suggestion, induce his body to succumb to insanity.

If we follow Sartre, Gustave during the months preceding January 1844 awaited something decisive that would come to him from outside — the quintessence of "active passivity." Certainly the timing of his nervous crisis suggests "intentional" hysteria and not a purely accidental epilepsy. After failing the second set of examinations, he had gone home for the winter holidays. If nothing happened to save him, he would have to return to the law books and try again. One night as he was driving with his brother a cart suddenly appeared out of the darkness, not colliding with the Flaubert vehicle, but coming close. As though it was a sign, Gustave fell rigid to the floor. He did not lose consciousness but suffered severe pains, hallucinatory perceptions of strange lights, etc. During the subsequent weeks attacks returned, accompanied now by convulsions, but Flaubert appeared strangely relaxed and without anxiety. It was as though the worst had happened and there was nothing more to fear. Was this simply because he had consented to the ignominy of failure and disgrace and now, having paid the price, could look forward to reaping the reward? Or was it also as Sartre suggests, relief that he had risked death and insanity but had avoided them? Dr. Flaubert died a little more than two years later, in 1846. Soon afterward, and despite the fact that his beloved sister had died in childbirth shortly before the father's demise, Gustave declared that at last he could get to work at writing again. The attacks diminished in frequency and finally, after ten years, ceased entirely.

Sartre is speaking of hysteria, of course, not playacting and knowing deception. Obviously the nervous crisis was not the effect of a rational act of will any more than Gustave's failure to pass the examinations was due to feigned ignorance. Yet Sartre insists that Flaubert had a certain comprehension of the intentional structure behind the crisis. This is implied in his many references to his having sacrificed everything for art, to his having renounced all real passions in order to be able to depict them in art. His language constantly suggests that some sort of bargain had been made. When the last years of his life were disturbed by financial worries, he regarded it not merely as unfortunate but unjust. His laments sound like complaints over a broken contract. Finally, at Flaubert's great moment of disillusion, there was another psychosomatic occurrence. The fall of the Second Empire and the Prussian invasion of France were cataclysmic for Flaubert, who looked on the defeat of France as the end of Latin culture. In retrospect he felt that the Court of Napoleon III, in whose circles he had been lionized, had all been a sham, like a staged court in an opera. Science had triumphed over art. Imagination, instead of creating a higher reality, had helped to insure the real humiliation of the German occupation of Flaubert's own home at Croisset. Sartre states that at this date Flaubert found his whole life called into question and felt that after all loser had been self-deluded in thinking he had won. Statements in Flaubert's letters testify to his acute sense of having outlived himself. In his anger at his fellow citizens he wrote, "I would like to drown humanity in my vomit" (III. 496). Significantly, it was at this time that he was afflicted with spells of nausea so severe that he was convinced that he had developed a stomach ulcer. He consulted a physician, who could find no organic cause. Gradually the symptoms disappeared. Sartre explains the imagined ulcer as the expression of Flaubert's wish that he could vomit up himself because of his guilt at having enjoyed and been an accomplice of the regime responsible for today's dust and ashes. He rejected both the fossil he saw himself becoming and the deluded man who had not foreseen the outcome. As Sartre expresses it, Flaubert could only wait for death since he had lived beyond the period for which he had programmed himself.

III

Who was Flaubert? Some critics of Sartre's biography of him have claimed that the study of conditioning has been carried to such an extreme that "Gustave" has been lost, that we are left with the feeling that any younger son in that family — or even a changeling — would have become the author of *Madame Bovary*. I hope I have shown, even by my few examples, that this is to misread Sartre, that Gustave as a passive agent still directed the course of his life. Sartre has remarked that Flaubert was at least free to choose to become the novelist we know, or a poor physician, or nothing but a typical bourgeois.[21] I would add that there are a number of places in the book at which one feels that his preference for the imaginary might also have induced him to choose psychosis.

John Weightman charged Sartre with a deficiency in his theory. In Weightman's view, Sartre's early rejection of "human nature" as a psychological given led him to miss "the physiological uniqueness, the given genetic identity of the individual Gustave." Weightman asks, "If there is no density of the given individual nature, if there is no weighting to be derived from the various possibilities within the temperament, how can anyone get the inner leverage necessary for the exercise of freedom? Freedom cannot be rootless; it must be the margin of uncertainty in the possibilities of the given."[22]

The last sentence we may dismiss with the observation that Sartre himself might have written it; but for him the margin of uncertainty would be located at the moment of internalization of the given, and the given would refer to the subject's situation, not to genetic coding. The rest of Weightman's accusation reveals an inability to grasp — or else an unwillingness to accept — the distinction between consciousness and ego. Like most people in our Western tradition, he is unable to conceive of life as a true self-making and wants to see it as an unfolding. The differences between a rolling snowball and a Roman candle! The free consciousness that made Flaubert continued to manifest itself through layers of personal ego which it itself laid down and within the structures of the life world it had formed out of its environment.

If to the question, "Who was Flaubert?" we were to reply, "He was himself," the statement is correct or incorrect, in Sartre terms, according to which use of self we have in mind. I like to think that there are two forms of self-realization consistent with Sartre's psychology.[23] The first is spontaneous self-realization and is based on my recognition that the core of my existence is inextricably bound up with nonbeing, the "nothingness" of which Sartre speaks, the separation between consciousness and all its objects (physical and mental) — my freedom itself. I need not (indeed *cannot*), in any absolute sense, *be anything*, but I am free to project being whatever I choose. I am separated from my past, from my future, even from my self (as fully personalized ego). Spontaneous self-realization is the realization of the power and the independence of the preflective consciousness.[24] In contrast, temporal self-realization depends on my acknowledging my responsibility for my own past and future; it necessitates that I relate them to the present in some coherent pattern. By my actions, Sartre tells us, I carve out my being — in the world; the image of what I have made myself is formed by the marks I have left on the total environment in which I have moved. What I am is what I have done — at this moment. "You are your life," Inez tells Garcin in *No Exit*. Obviously both kinds of self-realization are essential for full development of our freedom and responsibility. Spontaneous self-realization by itself results in the weather-vane personality, the irresponsible and finally valueless life. But to live wholly within the framework of one's chosen value system, even if once it was freely created, is to become "uptight," resistant to growth, incapable of enjoying the psychic refreshment of the "moral holidays" which, William James once said, are essential to our psychological well-being.

Sartre claims that Flaubert, insofar as he was able, refused spontaneous self-realization and chose to identify himself first with the ego "given" to him and then with his own carefully shaped self-image as artist. In reality both of these and the person history knows as Gustave Flaubert were the product of the original, nonpersonalized, prereflective self-consciousness, which neither Flaubert nor we could ever grasp and objectify.

Notes

1. *L'Idiot de la famille: Gustave Flaubert de 1821 à 1857* (Paris: Gallimard, Vols. I and II, 1971; Vol. III, 1972), p. 7. All translations in this paper are my own. Part One of this work has been published in English. *The Family Idiot*, translated by Carol Cosman (University of Chicago Press, 1981).

2. "Conscience de soi et connaissance de soi," *Bulletin de la Société Française*, Vol.

XLII, No. 3, April–June, 1948, p. 69. Sartre's example is *il se penche*, which literally means to lean but may also be used in the sense of "to take an interest in." My example seems to me to be clearer for English-speaking readers. In this discussion Sartre defends and explains in more detail the view of consciousness which he presented in the first part of *Being and Nothingness*. It has been published in English as "Consciousness of Self and Knowledge of Self," translated by Mary Ellen and N. Lawrence, in *Readings in Existential Phenomenology*, edited by Nathaniel Lawrence and Daniel O'Connor. (Englewood Cliffs, New Jersey: Prentice-Hall, Inc., 1967), pp. 113–42.

3. This is Sartre's image. *Being and Nothingness*, translated by Hazel E. Barnes (New York: Washington Square Press, 1972), p. 208.

4. Strictly speaking, the prereflective consciousness should not be qualified by personal pronouns, but I follow Sartre's custom in using them as we do in ordinary speech.

5. "Conscience de soi et connaissance de soi," p. 90.

6. *Being and Nothingness*, pp. 277–78. To be exact, Sartre's analogy refers to an attempt on the part of consciousness to escape from its own perpetual flight by making itself a fixed presence to the world. The image applies equally well in the context of my discussion.

7. Joseph S. Catalano, *A Commentary on Jean-Paul Sartre's Being and Nothingness*, (University of Chicago Press, 1980), p. 129.

8. In *Being and Nothingness* Sartre's discussion of pure reflection (pp. 211–21) does not mention any ethical implications. In the last paragraph of the book Sartre says that the ethical questions which he has just raised "refer to a pure and not an accessory reflection."

9. "Un Entretien avec Jean-Paul Sartre," with Michel Contat and Michel Rybalka. *Le Monde*, May 14, 1971. The interview has been published in English as "On the Idiot of the Family," translated by Paul Auster and Lydia Davis. In *Life/Situations* (New York: Pantheon Books, 1975), pp. 109–32.

10. "La Transcendance de l'Ego: Esquisse d'une description phénoménologique," *Recherches philosophiques*, Vol. VI (1936–37), p. 120. This has been published in English as *The Transcendence of the Ego: An Existentialist Theory of Consciousness*, translated by Forrest Williams and Robert Kirtpatrick (New York: Noonday Press, 1957).

11. On the surface Sartre seems to be simply wrong. The pleasure of drinking when one is thirsty is precisely one's awareness of desire in the process of being satisfied. Sartre appears to join in with Schopenhauer's gloomy appraisal of life as alternating between deprivation and satiety. Of course, Plato's more philosophical argument (in the *Symposium*) is relevant, too: that what love-as-lack desires is the continued (i.e., future) possession of the good and the beautiful; hence desire as such remains a deprivation or reaching toward that is not now possessed.

12. These are Sartre's examples. *The Emotions: Outline of a Theory*, translated by Bernard Frechtman (New York: Philosophical Library, 1948), pp. 62 and 31.

13. "La Transcendance de l'Ego," p. 115.

14. *Being and Nothingness*, p. 434. I have not listed the three dimensions in the same order as Sartre discusses them.

15. In this article I am not raising the question of the validity of Sartre's assertions concerning Flaubert so far as historical accuracy is concerned. I have discussed at length his interpretation of Flaubert in my book *Sartre and Flaubert* (University of Chicago Press, 1981). In referring to *L'Idiot de la famille* in this section, I will simply cite volume and page numbers.

16. Benjamin F. Bart, *Flaubert* (Syracuse: Syracuse University Press, 1967), pp. 93–7 and 752–53.

17. "Itinerary of a Thought," *New Left Review*, 58 (November–December, 1969), p. 45.

18. Sartre says that the motive of the prankster is to reassure himself. He himself knows

that all is within the bounds of normality even when things seem in utter disarray to the victim. "This momentary mini-scandal appears, therefore, to be a vaccine against the anguish of existing." Still, adds Sartre, the joker is an anxious type. (II. 1314).

19. Sartre admits that we have no evidence for the nature of the relation between Madame Flaubert and the infant Gustave but offers it as a hypothesis which fits what we do know of her background and personality as well as of Flaubert himself.

20. Sartre speaks of a "second castration," which was Dr. Flaubert's refusal to recognize his son's early aspirations to be an actor. I think Sartre has been guilty of exaggeration, if not actual distortion, at this point. The matter is discussed in my book, mentioned above.

21. *Sartre, un film réalisé par Alexandre Astruc et Michel Contat* (Paris: Gallimard, 1977), p. 76.

22. John Weightman, "Battle of the Century—Sartre *vs.* Flaubert," *New York Review of Books*, April 6, 1972.

23. I have discussed the two kinds of self-realization more fully in my book, *An Existentialist Ethics* (Chicago: University of Chicago Press, 1978).

24. I mean, of course, independence of psychological determination or inner necessity. Consciousness is always dependent on its objects in that it cannot exist without an object.

The Texts in the Self: Sartre and His Fiction

The Prolapsed World of Jean-Paul Sartre

W. M. Frohock*

Back in 1938, before France went under, long before he became the center of the Existentialist movement, and long long even before he was anything more than an obscure high school teacher, Jean-Paul Sartre wrote a novel called *La Nausée*: the title can be translated as "Disgust." I would like to talk of it here as if I had never heard of Existentialism.

Who wouldn't? But the Existentialists have us surrounded. To be perfectly honest, I have read a certain amount about the movement and am thus quite probably contaminated; fortunately I have been able to check my information and impressions by reading the proofs of Jean-Albert Bédé's authoritative note on Sartre in the forthcoming *Columbia Dictionary of Modern Foreign Literature*. What I mean is that I shall leave the reader to interpret *La Nausée* as an Existentialist document as much or as little as he likes.

The book stands by itself, and there is something in it for everybody: philosophers can read it for its philosophical groundwork; psychiatrists will find a long series of clinical notes on a curious emotional state; historians can use it as a document on the temper of pre-war France; and you and I can consider it as a rather expert novel in the traditional sense. It has a hero whose personality is modified during the story, and the extent of the modification is measured against the relative stability of the secondary characters — even though one of the characters has been dead a hundred years and more when the story opens. I am especially interested in it because as a novel of violence it ties up rather closely with the work of several Americans, including Hemingway, Steinbeck, Caldwell and Faulkner, of whose novels Sartre is, as a matter of fact, inordinately fond.

1

The hero is a negligible little specimen of pre-atomic man with a small but sufficient income, red hair and a homely face, named Antoine Roquentin. He is old enough to have acquired a considerable store of

*From *Accent* 7, no. 1 (Autumn 1946): 3–13. Reprinted with permission.

experience and a marked distaste for life. In many ways he sounds like the little man in *A vau-l'eau*, whose inability to struggle against the stream of life is finally reduced to a desperate and unavailing attempt to find a restaurant where he can eat without ruining his digestion, although of course Huysmans is true to his time in summing up his character's unhappiness in an easily understood symbol instead of trying to exhume the underlying neurosis. Roquentin's unhappiness is somewhat less definitive; at least he has loved once, although not very successfully, and he is looking forward to a reunion with the same woman which may prove to him that he is still capable of love. Meanwhile the insipid mediocrity of his existence is shown forth in the way that he has adopted, as an interim substitute for love, an entirely glandular relationship with the proprietress of his favorite café, who interprets her bedside prattle about the retail liquor business to express the hope that he "won't mind if she keeps her stockings on."

Roquentin is the kind of unhappy individual who contemplates himself in the mirror because, like an anti-Narcissus, he dislikes so much what he sees in the glass. "What I see," he reports, "is considerably beneath the monkey, down on the edge of the vegetable kingdom, on the level of the polyps. . . . Close up the eyes are horrible — vitreous, soft, blind, red-edged; you could take them for fish scales." Obviously such a man is what we agree to call abnormal. But let that pass. Novelists in France as well as America have been presenting abnormal types in their books so consistently during the last twenty years that we had better face the fact that, for their purpose at least, abnormality is the rule. What matters is the kind of abnormality and the degree, so far as it can be determined, of departure from whatever norm we can see through all the haze.

Several other symptoms have recently appeared. He is terribly lonely and envies people who move in groups because, as he puts it, "You have to be several men together to be able to bear existence"; he wonders whether it is his lack of friends which makes him feel so naked. Very lately he has had moments when he is absolutely afraid for minutes on end to look at his beer glass on the café table, and is unable during such times to make himself turn his head. He has also been unable to indulge a somewhat anomalous pleasure in picking up pieces of waste paper, clean or filthy, which he has always enjoyed finding in the gutter: lately something has made him withhold his hand. What bothers him even more, as he thinks of it, is another sudden inhibition which prevented him from throwing a pebble into the water; in this instance he has felt the psychic paralysis pass up his arm, as though it had started from the under side of the pebble.

He is aware of these things and they puzzle him. Once before in his life he has experienced a nameless upheaval of his instincts, which then precipitated his decision — for which he has never been able to think up a rational explanation — to give up a life of travel for one of scholarly retirement in the French coastal city where he now is. He wonders if once more his emotions are preparing to upset his entire way of life.

This is poor Roquentin as the story opens. Suspecting that he is going to get worse, he has started a journal into which he plans to pour his observations on his own condition, for the purpose of bringing the circumstances out into the open; he intends to avoid "making literature," and to put everything down as it comes to the pen, not searching for words. This, of course, is Roquentin's intention, not Sartre's; the latter is very self-consciously literary indeed.

From this point on, Sartre's hero is busy exorcising a devil. His basic trouble is something for which he has no pre-established vocabulary. It lies below the verbal level, and much of his effort is expended in bringing it up to where he can verbalize it. These recurrent attempts at verbalization, interspersed with descriptions of his affective states, form the core of the book.

By the time we have reached page thirty-four, Roquentin's disgust with existence, the *nausée* for which the book is named, is upon him. The first attack is brought on by sexual disappointment: the woman with whom he regularly goes to bed has missed their rendez-vous because of some errands in town. Subsequently, when the crises have become more habitual, it will take progressively less and less to push him over the edge of ordinary consciousness into his private slough of despond: a boresome conversation, the failure of someone to appear at an expected time, the sight of a decrepit or otherwise unfortunate individual, and finally anything at all that stimulates the senses (particularly visual) enough to renew his awareness of one small fact. The fact is small indeed — that he is alive. Let him become aware of his existence and almost nothing can bring him out of the state into which he quickly passes. Almost nothing — yet something always does, in the first attack something as simple as listening to a jazz record, *Some of These Days.*

The nature of the peculiar affective state itself seems to be an overwhelming awareness and sensitivity, and the ability to see the exterior world without the benefit of intervening preconceptions. For an illustration: we speak frequently of seeing things with special kind of eye — as, for instance, the "painter's eye," the "reporter's eye," the "dramatist's" or the "doctor's" or the "moralist's" or the "policeman's" "eye." By the phrase we admit that various individuals build up the habit of looking at the exterior world in ways characteristic of their personal pre-occupations. Let us call such a way a prejudice: they have, so to speak, habitual and probably salutary prejudices which affect their reception of stimuli. If there is anything in the way of psychological truth behind this metaphor at all, it must be extensible to all human beings, each of whom has built up his own prejudiced "eye." Now suppose that through some accident to his nervous system, one of us should momentarily shed these prejudices and see the exterior world not with a poet's or soldier's or iceman's eye, but with an eye *tout court*. Would he not report somewhat as Roquentin reports his sensations when standing, during a moment of such crisis, in a public park: "Existence had suddenly removed its veil and lost its usual character as an abstract category: it had become the dough out of which things are formed; this root had been kneaded up out of existence . . . or rather, the root, the garden fence, the bench, the rare grass of the lawn, had vanished; the diversity of things, the individuality of things was only an appearance, a varnish over them. The varnish had melted off and there remained masses, soft and disorderly, nude with a frightening and obscene nudity." This sounds a little as if the "buzzing, booming nothing" which psychologists tell us is the essence of a baby's consciousness has suddenly become about all that a perfectly adult and experienced mind can distinguish outside itself; for Roquentin there exists only himself and, exterior to himself, a sort of multi-morphous paste. Sartre's character, in other words, has contrived to have a particularly violent nightmare in the daytime, on his feet, and with his eyes open.

We had better drop this now, while we still can, and leave to the psychiatrist what is properly his.

2

Our business, as readers of his novel, is to examine the use Sartre makes of the remarkable instrument he has fashioned. What can he make of it as an artist?

Let us suppose—only for the purpose of seeing better what Sartre is doing—that Erskine Caldwell had something managed to see the characters of *Tobacco Road* as Roquentin, in the grip of his own clairvoyance, would see them. It is now impossible for Caldwell to use any of the "eyes" he has the habit of using: he may not see his people as figures in a particularly grotesque comedy, or as subjects for the reporter of the picturesque, or as objects of socially-conscious compassion: his three characteristic prejudices toward his material are out. No prejudice, as we understand the word, may come between him and the harelipped daughter, the dimwit son, the noseless bride and even old Jeeter himself. Now how—how indeed—would they look?

There is a page in *La Nausée* when Sartre makes Roquentin invite the humanity around him to look at itself. The world simply flies apart. Ordinary relationships between things break down. I paraphrase what is too long to quote. A man out walking sees coming toward him on the other side of the street a red rag, blown by the wind, which turns out to be a quarter of rotten meat, dust-spotted, dragging itself along the gutter and spasmodically spouting blood. A mother examines what seems to be a pimple on her child's cheek, sees the flesh swell, split, open up and a third eye appear. Others feel their clothes become living things. One man feels something scratching in his mouth and learns from the mirror that his tongue has become an enormous earwig, a part of himself which he has to tear out with his hands: "And he who has gone to sleep in his own good bed in the pleasant warmth of his own room, will awaken naked on the bluish earth, in a forest of rustling phalli, red and white and erected toward the sky like the smokestacks of Juxtebouville, with great culls half buried in the earth, hairy and bulbous, like onions. And the birds will flutter about the phalli and pick at them with their beaks and they will bleed. Sperm will run slowly and quietly from the wounds, sperm mixed with gluey, warm blood with little bubbles in it."

Enough of this. The literary end-product of Sartre-Roquentin's view of the exterior world is apparent: it eventuates here in the violent vision which we identify crudely as surrealist. Nothing in this passage is respendently new: the crawling, blood-spurting meat, the third eye, the live clothing, the earwig, are perfectly familiar in recent painting. The obscene forest with the flying figures was useful to Virgil and old stuff to Dante.

Working with words on paper instead of charcoal and paint, the technique consists of juxtaposing image-elements which are perfectly plausible to the imagination, but make the reason recoil because we know that the juxtaposition would be possible only if the world with which we are in contact were suddenly to disintegrate.

But what a difference between the mood of this and the sort of crazy playfulness which is so common to the surrealists. Part of the surrealist mood was of course pure snobbishness. This was the one revenge possible against the man of the nineteen-twenties who was master of all things because he could buy them. The artist could at least paint what he wanted to and then sell the painting, without enabling the rich man to purchase the understanding of the paint-on-canvas that he took home. This was perhaps the last phase in the long battle between the esthete and the bourgeois: intricate, wilful mystification. Now the technique of mystification here consists of hiding the intention of the artist. As a formula there is much to be said for it (so long as one does not apply it also to conduct, in which case it leads to the psychiatric ward), for if you paint a woman's torso with a crab in place of the umbilicus you may double your delight by telling the purchaser that you paint this way because you *feel* this way and then behaving as though he should be satisfied with this explanation. The reason that Sartre can use the vision-method of the surrealists without surrounding himself with an atmosphere of mystification is that he is not in the least hiding his intention, just as there is no mystification around Dante when he produces the violent metamorphosis of men and snakes. Such a thing is appropriate in hell—and what is appropriate in hell is appropriate in Sartre's world.

I have previously remarked that Roquentin lacks a vocabulary for bringing his trouble completely up to the verbal level. What he does instead, of course, is to resort to an imagery not unlike that of the symbolists in intention, since the aim of both is to evoke a mood. (The difference is in the mood evoked.) For the process of plausible-but-not-possible association of terms in a metaphor, illustrated above at the height of its power to shock, persists at a lower degree of tension through the book. I quote another simply to show how insidiously such metaphors can be slipped into the reader's consciousness: a sun which shines "with a reasonable and avaricious light, like the look one casts after a sleepless night over the decisions made in enthusiasm the day before." This is only one; a student of such things could find dozens.

Sartre is using them, it is hardly necessary to say, to undermine our confidence in what is conventionally called reality. It crumbles under Roquentin at nearly every step. I am not sure that the total symbolic effect does not amount to a mass murder of the race. Certainly for Roquentin, when under the sway of his nausea, certain common ideas about human-ity have to be radically revised. The philosopher, for whom I have said that I am not specifically writing, may see this as a new attack on the position of realism.

In the continuation of the particularly violent passage which has been quoted, Roquentin gives us the key to the readjustment. "Where then," he screams after the sufferers who have realized their plight, "where is your thinking reed, now?" I doubt that there is much profit in developing the association of the thinking reed with the rustling phalli of the passage, even though it should not go unobserved, but it is definitely necessary to keep in mind the general tenor of the thought of Pascal— Pascal not only sees the hope of man in the fact that while he is a reed, the feeblest thing in nature, he is a reed that thinks; he also points out that the human mind, that magnificent creation, can be rendered unserviceable by the buzzing of a fly. Man has thus a tenuous hold indeed on salvation. Roquentin would add that the feat of the fly is not at all stupendous. In the last of his life, Pascal lived with the hallucination of a great pit yawning beside him. Roquentin accepts the pit and rejects Pascal.

3

This is only one of an important series of rejections.

Most interestingly, Roquentin rejects as meaningless the central core of the teaching of André Gide. What happens to Roquentin may even be read as a specific and formal reply to Gide, although Gide's name is not mentioned. For Gide, as we most often think of him — he is many other things besides and this is not an effort to belittle him — is the apostle of self-culture through experience, of personal growth through exposure to the possibility of having things happen to you, of adventure in short. But Roquentin, who has been everywhere from London to Saigon until references to his past sound like a somewhat comic version of a Cook's advertisement, has come to the conclusion that experience does not exist except as a word. The lover of adventure in the story is a pitifully unattractive creature whom Roquentin to himself calls the *Autodidacte*, who is educating himself by reading his way through the library and after seven years has gotten through the alphabet as far as "L." He also composes maxims in a notebook and thinks that care in writing prose means avoiding inadvertent Alexandrines. This unfortunate would give his soul to have any adventure at all: "lose one's purse, miss a train, spend a night in jail." When he tries to buttonhole Roquentin on the subject, the latter sends him away delighted with a pocketful of postcard views from here and there, and the thought that travel is really-truly broadening. For Roquentin adventure is nothing but an attitude. "You used to kid yourself," he thinks, "with words. What you called adventure was the rattletrap of travel, love affairs with whores, street fights, dime-store stuff. . . ." Experience means nothing; something happens to you; for a time you remember the thing and then gradually you replace the thing by a word and after a while you have the word and nothing else. "My memories are like coins in the devil's purse; when you open it you find nothing but dead leaves." So much for Gide. The chance of growth through experience is in this case paltry indeed.

So also with history. At the beginning of the book Roquentin is still working on the life of an eighteenth-century adventurer named Rollebon, his own psychological antithesis. Rollebon, in spite of a physical ugliness as great as Roquentin's, had managed to contrive a life of constant action for himself. He had been greatly successful with beautiful and aristocratic women. The cold, practical, calculating wretch had passed through the best beds of France on his way eventually to conspiracy against the Czar and thence to virtual exile in Asia. On one occasion, when a priest had failed to bring a notorious freethinker to death-bed repentance, Rollebon won a bet from the priest by bringing the man to proper sentiments in two hours, not by Christian persuasion but simply, as he said, "by talking the fear of hell into him." He is so clearly Roquentin's opposite that for a while writing a book about Rollebon has been a delightful task, but now, as the biography is moving toward its end, the job has begun to pall. Rollebon strikes him less as a hero and more as a "vapid little liar." One of the reference points which permit us to measure the alteration in Roquentin's personality as the novel progresses is his increasing lack of stomach for Rollebon. He comes at length to the point of inability to imagine his man at all, has no confidence in his own data and conclusions, and abandons the study entirely. Experience and adventure have again turned out to be meaningless; the sense of the past is an illusion.

Much of the hope of the present is illusion also. There is no hope whatever of his being able to lose his loneliness by resorting to what he sees as the refuge of the bourgeois: the assumption of social responsibility. One afternoon he visits the local museum and contemplates at great length the collection of portraits which commemorate the builders of the municipality, the heads of powerful families, directors of flourishing businesses, partisans of success, prosperity and order. He knows their story, having studied the history of the town, and they offend him esthetically. What stuffed shirts! "I had gone the whole length of the gallery. Now I turned back. Farewell, beautiful lilies, delicate in your painted sanctuaries. Farewell, beautiful lilies, our pride, our reason for being. Farewell . . . you lice." And he is at the same time too honest to accept the Great Compromise. For him the bell-wether intellectuals of the bourgeoisie, symbolized for him in the portrait of a distinguished professor of medicine native to the place, are nothing but hypocrites: they have traded on a falsely acquired reputation as revolutionaries to win disgusted young men back to the ways of right thinking and of the established order. They are men like Renan, Melchior de Vogüé, Paul Desjardins, who have been tolerated by the bourgeoisie because nothing about them does anything but confirm the supremacy of the middle class.

But this does not mean that Roquentin places any hope in Revolution, whether of the Right or of the Left. There is no part of humanity which looks in any way lovable to him. Once the *Autodidacte*, having invited Roquentin to dinner, confides to Roquentin that he is a socialist and a humanitarian — he simply loves humanity. Immediately through Roquentin's head there runs a long list of humanitarian types: the middle-of-the-road "Radical," the Leftist, the Communist, the Catholic, the humanitarian who loves man as he is, the humanitarian who loves him as he ought to be, etc. When he tries to explain to the *Autodidacte* that such things are not for him, both of them are baffled, one because he can not comprehend how anyone can fail to feel such love and the other by the frustrating knowledge that his efforts to communicate his feelings can get absolutely nowhere. The total effect is to throw Roquentin into a particularly painful fit of his characteristic nausea.

Significantly, the *Autodidacte*, who personifies so much of what Roquentin rejects, comes to a sad end. Just before the finish of the book a schoolboy who has wandered into the library tempts humanity's lover into making a tentative homosexual gesture. For it he is beaten by the librarian and driven from the library in disgrace. With him the thirst for knowledge, desire for human betterment, respect for experience, and Gidian love of adventure which he incarnates, exit from the story.

One other of these rejections is especially significant because it helps identify Roquentin's peculiar state. "I began to laugh," says Roquentin, "because all of a sudden I thought of the redoubtable springtimes that are described in certain books, full of cracklings and gigantic buddings and explosive leafings-out. There were imbeciles who talked to you about the will to power and the struggle for life. . . . It's not posssible to see things under any such guise." Now the reference here is too pat not to be aimed at the work of Jean Giono, who, like Sartre, rejects much of modern life but, unlike him, takes refuge in a vision of nature — and of life in harmony with the ways of nature — compounded, as those who have read *Joy of Man's Desiring* already know, of Thoreau, Walt Whitman and Melville in about equal doses. Roquentin's words sound rather like a distant echo of Baudelaire's famous dismissal of nature with the declaration that he was incapable of bowing down before a lot of vegetables. I would not care to argue here for too close an identity of attitude because, among other reasons, Baudelaire reached his conclusion through self-contemplation, whereas Sartre seems to have reached his through contemplation of the world outside him, but the question is still worth asking: is not Roquentin's state of nausea very close to what Baudelaire meant by *ennui?* At least, Sartre does not, among all these rejections, specifically reject Baudelaire.

4

Meanwhile, what makes this a novel?

The fable — Roquentin's story — follows a mind as it progresses in the discovery of the nature of reality, which is another way of saying progress through constantly intensified affective states. On the plane of personal relationships, it is the account of the narrator's contacts in his recurrent meetings with Rollebon, the *Autodidacte*, the mistress pro tempore, the restaurant proprietor and other minor characters, up to the point where he is ready to put them all out of his life. It is also the story of a man who is moving toward a reunion with the woman he loved once and may possibly love again, who realizes that in the interim he is undergoing psychic experiences which must certainly change his character, and who expects some sort of conclusively revealing emotional experience at the meeting. The interview between this man and this woman will thus stand as the dramatic climax of the piece.

We know of Anny mainly that at one point in his life her stronger personality has thoroughly dominated Roquentin. He remembers her as a creature with the imperious ways and strange whims of a professional actress (which she is), such, for instance, as her insistence on decorating her hotel room even when she is determined to stay there no longer than the night. She has written him that she will be in his town on such and such a date, and expects him to come to her. All that Roquentin may expect and hope of the meeting is never clear; what the reader hopes for is an insight into Roquentin's character when the new contact with Anny brings home the difference between Roquentin then and Roquentin now.

But when Roquentin walks into Anny's room, he finds that she has sent for him because she needs him for this same psychological reason: she has changed and wants him near her for a moment because she is sure that he has remained unaltered. Her body is heavier; she no longer sets up her personal backdrop of room decorations; she tells him that she has given up the little "tragedies" in which she had once delighted and in which she had assigned him a role, and which had always resulted in the assertion of her will over his. She expects never to love again: she is, at present, being kept by an Englishman who means nothing to her and need mean nothing to Roquentin. The latter senses in the atmosphere around her some sort of despair and decides, somewhat against his will, not to tell her about the changes in himself. But she explains to him, as well as she can, what has happened: she has lost the feeling, around which her life had apparently been built, that there are times in one's life which are especially poignant and meaningful and heightened and emotionally tense—what she calls *moments parfaits* and *situations privilégiées*. The professional *actrice* has learned that drama does not exist. The artist has learned that there is nothing in her art! Shortly she sends Roquentin away, the final parting, and her face as he leaves is the face of an old woman.

"The past is dead," Roquentin thinks, "Rollebon is dead. Anny turned up only to take away my last hope. I am alone in this white, garden-bordered street. Alone and free." His life is over, although he knows that he will survive himself and go on living out of sheer habit. Suicide is impossible, since it is as meaningless as life. For some perverse reason he begins to cheer up at the thought of leaving this place, and this chapter, forever.

The cheerful mood does not last, because the scene in which the *Autodidacte's* homosexuality is revealed intervenes and throws Roquentin back in the mood of disgust. He has been cheered by the thought of leaving this town and going to Paris. Now he discovers that the town has already deserted *him*; the lady from the cafe, for example, is sleeping with someone else already. He then suddenly realizes that he no more wants to go than he does to stay. The feeling of loneliness *and* freedom has departed. He wants to do nothing whatsoever. "I know very well that I want to do nothing; to do something is to create existence. There is certainly enough existence without my doing that." And the book would leave him in that state if he did not wander into his café and listen once more to the record of *Some of These Days*. As before, the music lightens his mood. He thinks that perhaps, after all, if someone could create something like that tin-pan alley song, his life might not be unbearable. And we leave him with that thought.

Judging it first by the main impression which remains after the first reading, *La Nausée* is first of all a book in dispraise of life, after the manner of Céline. But it lacks Céline's essential bitterness and the anthropomorphism which gains expression through Céline's obscenity, for existence can be obscene only if man stays at the center of it. A large part of Roquentin's trouble is that existence has no place for him. "And here is the meaning of his existence: it is the consciousness of being *de trop*, in excess." He also feels a certain compassion occasionally, whereas Céline's people are swimming in misanthropy. What he does have most patently in common with Céline is violence.

I have quoted in this paper the page of *La Nausée* at which Sartre's violence reaches its climax; it will be noted that the violence is symbolic. Sartre's character comes to a moment when nothing will quiet him but a vision which simply tears apart the world men live in, a vision which condemns men either to suicide or insanity. I think that its impact on the reader is greatly impaired by its being so palpably literary—by the obviousness of the sources of the elements in the formula—but this is a comment on its success, not its nature or its intention. Sartre's character expresses himself, when the tension is greatest, through, I repeat, an act of violence.

It is possible to characterize so many novels in our time by this phrase that I have a growing conviction that we have here the central trait which marks most of the major novelists who wrote between the two world wars. I have named Céline and the connection is obvious; the statement fits Malraux equally well. The same judgment can be made of the four Americans named in the introduction to this paper. Within reason, of course: Sartre's violence is cerebral; it does not produce the rapid tale eventuating in a scene of physical brutality which so often appears in American fiction. But the same immediacy of sensation is immediately present in the Frenchman and in the Americans and it is equally true of both that the immediate sensation outruns the intelligence of the character; his intelligence is not equal to it—the main difference being that in Sartre's character there is more intelligence and the flood of sensation has a harder job. I do not feel particularly extravagant in suggesting that there is legitimate kinship at this point between *La Nausée* and *Death in the Afternoon*.

It would be possible to enmesh in the same web of implications this insistence on the immediacy of sensations with the Sartre-Roquentin attitude toward the past and the value of experience and adventure. Roquentin denies the value of adventure only when it has moved into the past tense. With adventure as a present source of sensation he has no quarrel. The point of focus in the novel is the dividing line where the things of the future become present. Such material as Roquentin gives the reader about the past, for instance his relationship with Anny, is what is necessary to understanding the advancing-present and is presented not as a narration of the events as they happened but as a lump of the past which is again impinging on Roquentin's consciousness in the present; they have the indefiniteness and distortion which clearly establishes this value. I mention this aspect of the novel here although it is out of place—since it leads fatally to a comparison of the usage of time by most of the interesting novelists who have written since 1910 or maybe since Flaubert—simply because it identifies the interest which Sartre displayed, at the time he was writing *La Nausée* in William Faulkner. What fascinated him with

Faulkner was precisely Faulkner's technique of mixing past and present through his familiar unannounced psychological flashbacks until for the reader the past exists only as an aspect of the present consciousness.

What really baffles me here is a rhetorical problem. If I had already published on the American novelists in question the proper basic discussion, which would have emphasized the appropriate aspects of their work, a referential technique would permit of explicitly detailed illustration. But otherwise it is impossible to put the matter of a book within the limits of an article. I am thus forced to take recourse to the expedient of inviting the reader to accept certain propositions as subjects for his own further meditation.

Thus, in place of a conclusion, here is an enumeration.

Do not the American and French novelists have in common the following characteristics? That the exterior world they see is, in one way or another, inadequate to the expectations of the human mind and thus one essentially of horror. That the immediacy of this vision is such that the intelligence of the characters is overwhelmed by it. That because of this immediacy the time plan of the novels tends always to emphasize the present. That this emphasis of the present tends to replace the older, time's-revenges sort of novel by one which is not lyrical-nostalgic in final effect but dramatic. That this naturally leads to an esthetic of the novel which places an increased value on success in effecting an impact on the reader, that is, on producing shock. That this in turn explains why so often the formula of a novel involves placing a character in a situation from which he may emerge only through one or more acts of some kind of violence. That this violence is particularly in harmony with the mood of violence which swept the world between the two world wars.

All this may make it seem that we have moved a long way from Jean-Paul Sartre, but I would argue that a consideration of Sartre makes these other considerations inevitable.

Sartre's *Nausea*: A Modern Classic Revisited   John Fletcher*

A man is always a story-teller; he lives surrounded by his own stories as well as those of others. Through them he sees everything that happens to him; and he tries to live his life as if he were fictionalizing it. (Sartre)

I

Nausea by Jean-Paul Sartre—whose seventieth birthday is, perhaps rather astonishingly, behind us—is a remarkably "significant" novel, even

*From *Critical Quarterly* 18, no. 1 (Spring 1976): 11–20. Reprinted with permission.

by French standards. So many tendencies meet at the nexus it provides, by virtue not only of its intrinsic nature, but also of the date of its publication: 1938. Ihab Hassan, writing in *New Literary History* (Autumn 1971), considers it a harbinger of postmodernism, a work (like Beckett's *Murphy*, which appeared the same year) that early on foreshadows — by over a decade, indeed — anarchic developments in literature and the arts characteristic of the post–Korean War era. "If we can arbitrarily state that literary Modernism includes certain works between Jarry's *Ubu Roi* (1896) and Joyce's *Finnegans Wake* (1939), where" — Hassan asks rhetorically — "will we arbitrarily say that Postmodernism begins? A year earlier than the *Wake*? With Sartre's *La Nausée* (1938) or Beckett's *Murphy* (1938)?"

II

To students and teachers within the necessarily narrower perspective of French literature, *Nausea* is the classic statement of proto-existentialism. The French novel in the thirties was torn between metaphysical despair and political commitment; the problem was to be resolved for most writers, of course, only in the frank camaraderie of the Resistance movement. All the intellectuals of the period betrayed something of the idealism of that eccentric of genius, Simone Weil, who gave up the relative comfort and security of a teaching post to take a job as an ordinary wage-earner on the factory-floor, martyring herself like any medieval nun; but, true to her vocation as an intellectual, she emerged from the harrowing experience with a book about it. There is something comic in the scourge the French intellectual creates to flagellate himself with, and it was an acute understanding of and sympathy with this often grotesque penchant that led Jean-Paul Sartre to write the novel which in political terms marks the end of the thirties in France. Its author's neo-Heideggerian philosophy, obscure (and even inconsistent) though much of it undoubtedly is, does render possible a radically new approach to literature and to man. That is why *Nausea* was such an original and important book, when it appeared at the end of the 1930s. It sounded a completely new note, which has been foreshadowed only by Céline's *Journey to the End of the Night* (1932). It's not without significance that Sartre quotes Céline in the epigraph to his novel: Céline, like Sartre, wrote fiction from a painfully systematic subjective point of view, very different from both the detached elegance of Gide and the impassioned but aloof humanity of Malraux.

In view of this, it is a matter for some surprise that Sartre casts his novel in one of the most hackneyed of forms, that of a diary which the "publisher" claims to have found by accident and which he prints without alteration, a device much used, of course, in the eighteenth century, either to pass the fiction off as a true story, or to forestall the accusation that the matter was too licentious for publication, or both. Sartre adopts a very similar technique — a "publisher's note" at the beginning claims that the diary was found among Roquentin's papers and is published as it stands. It's not clear why Sartre did this: he could hardly have thought it would make the story more real. The novel carries its own conviction which has nothing to do with our believing or not believing in the real existence of Antoine Roquentin; modern fiction has no place for such subterfuges. After this curious beginning the novel continues in the form of Roquentin's diary: we learn all about his everyday existence at Bouville; this is based on Sartre's own experience of life at the big seaport of Le Havre, where he taught before the war. The cold drabness of a provincial French town is vividly conveyed, and the people Roquentin associates with, like Françoise the café-proprietress or the Autodidact, are deftly drawn.

The novel of course is much more than the chronicle of a bachelor's life in a provincial town, where he is working on the biography of an eighteenth century aristocrat: it describes how a man — an ordinary enough man — comes suddenly to doubt not only the purpose of his existence, but also its very reality. He starts to question the consistency and solidity of material things, and to lose all bearings in the world. His diary (and that is no doubt the reason for the adoption of the diary form) is his only means of "keeping tabs" on the world, of not going mad. And it is through his diary — through the *literary* act — that he achieves salvation, the salvation of realizing that he must achieve something, even something quite modest like the blues singer's song (Sophie Tucker's *Some of These Days*), something quite different from the biography of an aristocrat, something which, as he puts it, "would have to be beautiful and hard as steel and make people ashamed of their existence" (Penguin Modern Classics ed., p. 252). It would enable him, as he says, to accept himself, at least retrospectively, and so would confirm his self-discovery. It is an intriguing fact that this self-analysis owes relatively little to the philosophy Sartre was elaborating at the time. It's true that we see "bastards" in the portrait gallery, and see a victim of "bad faith" in the Autodidact, but these elements, like Monsieur de Rollebon's atheism, are relatively peripheral and incidental. The central nub of the plot — how a man suffered a kind of metaphysical concussion and, slowly coming round, then saw life in a new light, is a profoundly original theme which (like Beckett's somewhat similar story, *Molloy*), has its roots more in the unconscious mind than in any consciously elaborated system of ethics. As such it makes *Nausea* the least didactic and most satisfying of Sartre's novels; the unfinished tetralogy *Roads to Freedom*, which started to appear after the war, is a pale achievement when set beside the anarchic, youthful vigor of this novel.

I do not myself find it very helpful or instinctive, in fact, to read *Nausea* as an existentialist work. It naturally bears a relation to Sartre's thinking as adumbrated in other books — just as Camus's *The Outsider* is not unconnected with *The Myth of Sisyphus* — but its roots run deep into his psyche. Simone de Beauvoir tells us, for instance, that he suffered for a time from a particularly unpleasant hallucination; he felt, she says, that he was being followed along the street by lobsters or crabs. This helps account for the fact that crustacea occur at least half a dozen times in *Nausea* and express — like the beetle image which is so disturbing and effective in Kafka's story *Metamorphosis* — feelings of revulsion and dread. In this passage Roquentin is running around the docks, in "absolute panic," until he stops at the water's edge and knows "a moment's respite." It is short-lived; he is suddenly seized with terror at the thought of what might lie under the calm surface of the black water: "A monster? A huge carapace, half embedded in the mud? A dozen pairs of claws slowly furrow the slime. The monster raises itself a little, every now and then. At the bottom of the water. I went nearer, watching for an eddy, a tiny ripple. The cork remained motionless among the black spots" (p. 116). Similarly, Roquentin remembers that when he was eight an old man in the Luxembourg Gardens terrified him because he was sure "he was shaping crab-like or lobster-like thoughts in his head" (p. 20). Just as some people are afraid of spiders — that is, project their psychological phobias on to these otherwise harmless insects — so Roquentin, and Sartre behind him, is terrorized by crustacea. An equally intense reaction — this time of disgust and revulsion — is contained in the sordid phallic imagery which comes naturally to Roquentin's mind. To express his overpowering sense of something fundamental having changed, the narrator, like Kafka, uses the symbol of emergence from sleep. On awakening "one fine morning" Joseph K. — we learn from the first sentence of *The Trial* — finds that he has been arrested; likewise, "Gregor Samsa awoke one morning from uneasy dreams" to find himself "transformed in his bed into a gigantic insect" (*Metamorphosis*, opening words). Roquentin's sense that the habitual names will no longer fit familiar things (the kind of epistemological concussion which Beckett's *Watt* also experiences) is expressed however in imagery even more violently sexual than either Beckett or Kafka would have considered appropriate:

> somebody who has gone to sleep in his comfortable bed, in his quiet, warm bedroom, will wake up naked on a bluish patch of earth, in a forest of rustling pricks, rising all red and white towards the sky like the chimneys of Jouxtebouville, with big testicles half way out of the ground, hairy and bulbous, like onions. And birds will flutter around these pricks and peck at them with their beaks and make them bleed. Sperm will flow slowly, gently, from these wounds, sperm mingled with blood, warm and vitreous with little bubbles. (p. 226)

A similar phallic image is employed to express Roquentin's disgust at the Autodidact's attempted seduction of the schoolboy in the Public Library: his finger is compared to "a brown hairy object" approaching, with "all the grossness *disgrace* of a male organ," the boy's hand, which lies "on its back, relaxed, soft, and sensual," looking "indolently nude," like "a woman sunning herself on the beach" (p. 234). Such imagery—arising evidently out of adolescent masturbation fantasies—contrasts oddly with the matter-of-fact way Roquentin describes his perfunctory, medicinal embraces with the café proprietress (for example in "I toyed absent-mindedly with her sex under the bedclothes," p. 88). The guilt feelings which he is careful to exclude from his blasé account of their "love on an *au pair* basis" (p. 17) are displaced on to other areas: hence Roquentin's pre-occupation with the perversions of various kinds, exhibitionism (p. 117), the rape and murder of little girls (p. 146), and the Autodidact's pederasty. It's perhaps not immediately clear to the reader of *Nausea* that such displacement is occurring in the novel. Similarly the reader of Kafka's *Metamorphosis* may not perceive at once the subtle intertwining of incest fantasies, Gregor's erotic feelings for his mother, and his consequent fear of his father who, significantly, fatally wounds him with an apple) with masochistic longings revealed by the frequent allusions to a "Venus in furs" figure which Gregor has cut out of an illustrated magazine; all this points to a punishment craving closely linked, as Gilles Deleuze has shown this phenomenon usually to be, with the Oedipus complex.

III

The "existentialist" reading of *Nausea* doesn't take us very far, therefore, in spite of some incidental remarks (such as "there's nothing, nothing, absolutely no reason for existing," p. 162), which might almost have been planted in the novel to mislead us into interpreting it exclusively on that level. There are, indeed, alternative ways of reading the book: as a unique moment in the development of the novel, for example; not only, as I have suggested, as a throw-back to the eighteenth century novel, but as a foreshadowing of contemporary formal experimentalism (the extensive use of what has come to be called "intertextuality" in a case in point, and one to which I shall return), and as a classic of late modernism in its featuring of jazz, its "portrait of the artist as alienated soul" motif, and its exaltation of salvation through art. It is remarkable, in fact, for so many currents in the history of fiction to meet in one work, particularly a first novel, a book which betrays all the strengths and weaknesses of the type: a naivety of manner, conventional approach to characterisation and form (as if Joyce, Proust and Virginia Woolf had not already altered all that), together with an intensity of vision, a success in fixing a mood which rightly makes it a "modern classic," and a considerable if curiously uneven achievement; a work, moreover, totally representative of its period, as is now, nearly forty years after, clearly apparent in retrospect. The contemporary cultural analogues are not hard to find: I have mentioned Céline already; and the attitude to women and love projected in Drieu La Rochelle's novels, particularly *Le Feu follet*, lies close behind the cynical romanticism (if that is not a contradiction in terms) of the very conventional story of Anny in *Nausea*; likewise the despair of utterances like "I haven't a single reason for living left" (p. 223) is equally reminiscent of Drieu's tone. Moreover even the neo-expressionist landscape of "Bouville" is characteristic of attitudes common throughout the period:

> Nothing is alive; the wind whistles, straight lines flee into the darkness. The boulevard Noir doesn't have the indecent look of bourgeois streets, which try to charm the passers-by: it is simply a reverse side. The reverse side of the rue Jeanne-Berthe-Coeuroy, of the avenue Galvani. In the vicinity of the station, the people of Bouville still look after it a little: they clean it now and then because of the travellers. But, immediately afterwards, they abandon it and it rushes straight on, in total darkness, finally bumping into the avenue Galvani. The town has forgotten it. Sometimes a big mud-coloured lorry thunders across it at top speed. Nobody even commits any murders on it, for want of murderers and victims. The boulevard Noir is inhuman. Like a mineral. Like a triangle. We are lucky to have a boulevard like that at Bouville. Usually you find them only in capitals — in Berlin near Neukölln or again towards Friedrichshain; in London behind Greenwich. Straight, dirty corridors, with a howling draught and wide, treeless pavements. They are nearly always on the outskirts in those strange districts where cities are manufactured, near goods stations, tram depots, slaughter-houses, and gasometers. Two days after a downpour, when the whole city is moist in the sunshine and radiates damp heat, they are still cold, they keep their mud and puddles. They even have puddles of water which never dry up, except one month in the year, August. (p. 43)

The oppressive, exclusively urban quality of those "straight, dirty corridors," threatened with invasion by "the Vegetation . . . crawl(ing) for mile after mile towards the towns . . . waiting . . . to clamber over the stones . . . grip them, search them, burst them open with its long black pincers" (pp. 221–2), is a curious amalgam of Friedrich Murnau and Marcel Carné. Indeed the release of films like Carné's *Quai des Brumes* and *Le Jour se lève* was almost exactly contemporary with the publication of *Nausea*; they similarly treat of the squalid sufferings of lower-class people, such as Lucie the charwoman of *Nausea* and her tubercular, alcoholic husband. And the attitude to a French provincial Sunday as something painfully to be endured is found not only in this novel but also in Camus's *The Outsider* which followed it four years later.

IV

In this diary-record of an alienated imagination the character of the diarist is naturally crucial. Roquentin is a *rentier*, a man for whom "there is neither Monday nor Sunday" (p. 82); a man moreover who has at his disposal an annual income of 14,400 francs (p. 245). This rentier is a scholar, a man who revels in the delights of literary composition and historical detection: "I had worked all day long in the Mazarine; I had just realized, from his correspondence of 1789–90, the masterly way in which he duped Nerciat. It was dark. I was going down the avenue du Maine, and on the corner of the rue de la Gâité I bought some chestnuts. How happy I was! I laughed all by myself at the thought of the face Nerciat must have made when he came back from Germany" (p. 25). Not unexpectedly this rentier-scholar is an introvert. He rarely talk or smiles, and even when he does smile, it is always for a reason: "I smile at him. I should like this smile to reveal to him all that he is trying to conceal from himself" (p. 104). And like those who stare a great deal, he is afraid of being caught staring. On one level, therefore, the novel is a brilliant evocation of an introvert's breakdown. He gazes at himself in the mirror:

> The eyes in particular, seen at such close quarters, are horrible. They are glassy, soft, blind, and red-rimmed; anyone would think they were fish-scales. I lean my whole weight on the porcelain edge, I push my face forward until it touches the mirror. The eyes, the nose, the mouth disappear: nothing human is left. Brown wrinkles on each side of the feverish swelling of the lips, crevices, mole hills. A silky white down runs along the wide slopes of the cheeks, two hairs protrude from the nostrils: it's a geological relief map. And, in spite of everything, this lunar world is familiar to me. I can't say that I *recognize* the details. But the whole thing gives me the impression of something seen before which numbs me. (p. 31).

It is characteristic of Roquentin's breakdown that frenzied, even hysterical prose alternates with temporary calm. The impassioned entry for a Monday, for instance, is followed by this laconic entry for Tuesday: "Nothing. Existed" (p. 149). Roquentin's crisis — which reaches its climax in the incident of the chestnut tree root — is a kind of Laingian collapse, a secular dark night of the soul, resulting in a form of health, certainly a radical rediscovery of the self. One is therefore not surprised to find that Roquentin's account, though alert and sharp, is oddly humourless. This is because he is given to satirical comments of the kind: "you get the impression that their normal condition is silence and that speech is a slight fever which attacks them now and then" (p. 76), or: "when his establish-ment empties, his head empties too" (p. 16). The whole episode of the Autodidact, at least until the explosion in the Public Library, is strongly satirical. Though we are offered wit of a kind, therefore, we find strangely little humour; perhaps because there is not sufficient distance between Roquentin and his creator, certainly less than between Beckett and his Murphy. It could be argued — although I would not wish to do so — that there is a hint of distancing at the very end of the novel; the narrator's gesture towards writing a novel is put in doubt by the evident fact that the novel was never written, thus undercutting the images of rebirth in the very last paragraph (Hotel *Printania*, *damp* wood, *rain* over Bouville). But if this is satire by the author at the narrator's expense, the motion is so velleitary as to be virtually imperceptible. It is thus difficult to avoid the conclusion that *Nausea* is a self-indulgent book. The curiously negative politics of the work—politics Sartre was later to repudiate of course—bear this out. Like young rebels of a later period. Roquentin does not shrink from theft (he tells us he stole letters from archives in Moscow). His resentment against the self-assured figures of the nineteenth-century city is unlimited, but he also dislikes the Left, Communist and Catholic human-ists alike. His iconoclasm embraces both Guehenno and Barrès, the liberal as much as the reactionary.

V

It follows from this that the diary which the novel offers us is a narcissistic document, stressing—as Anny does—the importance of its "privileged moments." Of course, Roquentin's journal is a diary in a rather special sense: really an address to a silent reader; Roquentin goes to some pains to explain his rather eccentric interest in garbage (p. 21), or he plays with—and teases—his hearer; for instance, he announces (on p. 30) that Rollebon bores him, but the reader isn't bored, on the contrary—these snippets in the book are like lumps of date in a piece of tea-time cake, the pleasant sweetness we all wait for, as Anny turns the page in search of the pictures in her copy of Michelet's *History of France*. Like the Michelet illustrations the tasty morsels about Rollebon have little "connection with the text on the adjoining pages" (p. 209). Roquentin doesn't hesitate to quote the most hackeyed stories ostensibly connected with Rollebon, such as his conversion *in extremis* of the moribund. This is an amusing if much-travelled anecdote, and one feels that Sartre's only justification for including it was that he enjoyed it as such.

The diary is, in fact, something of a sham. The editorial notes which grace the first few pages are extraodinarily naive: there is no need for the editors to pretend to any doubt that the undated sheet precedes the start of the diary proper, since there is clear internal evidence that this is the case—not least that on 30 January Roquentin talks about handling a pebble "the other day" (p. 22); the pebble is referred to in the undated sheet (p. 10). To clinch the matter, we have only to note that Roquentin talks about a "false alarm" on 29 January (p. 13), clearly referring to the "disgust" he felt on the seashore when he tried to play ducks and drakes alongside the children (pp. 10–11).

Roquentin narrates most episodes in the present tense, but it is clear that this is a kind of dramatic present, since he often "writes up" incidents some hours after they occur: he uses the present tense in as selfconsciously rhetorical a fashion as Meursault uses the past indefinite.[1] Some of his entries are long—almost short stories in their own right—while some are very brief, taking up a single line. There is evidence that the diary-form breaks down towards the end in any case, as if Sartre were losing interest in this artificial form of narrative: it was certainly convenient for

Roquentin's "editors" that his manuscript ended on the impressive note about rain on Bouville, and not, as it might well have done, in mid-sentence. In fact, the whole book is a highly-wrought artifact. Sartre is particularly adept at ironic counterpoint, for instance in confronting the "official" portrait of Blevigne with the unofficial one published in a satirical newspaper (pp. 134–5). The most extended example of this is, of course, the quotation from Balzac's *Eugénie Grandet*. This "intertext" serves many purposes. It subtly reminds us that Roquentin, like Eugénie, pins his hopes on the return of a long-lost lover. It also constitutes, in an impoverished world seemingly cut off from its cultural past, a reference to a literary tradition of stable values. Moreover, in striking an archaic note, it comments ironically on the social situation observed by the narrator in the restaurant where he is reading the book; even when he has left the restaurant, there is a kind of prolongation of the Grandet family situation, a sort of reflection-echo, in the three people he observes leaving for their Sunday walk: "I walked along the quiet rue Bressan. The sun had scattered the clouds and it was fine. A family had just come out of a villa called 'The Wave.' The daughter was buttoning her gloves out on the pavement. She could have been about thirty. The mother, planted on the first of the flight of steps, was looking straight ahead with an assured expression, and breathing hard. Of the father I could see only the huge back. Bent over the keyhole, he was locking the door. The house would remain dark and empty until they got back" (p. 77). There are other literary and sub-literary quotations in the text: a brand of cigarettes is known as "Salammbô," for instance, and the Vicar of Wakefield is possibly being referred to obliquely in the person of Dr. Wakefield (p. 129). At the sub-literary level, there are characteristically hyperbolic quotations from the local newspaper, which serve to emphasise the traditional quality of provincial life reflected in the novel. Although all of this looks forward to the manner of Claude Simon and other contemporary novelists, we should not confuse the two; Simon's recent works are almost collages, built up of a number of heterogeneous "intertexts" ranging from cigar labels to the transcript of the proceedings of a Writers' Congress. Although *Nausea* points in this direction, it is far from being a collage novel itself. It operates by more traditional methods: by symbolism, for instance (the name of the "rue des Mutilés" p. 10, hints that Roquentin is mutilated psychologically); by oxymoron ("I am afraid of towns. But you mustn't leave them," p. 221); and by metaphor, such as the curious instance of Roquentin's feeling "pregnant" with Rollebon:

> A little earlier he was there, inside me, quiet and warm, and now and then I could feel him stirring. He was quite alive, more alive to me than the Autodidact or the manageress of the Rendez-vous des Cheminots. Admittedly he had his whims, he could stay for several days without giving any sign of life; but often, on mysteriously fine days, like the man in a weather-box, he would put his nose out and I would catch sight of

his pale face and his blue cheeks. And even when he didn't show up himself, he weighed heavily on my heart and I felt full up. (p. 140)

This figurative patterning affects even the nausea which comes and goes. Roquentin feels no disgust at the idea of the sweaty American writing the jazz tune in the torrid heat of a New York summer, whereas there is something almost gothic about this image inspired by the thought of a red rag blown by the wind: "When the rag gets close to him, he will see that it is a quarter of rotten meat, covered with dust, crawling and hopping along, a piece of tortured flesh rolling in the gutters and spasmodically shooting out jets of blood" (p. 226). The truth is that Roquentin is attempting to fictionalize his own experience. He is "as happy as the hero of a novel" (p. 82), and yet warns himself about the danger of succumbing to the sublime, to "literature" (p. 85); there is something unintentionally comic about his thus reminding himself of his distrust of literature while enjoying the feeling of being a fictional character. Gradually, of course, the idea grows in his mind that he should himself write a novel. He begins by thinking that he would do better to use his accumulated material on Rollebon in fictional form, but at the very end he decides against this, and contemplates "another kind of book . . . the sort of story . . . which could never happen, an adventure" (p. 252). Such literary aspirations are ironic in the light of the fact that Sartre was later to lose all faith in writing fiction at all.

VI

Nausea is thus a curiously neo-symbolist novel, harking back to the *fin-de-siècle* belief that language aspires to the condition of music. It is, at the same time, a surrealist work, in which the surrealism is not fully integrated, as in this strange quotation: "Somebody else will feel something scratching inside his mouth. And he will go to a mirror, open his mouth: and his tongue will have become a huge living centipede, rubbing its legs together and scraping his palate. He will try to spit it out, but the centipede will be part of himself and he will have to tear it out with his hands" (p. 226). One thinks immediately of Kafka's *Metamorphosis*. But in that great story, the beetle image is fully integrated in the myth: it is a dream that is not a dream, a nightmare conducted with remorseless logic. *Nausea* is a more transcendental work, almost neo-platonic in the sense in which A. E. Dyson uses the term in his essay on *The Trial*: "Man moves in the world as an alienated being, cut off from his true life, yet as much the agent of his catastrophe as its victim" (*Between Two Worlds*, London 1972, p. 131). But Kafka — for whom man was a "suicidal notion forming in God's mind" — is an altogether more astringent author than Sartre. In his absurd universe man is blindly punished, the rigour of that necessity contrasting cruelly with the grotesque contingency of the world. His universe is one "where no assumption is safe, no technique works, no person can be trusted, no development can be 'placed' or understood" (Dyson, p. 120). It is for this reason that the first sentences of his stories — such as "It was late in the evening when K. arrived. The village was deep in snow. The Castle hill was hidden, veiled in mist and darkness, nor was there even a glimmer of light to show that a castle was there" — are the clearest statements the reader is ever to be offered. Sartre's terrors are limited by the fact that the real world is preserved: a chestnut-tree root writhes in a park in a provincial town in northern France. For all *Nausea's* aesthetic gothicism, therefore, it does not take us beyond the realm of the familiar; and Sartre's exploration of Roquentin's dilemma seems disturbingly tainted with "bad faith," a self-indulgent fantasy, especially when compared with the bleakness of Kafka's demonstration of the collapse into comic horror of Gregor Samsa's universe of cosy flats and easy jobs.

Notes

1. See my previous essay "Meursault's Rhetoric," *CQ* xiii, 2 (Summer 1971), 125–135.

The Ending of Sartre's *La Nausée*   Terry Keefe*

Reviewing Sartre's *La Nausée* in 1938, both Camus[1] and Nizan[2] found in its ending the hope of a solution to the problems of contingency raised in the book. Only Camus, however, went on to note ["a somewhat derisory disproportion between this hope and the revolt which has produced it"], and in fact, since 1938, few sequences in the whole of Sartre's fiction can have given rise to such widely divergent comments and such manifestly incompatible interpretations as the final few pages of his first novel. While Iris Murdoch claims that Sartre is "patently uninterested in the aesthetic solution,"[3] G. J. Prince argues that the ending ["admirably condenses . . . the atmosphere of the work"].[4] Susanne Lilar believes that the end ["gives its meaning to the work"], that Roquentin ["at the height of his ascesis reaches hope and even joy and love"],[5] and Sydney Mendel that "the last pages of *Nausea* foreshadow the main lines of Sartre's future development."[6] But Anthony Manser talks of Sartre's irony and considers the end to be based upon "a train of thought that is clearly intended to be fallacious as an argument."[7] Robert Champigny,[8] and George Bauer[9] insist that Roquentin did not go on to write any novel: Hazel Barnes[10] and Georges Raillard[11] hold not only that he did, but that *La Nausée* is that novel. While A. D. Nuttall[12] and Philip Thody[13] are convinced that this

*From *Forum for Modern Language Studies*, no. 12 (1976): 217–35. Reprinted with permission.

cannot possibly be the case, Geneviève Idt,[14] among others, seems to think that we cannot know for sure. And so on. . . .

I believe that here, as so often, a particularly close and careful reading of the text itself, with only very restrained use of external evidence, can take us much further than one might think towards the elimination of some of the contending views, thereby highlighting the importance of those questions that are less easily resolved, as well as enabling us to see the latter more clearly and tackle them with rather greater confidence. I should like, therefore, to clear the ground a little by criticising certain of the opinions that have been advanced, and, slightly more constructively, to draw attention to some features of the problem that have received either less attention than they deserve, or none at all.

Although, naturally, many of the issues involved radiate out into the book as a whole and especially into the preceding sections of the last entry in the diary, we should understand by the "ending" the last three pages or so of the book, from the point where Roquentin first begins to think about the man who composed the song, *Some of These Days*, to consider seriously the possibility of doing something comparable himself, and (in the final three paragraphs of the book) of writing a novel. Once the terms of reference are clear, the first question that we might wish to ask is whether Sartre "took, the ending of *La Nausée* seriously." The question is considerably less simple than it appears, but since the idea of Sartre not taking *any* of the book seriously is an obvious absurdity, we may assume that intially we are looking for reasons for singling out the ending (perhaps together with any general strand in the book to which it attaches) as something that he looked upon with particular detachment or indifference.

Some evidence for this view might exist if the ending stuck out like a sore thumb in the text and was radically discontinuous with the rest of the story. But it does not, and is not. It is certainly true, as has been pointed out, that the so-called aesthetic solution is "merely sketched in," and this is a fact to which we shall have to devote much of our attention. The ending as it stands, however, whilst undoubtedly raising explicitly for the first time matters hitherto scarcely touched upon in the book, is by no means ill-prepared. Establishing all of its connections with other aspects of the story would entail an examination of the whole book, but it is quite sufficient here to mention two particularly important links. Not only are we accustomed to the idea of Roquentin as a writer, since we are reading his diary, but there is also the question of his (eventually abandoned) biography of the Marquis de Rollebon. In connection with this latter work (which constitutes his major, or only, project during the first half of *La Nausée*), Roquentin twice indicates that he is coming around to the view that it needs to be a work of the imagination, that he would do better to write a novel based on Rollebon's life (p. 27 and p. 80).[15] Hence the possibility that he entertains at the end has already briefly been broached in relation to his historical research. Secondly, a parallel is quite unmistakably drawn between any novel that Roquentin might write and the popular song, *Some of These Days*, a recording of which he listens to many times in the book, and the significance of which he discusses in a number of separate sequences, including the one immediately preceding the ending proper. The song itself first appears early on in the book (p. 35) and very soon comes to stand for one of the two poles in the crucial philosophical distinction that underlies *La Nausée*: that is, for Being as opposed to existence, for necessity as opposed to contingency, for order and form as opposed to chaos, for structured as opposed to unstructured time. The ending of *La Nausée* is deliberately shown to be a certain kind of development of the theme of this philosophical contrast, and even the particular development has been foreshadowed in Roquentin's discussion with Anny:

> [I tell her about the *Rendez-vous des Cheminots*, about the old ragtime that I play to myself on the juke-box and about the strange happiness that it gives me.
> — I was wondering if, from that side of things, one couldn't find, or, at any rate, look for. . . .] (p. 191)

There is no substance at all, then, in the suggestion that Sartre is "uninterested" in the ending of his novel, or that it is unrelated to the rest of the book.

None of this, however, rebuts the claim that the ending is essentially ironical, that Sartre looks upon Roquentin's final hope of "salvation" with detachment and derision. Manser appears to believe that Sartre's irony extends to the whole "Platonic" strain in the book,[16] but he completely fails to substantiate this view on the basis of the text. He also fails to take account of Sartre's own testimony elsewhere: ["A born Platonist, I used to go from knowledge to its object; I found more reality in the idea than in the thing. . . . Whence came this idealism which has taken me thirty years to get rid of"].[17] And this last point serves to remind us that even when we concentrate on the ending of *La Nausée* in our own narrow sense, we need to remember that evidence external to the novel as such can come into play. Because this evidence is itself highly complicated, I believe that it tends, on the whole, to make the question of possible irony at the end of *La Nausée* look much more difficult than it really is, but having once been mentioned, such evidence cannot be entirely ignored.

Two points concerning the evolution of Sartre's views on relevant matters may be considered as established beyond any doubt on the basis of *Les Mots* and several important interviews published from the early nineteen-fifties onwards. Firstly, for a considerable length of time he himself believed in what may reasonably be described as the idea of salvation through literature: [". . . creamed off from catholicism, the sacred settled in Literature and the penman appeared, an *ersatz* of the

Christian that I couldn't be. His sole concern was salvation, his sojourn here below had no other goal but to earn him posthumous bliss through trials borne with dignity"].[18] Secondly, it is equally certain that at some perhaps fairly specific moment before the first publication of the text of *Les Mots* (in *Les Temps modernes* of October 1963 and November 1963) Sartre came to regard this belief as a rather serious illusion (he goes so far as to call it, in his own particular case, "une névrose"): ["The retrospective illusion is in pieces; martyrdom, salvation, immortality, the whole lot is going to rack and ruin, the building is tumbling down. . . . I see clearly, I am disabused, I know my true tasks . . . for about ten years now I have been a man waking up, cured of a long, bitter and sweet madness"] (*Les Mots*, pp. 210–11). But if these two facts are beyond dispute, the question of timing, of when Sartre's "awakening" took place is more problematic. The mention of "dix ans" in the last quotation settles nothing on its own, since it might refer either to the ten years before the *publication* of *Les Mots* in 1963, or to the ten years before the text was *written* in 1954.[19] But in any case, to argue that Sartre was being ironical about the notion of salvation through literature at the end of *La Nausée* presumably entails the view that he had lost his own illusions before the novel was written (that is, perhaps as early as 1934, but certainly no later than 1937), and neither *Les Mots* nor the published interviews offer a single shred of evidence to support *this* view. It is all too easy to be more impressed by Sartre's later, disabused attitude towards literature than by the fact that he was under the "illusion" concerned for a long time, but a careful reading of the one passage about *La Nausée* in *Les Mots* unmistakably brings out — in spite of the rather complex nature of what he has to say — Sartre's claim that, at the moment of writing the novel, he still believed he could be "saved" through literature (["I wanted to save myself through my works. . . . I was blind to the facts"] p. 209).

It is true that at least three commentators have denied the substance of his claim, but two of them were writing before the publication of *Les Mots* and the third simply omits to refer to that text in his remarks. Moreover, as soon as we depart from the matter of Sartre's own later comments on his "névrose," the whole issue becomes cloudier, and the precise relevance of particular pieces of external evidence to the ending of *La Nausée* becomes uncertain. For example, all three of the critics just referred to stop short of actually talking of *irony* at the end of the novel and are content to argue, vaguely, that Sartre had "gone beyond" Roquentin's final perspective at the time of writing. But while Francis Jeanson[20] offers no external evidence at all to support this assertion, G. J. Prince at least refers to a section of *L'Etre et le Néant* by way of support,[21] and Claude-Edmonde Magny clearly sees the view as substantiated by her reading of *L'Imaginaire*.[22] The difficulty over anything in *L'Etre et le Néant*, however, is that this philosophical work was written and published some five years after *La Nausée*, and without some additional evidence there seems no particular reason to simply *assume* that Sartre's views could not have changed between, say, 1936 and 1941 — indeed, in view of the political events of this period, such an assumption is intrinsically implausible. The case of *L'Imaginaire* is rather different, for although it was not published until 1940, one part of the text appeared as early as 1938 and the whole book is known to be based on work that Sartre carried out much earlier. The problem here is, rather, that the suggestion that this work shows us Sartre repudiating the idea of salvation through literature seems to be seriously mistaken. Another critic has actually drawn exactly the opposite conclusion to Magny's from his own reading of *L'Imaginaire*: "the 'aesthetic solution' adopted by Roquentin is identical with Sartre's treatment of the aesthetic object in *L'Imaginaire*."[23] But in any case, close scrutiny of the last section of the work ("L'œuvre d'art"), where Sartre makes one or two explicit references to the novel in general, reveals nothing whatever that is incompatible with Roquentin's views in the last few pages of *La Nausée*.

We may return, then, to the text of the novel itself and consider what kind of internal evidence might point to irony on Sartre's part at the end. I can see only two or three directions in which the search might proceed. It has been suggested that the irony attaches to the banality or triviality of the song, *Some of These Days*, which plays such an important role as a point of reference at the end; that in the last few paragraphs of the book Roquentin's project is in direct contradiction with his own stance earlier in the novel; and that one particular major step in his argument is "clearly intended to be fallacious." The first suggestion, however, is not at all difficult to refute, for there is no reason to believe that Sartre ever regarded songs like *Some of These Days* or the ragtime genre as a whole as banal or trivial. On the contrary, his liking for ragtime, blues, negro spirituals and jazz is quite well documented (particularly by Simone de Beauvoir, who mentions *Some of These Days* as an example of the sort of music by which they were both "passionnément émus"), and he himself mentions by name in *Les Mots* Sophie Tucker, almost certainly the "Negress" whose recording he was thinking of in *La Nausée*.[24]

The second and third points, which may be taken together, deserve more detailed consideration, for many critics have suggested, in one way or another, that at the end Roquentin is no better than the bourgeois that he so despises, in that he too is hoping to justify his existence by reference to Being, to escape from existence into Being. Yet this is not the case at all, and there is even a vital paragraph just before the ending proper where Sartre might be taken as warning us explicitly against just such an interpretation: ["And I, too, wanted to *be*. I have never wanted anything but that; there's the fine word of my life. . . . It could even be an *apologia*: he was in the wrong world. He existed, like other people, in the world of public gardens, bistrots, commercial towns and he wanted to persuade himself that he lived elsewhere, behind the canvas of paintings, with the doges of Tintoretto. . . . And then, after really having played the fool, he understood, he opened his eyes, he saw that there had been a misdeal"] (pp. 218–19). Again, it is made plain that Roquentin is not hoping to escape existence, or even the feeling of existing, by writing a novel: ["Of course, at first, it would be just a boring and tiring job, it wouldn't stop me existing nor from feeling that I exist"] (p. 222). And neither, incidentally, was the composer of *Some of These Days* (["He must have thought: with a bit of luck, this number'll bring me fifty bucks!"] p. 220). There is, after all, an important difference between what Roquentin may do and what he attacks the bourgeoisie for doing: rather than claiming that his own existence is justified by reference to certain pre-existing samples of Being (Religion, Rights, etc.), he would actually be consciously bringing something—a work of art—*into* Being.[25] Contrary to what has sometimes been supposed, there is nothing in the novel to suggest that this is an illegitimate process, and the crucial step in Roquentin's thoughts from *Some of These Days* to its composer (p. 219), from the work of art to its creator, although opening up complicated issues, is *not* intended to be seen as fallacious; it is the step that lets a tiny ray of hope into the book right at the end, and there is no positive encouragement in the novel for us to see such hope as illusory.

Yet in spite of all this, it is undoubtedly a fact that the ending of *La Nausée* is sketchy, for the complex ideas that it raises are certainly left in an unusually fragmentary and undeveloped state. As a matter of fact, the end is even more restrictive and tentative than critics have so far acknowledged. We have pointed out that the aesthetic solution proper is confined to the final three pages of the book, but the way in which this is geared into the time-scale of the events of the final entry in Roquentin's diary is also revealing. Examination of the material under the heading ["One hour later"] (which follows the entry under ["Wednesday: My last day in Bouville"]) shows that the narrator's actions and thoughts are plotted in relation to the time of departure of his train for Paris: ["the train is leaving in two hours"] (p. 211); ["the train is leaving in three quarters of an hour"] (p. 215); ["in a quarter of an hour I will be on the train"] (p. 219). Roquentin may actually be at the station at the moment of writing the last few lines of the book. Remarkably then, the one specific positive measure that he considers taking to overcome contingency occurs to him for the first time during the last quarter of an hour of his stay in Bouville, or, if one could speak this way, during the last quarter of an hour of the book! And there is one further unnoticed point that has a bearing upon the essentially undeveloped nature of the ending: contrary to what virtually every commentator has said or implied, *Roquentin does not decide to write a novel*. He is, of course, entertaining the possibility of doing so, but his general state on recognising that ["one can justify one's existence"] is explicitly described as one of indecision. The last three paragraphs of the book are predominantly in the conditional tense (["A novel. And there would be people who would read this novel who would say . . ."] p. 222). The conditionals of the crucial penultimate paragraph depend grammatically upon the antecedent, ["If I was sure I had any talent"], and this follows directly upon the entirely unambiguous statement: ["*I dare not take a decision*"]. It is rather surprising that this particular aspect of the tentative, inconclusive nature of the ending has not been noticed and emphasised, for it has its importance. Had one of Sartre's aims been to treat the notion of salvation through literature ironically, he would surely have had Roquentin do more than entertain the *possibility* of writing a novel. It seems that for some reason he does not wish his character to do more than catch a glimpse of a possible "solution" at the end (["It's not that I'm very hopeful"] p. 221): ["he glimpses a chance, a slim chance of accepting himself"].[26]

Some critics, however, have claimed or implied that there is more to the ending than this, that *La Nausée* as a whole gives us grounds for believing that Roquentin not only eventually decided, but also actually executed his project and wrote a novel. The point is a vital one, since if we were in a position to say this, we should at least be on the way towards knowing whether the idea turned out as well as Roquentin had hoped. Are we to understand, then, that he did go on to write a novel? Robert Champigny, who was one of the first critics to emphasize the importance of the "Avertisement des éditeurs" in this connection, argues that the preface to *La Nausée* shows that he did *not*.[27] It is certainly true that, on the basis of that preface, we may reasonably presume that Roquentin is dead: ["These notebooks have been found among the papers of Antoine Roquentin"]. But even if it were legitimate to infer, as Champigny does, that if he had written a novel the preface would have been bound to mention the fact, this would still leave room for very different opinions: did Roquentin simply die before his novel was completed, or had he already, as Bauer seems to think, abandoned the project anyway?[28] In any case, Champigny's initial inference does not appear particularly well-grounded. Is there any specific reason why the "editors" should have mentioned a novel, had Roquentin written one? Could it not equally well be argued that he *must* have done something rather more special than anything recorded in *La Nausée* for the posthumous publication of his personal diary to be justified?

In fact, all of this is *so* speculative that we do better to examine the more determinate suggestion that *La Nausée* is itself to be taken as the novel that Roquentin was considering writing, or at least the one that he in fact went on to write. This is undoubtedly a highly important, but also a peculiarly complicated matter, which deserves the most careful scrutiny. I would suggest that while the nature of the evidence is such that this possibility cannot be utterly excluded, probabilities of a variety of different kinds all point in the other direction and thereby amount to something close enough to certainty. It is revealing, for example, that no good, direct evidence has been provided by critics like Lilar, Barnes and Raillard to substantiate their claim that *La Nausée* is Roquentin's novel. There *may* be some genuine difficulty over what such evidence could consist of, but one is strongly tempted to believe that if Sartre had really wanted his reader to clearly see *La Nausée* as Roquentin's novel, he would have given some explicit indication to that effect, particularly in the presence of *prima facie* evidence to the contrary. For such evidence there certainly seems to be. *La Nausée*, in fact, seems the very antithesis of a book conforming to the description of the sort of novel that Roquentin would want to write: ["My mistake was to want to resuscitate Monsieur de Rollebon. Another kind of book. I'm not quite sure what kind – but one would have to guess, behind the printed words, behind the pages, something which wouldn't exist, which would be beyond existence. A story, for instance, which couldn't happen, an adventure. It would have to be beautiful and hard as steel and it would have to make people ashamed of their existence"] (p. 222). We cannot help bearing in mind how very different *La Nausée* is from what would have to be its model, *Some of These Days*, a song whose notes ["Know no rest, an inflexible order produces them and destroys them without ever giving them the time to recover or to exist by themselves"] (p. 36). Can it be said with any plausibility at all that *La Nausée* resembles or reads like "une aventure" (especially when the diary itself is so critical of this concept, at least in certain respects), or that it is ["beautiful and hard as steel"]? Does it not, rather, reflect life (as opposed to adventures, or Art) as Roquentin sees it, repetitive, rather uneventful, disordered and messy? And yet there is a theoretical reason for being somewhat hesitant in these judgements. It is only to be expected that criticism will progress by finding new connections between different entries or passages in *La Nausée*, and the curious result is that the more (hidden) structure that we come to recognise in the book, the more it will appear to approach Roquentin's stated ideal for the "histoire" he would like to write! But although Raillard talks of "la 'rigueur' de l'œuvre," it might be suggested that *still La Nausée* does not come very close to that ideal. Moreover, the crucial question is whether we are prepared to make the assumption that Roquentin himself is fully aware of such structure as his diary has. Recent findings concerning structure are almost certainly not evidence that *La Nausée* is Roquentin's novel, but a sign of the difficulties that Sartre is in in trying to convey the shapelessness and purposelessness of existence in a book which, if it is to be readable at all, must have some shape and purpose. He does, after all, go as far as he could be expected to have gone in 1938 towards making his novel loose in structure in a way conforming to the contingency of life itself, and this is certainly the main reason behind the diary form adopted in the book.

This raises the further point that seeing such shape as *La Nausée* has as a deliberate, fictional structuring of experiences after the event *by the narrator* involves seeing the diary form of the book as something of a fraud on Roquentin's part. If he is taken to have written all of it *after* going through the experiences it describes (that is, after the project of writing a novel first occurred to him), then we have to accept that it was not written in the way that a diary is written at all. But then why should Roquentin himself present it in that form, since his aim is to write ["a story . . . which couldn't happen"]? And why the elaborate charade of stressing the importance of honsty and plain speaking (["I haven't told the truth"] p. 21; (["mistrust literature. One must write spontaneously"] p. 77) in a work that would be flagrantly breaching these principles? Of course, the argument could be made more sophisticated at this stage, and it could be suggested that, after leaving Bouville, Roquentin selected, possibly revised, and put together pages from a diary already written in Bouville, thereby composing the novel, *La Nausée*.[29] At least the "deception" is not quite so great if we suppose him to have originally written his diary day by day at the times the headings indicate. But the trouble is that there is no particular evidence to support this rather complicated hypothesis, and that once more we seem to have reached the realms of the highly speculative. Whichever way one looks at it, the fact that *La Nausée* takes the form of a diary makes it more, rather than less, difficult for us to assume that it is Roquentin's novel.

Furthermore, the "Avertissement des éditeurs" forms an additional obstacle in this respect. It is true that it is something of an oddity on any account of the book,[30] but both the simple and the more complex versions of the hypothesis under discussion would presumably make it some kind of extra, and quite gratuitous, deception on Roquentin's part. If *La Nausée* was from the first conceived by Roquentin as a novel (and not as a diary), what does he achieve by presenting it as a set of notebooks found among his papers? On the other hand, why, having structured or revised his original diary to make it more like "une aventure" (!!), or ["a story . . . which couldn't happen"], should he then add a preface that makes the diary look more like a simple personal record of part of his life? In any case, the notion of Roquentin himself adding the preface raises other problems: Is he pretending to be dead? Did he arrange for posthumous publication? etc. It is much easier—and more plausible—to regard the "Avertissement" as quite separate from the text itself, as something we must not see as supplied by Roquentin himself. And this in turn brings us back to the idea that the preface constitutes some sort of comment *about* Roquentin that Sartre wishes to make, albeit indirectly, on his own behalf. Champigny is almost certainly right to this extent, but he is mistaken in his claim that it is there to give us additional information on whether or not Roquentin wrote his novel. Sartre, in fact, gives us no such information, but deliberately leaves the question open. What he does in the "Avertissement" is, precisely, to say clearly that, in any event, this is certainly *not* Roquentin's novel: ["These *notebooks* have been *found* among the papers of Antoine Roquentin. . . ."] The whole point about the critical paraphernalia at the beginning—preface, undated page that does not belong to the diary proper, footnotes about words omitted or crossed out—is surely to emphasise the point that Roquentin's diary was not intended for publication (which is perfectly consistent with his stated purpose in writing it: (["Keep a diary in order to see clearly"] p. 11). If Sartre had wished us to take it that *La Nausée* is Roquentin's novel and/or that Roquentin himself had it published as such, it is very difficult indeed to see any reason why he should have added the preface.

Apart from the matter of the form of *La Nausée*, there is the general question of its subject-matter. Is it not highly unlikely (although perhaps Geneviève Idt is right to argue that it is not wholly impossible)[31] that Roquentin's novel would be about his own life at all? He is emphatic that it would be nothing like a biography: ["But not a history book, they speak about what has existed and an existent can never justify existence to another existent. . . . Another kind of book"] (pp. 221–22). And he insists that ["never, never have I written anything of this kind"], in spite of the fact that he has by then been writing his diary for some time. Moreover, if Roquentin were to write his novel about his own life and sufferings, there would be an obvious sense in which he would be opening himself to the objections he raises against the "imbéciles" who believe that when they listen to music ["their sufferings become music"] (p. 217)—["The idiots"]; much as he would still like to ["suffer in tempo"] as *Some of These Days* invites him to, he now knows that this is impossible. Again, we must not lose sight of the analogy between Roquentin's novel and the song. *Some of These Days*, we should remember, is certainly not an account of the life of its composer (even though the lyric, "Some of these days, You'll miss me honey . . . ," may vaguely reflect one of his preoccupations [p. 220], just as it may reflect Roquentin's longing for Anny), much less of that of the "Negress" who sings it. What "saves" these two is not that their lives are transformed *within* the song, but that they are both, in their different ways, involved in the creation of an ideal object, of an instance of Being as opposed to existence. Roquentin, after all, learns nothing about the lives of the composer and performer from the song, but wants to imagine them when he hears it: ["I'm trying to think of him *through* the melody, through the white, acid sounds of the saxophone. . . . I don't want to meet him. . . . Just want to obtain some information about him and to be able to think of him while listening to the record"] (p. 220). It is wholly reasonable, therefore, to assume that he would wish the same relationship to pertain between himself and the readers of his novel: ["But *I'd* be happy in his place. I envy him"] (p. 246). And this is confirmed in the penultimate paragraph of the book: ["And there would be people who would read this novel and who would say: 'It was Antoine Roquentin who wrote that, a red-haired guy who used to hang around in cafés,' and *they would think of my life as I am thinking of that of this Negress*: the way one thinks of something precious and half legendary"] (p. 222, italics added).

If the analogy is to hold, then, Roquentin's novel would not be about his own life at all. In saying to themselves, ["It's Antoine Roquentin who wrote it . . ."], his readers would not be senselessly stating what would be perfectly obvious if *La Nausée* were that novel, but reminding themselves of the man *behind* rather than *in* the novel, just as Roquentin has to remind himself of the composer behind *Some of These Days*.

In short, there is no positive reason for assuming that *La Nausée* is Roquentin's novel, and a great deal of evidence to the contrary. We must fall back on the view that Sartre wished to show Roquentin simply catching a glimpse of a possible way out at the end of the book, and to refrain from building into the novel any kind of assessment of the legitimacy or efficacy of the putative solution. But *why* does Sartre do no more than this? Why is the ending so tentative and fragmentary, so indecisive and incomplete, with loose ends of many different kinds? I believe that Sartre's reasons for deliberately doing no more than sketching in a new development of his themes at the end of the book fall into two categories, both aesthetic and moral considerations being involved.

It is important to recognise that Sartre was faced with rather difficult aesthetic problems in having to bring *La Nausée* to an end at all. There is, for instance, the matter of consistency in Roquentin's character. The very last thing that could be said of Roquentin is that he is a positive and decisive figure (Anny is much more active and forceful, and herself points out the contrast: pp. 189–90), so that to have him reacting quickly and decisively in any way to his discovery of contingency might have greatly strained the credulity of the reader. But above all, there is the difficulty that in the course of the book Roquentin discovers that life as we live it is not neatly divided up into adventures: ["There are no beginnings. . . . There's no end either: one never leaves a woman, a friend, a town at one go"] (pp. 57–58). If this discovery is to carry any weight, therefore, Roquentin's diary — which purports to be an accurate record of part of his life — cannot finish on a high note, or have a strong, definite ending. It is unlikely to be coincidental that all of the three examples that Roquentin gives in the above comment can be seen to relate to the end of *La Nausée* itself: he has parted from Anny ["one never leaves a woman"]; he has lost the Autodidact, his "ami"; and he is about to leave the town of Bouville. In fact, apart from the highly abstract entry under ["Tuesday in Bouville"] (pp. 196–201), these three episodes entirely dominate the book after the account of Roquentin's discoveries in the Jardin Public. But far from contradicting his earlier reflections, the last quarter of *La Nausée* is calculated to confirm them. He *may* never see Anny again, but it is just as likely that at some future date he will once more receive her summons: ["Perhaps I'll see her again in ten years' time"] (p. 193). Equally, it may be unlikely that he will ever meet the Autodidact again, but Roquentin has not exactly broken with him in any clear-cut, definitive way: after the incident in the library, he had wanted to stay with him to help, and indeed just before retrospectively recounting what happened in the library, he has been all over the town looking for the Audodidact (p. 201). For a time, his concern is so strong that it prevents him from really "feeling" that he is leaving Bouville (p. 201), but in any case it cannot be said that the end of *La Nausée* sees him making a clean break with the town either: he is, after all, still in the town when the book ends (Indeed, the very last sentence envisages the following day in Bouville), and the "patronne" of the *Rendez-vous des Cheminots* has insisted that Roquentin will come back: ["with us, folks always come back"] (p. 214). In other words, granted that Sartre wants to include certain incidents and relationships, he ends *La Nausée* just about as inconclusively as he can, with the present (Bouville) running into the future (Roquentin's *possible* project) as messily and indistinguishably as Roquentin sees it doing in life itself. All of this, together with the uncertainties already noted, suggests that Sartre is doing his best with the problem of ending the diary of a man who says there are no endings in life.

Perhaps the only feature of the end that appears difficult to reconcile with this general view is Roquentin's suggestion that he may come to see his very last day in Bouville as a crucial one, a day when something vitally important started (and therefore, presumably, other things ended):

> [But a moment would certainly come when the book would be written, would be behind me and I think that a little light would be shed on my past. Then, perhaps, I would be able, through it, to recall my life without repugnance. Perhaps one day, thinking precisely of this very hour, of this dreary hour waiting, round-shouldered, for it to be time to get in the train, perhaps I would feel my heart beat faster and would say to myself: "It was that day, that hour that everything began." And I would manage — in the past, only in the past — to accept myself.] (p. 222)

But apart from the general tentativeness of this sequence (conditional tense, "peut-être" three times, "je pense que" once), what needs to be retained for present purposes is Roquentin's emphasis that his new ploy will, at best, be successful only in relation to his past: "sur mon passé," "me rappeler ma vie," "au passé — rien qu'au passé." We saw earlier that he is not hoping to gain relief from existence *as he writes* his novel (any more than did the composer of *Some of These Days*), and there is a closely related point about his attitude towards the concept of "adventures," which has also been much misunderstood by commentators. Roquentin's crucial discovery, ["I have not had any adventures"] (p. 54), has to be clearly understood as the recognition of the fact that there are no adventures in life while we are living through the "events" themselves ["When one lives, nothing happens"] (p. 57), that adventures are essentially constructions *after the event* ["in order for the most banal event to become an adventure, it is necessary and sufficient that one begins to *recount* it"] (p. 57). He discovers that there is something illusory in any impression or feeling that we are actually in the process of having an adventure,[32] and therefore something mistaken in any later claim that we have had adventures, if it be based on that impression. But this does not commit Roquentin to ruling out, or even deprecating, the possibility of looking back on a sequence of events and calling it an adventure, provided that one is aware of exactly what one is doing. It is true that he urges: ["But one must choose: to live or to recount"] (p. 57), but he also admits: ["From time to time, one does a partial totting-up . . . Occasionally — rarely — one fixes one's position"] (pp. 57–58), and it is clear that he does not see the dichotomy in the way that he is sometimes taken to see it. For him, the important thing is not to avoid all retrospection — which is surely an impossibility — but to avoid conflating and confusing on any given occasion the two distinct processes of "vivre" and "raconter." It is this type of confusion that he himself had failed to avoid before coming to understand what "adventures" really are: ["I wanted the moments of my life to follow each other and to be ordered like those of a life that one remembers. One might as well try to catch time by the tail"] (p. 59). What Roquentin is saying, then, at the end of *La Nausée* is: "*If I were to* decide to write a novel, then *perhaps* one day when the project was completed, *I might* look back and see the day of decision as an important beginning." This attitude is an extremely hesitant one, but in any case there is nothing in it that contradicts his earlier discoveries about the nature of adventures: he is anxious to avoid living *as if* one were looking back, but he has said nothing against looking *forward* to a time when one may occasionally wish to look back.

Yet although there is no self-contradiction in Roquentin's views, Sartre could not afford to make the ending of his novel any stronger or any more definite, for fear of opening himself *as author* to the charge that his book has a sharp, decisive cut-off which is inconsistent with what the narrator is supposed to believe about life. In short, precisely in order to *avoid* irony at the end, Sartre has to have *La Nausée* end with a whimper rather than with a bang. And again the "Avertissement des éditeurs" is useful here, since it enables him to add another dimension of uncertainty and inconclusiveness to the end. It implies that Roquentin is dead, but without telling us when or how he died (or whether he wrote a novel). Now, as Roquentin himself points out: ["when one recounts a life. . . . One gives the impression of beginning at the beginning. . . . And in fact it's by the end that one has begun"] (p. 58), and Sartre indicates in *Les Mots* that this applies just as much to a man's life as a whole as to a single adventure: ["in a completed life, it is the end that one takes for the truth of the beginning"] (p. 166). If, then, we were to be told when and how Roquentin died, we should find it very difficult not to see his whole life in the light of its end, as a kind of adventure, whereas Sartre wishes

Roquentin's diary, above all, to give us something of the flavour of life as Roquentin lived it.

Over and above these aesthetic considerations, however, a number of features of the text give the ending a markedly moral dimension. Not the least of these is the fact that Roquentin has earlier linked his discovery of contingency with what we would have to call the "morality" of the bourgeoisie: ["there's Nausea; there's what the Swine — those of the Coteau Vert and the others — try to hide from themselves with their idea of right"] (p. 166). When, therefore, he finally begins to adopt a stance of his own designed to counteract the debilitating effects of that discovery, we have to consider this, equally, to be a moral matter. In any case, the key terms in the last few pages of the book are undoubtedly moral ones: ["Saved," "washed of the sin of existing," "to justify one's existence," "shame," "to recall my life without repugnance," "to accept myself"]. What I should like to suggest is that while there are moral issues present throughout La Nausée, by the end the earlier ones are beginning to merge into, or open up, other more complex ones, which Sartre wanted to air but could not possibly have undertaken to tackle in his novel — issues to which he himself, in 1938, was probably only just beginning to address himself. This fact is superimposed upon, and reinforces the aesthetic factors already discussed, making it even more necessary for Sartre to end his novel by simply touching upon certain questions and suggestions, rather than by developing them in full.

It has not, perhaps, been sufficiently emphasised in connection with La Nausée that one of Roquentin's principal preoccupations — and indeed his main reason for writing a diary — is that of regaining and retaining full control over himself in the face of the onslaught of Nausea. His desire to see clearly ["To keep a diary so as to see clearly"] (p. 11) is dictated by fear of what is happening to him (["I am frightened of what is going to happen, going to seize hold of me"] p. 17), and he needs to take a grip because he feels he is losing his freedom of action (p. 23) and being taken over by his Nausea (pp. 32–33). The urgency of the matter only begins to disappear with Roquentin's insight into contingency in the Jardin Public: [". . . I know what I wanted to know; everything that has happened to me since the month of January I now understand. The Nausea has not left me and I don't believe that it will leave me so soon; but I am no longer submit to it, it is no longer a sickness nor a passing spasm: it's me"] (p. 161). But it is clear that Roquentin's discovery leaves him with a greater problem than ever, namely that of "accepting" himself, or justifying his existence, and for some time he can make no progress at all with this. Indeed, he is subsequently stripped of his one remaining "raison de vivre," that is his relationship with Anny (p. 196), and right into his last hour in Bouville he is still at a loss, failing to do or think anything on his own behalf that would go any of the way towards self-justification (["I know very well that

I don't want to do anything"] p. 216). Hence an important feature of the very end of *La Nausée* is that Roquentin is at last considering *doing* something for himself, considering taking some kind of positive action that may partially justify his existence in his own eyes, at least retrospectively. There is a shift in the moral centre of gravity of the book, and having, as it were, made up some lost ground by understanding certain things, now for the first time Roquentin begins to look forward constructively to the possibility of actually giving his life some shape.

Nevertheless, although we are compelled to class this as a moral matter, the signs are that Sartre himself has not yet fully worked out the implications of such a classification. We have seen that there is no likelihood that he was being ironical about Roquentin's hope of salvation through literature, but we have to acknowledge also that he shows no inclination in *La Nausée* to extend this response to contingency beyond Roquentin himself, no inclination to universalise it into a moral prescription or recommendation.[33] On the contrary, he appears to fall back on the notion that Roquentin is ["a lad without collective importance . . . scarcely an individual"] (Epigraph). This is perhaps understandable in the light of the intrinsic nature of the measure that Roquentin is considering adopting, since not everyone can justify himself by writing, or composing, or embarking on creative artistic work of any kind. But it is almost certainly also the case that Sartre, far from being detached in this respect, was too close personally to Roquentin's solution to be able to judge its *moral* status in an objective way. Whilst in 1938 his own private faith in salvation through literature remained unshaken, he was undoubtedly already dimly aware of a discrepancy between the highly general or universal truths about the human condition embodied in Roquentin's discovery of contingency, and a specific "solution" to the problem that may not have very much more than personal significance. This dim awareness is one of the factors reflected in the unresolved nature of the ending of *La Nausée* and the rather curious proportions of the book, with the bulk of it dwelling on contingency and only a few pages at the end touching on Roquentin's response to it in the form of a hope of ["literary afterlife"]. Yet it was only some years later that Sartre came to fully understand the underlying discrepancy: ["I used to think of nothing more than achieving my salvation. . . . I didn't realize this until I was forty, and simply because I never questioned myself about my motives for writing. I contested everything, except my profession. So much so that one day, while writing down some thoughts on morals, I noticed that I was constructing a writer's ethics for writers, whilst claiming to speak to those who didn't write!"] (*Situations IX*, p. 33). The fact is that Roquentin's project at the end of *La Nausée* is extremely difficult to situate in relation to the borderline between those purely personal choices that affect an individual's own life (often profoundly) without being moral matters in any strong sense, and moral choices proper. Roquentin doubtless sees the business of writing a novel as a highly personal one, but quite apart from considerations mentioned above, certain points in his reflections at the end appear there more or less for the first time in the book and begin to pull his proposal ineluctably into the moral arena.

His project does, after all, involve crucial reference to others, although the exact nature of the reference is less than clear. Roquentin is essentially a solitary figure throughout most of the book, and when in the last few pages his begins raising issues that have to do with others in rather complex ways, the end is bound to fail to elucidate these issues adequately. But if the details of his new awareness of the importance of others are unclear, the new awareness itself is beyond dispute. It is when, in the middle of a fit of depression about his future life in Paris, he comes to think of someone other than himself that he first sees a chance of salvation: ["She turns the handle and there it is beginning again. But I'm no longer thinking of myself. I'm thinking of that guy from over there who composed this tune . . ."] (p. 220). Although he insists that there is no humanism involved, it is noticeable that his feelings towards the composer are ones of sympathy: [". . . I find his suffering and his sweating . . . moving . . . it's the first time in years that a man has appeared moving to me"] (p. 220). As we have seen, he himself would like to be remembered in the way that he remembers the composer, that is not simply to be in the minds of others (as Iris Murdoch points out, "if this were salvation then Herostratus is saved too"),[34] but to be remembered as someone who has brought Being into the world. This leaves many obscurities, including a general one about what such salvation could possibly amount to. And in an undeveloped and even enigmatic form, the notions of looking at, or being aware of others, as well of being looked at *by* others are now right to the fore in the book, and are presented in a very complex way. Anny has already mentioned the difference between the point of view of the (theatre) spectator and the performer (p. 191), but here at the end we have to add the third figure of the composer, and even the idea of the work of art itself as a ["pitiless witness": "I am ashamed for myself and for what exists *confronted* with it [the song]"] (p. 218). There is also the problem of deciding to what extent Roquentin believes that he has something to communicate to his fellow-men (Mendel),[35] and to what extent he is adumbrating a way of imposing his own personal existence upon others (Jameson).[36] He himself is made to feel ["shame"], at a moment when he has abandoned himself to existence, by the song, *Some of These Days* (pp. 217–18), and one of his expressed aims is that any novel he may write should have that effect upon others: ["It would have to . . . make people ashamed of their existence"] (p. 222). But the evidence is just too scanty for us to be able to say whether he wishes this for the good of others or for reasons of personal satisfaction.

In its way, then, the very sketchiness of the ending constitutes an acknowledgement on Sartre's part that much more reflection was needed on the appropriate moral reactions to contingency than he himself had managed by 1938, and that he was far from sure about the moral implications of his own personal belief in salvation through literature. In saying in 1964 that ["From the time when I was writing *La Nausée* I wanted to write a book on ethics"],[37] he may well have been confirming that his first novel marked a kind of transitional phase when his central concern with metaphysics (or ontology) was beginning to force him to consider specifically moral problems. This is also implied in a comment reported by Claudine Chonez just a few months after the publication of *La Nausée*: ["*La Nausée* has been accused of being overly pessimistic. But let's wait until the end. In my next novel, which will be a sequel, the hero will right the machine. One will see existence rehabilitated, and my hero acting and enjoying the taste of action"].[38] This picture, furthermore, fits perfectly with what we learn of the development of Sartre's moral views from Simone de Beauvoir's memoirs. By the very nature of the case, the exact timing of the "moral awakening" of Sartre and de Beauvoir is difficult to pin down accurately, but it is clear that up to the early thirties they espoused a kind of "individualisme" that involved positive hostility to ethics: ["Neither one of us wanted what is classically called morals. . . . We challenged, I through an old-fashioned taste for the absolute, Sartre through a disgust with the universal, not only the precepts current in our society, but any maxim whatever that claimed to impose itself on all"].[39] One of the main historical events to begin causing them to change this perspective was the Spanish Civil War, but even before going to Berlin (1933–34), where he finished a second version of the work that was to become *La Nausée*, Sartre is described by de Beauvoir as having, like himself, a rather more complex attitude towards individualism than before:

> [To justify myself, I used to invoke the theory of "man alone." Sartre objected that "man alone" is not uninterested in the course of things. . . . Sartre's position, in relation to his fellowmen, was not very clear either. He used to make fun of all the humanisms; impossible, he would think, to cherish — or even to detest — that entity "Man." Both of us however . . . took pleasure in rubbing shoulders with crowds . . . it's that we weren't indifferent to men. We questioned ourselves without finding any answer.][40]

In short, at the time of writing *La Nausée*, Sartre was in a transitional phase with regard to morality, and the undeveloped, fragmentary nature of the ending of the novel, which shows Roquentin conscious of the need to relate to others but hardly certain about the exact purpose and means of doing so, is as much a reflection of this fact as of the aesthetic exigencies outlined above. The end *does* leave us dissatisfied and, in various ways, puzzled, but part of the reason for this is that Sartre himself was puzzled at the time (["We questioned ourselves without finding any answer"]). Doubtless, he did not believe, by 1938, that Roquentin had the moral answer to the most pressing moral problems of the time, but it is a grave error to see him looking on Roquentin's "solution" to his own problems ironically or with derision, and a still graver one to claim that the unelaborated character of the ending indicates that Sartre did not take it seriously, or was uninterested in it. Those critics who have claimed that the end of *La Nausée* was effectively a new beginning in Sartre's thought are quite right, but the particular questions raised for the first time there were not his central preoccupations in the body of the novel and, even had he known how to develop them fully, the aesthetic factors hemming him in would have prevented him from doing so without marked inconsistency in the form and content of Roquentin's diary.

Notes

1. *"La Nausée* de Jean-Paul Sartre," *Alger républicain*, 20 octobre 1938 (quoted in J. Lecarme [ed.], *Les critiques de notre temps et Sartre*, Garnier, 1973, pp. 36–39).

2. *"La Nausée*, un roman de Jean-Paul Sartre," *Ce soir*, 16 mai 1938 (also quoted in Lecarme, pp. 35–36).

3. *Sartre. Romantic Rationalist*, Bowes & Bowes, 1953.

4. *Métaphysique et technique dans l'œuvre romanesque de Sartre*, Droz, 1968.

5. *A propos de Sartre et de l'amour*, Grasset, 1967.

6. "From Solitude to Salvation: A Study in Development," *Yale French Studies* 30 (1962), 45–55.

7. *Sartre. A Philosophic Study*, Athlone Press, 1966.

8. "Sens de *La Nausée*," *PMLA* LXXX (1955), 37–46.

9. *Sartre and the Artist*, University of Chicago Press, 1969.

10. *The Literature of Possibility*, University of Nebraska Press, 1959.

11. *La Nausée de Jean-Paul Sartre*, Hachette, 1972 ("Poche Critique").

12. *A Common Sky. Philosophy and the Literary Imagination*, Chatto & Windus, 1974.

13. *Jean-Paul Sartre. A Literary and Political Study*, Hamish Hamilton, 1960.

14. *La Nausée*, Hatier, 1971 (Profil d'une œuvre").

15. All references to *La Nausée* in the body of the text are to the standard 1938 Gallimard edition.

16. "Sartre makes his *final attack* on the notion of ideal objects existing in a timeless world by means of irony," op. cit., p. 14 (my italics).

17. *Les Mots*, p. 39; this and subsequent references are to the standard Gallimard edition of 1964.

18. *Les Mots*, pp. 207–208. Cf. pp. 150, 160, 164, 209, 212. And see *Situations* IX (Gallimard, 1972), pp. 32–33: *Le Monde*, 18 avril 1964.

19. In spite of the fact that just after the publication of *Les Mots* in book form Sartre answered a question on this subject by saying that the discovery of his "névrose" took place around 1954, a great deal of evidence suggests a date some ten years earlier. As early as 1951 he was already talking about his belief in salvation through art as a thing of the past ("Recontre avec Jean-Paul Sartre," *Les Nouvelles littéraires*, 1er février 1951). And when in a letter interview with Madeleine Chapsal (reprinted in *Situations* IX) he indicated that his

awakening took place when he was forty (1945), he offered a dating that is perfectly consistent with much else that is known about the evolution of his thought. Interestingly, the interview where he apparently claims 1954 as the moment of his awakening ("Jean-Paul Sartre s'explique sur *Les Mots*," interview par Jacqueline Piatier, *La Monde*, 18 avril, 1964) begins with his admission that ["There are chronological contradictions in *Les Mots* . . . I haven't standardized the dates"]. It seems highly probable that either the exact question and answer concerning his awakening are inaccurately recorded, or that some misunderstanding was involved.

20. ["At the time, moreover, when Sartre was writing his, he had himself gone beyond this perspective"], *Sartre par lui-même* (Ed. du Seuil, 1956), p. 122. Elsewhere Jeanson's view does not appear to be the same (see *Le Problème moral et la pensée de Sartre*, Ed. du Seuil, 2nd ed., 1965, pp. 96–98).

21. ["It is, moreover, obvious that the aesthetic solution cannot be satisfactory for the author of *Being and Nothingness*"], op. cit., p. 28.

22. ["The unfortunate thing is that, at the very moment when Sartre was writing *La Nausée*, he already knew that this salvation is also illusory. An unreal universe is not even really a world, any more than that of the novelist or of the painter, or those of the madman or mythomaniac"], "Système de Sartre," *Esprit* 13 (mars 1945), 570. This critic, too, has failed to repeat her claim elsewhere (see *Essais sur les limites de littérature. Les Sandales d'Empédocle*, Neuchâtel, La Baconnière, 1945, p. 140).

23. A. J. Arnold, *La Nausée* revisited," *French Review* XXXIX, No. 2 (Nov. 1965), 199–213.

24. For some fascinating information on this particular subject, see E. N. Zimmerman, " 'Some of these days': Sartre's *Petite phrase*," *Contemporary Literature* 11, No. 3 (summer 1970), 375–81.

25. A point well recognized and expressed by Jeanson: ["One must not seek to be in the manner of works of art; one must try to bring a work of art into being"] (*Le Problème moral*, p. 96).

26. Sartre's own *Prière d'insérer*, quoted by M. Contat & M. Rybalka, *Les Ecrits de Sartre*, Gallimard, 1970, p. 61.

27. Op. cit., p. 44.

28. Op. cit., pp. 40, 43, Cf. Prince, op. cit., pp. 28. Other critics have speculated on the possibility that Roquentin has become insane, or committed suicide.

29. Rather curiously, this suggestion is virtually identical with one of the more recent attempts to offer a solution to the problems of narrator and narration in Camus's *L'Étranger*; see Jean-Claude Pariente, "L'Étranger et son double," *Albert Camus I. 'Autour de L'Étranger,'* Lettres Modernes, 1968 (*La Revue des lettres modernes*, Nos. 170–74), pp. 53–80.

30. To say that it parodies an eighteenth-century convention is unhelpful, since that goes no way towards explaining how that parody fits into the central themes of the work as a whole.

31. Op. cit., p. 35.

32. There is an interesting sequence later, where Roquentin experiences ["a great feeling of adventure"], and goes on to analyse this feeling as simply that of ["the irreversibility of time"] (pp. 74–78).

33. In *L'Existentialisme est un humanisme* (Nagel, 1946), he was to make a great deal of universalisability in ethics, the idea that in choosing for ourselves we choose for others too.

34. Op. cit., p. 17.

35. Op. cit., pp. 53–54.

36. F. Jameson, *Sartre: The Origins of a Style*. Yale University Press, 1961.

37. Interview with Jacqueline Piatier referred to in note 19.

38. Quoted by Contat & Rybalka, p. 66. It is well-known that things did not work out nearly so well as Sartre intended: he has published neither the fourth volume of *Les Chemins de la liberté*, nor the *Morale* promised in *L'Etre et le Néant*.

39. *La Force de l'âge*, Gallimard, 1960, p. 47.

40. Ibid., pp. 154–55.

"The Nine of Hearts": Fragment of a Psycho-reading of *La Nausée*   Serge Doubrovsky*

I have selected for our attention a rather insignificant detail in a rather famous scene: the scene at the café, the "Rendez-vous des Cheminots," where Roquentin finally experiences Nausea with a capital "N": "Things are bad! Things are very bad: I have it, the filth, the Nausea" (p. 18).[1] Along with the print, Nausea here assumes capital importance: it attains a status which is *clinical*, as the symptom of a malady, *ontological*, as the revelation, through this malady, of the subject's mode of being-in-the-world, and *esthetic*, as the call to salvation through art, which is offered here by the "rag-time with a vocal refrain" and which will be taken up again by the "book," the "novel" planned by Roquentin in the conclusion. Sartre produces a discourse which "totalizes," or rather, which progresses by a process of totalization until the moment when Roquentin can say: "I understood that I had found the key to Existence, the key to my Nauseas, to my own life" (p. 129). Fictional language is equipped, is coupled with a metalanguage which is imperious, even imperialistic, and which seems, from the beginning, to exclude commentary, or, what amounts to the same thing, to include it. For years, the critical result has been paraphrase. After the wealth of explanations offered by the narrator himself (an ironic, post-Proustian tribute?) what more or better, or simply, what else, can be said of Nausea than what is said in the text? What remains for the critical eye to see? Nothing, certainly, except this unimportant detail: the Nausea scene closes upon a card game which is fairly intricate, and the game itself, just at the moment when Roquentin gets up, closes upon an exclamation by the "dog-faced young man": "Ah! The nine of hearts" (p. 24). This paper is therefore entitled: " 'The Nine of Hearts': Fragment of a Psycho-reading of *La Nausée*."

At the level of stylistic analysis, you might call it a purely realistic effect; verisimilitude in the narrative code demands that a card game be played, preferably "manille" or "belote," in a French café in the provinces. From this point of view, the ace of clubs or the nine of hearts would do the trick equally well. For me, psycho-criticism begins right where other

*Translated by Carol A. Bové. From *Boundary 2* 5, no. 2 (1977):411–20. Reprinted with permission.

forms of criticism stop: at the production, in the text, of an insignificant detail which cannot be accounted for by either the Sartrian meta-text or by another meta-discourse. Sartre might certainly just as well have written: "Ah! The ace of clubs" or the "nine of hearts" with the same narrative-stylistic effect. It remains that he has written "nine of hearts," and it is precisely this *remains* which remains for the critical eye to see, all the more since, strangely enough, this card, displayed right in the middle of the table, *is not seen* by the players: "One of the players pushes a disordered pack of cards towards another man who picks them up. One card has stayed behind. Don't they see it? It's the nine of hearts" (p. 23). What is insignificant now begins to signify, since the invisible card which is right in front of their eyes is perceived only by Roquentin. This perception must in turn be perceived, and, hopefully, penetrated, by the psycho-critic.

Don't worry, I'm not going to do or redo "The Purloined Letter" act, nor will I play or replay some "instance of the card." Abandoning for now this signifier at the end of its chain (which is our own in this discussion, since it closes precisely the narrative sequence of the café), and hoping to find it later in its place, let's leave Lacan for Freud and direct our attention straightaway to sex. Like Roquentin, as a matter of fact: "I was coming to screw, but no sooner had I opened the door than Madeleine, the waitress, called to me: 'The patronne isn't here, she's in town shopping.' I felt a sharp disappointment in the sexual parts, a long, disagreeable tickling" (p. 18). Before it makes your head "whirl," it "tickles," then, uncomfortably, in a definite erogenous zone. Like honor, Roquentin's penis is "ticklish," and of course, only what is by nature delicate, vulnerable to attack, can be ticklish in this way. Now, it strikes us immediately that there is a lack of proportion between the process which sets off Nausea (what in Sartrian terms might be called the "teleological circuit" of fornication: "I was coming to *screw*") and Antoine's usually very lukewarm ardor for the owner: "I dined at the *Rendez-vous des Cheminots*. The patronne was there and I had to screw her, but it was mainly out of politeness. She disgusts me a little, she is too white and besides, she smells like a newborn child. . . . I played distractedly with her genitals under the cover" (p. 59). Without having read Freud, we rightfully wonder why, when the *owner is not there*, he experiences such "sharp disappointment" in a zone which, when she *is there*, is, we must admit, hardly erogenous. Why this "long uncomfortable tickling" in a penis which is definitely more ticklish than it is capable of being tickled? Having read Freud, of course, we may wonder whether there is not an unconscious denominator common to the two complementary and antithetic sequences (*I was coming to screw/I had to screw her*), an operating chart common to the pleasure which is disappointed or received; or again, having read Mauron, we wonder whether the two texts are not superimposable.

Once the act is more or less completed, sequence 2 (*I had to screw her*) produces something which makes the analyst happy: a "dream": "I let my arm run along the woman's thigh and suddenly saw a small garden with low, wide trees on which immense hairy leaves were hanging. Ants were running everywhere, centipedes and ringworm. . . . Behind the cactus and the Barbary fig trees, the Valleda of the public park pointed a finger at her genitals. 'This park smells of vomit,' I shouted" (p. 59). Since we cannot go into the problematic of the written pseudo-dream, which is not a dream, but can be analyzed as if it were (see Freud on Jensen's *Gradiva*), and since we don't have the time to undertake a detailed analysis, we will confine ourselves to two remarks: (1) the "dream" subsequent to the consummation of the sex act shows the vagina to be an extremely anxiogenic source, precisely the *nauseating* site of a nightmare ("this park smells of vomit"), and (2) if we grant the traditional Freudian decoding, vermine = children, in dream language, we understand the nature of Roquentin's "disgust" for the owner who "smells like a newborn child." The parturient organ of the woman anticipates the final horror of a kind of swooning fecundity (the chestnut root scene): "my very flesh throbbed and opened, abandoned itself to the universal burgeoning. It was repugnant" (p. 133). *Throbbing, opening, abandoning itself*: Roquentin experiences his final Nausea as if his entire body had become *the female organ*, which is, moreover, "burgeoning," in gestation. It's an absolute nightmare. For whom? "I was coming to *screw*." For a man. Recalling sequence 1, we observe that the disappointment of a kind of ticklish masculinity is accompanied by another symptom: "at the same time I felt my shirt rubbing against the tips of my breasts and I was surrounded, seized by a slow, coloured mist" (p. 18). Usage demands that the word *breast* (and the Robert dictionary, I venture to add, confirms it), especially in the plural and in the expression: "the tips of my breasts," refer to a fundamental signifier of femininity, one of its essential appendages and endowments. A man usually speaks of his chest. Everything occurs, then, exactly as if this radical disgust for the female sex, projected as dream at the end of the completed sexual act, is introjected as *phantasy* in the aborted act, the failure to screw being in no way a failure to *enjoy* but a failure to *prove*: from the minute I become unable to prove that I am a man, *I am immediately transformed into a woman*. Such is the logic of Sartrian phantasy which thoroughly regulates the unfolding of Nausea. We could demonstrate in detail, in its four successive stages (pebble, café, little Lucienne, and chestnut root scenes), the inevitable progression of the phantasy, experienced in the merry-go-round of ambivalence, "whirling" from disgust to desire. That is, the phantasy is experienced as a number of stations of the cross at which the man-woman stops, obsessed by the sudden, forced substitution of a female sex for a precarious, masculine one: "How strange it is, how moving, that this hardness should be so fragile" (p. 22). This constitutes, at one and the same time, a malady and remedy, since, in short, by assuming a femininity which makes you nauseous ("the viscous puddle at the bottom of *our* time" [p. 21]), it is a question of bartering actual masculinity for a kind of inexpugnable, imaginary one, inscribed in the symbolic domain: the "steel band" of music or the "beautiful," "hard as steel" story into which Roquentin dreams of transposing himself.

Those who are suspicious of this analysis can at least give credence to "Sartre Through Flaubert," or, if they prefer, to "Sartre: A Self-Portrait." Thus, by reading Sartre reading Gustave, we reread precisely *La Nausée*: "Flesh is complete inaction. . . . now, according to Gustave, pleasure arises from a kind of swooning abandonment, from a passivity which is ready and willing; the woman feels pleasure because she is taken. She feels desire, too, of course, but in her own way. . . . female desire is passive waiting. The text speaks for itself: if Gustave wants to be a woman, it is because his partially female sexuality demands a sex change which will allow the full development of his resources." In this respect, Antoine is Gustave's guilty conscience. "The text speaks for itself," said Sartre: yes, especially when it believes it is talking about the Other. Let's take a look at Sartre as he imagines Flaubert looking at himself in a mirror: "At the start, out of his natural passivity, he creates the *analagon* of a femininity which is concealed. . . it is possible for him, at the cost of creating a double illusion, to imagine that he is someone else, who is caressing an actual woman — himself — behind the mirror. . . . There are two *analoga* here: his hands, his reflection. In the latter, he apprehends only his caressed flesh, overlooking insignificant details like his penis or his youthful male chest."[2] In this "Sartre Through Flaubert," then, we surprise Jean-Paul as he rewrites precisely the progression of Nausea, that is, the progressive feminization of his flesh, which goes from his *hands* (pebble scene), to his *face* in the mirror ("An entire half of my face yields. . . . the eye opens on a white globe, on pink, bleeding flesh" [p. 17]), preceding the entrance into the café where the narrator suddenly "loses" the insignificant detail which is his *penis* and where his *youthful, male chest* becomes "the tips of his breasts." The discourse of fiction and the discourse of criticism display a strange kind of intertextuality/intersexuality. In fact, if Madame Bovary is a man disguised as a woman,[3] there is no reason why Antoine Roquentin cannot be a woman disguised as a man. But if we prefer to believe "Sartre: A Self-Portrait," let's listen to him directly as he answers the formidable questions of the formidable Simone: "Now then, Sartre, I would like to question you on the subject of women. . . . you've never talked about women. . . . how do you explain that?" — "I think it stems from my childhood. . . . girls and women formed, in a way, my natural milieu, and *I have always thought that there was a kind of woman in me*."[4]

But, not as "natural" as all that, as *La Nausée* demonstrates, and this reticence on the subject of women is no way innocent, analytically speaking (I'll have leave ideology to Simone). At the level of unconscious discourse, *La Nausée* fills precisely the strange gap in the writer's conscious discourse, and the trio "Antoine — Jean-Paul — Gustave" reveals more about it than Sartre would like to say or to admit to himself. We know that the notion of "bisexuality," introduced both as a major and as a poorly defined element in Freudian thought, receives a good deal of attention from psychoanalysts, at least from those of the Psychoanalytic Society of Paris, which devoted its April 1975 meeting to it. According to a recent report by Dr. Christian David, every successful cure implies the integration of the subject's psychic bisexuality; inversely, he tells us: "every serious threat concerning sexual identity or integrity is likely to lead to a variety of disturbances to psychic organization, to the point of psychosis." And the French psychiatrist Kreisler formulates the same idea in a vocabulary which is of particular interest for us: "Belonging to a sex constitutes one of the firmest kernels enabling the personality to cohere, and sexuality may be the most primitive and most powerful form rooting us in existence."[5] That Roquentin's final Nausea takes place in front of an eminently phallomorphous root ("the bark, black and swollen, looked like boiled leather. . . . this hard and compact skin of a sea lion" [pp. 127–28, 129]) clearly indicates that the form taken by the subject's existential crisis consists in a kind of rooting in masculinity. "I am not at all inclined to call myself insane," writes Roquentin (p. 2). He shouldn't feel this way, especially at a time when neurosis is terribly devalued and when only psychosis gives status to the writer.

The critic, however, is not a psychiatrist, and the diagnosis (if you wish, the so-called "construction" element) is of interest only if it produces something which is equivalent to the stream of new, repressed material which Freud sees (*Construction in Analysis*, 1937) as the touchstone of a correct interpretation. Here, this equivalent would be the increasingly thorough integration of metonymically discreet elements of the text into a coherent, metaphoric sequence. At bottom, a psycho-reading simply establishes what may be called a rigorous logic of details, to the extent that the logic which underlies the possibilities of the narrative is reinserted into the operation of the phantasy. If we fold erotic sequence 1 ("I was coming to screw") down upon erotic sequence 2 ("I had to screw her"), we might say that the masculine obligation which has been fulfilled avoids the crisis of sexual identity, if it is true, according to R. R. Greenson's remark, that "the adult neurotic behaves as if the sex of his sexual object determined his own sex." But traces of the signifiers' first logic subsist in the second: no sooner does the Valleda in the public or pubic garden point to her genitals as the "sinful parts," in this way reassuring the male sleeper, than upon waking, the latter hears the owner say to him: "I didn't want to wake you up . . . but the sheet got folded under my backside" (p. 59). The syntagmatic order is revealing: this vestige of "daytime" sets off *immediately afterwards* another "dream" in the fictional text, a dream in which the "backside" signifier proliferates, having been repressed as a simple detail pertaining to the "real" in the vigil scene (the fold in the sheet). The obsession is fully manifested: "I gave Maurice Barrès a spanking. We were three soldiers and one of us had a hole in the middle of his face. Maurice Barrès came up to us and said, 'That's fine!' and he gave each of us a small bouquet of violets. 'I don't know where to put them,' said the soldier with the hole in his head. Then Maurice Barrès said, 'Put them in the hole you have in your head.' The soldier answered, 'I'm going to stick them up your ass' " (p. 59). Once again, a detailed analysis is impossible here. Let us mention only the triple associative constellation: head with hole — put up your ass — bouquet of violets; and, with a movement reversing the first, let's fold it back upon erotic sequence 1.

In the café where we left him, we find Roquentin in the throes of Nausea, flopping on the bench: "The bottom of my seat is broken. . . . I have a broken spring. . . . My head is all pliable and elastic, as though it had been simply set on my neck; if I turn it, it will fall off" (p. 19). Having become the "little, detachable object," the "broken spring," the head which turns to the point where it risks falling off, reveals severe castration anguish at the source of Nausea: in vertigo, Roquentin actually *experiences* his head *as a penis*, facing the castration threat which takes aim at his narcissistic identification. "I dropped to a seat, I no longer knew where I was" (p. 18): the text, however, *knows* exactly where he is; when he (his head) drops, Antoine is in the spot where the "seat is broken" (*défoncée*). Now, in the crude slang which is dear to Sartre, "se faire défoncer" (to get buggered) designates the greatly feared act which transforms the masculine subject into a "queer." The anguish of castration, which feminizes, causes a return to a vulnerability which is fundamental to him: the anus is the male's vagina. Disgust (desire) for the feminine sex becomes interiorized in the phantasmatic register as the obsession to possess a potential female sex, which is actualized in Nausea. The fear of castration is accompanied by a severe complementary fear of sodomization. Let's not forget the answer to Maurice Barrès who tells the soldier to put the bouquet "in the hole you have in your head" (the soldier's head with a hole in it, Roquentin's head which has been cut off): "I'm going stick them up your ass." Now what is stuck up this ass, if I may inquire? A bouquet of *violets*. The obsession with sodomization, experienced as feminization, (phantasy being along with common sense the most widely shared thing in the world, Roquentin finds himself here in the excellent company of Freud's President Schreber who is "God's wife") is, moreover, designated, in the Sartrian text, by a special signifier, *violet*, since, let's not forget, Roquentin's Nausea is also a *colored* vertigo: "I saw the colors spin slowly around me" (p. 18). A thematic analysis of the signified would easily show that, in the Sartrian text, this color is the emblem for a sexuality which is feminine and lethal. (A case in point, the cashier with whom Roquentin spontaneously identifies: "she's red haired, as I am; she suffers from a stomach disorder. She is rotting quietly under her skirts with a melancholy smile, like the odour of violets given off by a decomposing body" [p. 55].) We are, then, less surprised than Annie at this esthetic repugnance on Antoine's part: "You swore indignantly for a year that you wouldn't see *Violettes Impériales*" (p. 140). But, still more important, violet is the Sartrian color for a formidable female sexuality even at the level of signification as "*viol*" (rape), as *violated*. This is affirmed in the next stage of Nausea when the narrator identifies with "little Lucienne" after he has done so with the putrescent cashier: "Little Lucienne was raped [*violée*]. Strangled. Her body still exists. . . . *She* no longer exists. Her hands . . . I . . . there, I . . . Raped [*Violée*]. A soft, bloody desire for rape takes me from behind" (pp. 100–01). The very ambiguity of the expression: "bloody desire for rape" (to rape, to be raped?), which is none other than the ambivalence of active/passive desire, is momentarily resolved for the benefit of a transsexualization which is phantasmatically assumed by way of the *place* where desire takes hold of the subject: *from behind*. There is in this an exact symbolic equivalence between the way that he experiences his flesh as feminine ("My body of living flesh which murmurs and turns gently, liquors which turn to cream . . . the sweet sugary water of my flesh" [pp. 101–02]) and his universal Schreberian sodomization: "existence takes my thoughts from behind and gently expands them *from behind*; someone takes me from behind, they force me to think from behind. . . . he runs, he runs like a ferret, 'from behind' from behind *from behind*, little Lucienne assaulted from behind, violated by existence from behind" (p. 102). Little Lucienne, having reappeared just in time as the last link in the chain of verbal delirium, is necessarily "assaulted from behind," if Roquentin is to be able to "become" her. Here, according to the law which Freud assigned to the development of the dream sequences of a single night, which progress from what is most hidden to what is most manifest, all elements of the Sartroquentinian phantasma appear unrepressed in the delirious writing (desyntaxization, degrammaticalization, decodification in the narrative indicating that "textual work" is fulfilling sexual impulse). We have not yet arrived at that point, and in the café scene, the elements mentioned only show through something else, are a little obscured, hesitant: like cousin Adolph's *suspenders* (the traditional emblem, if ever there was one, of proletarian machismo, the Gabin-suspenders of the Prévert-Carné films), which "hesitate" between blue and mauve ("You feel like saying, 'All right, *become* violet and let's hear no more about it' " [p. 19]). But, at this stage, and it is for this reason that they are discussed, that is, written about, the suspenders cannot, *do not want* to become violet; and where Robbe-Grillet formerly saw naive anthropomorphism in Sartrian description, we see the very clear, precise inscription of phantasy, which already articulates "the time of violet suspenders and broken chair seats" (p. 21) in a strangely condensed form. The drive which is yearning and delirious is controlled by the call already mentioned to a kind of imaginary masculinity, to this "band of steel, the narrow duration of the music which traverses our time through and through" (p. 21), whose effect is indicated as specifically as is its cause: "When the voice was heard in the silence, I felt my body *harden* and the Nausea *vanish*" (p. 22).[6] A controlled drive, we might say, but nevertheless one in which a dangerous and latent feminization is retained, not only in the *female* vocalist's song, but also in the very reaction of the veterinarian's little girl listening to the music: "Barely seated, the girl has been seized by it: she holds herself stiffly, her eyes wide open" (pp. 21–22). A phallic, female child, we might say, in whom what holds itself stiffly is a woman's penis. We are hardly surprised that the book's final solution constitutes a kind of fetishism of art.

Yet the café scene doesn't end with the disappearance of Nausea under the spell of the music; it closes upon that innocuous card game which demanded our attention in the beginning—less innocuous, perhaps, for being "manille," if we consider that Nausea originally attacks the "*main*" (hand), which is punished later on ("I . . . stab the knife into the palm" [p. 100]). Having averted obsession with sodomization, Roquentin has yet to confront the threat of castration, in order that the well-known "masculine protest" be complete. This second phase of the phantasmatic operation is carried out vicariously in the card players scene. When the "great, red-faced young man" throws down his diamond "manille," the "dog-faced young man" immediately trumps him (this head, like that of a domesticated, male animal, is an improvement over Roquentin's "pliable," "elastic" one): "Hell. He's trumped" (p. 23). You *coupe* (trump) in cards; you also *coupe* (castrate) on the analyst's couch; and there, when it comes to the father, there's no cutting out. It's precisely he who appears, only to disappear in his most classic form: "The outline of the *king of hearts* appears between his curled fingers, then it is turned on its face and the game goes on. Mighty king, come from so far, prepared by so many combinations, by so many vanished gestures. He disappears in turn so that other combinations *can be born*, other gestures" (p. 23). The unexpected lyricism in this passage has no meaning in terms of the "realistic" code of a narrative in which Roquentin is not known to be a great "cardomaniac" or "manillephile." On an Other Stage and in another code, the reading is perfectly logical: the "son" castrates (*coupe*) the "father," liquidates the Oedipal complex by reversing the threat; in order that the son *be born*, the "king of hearts" disappears, as Mr. de Rollebon does later on (another imaginary murder of the father). Dubbed male, consecrated truly virile, he is struck by an otherwise unexplainable "emotion" which we can well understand: "I am touched, I feel my body at rest like a precision machine" (p. 23), a rest which is well deserved after such transsexual terrors. We understand equally well the stream of memories which suddenly overwhelms Roquentin precisely at this point in the phantasmatic chain: "I have . . . plunged into forests, always making my way towards other cities. I have had women, I have fought with men" (p. 23). In keeping with a masculinity which is from now on homologized, reassured concerning his two essential attributes, the screwer-fighter is at peace with his "human machine": it is normal that he *should see* what others *do not see*, since this is the site of his phantasy: the "neuf de coeur."[7] "New of heart," he can set out once again ("That's it, I'm going to leave" [p. 24]), and gets off on the right foot, except, alas for one gauche move. It's the card which "has stayed behind": "someone takes it at last, gives it to the dog-faced young man. . . . Ah! The nine of hearts" (pp. 23–24). There is certainly reason for this surprise. As far as the phantasy's resolution is concerned, you are not "given" masculinity, you have to "take" it yourself, that is, to apprehend it, unless you have "stayed behind," or as we say, "are left back." Not knowing what to do with it and not having yet decided to transmute or to "transmalize" it into writing, "the young man turns and turns the nine of hearts between his fingers" (p. 24). But, along with this failure, there may already be the promise of a (re)solution to come, since, next to the young man, "the violet-face man bends over a sheet of paper and sucks his pencil."

Notes

1. I have revised several passages of Floyd Alexander's translation of *La Nausée, Nausea* (New York: New Directions Paperbook, 1964), for use in this article. Page references are to this edition.

2. These two quotations on Flaubert are from Sartre's *L'Idiot de la famille. Gustave Flaubert de 1821 à 1857*, I (Paris: Gallimard, 1971), 685, 693. My translation.

3. Jean-Paul Sartre, *Critique de la Raison dialectique* (Paris: Gallimard, 1960), p. 90.

4. Simone de Beauvoir, "Simone de Beauvior interroge Jean-Paul Sartre," *L'Arc*, 61 (1975), 3. Doubrovsky's italics. My translation.

5. Both of these quotations appear in the report by Dr. Christian David, *La Bisexualité psychique* (Paris: Presses Universitaires de France, 1975), p. 52. My translation.

6. Doubrovsky's italics.

7. *Neuf*, of course, means both *nine* and *new* here.

"Looking for Annie": Sartre's
La Nausée and the Inter-War Years   Nicholas Hewitt*

"If you want a really reliable cure for sea-sickness,
I suggest you come down . . . and start looking for Annie."
Charles Causley

In her article, "De Roquentin à Mathieu," in *L'Arc*, of 1966, Annie Leclerc comments on Sartre's first novel: ["Can one read *La Nausée*

*From *Journal of European Studies* 12, part 2, no. 46 (June 1982): 96–112. Reprinted with permission.

otherwise than as the confused, living expression of a certain philosophical enterprise, an adventure of the mind and not an adventure of the hero in the world?"][1] thus encapsulating what has become a stock critical reaction to the balance between fiction and philosophy in *La Nausée*. Most writers on Sartre's work have been quite content to follow Simone de Beauvoir's reference to the novel as "un factum sur la contingence"[2] and therefore to see the major problem presented by the work as being the decyphering of a complex philosophical argument, with the help of later essays, particularly *L'Etre et le néant*. This approach to *La Nausée* is carried to its extreme in Rhiannon Goldthorpe's two-part article, "The Presentation of Consciousness in Sartre's *La Nausée* and its theoretical basis,"[3] but it also constitutes the unquestioned centre of most critical works dealing with the novel. Even Michael Edwards, in his treatment of *La Nausée* as a Symbolist text, feels obliged to begin his essay with the recognition that it is "almost a philosophical novel."[4] Nor has this mainstream interpretation been affected in any way by the publication of *Les Mots* in 1964 and its attendant interviews: the view of *La Nausée* as a philosophical demonstration has emerged reinforced from a reading of the autobiography, which, moreover, has appeared to provide factual evidence to identify Sartre even more closely with his fictional creation Roquentin.

Such a reading of the novel, however, presents serious difficulties, of a both technical and aesthetic nature. The interpretation of *La Nausée* as a major illustration of Sartre's philosophy begs the question of the status of the text when it was published in 1938, and ignores the possibility that the novel may to some extent have been recuperated by the author's subsequent success and prestige. Certainly, Simone de Beauvoir's rather complacent reference to the ["success of *La Nausée* that the critics had greeted as a kind of event"][5] is not born out by Marcel Arland's review in the *Nouvelle Revue Française*. Referring to the appearance of "Le Mur" in the *NRF* and of "La Chambre" in *Mesures*, he comments: ["*La Nausée* is far from offering such a success"],[6] and goes on to see the novel's failure precisely in its unsatisfactory combination of fiction and philosophy: ["A novel? Truth to tell, it would be better to speak of an essay, a satire, or a philosophical meditation"].[7] Similarly, Michel Contat and Michel Rybalka, commenting on Sartre's own "prière d'insérer" for the first edition of the novel, conclude: ["With its half-ironic, half-serious tone, this *prière d'insérer* appears to constitute a compromise between the anecdotal contents of the book and its philosophical meaning"].[8] Finally, if *La Nausée* cannot be seen to resolve adequately its philosophical and fictional ambitions, it also contains minor errors of detail, due probably to the extended period of its composition, which might point again to its unfinished status. Interestingly, these errors of detail concern Anny: her letter to Roquentin which arrives on *mardi gras* summons him to Paris on 20 February,[9] a Tuesday, but it is not until the following Saturday, the 24th, that Roquentin finally goes to the *Hôtel d'Espagne*.[10] Similarly, whilst on receipt of the letter, Roquentin comments: ["It's been five years since I've heard from her"], he reproaches Anny at their meeting with the words: ["Have you needed me during these four years that you haven't seen me?"].[12] Minor though these errors are, combined with the uneasy mixture of philosophy with fiction, they point either to a certain mismanagement on Sartre's part which may serve to weaken the force of his novel as a philosophical parable, or to a considerably different practice within the novel itself, by which its psychological and fictional elements become dominant.

A further preliminary difficulty of a technical nature concerns the legitimacy of applying to a study of *La Nausée* information only applicable to Sartre's work after 1940, especially since the novel was begun in 1931 and completed in 1936.[13] Philosophical interpretations of the novel depend all too often upon a view of Roquentin as a pre-existentialist hero, a view to some extent encouraged by Sartre himself in his highly ambiguous "prière d'insérer" and in his interview with Claudine Chonez after the publication of *La Nausée*.[14] This ignores the fact that Sartre's intellectual preoccupations during the 1930s were centered upon contingency, phenomenology and psychology,[15] an interest which lies at the heart of the short stories in *Le Mur*, and that between the pre-War Sartre and the Existentialist hero of the Liberation, there lies the crucial dividing-line of his experience in a German prisoner-of-war camp and his first *engagé* text, the play *Bariona*. To read *La Nausée* with hindsight, therefore, through *L'Etre et le néant* and later texts, is a dangerous activity, even though certain sections, especially those used by Rhiannon Goldthorpe and the description of *mauvaise foi*, appear to be highly pertinent: it encourages an unjustified moulding of the text into a philosophical pattern established long after its creation. Above all, the mere similarity between passages in *La Nausée* and analyses in the later philosophical works is not enough to establish an interpretation of the novel, since it offers no guide to the status and tone of these passages and hence no means of understanding their role within the novel.

If a purely philosophical reading of *La Nausée* presents difficulties on its own terms, concerning the status of the text and the precise role and nature of the philosophy within the novel, it is additionally problematic in that it necessarily relegates the literary content of the text to a subordinate or non-existent level. In so doing, whilst having the merit of by-passing the ambiguities raised by the mixture of philosophy and fiction, it ignores the fact, recounted at length in *Les Mots*, that Sartre's early dominant ambition was, precisely, literary, and obliges the reader to evade or relegate whole sections of the novel. As a counter-balance to the traditional view of *La Nausée* as a philosophical parable, it seems useful, therefore, to reduce and change the context in which the novel is usually discussed, to momentarily place the philosophical over-view to one side and to concentrate on the purely fictional quality of the work in the context of the pre-War Sartre and French intellectual and literary life of the Inter-War Years.[16] As Contat and Rybalka observe:

> [Sartre's original ambition was "to express in a literary form metaphysical truths and feelings" (*La Force de l'âge*, p. 293). Critics seem to have followed this direction too literally by constantly giving more weight to the philosophic aspect of *La Nausée* at the expense of the other possible approaches. It appears to us today, however, that the images and metaphors of the work are not always there to illustrate a system but that, on the contrary, Sartre invents a philosophy to unify these images and to account for his own obsessions. *La Nausée* is, on the one hand, a piece of research work in which Sartre reveals himself entirely, and, on the other hand, a work of transition that, even before the publication of the book in 1938, marked an already completed stage in the evolution of his thought.][17]

As a literary work, with the balance redressed in its favour, the novel may lose some of its metaphysical didacticism, but it begins to provide an important insight into French literary and intellectual preoccupations of the 1920s and 1930s.

In order to recuperate the literary status of the work, it is necessary first of all to distinguish between author and creation and then to proceed by testing the validity of Roquentin's aesthetico-metaphysical solution at the end of the novel by examining the personal and psychological factors which determine it: an area in which the role of Anny is crucial. It then becomes possible to view Roquentin as representative, not of a positive general philosophical position, but of a particular intellectual *malaise* of the Inter-War Years.

In distinguishing between the author Sartre and his creation Roquentin, the reader is assisted by Sartre's own comments in *Les Mots*, which weigh strongly against an interpretation of Roquentin purely as a representative of the authorial view: ["*I was* Roquentin, I showed in him, without any accommodation, the thread of my life; at the same time I was *me*, the elect, the annalist of Hades, with my photomicroscope of glass and steel leaning over my own protoplasmic syrups"].[18] At the same time, within the text itself, Sartre stresses the autonomous, *fictive* nature of Roquentin, through the device of the "Avertissement des Editeurs." As Michael Edwards points out, the use of such a hackneyed contrivance as the eighteenth-century convention of a fictional "editor" serves primarily to fit the work into a recognisable fictional category. The very presence of the "Avertissement" signals the work's nature as a novel,[19] and not as a philosophical "factum." In addition, the "Avertissement" fulfils its original eighteenth-century purpose, that of acting as a disenculpation-device by which, since the events of the novel are manifestly *true*, the author is absolved of the guilt of creating them and is separated in the mind of the reader from the protagonist. In this context, Sartre doubly profits from the benefits of the disenculpation-device, by using the stronger indication

"Avertissement," rather than the milder "Avis," and by using an undefined number of "éditeurs," rather than one, preventing even the identification of the editorial voice with that of the author. Finally, the use of footnotes and blanks in the early pages of the novel again follow a convention by which a semblance of veracity is given to the fictional diary-form.[20] The importance of this for *La Nausée*, however, lies in the fact that, if the diary is *true*, then the protagonist Roquentin is *real*, not merely external to his creator Sartre, but also irremediably *specific* and individual. Hence the weight of the *exergue* from Céline's *L'Eglise*: ["He's a lad without collective importance . . . scarcely an individual"]. A final warning against viewing Roquentin immediately as an exemplary character is conveyed by the fact, as Contat and Rybalka point out, that he presents many similarities with the hero of ["The Childhood of a Leader"], Lucien Fleurier, whom they term "un anti-Roquentin."[21] The first-person narration of the diary-form in *La Nausée* is not enough, *a priori*, to confer upon Roquentin an exemplary status plainly denied his young fascist counterpart who nevertheless undergoes similar obsessional experiences. The reader is therefore invited to transfer his attention from the metaphysical message that the novel appears to be trying to convey to the precise explorations, in their totality, that Roquentin is undertaking in the course of *La Nausée*, and the reason for them.

Nevertheless, it is from the ostensible philosophical message of the novel that it is most convenient to proceed, since the significance of *La Nausée* lies, in large part, in the way in which that message breaks down under its own weight. Broadly summarised, the philosophical exploration in the novel is concerned with two distinct but connected areas of experience. One, which runs from the initial attack of Nausea when Roquentin is confronted with the "galet" in the "Feuillet sans date," to the final revelation of the significance of that and other similar experiences in the final *Jardin public* scene, may be said to be working towards a vision or intuition of the contingency of all phenomena and hence of Man's absurd position in an inescapable existence. This progression towards the intuition of contingency of phenomena is accompanied by a much weightier and continuing reflexion on the notion of "aventures," introduced by the Autodidacte when he visits Roquentin in order to see the latter's post-cards,[22] and which casts the same light, ultimately, on the structuration of human experience as does the discovery of "contingence" on that of phenomena. An adventure, decides Roquentin, cannot by definition exist in the present, but only in the past, and the only way that it exists in the past, and is brought *back* to the present, is through an aesthetic mediation: ["in order for the most banal event to become an adventure, it is necessary and sufficient that one begins to *recount* it"].[23] Hence, ["adventures are in books"].[24] The belief in "aventures," therefore, testifies to the same "mauvaise foi," and for the same reasons, as the belief that a ["chestnut tree"] is part of a great chain of being in which all the

components may be conveniently categorised, labelled, and thus neutral-
ised. It is for this reason that Anny's attempt to have ["adventures"] in the
present, in the form of ["perfect moments"], constitutes, literally, play-
acting and is doomed to the failure revealed in her final meeting with
Roquentin.

It is precisely in this early reflection on the aesthetic properties of
"aventures," in which Roquentin records his fascination with Jazz, café
music, gramophones and "Négresses": ["I am so happy when a Negress
sings: what summits will I not reach if my *own life* were the material of
the melody"],[25] that he begins to work towards the final aesthetic solution
of the novel, revealed with the same suddenness as the sense of "contingence" in the *Jardin public*, in the final scene in the *Rendez-vous des
cheminots*, through the playing of "Some of these days."[26] The line of
argument which leads to this apparently positive conclusion of the novel
begins formally in the reflections on the *Jardin public* vision, concentrating on the properties of the circle. As Roquentin concludes: ["A circle is
not absurd, it is very well explained by the rotation of a segment about one
of its extremities. But then a circle doesn't exist either"].[27] Yet it is precisely
existence which is the central problem and which condemns Roquentin to
be ["superfluous for eternity"]:[28] thus, what appears as a black joke, by
which the positive qualities of the circle are negated by its non-existence,
becomes a highly serious project, by which the quest for non-existence is to
be sought through the properties of the circle and its equivalents. Among
these equivalents are the "aventures" and the song, "Some of these days," a
circle by virtue of being a "disque" and saved from existence: ["She doesn't
exist since she has nothing superfluous: it's everything else which is
superfluous in relation to her. She *is*"].[29] Hence, if in Roquentin's eyes, the
"Négresse" and the "Juif" justify themselves by the creation of the song,
then the construction of a similar artefact can lead to salvation: Roquentin
will escape from "contingence" by writing "une histoire," "une aventure."
As Keith Gore concludes: "He too, by the creation of a work of art owing
its existence to his imagination, would be cleansed of the sin of existing."[30]

The initial problem posed by this interpretation of the philosophical
material in the novel is that the ending is plainly calqued upon that of
Proust's *A la Recherche du temps perdu*. This feature has caused some
embarrassment to those critics who have recognised that Sartre may not be
opting for the Proustian solution but have been unable to satisfactorily
integrate the Proustian presence into an overall reading of the novel.[31] Not
only does *La Nausée* as a whole present undoubted coincidences with
Proust's work: the isolation of the narrators, the rooms to which they
retreat in order to digest and create their experiences, their love of
aphorism, their preoccupation with time, but the role played in the novel
by the Jazz tune "Some of these days" appears exactly similar to that
played by the Vinteuil sonata in *A la Recherche*. The presence of a ["Swan
toothpaste"][32] in the novel, and the fact that the record of "Some of these

days" is played for Roquentin by the "serveuse" in the café who happens to be called Madeleine, whilst the café's owner is called Françoise,[33] serve to make the parallel inescapable.

Yet, if the parallel is obvious, the humorous allusions to Proust prevent it from being serious or even neutral. As a literary reflection within the text, the Proustian material forms part of a pattern which is uniformly parodic. Not only is parody a device of which Sartre makes important use in the last two stories of Le Mur, "Erostrate" and "L'Enfance d'un chef," where the principal target is Surrealism, but it plays a major role throughout La Nausée, to the extent that Germaine Brée can refer to it as a "literary graveyard."[34] Thus Roquentin's past in South-East Asia, his theft of the Rollebon manuscript and the whole reflection on "aventures" are clearly directed at Malraux.[35] The ["chestnut tree"] which reappears, incidentally, in "L'Enfance d'un chef,"[36] and which becomes for Roquentin the very image of "contingence," is the exact negation of the "Arbre de M. Taine" in Barrès's Les Déracinés, which symbolised the unity of human existence,[37] and the satirized humanism of the Autodidacte, who admits to having impulsively followed the funeral of a total stranger, is an ironic reflection of Jules Romains's Mort de quelqu'un.[38] In this context of parody, therefore, the debasement of the Vinteuil sonata into Sophie Tucker's Jazz song can only constitute a warning that Roquentin's conversion to art is not to be read on the same level as the aesthetico-metaphysical solution at the end of A la Recherche.[39] Further evidence for this is contained in Sartre's comment in his essay of 1939, "Une Idée fondamentale de la phénoménologie de Husserl: l'Intentionnalité": ["And now we are rid of Proust"],[40] and in the fact that La Nausée, because of the device of the "Avertissement," is open-ended, in contrast to the closed circle of Proust's novel.

Doubt is cast upon the ending of the novel, however, not merely by its status as ironic calque upon Proust: Roquentin's reasoning as he listens to the record and constructs his new project is seriously defective. Not only does his plan to write an adventure-novel contradict his earlier conclusions, without bringing to bear any new data which might justify such a reversal, but the theoretical meditation on which his decision is based is not totally logical. The song has the same properties as the circle: it is self-justificatory, it is not de trop. It is not absurd because it does not exist. A posteriori, it may justify the Jewish author and the black singer, though this is by no means certain: Roquentin is the only person to think of them, and even he does not bother to recall their names. What it does not do, is to justify the process of its own creation, nor those who participate in it. In other words, whilst the song, as a circle, as a "disque," is charmed, outside existence, the "Négresse" and the "Juif," even though they sing and write it, are "de trop" and absurd. In that sense, their work can by no means serve as a useful model for Roquentin: his projection to the moment when the book, like the song, will live autonomously apart from being couched in the terms of the most naïve and adolescent ambition, will do nothing to spare him his present and continuing anguish. What Roquentin is doing is confusing two totally separate categories: the Platonic realm of the work of art, and the real world in which he has to live, much in the same way that Descartes, in his ontological proof of God, confuses attributes with existence and erroneously uses the former to prove the latter.[41]

The ending of the novel, therefore, is ironic in its use of the Proustian model, and comprises by no means unassailable reasoning and a strong negation of previous tenets. It constitutes not so much a triumphant grasp of an ultimate solution as a flight into self-delusion, and has the effect of shifting the area of interpretation of the protagonist from the philosophical to the psychological. It is important to recall that Sartre's original title for the novel was *Melancholia*, changed at a late stage to *La Nausée* at the suggestion of Gaston Gallimard,[42] from the engraving by Dürer. The importance lies, not so much in the relationship between the novel and the engraving (though the fact that the engraving is a puzzle, to be decoded, is not without significance),[43] as in the way in which the original title evokes a psychological state by no means uncommon in French literature of the time, as Léon Daudet's *Melancholia*, of 1928, and Louis Guilloux's *Le Sang noir*, of 1935, indicate.[44] In this context, it is helpful to read *La Nausée* in conjunction with Freud's essay of 1915, *Mourning and Melancholia*,[45] although some caution must be exercised, since Sartre's dislike of the Freudian theory of the Unconscious is well-known. Nevertheless, the stories in *Le Mur* point to an unironic concern with the psychologically abnormal, by which sexual and family tensions lead to a state of *mauvaise foi*, and this would appear to permit a serious exploration of Roquentin on the same terms. In what Freud himself admits is a tentative and preliminary study, he defines the major features and causes of melancholia as "a profoundly painful dejection, cessation of interest in the outside world, loss of the capacity to love, inhibition of all activity, and a lowering of the self-regarding feelings to a degree that finds utterances in self-reproaches and self-revilings, and culminates in a delusional expectation of punishment."[46] What distinguishes these symptoms from those of mourning is that, while both depend on the disappearance of a love-object, in the case of mourning: "Reality-testing has shown that the loved object no longer exists, and it proceeds to demand that all libido shall be withdrawn from its attachments to that object."[47] In the case of melancholia, however, the break is less clean and more subtle. "Melancholia too may be the reaction to the loss of a loved object,"[48] although in this case "the object has not perhaps actually died, but has been lost as an object of love (e.g. in the case of a betrothed girl who has been jilted)."[49] The important point, however, is that the patient "knows *whom* he has lost but not *what* he has lost in him. This would suggest that melancholia is in some way related to an object-loss which is withdrawn from consciousness, in contradiction to mourning, in which there is nothing about the loss that is unconscious,"[50] and Freud is then able to reconstruct the process by which melancholia is formed:

> An object-choice, an attachment of the libido to a particular person, had at one time existed; then, owing to a real slight or disappointment coming from this loved person, the object-relationship was shattered. The result was not the normal one of withdrawal of the libido from this object, and a displacement of it on to a new one, but something different, for whose coming-about various conditions seem to be necessary. The object-cathexis proved to have little power of resistance and was brought to an end. But the free libido was not displaced on to another object; it was withdrawn into the ego. There, however, it was not employed in any unspecified way, but served to establish an *identification* of the ego with the abandoned object. Thus the shadow of the object fell upon the ego, and the latter could henceforth be judged by a special agency, as though it were an object, the foresaken object. In this way, an object-loss was transformed into an ego-loss and the conflict between the ego and the loved person into a cleavage between the critical activity of the ego and the ego as altered by identification.[51]

This process, which is "effected on a narcissistic basis,"[52] leads to a state of self-denigration and self-hatred on the part of the patient. Yet, for Freud, this self-hatred is in reality a screen for a sadistic hatred of the departed loved object, and can be carried to an ultimate extreme: "It is this sadism alone that solves the riddle of the tendency to suicide which makes melancholia so interesting — and so dangerous."[53]

Freud's study is illuminating for certain features of Roquentin's psychological state: the persistent misanthropy, the self-denigration, the retreat from the real world into a purely metaphorical one (surely, the major significance of the name, Bouville) constructed from Roquentin's own obsessions, the all-pervading sense of threat: ["A great menace hangs over the town"].[54] Perhaps more importantly, it directs the reader to an all-too-neglected aspect of *La Nausée*: the role of Anny. When she is discussed in analyses of the novel, it is only in connection with her conception of "moments parfaits," expressed in the scene of her final encounter with Roquentin. The advantage of momentarily setting the philosophical interpretation of the novel on one side, however, is that it allows the reader to see that Anny's role is considerably more important, to the extent that she can be seen to constitute the absent moving-force of the work. And it is in this context that her disruption of Roquentin's sense of a time-scale must be seen. Roquentin's first reference to Anny is near the beginning of the novel, and is illuminating in the light of Freud's comment on melancholia and the unconscious: ["Formerly — even a long time after she left me — I thought for Anny. Now I no longer think for anyone"].[55] Roquentin is the victim of the loss of a love-object, believing that loss is no longer important to him. That he is deluded is indicated by the frequent and persistent references to Anny throughout the novel, long before the letter summoning him to Paris, and by the way in which the relationship with her, as discussed earlier, somehow disrupts Roquentin's conscious grasp of the flow of time. The unconscious effects of Anny's departure can therefore be seen in Roquentin's retreat into the melancholic capital of Bouville and in his transfer of interest to the misanthropic and cynical Rollebon. At the same time, Freud's schema by which the ego of the melancholic is forced to identify with the abandoned object, to the extent that the abandoned object casts a shadow over the ego, throws light upon the way in which Roquentin, absent from Anny, undergoes a parallel, albeit tardy, development. His meditation on "aventures" *reflects* Anny's fascination with "moments parfaits"; similarly, he reaches the same conclusion as Anny regarding their spuriousness, though again after her discovery.

If Anny remains throughout the novel a constant object of Roquentin's preoccupations, to the extent that she may constitute the psychological motivation for an ostensibly philosophical position, Freud's comment on hatred/self-hatred would provide valuable information on the direction to which Roquentin's writing is turned. In this sense, it is possible to read the diary as having Anny not merely as hidden subject, but also as hidden object (the necessary hidden reader of any diary): the butt of Roquentin's reproach and remorse. For this reason, the choice of Sophie Tucker's record is by no means as gratuitous as it may at first sight appear: "Some of these days / You'll miss me honey," with its mixture of condemnation and anticipated revenge, mirrors exactly Roquentin's dismay at Anny's original departure and his anticipation of a reconciliation at the *Hôtel d'Espagne* (Château en Espagne). It is highly significant, therefore, that once Anny, the implicit object of the diary, has made her quasi-definitive departure, Roquentin is left in a total limbo, is receptive to the temptations of the bogus aesthetic solution, and the diary, and the novel, end.

Roquentin's projection towards Anny also serves the purpose of indicating a constant feature of his personality: his bad faith, which takes one form of attempting to give himself meaning by situating himself in a time-scale which runs from the present to the future. Thus, his anticipation of the meeting in Paris with Anny, reflected by his subsequent decision to leave Bouville on 1 March, allows him to exist in the time-scale which he affects to despise. He is able to dismiss the past, his own and that of M. de Rollebon, without, by so doing, cutting himself adrift entirely. He is a victim of the same syndrome analysed by Beckett in *En attendant Godot*, by which the artificially-sustained hope of Godot's arrival *in the future* still confers meaning on Vladimir and Estragon, even though their past is lost day by day.

This example of bad faith on Roquentin's part suggests another, connected feature: the fact that he is considerably more ambiguous socially than initially appears. On one level, Roquentin is very much the subversive, despising the bourgeoisie of Bouville and their attempts to immortalise themselves in their portraiture. For this reason, he experiences close fellow-feeling with those like Anny, who exploit the system consciously, or those like the Autodidacte or M. Achille, who are the victims of bourgeois society, albeit petit-bourgeois victims, the proletariat being strangely absent from Roquentin's metaphorical universe. Hence his shame at M. Achille's subservience to *docteur* Rogé: ["We're on the same side, we should have united against them. But he left me in the lurch . . ."],[56] and his comments on the Autodidacte: ["he had to find himself alone one day. Like M. Achille, like me: he's my kind, he has goodwill"].[57] At the same time, there is something rather assumed about his fellow-feeling, and there is more than a suggestion that Roquentin's disgust with bourgeois society comes, not from below, but from above. He is, after all, a *rentier*, removed from the day-to-day economic system, a snob, who despises the innocent pastimes of the Bouvillois as inauthentic "divertissements," a man, in fact who may be closer to *docteur* Rogé than he cares to admit. In his disparaging analysis of the microcosm of Bouville, he certainly shares the aristocratic cynicism of Adhémar de Rollebon, as well as his subject's initials:[58] and Rollebon, we are told, is a ["a conceited little liar"].[59] In all, Roquentin, with his retreat to Bouville, his withdrawal to the Hôtel Printania, his aesthetic enterprise, his reflections on painting and his elitist isolation reflects no-one so much as Huysmans's Des Esseintes, that earlier distinguished victim of "nausées":[60] ["Since his earliest youth he had been tortured by inexplicable loathings, by shudderings which froze his spine, which made him grit his teeth for instance when he saw the wet linen that a maid was wringing out. These effects had always persisted; even today he suffered for real when he heard a cloth ripped, or when he rubbed a finger over a piece of chalk, or when his hand felt a piece of watered silk"].[61] A problematic metaphysical hero, a parodied artistic decadent, socially ambiguous and psychologically melancholic, Roquentin appears to defy synthesis, and it is undoubtedly in this multifaceted nature of the protagonist that the novel comes under maximum tension. The problem may be resolved to some extent, however, by returning to the *exergue*: ["He's a lad without collective importance, just an individual"]. It is an interesting quotation when read in the context of Céline's *L'Eglise*, occurring during a dialogue between the hero, Bardamu's, two employers at the *Société des Nations* in Geneva, who are just about to sack him. His immediate superior, Yudenzweck, remarks, of Bardamu, to his friend Mosaïc: ["I'm going to treat him as a friend; anyway I saw him yesterday evening. He's going away; he explained it to me. He's a lad without collective importance, he's just an individual"],[62] but then goes on to make an important qualification:

[YUDENZWECK: Yes, Bardamu, I'm telling you, I felt that he was judging me. He was judging me, I understood it later, because we don't speak the same language. He spoke the lingo of the individual; me, I speak the collective lingo. He used to interest me quite a bit until the moment I understood that. Then, I stood listening to him, out of discipline. It's poison what they speak these individuals.

MOSAÏC: Yes, poison that serves no purpose.

YUDENZWECK: There are lots of individuals among the French. The Germans, the Japanese, the English too—but they're too proud—are almost the only ones who are a little bit collective.][63]

The "individu," therefore, is set against the "collectif" and acts subversively towards it. In reading *L'Eglise*, Sartre has recognized the "Homme seul" who is the hero of his unpublished *La Légende de la vérité* of 1931 (the year in which he began *La Nausée*) of which only a fragment was published in *Bifur*.[64] Sartre's view of the "Homme seul" is neatly summarised by Simone de Beauvoir: ["He reserved his sympathy for the thaumaturges who, excluded from the City and from its logic and its mathematics, wander, solitary, in the wild places, and, in order to know things, believe only their eyes. Thus, he only granted to the artist, to the writer, to the philosopher, to those men he called 'the men alone,' the privilege of grasping reality from life"].[65] At the same time, however, the "individu/homme seul," cut off from the "collectif," is not merely a prophet, he is also a highly vulnerable man, and it is this tension between the official and private roles that *La Nausée* explores. Believing only the evidence of one's own eyes is heroic, but is also open to danger and distortion: hence the ultimate doubts about Roquentin's reasoning. Similarly, in his predilection for aphorism and his philosophical system-building from an acute psychological state, he can be interpreted as an "individu" who is claiming for himself an "importance collective" to which he may not be entitled. The question raised by Roquentin's ironic role as *Homme seul* is: can he stand the tension, the ambiguity and the isolation? The flight from reality at the end of the novel and the references to Roquentin's *papiers* in the "Avertissement" suggest that he cannot. Possibly the most revealing phrase in the final scene is the one which runs: ["I am like some guy completely frozen after a journey in the snow who suddenly enters a warm room"].[66] Roquentin can no longer stand the cold of his self-created philosophical world, and by the end of the novel he is looking for refuge.

That the refuge should be an "histoire" is of less importance, finally, than the words in which the flight is couched: ["It should be as beautiful and as hard as steel . . ."].[67] It is vital in this context to recall that Drieu la Rochelle's novel *Le Feu follet*, published in 1931, and which recounts the inexorable path to suicide of a young, isolated dilettante, Alain, concludes with the words: ["A revolver is hard, it's made of steel. To strike the object at last"].[68] Roquentin's projected novel, therefore, fulfils the same function as the revolver in *Le Feu follet*: that of suicide-symbol, be the suicide literal or metaphorical, although the implication of the "Avertissement" is that Roquentin is no more. In such a conclusion, *La Nausée* enters a major area of preoccupation of French Inter-War writing, that of the intellectual suicide. Explorations of the reasons and justifications for such a suicide are contained, for example, in the "Enquête sur le suicide," in *La Révolution surréaliste*,[69] in the black humor of Jacques Rigaut's *Agence Générale du Suicide*,[70] in Drieu's "La Valise vide," as well as in *Le Feu follet*,[71] in debates between Claude Vannec and Perken in Malraux's *La Voie Royale*,[72] and in the tragic dénouement of Louis Guilloux's *Le Sang noir*.[73] Moreover, the period is dotted with real literary and intellectual suicides: Georges Plante, Jacques Rigaut, René Crevel and that of Drieu himself at the end of the War. It is not sufficiently remarked upon, though *La Nausée* reminds us that this is so, that, if the French Inter-War Years are a period of speculation on ideas, then those ideas are quite capable of killing.

Read in this light, *La Nausée* appears less as a philosophical novel than as a novel about a philosopher. It can stand as the evocation of an intellectual of the Inter-War Years who, through a dangerous mixture of psychological vulnerability and social isolation, of which the loss of Anny is the cause, is led to invent a metaphysical system which proves hard and cold indeed and from which, finally, refuge must be sought.

Notes

1. Annie Leclerc, "De Roquentin à Mathieu," *L'Arc*, 30 (1966), 71–76.

2. Simone de Beauvoir, *La Force de l'âge* (Paris, 1960), 111.

3. Rhiannon Goldthorpe, "The Presentation of Consciousness in Sartre's *La Nausée* and its Theoretical Basis: Reflection and Facticity," *French Studies*, xxii (1968), 114–32; "The Presentation of Consciousness in Sartre's *La Nausée*: 2, Transcendance and Intentionality," *French Studies*, xxv (1970), 32–46.

4. M. Edwards, "*La Nausée*—a Symbolist Novel," *Adam*, Year 35, nos. 343–5 (1970), 9.

5. De Beauvoir, *La Force de l'âge*, 335.

6. Marcel Arland, "Essais critiques," *Nouvelle Revue Française*, 298 (juillet 1938), 130.

7. *Ibid.*, 130.

8. Michel Contat and Michel Rybalka, *Les Ecrits de Sartre* (Paris, 1973), 61.

9. Jean-Paul Sartre, *La Nausée* (Paris, coll: "Livre de poche"), 90.

10. *Ibid.*, 191.

11. *Ibid.*, 89.

12. *Ibid.*, 194.

13. See: de Beauvoir, *La Force de l'âge*, 111; Contat and Rybalka, *Les Ecrits de Sartre*, 62.

14. Claudine Chonez, "Jean-Paul Sartre, romancier philosophe," *Marianne*, 23 novembre 1938; "A qui les lauriers des Goncourt, Femina, Renaudot, Interallié," *Marianne*, 7 décembre 1938.

15. As indicated by his work with Nizan, in 1928, on the French translation of Jaspers's *Psychopathologie générale*.

16. The affinities between *La Nausée* and German literature, particularly Kafka's *Die Verwandlung* and Rilke's *Die Aufzeichnungen des Malte Laurids Brigge*, lie outside the scope of this essay.

17. Contat and Rybalka, *Les Ecrits de Sartre*, 63.

18. Jean-Paul Sartre, *Les Mots* (Gallimard, Paris, 1964), 210. It could be argued that it is as illegitimate to use *Les Mots* in a discussion of *La Nausée* as it is to refer to *L'Etre et le Néant* and subsequent philosophical works. I would maintain, however, that there is considerable difference between Sartre's ability to comment usefully on his own work and the arbitrary application to early works of fiction of later philosophical argument.

19. Edwards, "*La Nausée* — a Symbolist Novel."

20. As, for example, in Bernanos's *Journal d'un curé de campagne*.

21. Contat and Rybalka, *Les Ecrits de Sartre*, 70.

22. *La Nausée* 49–60, the section headed: "Vendredi, 3 heures."

23. *Ibid.*, 60.

24. *Ibid.*, 58.

25. *Ibid.*, 59.

26. It is worth emphasising at this point that the song constitutes a strong link with "L'Enfance d'un chef," where Lucien and Berliac ["smoked English cigarettes, played some records, and Lucien heard the voices of Sophie Tucker and Al Johnson [*sic*]"] (*Le Mur* (Paris, coll: "Livre de poche"), 183). The use of the song also testifies to a certain confusion on Sartre's part, Sophie Tucker not being a "Négresse" and "Some of these days" hardly qualifying as a Jazz piece. Finally, to settle a long-standing controversy over the accuracy of the lyrics, whilst later versions undoubtedly read "Some of these days / you're gonna miss me honey," the original Sophie Tucker lyric is that recorded by Sartre.

27. *La Nausée*.

28. *Ibid.*, 182.

29. *Ibid.*, 244.

30. Keith D. Gore, *Sartre: "La Nausée" and "Les Mouches"* (London, 1970), 43.

31. See, for example: Pierre Bost, "Proust devant une sonate, Sartre devant un air de jazz entendent une seule voix," *Le Figaro littéraire*, 8 janvier 1949, pp. 1, 3; Robert Champigny, "Sens de *La Nausée*," *PMLA*, lxx (1955), 37–46; Robert G. Cohn, "Sartre versus Proust," *Partisan Review*, xxviii (1961), 633–45. In particular, P. Newman-Gordon, in "Sartre, lecteur de Proust ou le paradoxe de *La Nausée*," *Bulletin de la Société des Amis de Marcel Proust*, no. 29 (1979), is unable to reconcile Sartre's use of Proustian material in *La Nausée* with his stated antipathy to *A la Recherche*.

32. *La Nausée*, 158.

33. *Ibid.*, 32.

34. Germaine Brée and Margaret Guiton, "Jean-Paul Sartre: The Search for Identity," *An Age of Fiction* (New Brunswick, 1957), 207.

35. See: J. Dale, "Sartre and Malraux: *La Nausée* and *La Voie Royale*," *Forum for Modern Language Studies*, iv (1968), 335–46.

36. *Le Mur*, 160.

37. See: Denis J. Fletcher, "Sartre and Barrès: Some Notes on *La Nausée*," *Forum for Modern Language Studies*, iv (1968), 330–34.

38. See: Clothilde Wilson, "Sartre's Literary Graveyard: *La Nausée* and *Mort de quelqu'un*," *French Review*, xxxviii (1965), 744–53.

39. The song "Some of these days," combining Jazz and a Negro singer, could contain a further ironic reference, directed at the fashionable craze amongst the Inter-War Years intelligentsia for Jazz and the "bal nègre."

40. Jean-Paul Sartre, "Une Idée fondamentale de la phénoménologie de Husserl: L'Intentionalité," in *Situations*, I (Gallimard, Paris, 1947), 34.

41. In this context, Roquentin's insistence upon geometrical examples: the circle, and the triangle created by the Boulevard Noir, may well be a specific allusion to Descartes's use of the triangle in his ontological proof of God. Roquentin does refer to himself as a "young Descartes" (p. 84).

42. See: de Beauvoir, *La Force de l'âge*, 308.

43. For a full account of the possible influence of Dürer's engraving upon *La Nausée*, see: G. H. Bauer, *Sartre and the Artist* (Chicago, 1969).

44. Léon Daudet, *Melancholia* (Paris, 1928); Louis Guilloux, *Le Sang noir* (Paris, 1935). It was probably the existence of Daudet's volume that led Gallimard to insist upon a change of title. "Le Sang noir" is, of course, a synonym for melancholy.

45. Sigmund Freud, "Mourning and Melancholia," in *The Standard Edition of the Complete Works of Sigmund Freud*, ed. James Strachey (London, 1953–66), xiv, 283–60.

46. *Ibid.*, 244.

47. *Ibid.*, 244.

48. *Ibid.*, 245.

49. *Ibid.*, 245.

50. *Ibid.*, 245.

51. *Ibid.*, 249.

52. *Ibid.*, 249.

53. *Ibid.*, 252.

54. *La Nausée*, 116. In one sense, the entire topography of Bouville can be seen to be generated by Roquentin's intellectual and literary obsessions: hence, the interest in "ordures" and Bouville, the Proustian presence, the café Mably and the abbé Mably, and the fact that the café's proprietor is a M. Fasquelle, the name of a famous publishing-house. This opens out into a general obsessional and hallucinatory world, as, for example, in the dream sequence on pp. 87–88, which could serve as a *mise en abyme* of the novel.

55. *Ibid.*, 17.

56. *Ibid.*, 99.

57. *Ibid.*, 225. An interesting echo of Dr. Delbende, in Bernanos's *Journal d'un curé de campagne*.

58. An interesting pattern between the use of the letters A and R emerges in the novel.

59. *La Nausée*, 86.

60. J.-K. Huysmans, *A rebours* (Paris, coll: "Diamant"), 120.

61. *Ibid.*, 120. For a further study of Huysmans and *La Nausée*, see: Jean Onimus, "Folantin, Salavin, Roquentin: trois étapes de la conscience malheureuse," *Etudes*, 296 (janvier 1958), 14–31.

62. L.-F. Céline, *L'Eglise* (Paris, 1952), 161.

63. *Ibid.*, 163. The deep impression made on Sartre by *Voyage au bout de la nuit* (see: de Beauvoir, *La Force de l'âge*, 142) is probably translated into *La Nausée* more in terms of the cynical, detached tone than in specific stylistic features.

64. Jean-Paul Sartre, "Légende de la vérité," *Bifur*, 8 (juin 1931), 77–96. See: Contat and Rybalka, *Les Ecrits de Sartre*, 52–53, and Appendix, pp. 531–45.

65. De Beauvoir, *La Force de l'âge*, 49–50.

66. *La Nausée*, 248. Another echo of Bernanos's *Journal d'un curé de campagne*.

67. *Ibid.*, 249.

68. Pierre Drieu la Rochelle, *Le Feu follet* (Gallimard, Paris, coll: "Folio"), 172.

69. "Enquête sur le suicide," *La Révolution surréaliste*.

70. Jacques Rigaut, *Agence générale du suicide*, reprinted in *Ecrits* (Paris, 1970).

71. Pierre Drieu la Rochelle, "La Valise vide," *Nouvelle Revue Française*, nos. 118–23 (1923), 162–205.

72. André Malraux, *La Voie Royale* (Paris, 1930).

73. See also: Francis J. Green, "Louis Guilloux's *Le Sang Noir.* A Prefiguration of Sartre's *La Nausée*," *French Review*, xliii (1969), 205–14.

Erostrate: Sartre's Paranoid

Gary Woodle*

Although the collection of short stories under the title *Le Mur*[1] contains some of Sartre's finest work, it has been almost ignored by criticism, which tends to focus on his theater and on his philosophy proper, even at the expense of *La Nausée*. The third story, *Erostrate*, was completed in 1936 but seems to belong to a slightly earlier period; it makes specific reference to the sensational murder by the Papin sisters of their mistresses, which occurred in February, 1933. *Erostrate* is playful and amusing, and simply told, with none of the labored phenomenological performances which mar so much of his last novels. It provides an accessible, perhaps indispensable introduction not only to *La Nausée*, which it anticipates in many ways, but to Sartre's work in general.

Paul Hilbert, the narrator and semi-hero, has isolated himself on the seventh floor of a hotel in Montparnasse, not far from the bustle of the great Boulevard, with, in those days, its railroad station and its cluster of celebrated cafés. He leaves his room only when absolutely necessary, to eat and to go to work, anxious to avoid contact with the "enemy," his fellow man. Things get better for him, he says, after he buys a revolver. From time to time he fondles the heavy object; knowing that it is loaded and ready to explode at any time gives him a new sense of power, and he no longer fears strolling the crowded Paris streets. He is aware that the gun in his pocket must make him walk like a man with a constant erection.

On the first Saturday of every month Hilbert takes a prostitute, Léa, to a hotel room where he manages sexual gratification of sorts by watching her undress. Once, unable to find the willing Léa, he uses his new revolver to force a reluctant surrogate to strip and parade and humiliate herself before him; he realizes that his pleasure increases in proportion to the helplessness of the victim. She is no longer young, and her very maturity makes her seem more "nude" to him and thus more vulnerable. The gun, of course, makes her totally defenseless and him absolutely powerful. Later he recalls her terrified eyes and regrets not having shot her in the stomach; he soon dreams of bullet holes grouped around a navel and

*From *Review of Existential Psychology and Psychiatry* 13, no. 1 (1974): 30–41. Reprinted with permission.

begins to imagine the pleasure he would take firing point-blank at his fellow men. Having horrified a prostitute (which, he claims, is not easy), Hilbert hatches a plan to astound the world by the gratuitous murder of a random selection of people in the street, to be followed by that ultimate refusal of the Human, his own suicide. He prepares his publicity in advance by mailing an explanatory letter to 102 French Humanist writers, the benevolent shepherds of the Human Race who imagine they perform great works dispensing to the masses the false comfort of Universal Brotherhood. Eventually he stops going to the office, loses his job, and spends the last of his savings. When his food is gone he goes down to the rue d'Odessa, fires his revolver at a man, finds himself pursued by a mob and finally run to ground in the toilet of a café.

Hazel Barnes suggested once that *Erostrate* might be read as the work of a traditional Freudian,[2] and then, in her latest study, that a follower of Adler might have written it.[3] There is no question that Hilbert is a pathological case, and getting worse. Broadly speaking a paranoid, he exhibits an array of related symptoms around a basic sexual inadequacy. He has never slept with a woman and is convinced, from what he has heard, that she gets more from it than the man.[4] At best he would need a pious and frigid woman who would submit with disgust. He claims that he wants nothing from anyone and wants to give nothing (having nothing to give, of course, given his rigidity and flattened sensibilities). Clinically speaking, he fears loss of control; by his sadistic manipulation of the whore he turns the tables on his own passivity and takes revenge against some lost authority figure. Sartre would add that he captures the free subjectivity of the Other, dangerous to his own, by making it as far as possible an object for his mute gaze. The most serious of his evident problems are, in no particular order, his sadism, his voyeurism, his fear of crowds and of being touched, and of course his sense of moral superiority and growing megalomania, the exaggerated response of the paranoid to the increasing debilitation of the Ego. Repetitions conforming to the calendar, a fastidious attention to detail in his planning, and a ritual hand-washing before leaving his room at the end might also count as symptoms. Prior to his crime he experiences visual hyperacuity and hallucinations. Conspicuous by its absence is any indication of the latent homosexuality (or even fear of it, or confusion of sexual identity) intrinsic to Freud's formulation of paranoiogenesis. A paranoid without homosexuality may be as disturbingly anti-Freudian as Sartre's later portrayal of the homosexual Genet, especially in light of the fact that the obvious model for the gun-toting paranoid was a friend of his who was indeed a homosexual.[5] Suffice it to say here that any final assessment of Sartre's system will have to come to grips with his radical anti-Freudian interpretation of Genet's homosexuality.

It is impossible now to say whether Sartre had read Freud's analysis of Dr. Schreber. Simone de Beauvoir says that by around 1930 he had read

the *Interpretation of Dreams* and the *Psychopathology of Everyday Life.*
We also know that by then he had read Adler's *Neurotic Constitution* and
preferred it to Freud because it gave less importance to sexuality. In
general, Sartre was suspicious of psychoanalysis, put off by what he saw as
dogmatic symbolism, mechanistic explanation, a preponderant role for the
unconscious and sexuality, and an analytic method dividing the personality into hermetic components rather than attempting to comprehend it
both in its singularity and, synthetically, as an indivisible totality.
Beauvoir grants that at the time their knowledge of psychoanalysis was
superficial and that they confused readily the serious analysts and their
amateur counterparts. A serious study of it, she says, could have tempered
their exaggerated notion of human freedom, according to which the lucid,
"normal" individual could triumph over complexes, trauma, influences,
and memories. They were ready to admit, however, that the psychoses,
neuroses, and their symptoms have meaning, and that the meaning refers
to the infancy of the subject.[6]

Hilbert makes much of his physical deficiencies and of certain
unspecified frustrated ambitions, which might prompt an Adlerian, rather
than Freudian approach. He claims that the police, after his arrest,
worked him over for two hours, breaking his lorgnon and repeatedly
kicking his rear while he groped helplessly on the floor. This did not
surprise him, however, because "they," the big guys, had been waiting for
years to take advantage of his weakness and inability to defend himself.
Bullies in the streets, after all, had long been bumping into him for laughs.
Just before the shooting a passer-by clucks his tongue at him. These kinds
of outrages are clearly imaginary, and his physical weakness itself must be
exaggerated for at one point he brags of his hard, wiry body and his ability
to climb more than four flights of stairs, in spite of his paunch, without
breathing hard. It doesn't much matter, in any case, whether his paranoia
and over-compensating megalomania are due to an unhappy infantile
sexual experience with self-hatred and guilt projected outside or represent
a response to real or imagined inferiority and thwarted ambitions, since
Sartre would set up a case for psychoanalysis only in order to break it
down and use it to the ends of his own psychology.

Traditional complexes are important in Sartre's scheme but remain
merely "secondary" structures which only partially explain behaviour. We
cannot reduce Hilbert simply to a paranoid whose grandiosity has become
dangerously anti-social. A psychoanalytic interpretation doesn't exhaust
the meaning of his act any more than a reduction to complexes exhausts, in
Sartre's view, human reality. The inferiority complex, for example, is a
way we freely choose our relation with others. Inferiority as felt and lived
is the instrument we choose, in shame and anger, to make ourselves as
much as we can like things, objects for others. The recognition of a
fundamental inferiority is not unconscious, it is free choice and flight from
freedom.[7] Hilbert's poor eyesight, his potbelly are real enough, but he

seems to have largely invented his physical weakness for the cause, that is, to guarantee the superiority of his enemies and his own inferiority in their eyes, as if they were looking. Hilbert, besides being a subject for therapy, is a study in Sartrean "bad faith." Since this concept is supposed to replace the Freudian unconscious, *Erostrate* has to be seen as at least a partial repudiation of psychoanalysis.

We may approach the story by viewing Hilbert first from the outside, as he might be seen by the newspapers or in a case-study, then from the inside, as he "lives" his crime and the events leading to it. Sartre has managed with remarkable skill and consistency to wed at every point in the narrative this "psychoanalytic" Hilbert — a bundle of neurotic symptoms the gradual deterioration of which leads to acute paranoid turmoil and a potentially tragic anti-social act — with the "Sartrean" Hilbert — a free consciousness making its way toward the crime according to Sartrean categories, "faisant pour se faire et se faisant pour etre"[8] ("doing in order to make itself and making itself in order to *be*") against an objective background which includes those "secondary" structures, the pathological symptoms. One might be tempted, from the outside, to account for all of Hilbert's behaviour in psychoanalytic terms, in which case the various contents of his ravings would appear as simple rationalizations. His doctrinaire anti-Humanism, given a certain culture and the relatively high intelligence usually associated with the paranoid, would express conceptually his neurotic fear and aggression and above all the special irritation provoked by the purveyors of Brotherhood, the Humanists of whatever stamp, irritating enough to set most to raving, but the particular enemy of the paranoid temperament. His hatred of emotional promiscuity would be a simple extension of his fears of losing control and of being touched and crowded. The moral superiority he claims for himself would serve to rationalize his megalomania, in turn the last-ditch effort of the inferior Ego to save itself. His desire to astonish the world would be an extension of his sadistic joy, "comme un enfant" (88), in horrifying the prostitute. The projected crime itself would be classed as the acting out of his problem in a mode characteristic of the paranoid — assassination to gain attention. The crime as projected doesn't come off at all but its failure is perfectly consistent with Hilbert's role both as Sartrean example and as paranoid type. When he first contrives the plan, Hilbert makes no decision to carry it through but chooses to act as if he has, preoccupying himself with the necessary details — practicing his marksmanship at the shooting gallery and attending to his advance publicity by elaborating his notion of the "black hero" to his colleagues at the office. He never does make the decision and "wakes up" one day to find himself in a no-longer recognizable street, as he really is, stripped of his delusional system, "horriblement seul et petit" (96). Mechanically, he follows a man down the rue d'Odessa. When the man turns and sees his gun, Hilbert asks him where the rue de la Gaîté, of all places, is. Fearful of humiliating himself by screaming in the middle of the street, retaining a minimal sense of "dignity" by refusing to lose control in that way, yet needing to relieve the intolerable pressure, he fires. He tries to manufacture some emotion to accompany the shots by shouting "salaud" at the man, then runs down the street towards the crowded Boulevard du Montparnasse. He fires a second time because he feels a hand on his shoulder and fears "suffocation" by the crowd. His act is a failure not because he lacks the courage of his conviction, as Philip Thody has suggested,[9] but because he never had conviction in the first place.

But Hilbert is more than a crystallized paranoid type; he is an anti-Christ (a comic Sartrean version of the religious paranoid) and a study in bad faith. That Sartre is playing with the Christ-figure is obvious: Hilbert is thirty-three years old and spends his last three days locked in a dark room, with food placed before his door. Unlike Christ and Dr. Schreber, however, whose missions were to redeem Mankind and restore a lost state of bliss, Hilbert's mission is to redeem his fallen Ego, for himself alone and against Mankind, not only because the redemption of the "I" is the constant passion of the depressed, or inferior, or depersonalized neurotic, but because in Sartre's system it is the principal occupation of all of us most of the time. Hilbert has already attempted to refortify his lost sexual "I" by carrying the symbolic revolver-penis, but there is a crucial moment in the narrative when this no longer suffices, when the "Sartrean" hero takes over, as it were, and consciousness "overflows" the secondary, sexual structures to begin work on the imaginative construction of an acceptably powerful and respectable "I" in the image of Erostratus, who burned the temple of Ephesus to achieve immortal notoriety: "Quand je descendais dans la rue, je sentais en mon corps une puissance étrange. J'avais sur moi mon revolver, cette chose qui éclate et qui fait du bruit. Mais ce n'était plus de lui que je tirais mon assurance, c'était de moi: j'étais un être de l'espèce des révolvers, des pétards et des bombes" (91). ("When I would go down to the street, I would feel in my body a strange power. I had my revolver on me, that thing which explodes and makes noise. But it was no longer from it that I was getting my confidence, it was from me: I was a being in the nature of revolvers, firecrackers and bombs.")

The figure of Erostratus, supplied by one of his colleagues at the office, is timely; it encourages him to begin seeing himself not as a lonely, petty-bourgeois clerk, but as a "destiny," short and tragic and atrocious to be sure, but celebrated and immortal. Hilbert's imagination, which is considerable, works hard to create his new self-image. He repeatedly visualizes himself firing at a crowd. He attempts to convince himself that his very physiognomy is changing little by little (a frequent paranoid delusion), the eyes growing bigger and more beautiful, resembling those of an artist or assassin. Towards the end he desperately tries to maintain his fragile image as assassin by describing himself from the outside as terrified humanity must see him, a monster crouched in his dark room without food, awaiting only his moment to go down to the street to kill. His effort is to "become" the Assassin so completely that the decision to murder will not have to be made freely but will in some way follow necessarily from the nature of the beast. He thinks that a crime will change him even more than it did the Papin sisters, whose prim rectitude and comforting family resemblances disappeared from their photos. By their murderous act they achieved a certain individuality, each portrait now representing in its own way the common crime. Hilbert wants more, an individuality that will cut him off from the Human Family altogether. He plans for an hour of freedom in his room to feel the "weight" of his crime and to savor his new identity, a futile hope given Sartre's theory of consciousness.

Consciousness, for Sartre, is empty, impersonal, and contingent, but it would rather be full (like his other term, Being-in-Itself), individualized, and necessary. It has no Ego behind it from which the content of its behaviour might emanate and no Human Nature further back which would stand as everyman's permanent definition, securing for all time the individual's inclusion in the species, his "dignity" and his ascendance over beasts — to whom we feel superior, as Hilbert reminds us scornfully, because they walk on four legs and can't look us in the eye. The Ego as permanent and personalized Self, and Human Nature as guarantor of a permanent and privileged Creature represent together a lost paradise and state of bliss which the free consciousness, foot-loose and frightened, is perpetually trying to regain (pointing to an even more fundamental drive, to become God or the *ens causa sui*). Consciousness faces the constant temptation to create out of whole cloth a convincing Ego, as if substantized, which would endure as permanent explanation for and justification of any and all conduct. Consciousness undefined, existing as flux and utter potentiality (within a concrete situation), strives to save itself from the burden of perpetually choosing values, tentative and risky ones at that, as it goes along in Time, or, if you wish, *as* Time. The easiest way is to build an Ego around the expectations of others. Hilbert's choice of a permanent Being is neither the established norm of good conduct and values rationalized in morals, liberal politics, and idealistic philosophies (as in the *esprit de sérieux*), nor the desire to be loved, like Jesus, or to be virtuous — a disguise for rigidity and bigotry — like Dr. Schreber; he chooses to set himself against that establishment, radically, as Public Enemy Number One. Hilbert will go one step further by attempting, like Erostratus, to secure his identity for all time in the minds and hearts of his enemies. His effort is to bring about, if only for an instant, the coincidence or fusion of the Hero with his Act; of consciousness with the Self, of Existence with Being, and to present this fusion to his pseudocommunity, posterity, in a splendid baroque *tableau vivant*, featuring the anti-Christ, in a desperate attempt to pin down his "nature" as unique and superior, murdering his fellow creatures. The attempt is doomed to failure because consciousness constantly "overflows" the precarious "I" that it has created, and the only way to stop the action and guarantee the coincidence is to take one's life, so that Eternity can change you into Yourself, and who wants to do that? Certainly not Hilbert, who can't bring himself to commit suicide and surrenders meekly to the police. The surviving consciousness is condemned to go freely on its way where it will find, inexhaustibly, new worlds to organize, deal with, and escape from. Left behind, Hilbert's Act will supposedly divide his life in two and remain like a "glittering mineral" to shore up forever the newly-created Ego and prevent any backsliding (95). Instead it goes unrecognized, as if committed by somebody else. Hilbert hears the cries of "assassin" behind him as he runs but cannot identify with the criminal being chased. Even death is no guarantee of success, since posterity doesn't always see you as you want to be seen, in your Sunday best, or, in this case, worst. In his letter to the Humanists Hilbert is careful to point out that the tabloids will undoubtedly betray his purpose by making him out a raving maniac; he wants to make it absolutely clear that he killed in perfect calm and that he had sound objective reasons for his act (his doctrinaire anti-Humanism).

A further way for posterity to betray Hilbert's intentions is to treat him as a political anarchist, as an example, by Sartre, of misguided revolutionary zeal. Readers familiar with the period will notice at once that Hilbert, by firing indiscriminately at people in the street, performs the "simplest surrealist act" as proclaimed by Breton in the *Second Manifesto* of 1930; one might presume a sly attack by a Leftist on Surrealist revolutionary pretensions. Breton had anticipated and tried to answer in advance the inevitable criticism of the text in question. An attack of this kind would be consistent enough with Sartre's later politics and conceivable even in 1936, for although he was politically inactive before the War, not bothering to vote even for the Popular Front, he was not politically neutral by any means. His hatred of middle-class rectitude and hypocrisy, as well as its ideology and the fact of its dominance, is well-known, so that a corollary sympathy with the factory worker and the artisan is not surprising. Though Simone de Beauvoir tells us that as late as the early thirties they hadn't as yet any opinion about peasants.[10] Even in 1936 Sartre would surely have held that, from the point of view of real revolutionary activity, Hilbert's act is individualistic, counter-revolutionary, and sick, a futile and self-defeating gesture acting out a romantic posture best associated with middle-class sons in revolt against their temporal and eternal fathers, an anarchist's *propagande du geste* coming, not from outside the power structure but from within the closed bourgeois world, therein muffled, absorbed and forgotten, a pop-gun explosion that destroys nothing, except a few lives, and doesn't even frighten. After the War Sartre did undertake (in *Qu'est-ce que la littérature*), from the polemical point of view of "committed" literature, a serious analysis of Surrealist revolutionary claims. It would be a mistake, however, to view the story from a narrow political point of view, not only because internal evidence is against it, but because it would prevent the understanding of an important element in Sartre's development, predominant in the early thirties, but which to a certain extent has never been abandoned. Although he would not have confused Hilbert's act with genuine revolutionary activity, Sartre would have surely agreed with Breton that the purely negative act has a certain validity in itself,[11] and this would in no way run counter to his later political thought, one of whose principal tenets is to maintain the free, critical, or "negative" moment at the heart of Marxist philosophy and Socialist practice. Simone de Beauvoir writes that in the thirties Sartre was interested only in the negative side of Socialist revolution.[12] His broad negativity in general, his radical refusal of any restraint from the outside, and his deep hatred of the established order, its culture, its ideology, and its very language is consistent with the climate of the time and with the mood of the Surrealist movement that dominated it. Though his hostility towards bourgeois culture, spoon-fed to him by his grandfather Schweitzer, can be partly understood on the level of psychology, it would draw later on attitudes which came to a head in the Surrealist explosion. According to Beauvoir, the movement itself, although they were outside it by virtue of their age and university background, had been at least indirectly very important in their lives.[13] Sartre would diverge from the Surrealist current in that he would demand, not the death of intelligibility, communication, and language itself, but the creation of a new kind of intelligibility, a use of all language for communication (and communication for change).

Hilbert goes to some lengths to establish the non-political character of his act. He elaborates to his co-workers at the office his ideal of the "black hero," who would definitely not be an anarchist because in his own way the anarchist, too, loves Mankind (90). He makes it clear that through his act he will attempt to do something *against* humanity. Later, in his letter to the Humanists, he reiterates: they will be all the more scandalized by the murders *because* they are non-political. Hilbert's act, rather than representing an attack on Breton and the political failure of impatient anarchist violence as against true revolutionary patience, must be seen as positive, in Sartre's view, at least in its inspiration. Although Hilbert's solution, which attempts to prolong the "abstract, negative moment of freedom," not only as long as he lives, as in Sartre's version of Genet,[14] but forever, is negative from the point of view of "authentic" moral commitment, it is positive and admirable in so far as it represents the naked explosion of a human freedom. As such, it takes its place alongside Mathieu's broken vase in *L'Age de raison* and the black pilot who steals the plane in *L'Etre et le néant*, and, in real life, with increasing social and political content, it takes its place alongside the Papin sisters, Tito's defection, and the "events" of May, 1968. Its source can be traced to Sartre's uncompromising cult of freedom of the early thirties. He refused categorically any definition of man that would extend to him personally, and any definition of himself that would square with ordinary social role-playing or with any accepted notion of rights, duties, virtues, and obligations of the citizen. He claimed that no real knowledge of the world was possible within traditional modes of thinking; it was only accessible to the "solitary man," and "thaumaturge" who, as writer, artist, or philosopher, would remain outside the academy and believe only what he saw with his own eyes.[15] Hilbert is the caricature of what Sartre would have considered a lonely but legitimate negative force, blown up into an extreme, pathological, and thus instructive, case-history.

Simone de Beauvoir writes that in the early thirties she and Sartre were fascinated by newspaper accounts of extreme cases of abnormal behaviour, which, like the psychoses and neuroses, presented in exaggerated form attitudes and passions common to so-called normal men and women. They were convinced that these anti-social explosions always entailed the revelation of some important truth. They gave special importance to those which seemed to indicate a personal liberation for someone and to those which laid bare the *tares* and hypocrisies that were concealed behind the facades of bourgeois households and conduct. They paid special attention to those crimes and trials which had psychological or social significance and were quick to smell out the mystifications involved when the social order was in question and defending itself. Like Hilbert, they were intrigued by the case of the Papin sisters, wanting to see in the murder by the maids of their tyrannical mistresses, as did Janet Flanner, not a murder so much as a mini-revolution, a drama of social and political retribution, the revenge by members of an exploited working class against a society responsible for the orphanage where they grew up and their servant status, an absurd and unjust social system created by and for the *bien pensants* and which systematically spawned all manner of psychotics, murderers, and freaks. The horror inspired by the system could be properly denounced only by an exemplary counter-horror: the two sisters had made themselves the instruments and the martyrs of a "somber justice."[16] When in the course of the trial it became evident that the elder sister was an out-and-out psychotic and that the younger one had participated in her illness in a bizarre, incestuous, Lesbian *folie à deux*, Sartre and Beauvoir were disappointed, concluding that the crime was not, as they had hoped, the "savage unleashing of a freedom" against a repressive establishment, but merely the blind, terrified striking out of a psychotic, and with no social meaning. They were wrong, of course; that the raving Christine lacked the class consciousness necessary for a political murder would take little away from whatever social significance there might be. She did strike, after all, as opposed to, say, cutting out paper dolls, and it was the mistresses who were slain, and not some random dog or cat. Hilbert, in any case, seems to represent what Sartre might have wished the Papin sisters to be. He, at least, had "more serious reasons" for killing, more serious, that is, than the fancied ones, that "they" hated him and were forever jostling him in the street.

Hilbert's more serious reasons (his theoretical anti-Humanism) would have been shared by Sartre, who possessed a generous dose of good feeling for his fellow men but an exasperated antipathy towards the liberal intellectual Establishment whose timeless, abstract values, silly optimism (200 years after Doctor Pangloss) and systematic reverence for Culture called nothing into question, fled any genuine attempt to understand the human condition, and rationalized handily any real problem, such as the brooding presence of an exploited working class on the edge of town. Hilbert tells us in his letter that the Humanists have monopolized the meaning of life. Not sharing their state of grace, he has been forced to abandon everything he has undertaken; otherwise "they" would turn it sooner or later to their profit. All of the available tools, including language, come down to us from "them," so that a man can't even formulate a thought by himself: ". . . j'aurais voulu des mots à moi. Mais ceux dont je dispose ont traîné dans je ne sais combien de consciences; ils s'arrangent tout seuls dans ma tête en vertu d'habitudes qu'ils ont prises chez les autres et ça n'est pas sans répugnance que je les utilise en vous écrivant" (93). (". . . I would have like to have my *own* words. But those at my disposal have kicked around in I don't know how many other consciousnesses; they arrange themselves in my head on their own, thanks to habits they've picked up in other people's brains and it's not without repugnance that I utilize them in this letter.") One is reminded of Sartre's own situation (which, in *Qu'est-ce que la littérature*, he extends to his class): condemned by his bourgeois situation (and a doting grandfather) to a *lycée* education, the University system, and a career in letters, all within an ordered culture and a policed society — in which books "grow naturally" like trees in a garden, make their appearance fully-grown in their perfected, classical form, received as a matter of course the seal of collective approval, are accepted automatically as national monuments (Didn't De Gaulle say that Sartre, *also*, is France?), and provide material for the *explications de texte* of the future[17] — Sartre felt obliged to spend a lifetime contesting this enforced patrimony and to this day does his best thinking "against himself." Hilbert finds himself alienated and uncomfortable in a material and social world contaminated with *a priori* meaning and value and unable to share with others their complaisant acceptance of it and the smug sense of their own preordained legitimacy in the scheme of things. Incapable of doing anything *with* them, he can at least, with his revolver, do something *against* them; he can really and symbolically blow a few of them out of the human tub (taking, of course, the baby with the bathwater) in a futile, symbolic attempt, as Sartre said of the Surrealists, to leap outside the human condition,[18] or, like Abraham's paranoid, destroy the world.

Hilbert's inhibited thought processes are typical of the paranoid, who often feels that others can read his mind, steal his thoughts, and put ideas in his head, or that his brain, like his body in a crowd, is entrapped and suffocated by any concrete environment — originally within the family where, as a child, all his thinking and responses were felt to be restricted and imposed upon, and later within the family's neurotically-sustained extensions, such as marriage, as if thought itself were impossible without first breaking away from the stifling presence of the Other. But we don't want to reduce Hilbert to psychology, because for Sartre the delusion of influence is a fundamental aspect of human reality, implicit in the very fact of verbal communication. In a world populated, scandalously, by other people any verbal expression at all needs, for better or for worse, the collaboration of the Other in order to come to have objective meaning. The presence of the Other is always in some sense "alienating" because our utterance, once in the public domain, is at the mercy of interpretations and its intention is always more or less distorted. Likewise, one must read Hilbert's conviction that his projects were doomed to failure, or absurd and frowned upon, or diverted to the profit of "them," as both the rationalization of failure by a clinical paranoid and the ground for a serious theory of alienated effort which poses the very necessity of alienation from available socializations. In Sartre's system, the presence of the Other makes any expression of "self," verbal or otherwise, alienated by definition: ". . . je m'éprouve dans mon aliénation au profit de l'Autre."[19] (". . . I experience myself in my alienation to the profit of the Other.") And being in the world with others, from the point of view of L'Etre et le néant and common sense, is an inescapable aspect of the human condition.

Sartre himself, in the blurb he prepared for his publisher, emphasizes Hilbert's attempt, and failure, to deny his "human" condition, which involves, besides an ontological relation to the universe at large, a social or intersubjective element which even supplies a necessary, if bothersome, dimension of ourselves, the Being-for-Others. The fainting scene at the beginning provides a preview for Hilbert's ultimate failure to put himself "above the human" that he admits is in him (81). Seeing a man dead and bleeding in the street, Hilbert claims emotional invulnerability, telling himself that there is nothing "human" about the tragic scene, that the blood is no more moving than fresh paint. It doesn't work; he feels weak and chooses to faint, what Sartre would probably call a "magical" attempt to alter a world with such creatures in it. He is brought to his senses by some anonymous passers-by and is of course furious at their intervention, the fraternity of their act, and his dependence on them.

His attempt at assassination is no less a failure, from the points of view both of psychology and "Existential" humanism. Psychologically, Hilbert's sensibilities are so blunted that by the time of the shooting his "hatred" has no substance and his project founders in useless agitation. For Sartre, Hilbert's "hatred," which fails in real life, is no different from the abstract "love" of the Humanist, which fails on the political level: it is just as impossible to hate Man as an entity as to love him.[20] Hilbert wants no more to inflict pain on others than on himself. Cornered in the toilet, he finds excuses not to shoot himself and wonders, hopefully, if his victim might not live. In the end he puts off his project as long as possible and assures his capture by "forgetting" to leave his door unlocked, then conveniently running the wrong way in the rue d'Odessa, towards the populated Boulevard du Montparnasse instead of back up the street to the relatively quiet Boulevard Edgar-Quinet, as planned. Like the depressed suicidal, Hilbert wants nothing more than to reestablish human contact, but he can't bring himself to understand it or do it; thus the ironic: "J'aurais donné n'importe quoi pour quitter ma chambre, mais je ne pouvais pas descendre à cause des gens qui marchaient dans les rues" (97). ("I would have given anything to leave my room, but I couldn't go out because of the people walking around down there in the streets.") Freud's view that the paranoid's hatred is disguised love seems applicable to Hilbert's case. His solitude, like that of Sartre's Baudelaire, is, ironically, a kind of social tie, a superior isolation being his only means of participation; and ultimately, the crime constitutes a kind of twisted link with humanity, a way of forcing attention, recognition, and perhaps love. In his study of Baudelaire Sartre quotes (twice) a remarkable statement from *Fusées* which could serve accurately as Hilbert's epitaph: "Quand j'aurai inspiré le dégoût et l'horreur universels j'aurai conquis la solitude."[21] ("When I will have inspired universal disgust and horror, then will I have conquered solitude.") Taken in its broadest significance, *Erostrate* can represent the foundation in fiction of what will later become an "Existentialist" humanism having its ground, not in some abstract myth of static Human Nature and so-called Human Dignity, but in the lucid comprehensions of the reality of the human situation intrinsic to which is a fluid, immediate relationship with others, alternately free and alienated, sadistic and masochistic, and from which derives a dimension of ourselves that must be dealt with constantly—the Being-for-Others. Sartre will spend much of the rest of his life grappling with this social problem, first in terms of close intersubjective relations, in *L'Etre et le néant*, and finally within a much broader, Marxist context, in the *Critique de la raison dialectique*.

Notes

1. Jean-Paul Sartre, *Le Mur* (Paris: Gallimard, 1972). Page references are in the body of the article. All translations are mine.

2. Hazel Barnes, *Humanistic Existentialism: The Literature of Possibility* (Lincoln: University of Nebraska Press, 1959), p. 261.

3. Hazel Barnes, *Sartre* (Philadelphia, New York: J. B. Lippincott, 1973), p. 19.

4. When Hilbert says that the female devours you with her big hairy mouth he is

expressing, according to Sartre, both a pre-sexual "appeal to Being" and a male fear of castration, thus Adler's "masculine protest." Jean-Paul Sartre, *L'Etre et le néant: Essai d'ontologie phenomenologique* (Paris: Gallimard, 1943), p. 706.

5. Simone de Beauvoir, *La Force de l'âge* (Paris: Gallimard, 1960), p. 292.

6. Beauvoir, *La Force de l'âge*, pp. 24–26, 47, 75, 133, 144.

7. Sartre, *L'Etre et le néant*, p. 552.

8. Sartre, *L'Etre et le néant*, p. 507.

9. Philip Thody, *Sartre: A Biographical Introduction* (New York: Charles Scribner's Sons, 1971), p. 50.

10. Beauvoir, *La Force de l'âge*, p. 38.

11. See André Breton, *Manifestes du surréalisme* (Paris: Gallimard, 1971), p. 79.

12. Beauvoir, *La Force de l'âge*, p. 37.

13. Beauvoir, *La Force de l'âge*, p. 586.

14. See Barnes, *Humanistic Existentialism*, p. 353.

15. Beauvoir, *La Force de l'âge*, pp. 47–50.

16. Beauvoir, *La Force de l'âge*, pp. 135–137.

17. Jean-Paul Sartre, *Situations II* (Paris: Gallimard, 1948), pp. 202–205.

18. Sartre, *Situations II*, p. 219.

19. Sartre, *L'Etre et le néant*, p. 428.

20. Beauvoir, *La Force de l'âge*, p. 155.

21. Jean-Paul Sartre, *Baudelaire* (Paris: Gallimard, 1947), pp. 62, 99.

Paris as Subjectivity in Sartre's *Roads to Freedom*

Prescott S. Nichols*

The Paris of Sartre's trilogy, particularly that of the first novel, *The Age of Reason*, is generally seen as a bohemian demi-monde. It is the exotic world of the Sorbonne area and the streets and cafés of the Latin Quarter; it is the colorful if sometimes sordid milieu of the intellectual Mathieu Delarue and his circle of friends. Sartre's Paris is indeed all of this, but it would certainly be a misinterpretation to see it as no more than a backdrop against which the existential dilemmas of his work are played out. For I think it can be demonstrated that the Paris depicted by Sartre is the physical manifestation of, and almost an objective correlative for, the petit-bourgeois subjectivity in which so many people of Sartre's generation were engulfed prior to World War II.

It must be emphasized, first of all, that Sartre portrays his Paris with painstaking realism. He does not sketch a little of it here and there in order to suggest the *atmosphere* of Paris but rather he gives us actual streets, bridges, cafés, parks, and landmarks. Throughout the trilogy forty-seven

*From *Modern Fiction Studies* 24, no. 1 (Spring 1978):3–21. Copyright © 1978 by Purdue Research Foundation, West Lafayette, Indiana 47907. Reprinted with permission.

different streets are mentioned by name at least once, and some—such as the rue Vercingétorix, rue Montmartre, rue Réaumur, boulevard Saint-Michel, rue Royale, rue Huyghens, boulevard Montparnasse, and rue Denfert-Rochereau—are referred to several times. These are, of course, streets that actually exist, though at least one of them, avenue d'Orléans, has since changed its name.[1] In addition to the streets, Sartre mentions four of the Seine bridges by name, eight different places, squares, and fountains, several parks or landmarks such as the Luxembourg Gardens, frequented by Mathieu in his walks, the Bourse stock exchange, where Daniel is a broker, the Santé prison, outside of which Boris and Ivich sit on a bench to have a little chat, and les Halles, the famous open market where Mathieu has his nighttime encounter with Philippe and Irène.[2] Again Sartre presents us with the names of a number of different cafés: the Dupont Latin, where Mathieu meets Ivich early in *The Age of Reason*;[3] the Café des Deux-Magots, where Mathieu sits contemplating the Church of Saint-Germain-des-Prés on the night before he reports for duty; and above all, the Dôme, which is Mathieu's regular hangout.

More remarkable, perhaps, than Sartre's specification of public places such as cafés is his listing of eight different street addresses. We not only learn the addresses of some of the minor figures (the old abortionist woman with the "strangler's hands," who is located at 24 rue Morère or Daniel's homosexual friend, Ralph, at 6 rue aux Ours), but also those of such major characters as Sarah, 16 rue Delambre, Daniel, 22 Montmartre, Ivich, 173 rue Saint-Jacques, and Mathieu, 12 rue Huyghens. Sartre's technique in regard to addresses, however, is not that of straightforward realism. All of the street addresses given are real in the sense that the street exists and the number *could* exist but bogus in the sense that in almost all cases the kind of building described, usually an apartment building, simply is not, and probably never was, present at the address given. A good example is Mathieu's address at 12 rue Huyghens; the actual street, which is only one block long, is not at all what one visualizes from such vague comments as that of Boris when he leans out over Mathieu's balcony and informs him, "I like your street . . . but you must get bored with it in the long run" (p. 126).[4] From this remark one would expect the street to look a little too settled and residential for Boris' taste—maybe some comfortable looking apartment buildings, possibly some chestnut trees—but not at all what rue Huyghens is—almost an entire block, on both sides of the street, of municipal buildings.[5] No doubt Sartre was reluctant to carry his realism to the point of pinpointing actual apartment buildings, because addresses pertain to people as well as to physical reality, and just as a novelist creates fictional names for his characters, he will generally want to create fictional addresses for them.

The point is that Sartre is being as meticulous as one can be in setting the Paris scene. We see this even better if we follow carefully some of the characters as they move about through the streets, for Sartre always enables us to perceive that they are following a definite route, that they are moving concretely from one part of the city to another. Some characters, to be sure, appear not to move at all. Mathieu's brother Jacques, for example, is comfortably ensconced in his bourgeois law office on rue Réaumur, which is also his home. And Marcelle, Mathieu's mistress, almost never emerges from the seclusion of her pink room above her mother on the rue Vercingétorix, but as if to accentuate her general lack of mobility she tells Mathieu: "I did go out today . . . I felt I ought to get some air and see some people on the street. So I walked down as far as the rue de la Gaîté, and enjoyed it . . ." (p. 5). But then she adds that after visiting with a friend, it started to rain, so she hurried home by taxi.[6] The other woman in Mathieu's life at this point, Ivich, also is not too inclined to walk about much, at least not in the company of Mathieu. After meeting him at the Dupont Latin, they take a taxi over to the Right Bank to the Gauguin exhibit at a gallery on faubourg Saint-Honoré, and when they start walking toward Daniel's place on rue Montmartre after the exhibit, she professes to be getting tired, and Mathieu has to get a taxi home. One character, Brunet, the Communist organizer, is always on the move, but in *The Age of Reason*, where he is not yet a point-of-view character, we only see him coming and going. Even this has its significance, however, as when Brunet leaves Mathieu after trying unsuccessfully to get him to join the Party, and Mathieu pictures him "walking along the streets, with the pitching, rolling gait of a sailor, and the streets become real one by one" (p. 137).

Next to Mathieu himself the two most ambulatory characters in *The Age of Reason* are Boris and Daniel. Early in the novel we see Boris walking along the avenue d'Orléans with the air of an appreciative tourist. He is delighted to find himself on the outskirts of Paris, "near one of the gates" (Porte d'Orléans), and he savors the "russet-muslin" of the summer evening as he saunters down the avenue toward the boulevard Raspail. It is true that his walk has a goal — he is headed for the Garbure bookstore in order to steal their Thesaurus just before closing time — but even this "appointment" has an aesthetic quality; it is something on the order of the tourist who wants to get to Notre Dame in time to hear the organ concert. Boris crosses the boulevard Raspail, proceeds down the rue Denfert-Rochereau, for which he detects "a faint sense of dislike" (p. 155), and turns on to the boulevard Saint-Michel. The Garbure bookstore is located on the corner of the boulevard Saint-Michel and the rue de Vaugirard, and it has a doorway on each street.[7] Apparently, Boris' plan is to pick up his coveted Thesaurus from one of the sidewalk tables, enter the store, stuff it in his portfolio, and exit from the other door. He executes his plan, but only after a disturbing coincidental encounter with Daniel, who has been walking up the boulevard Saint-Michel on a mission of his own. Earlier in the day Daniel has taken the Number 72 bus to Charenton, on the outskirts of Paris, in order to drown his cats in the Seine, but he has returned to his apartment by taxi with his cats intact. Now, after walking about the boulevard Sébastopol and encountering one of his homosexual acquaintances at the fair, he is crossing over to the Left Bank to see Marcelle. Following his encounter with Boris at the bookstore, he continues up the boulevard Saint-Michel and finally reaches the rue Vercingétorix and Marcelle's apartment. It is not our purpose here to get into the complex sado-masochistic motives of Daniel's various clandestine missions. It is enough to see that his movements are depicted accurately and with attention to realistic detail.

What we have, then, in *Roads to Freedom* is not a Parisian atmosphere but Paris itself. We shall now examine the way in which Sartre uses the reality of Paris to convey, paradoxically, the illusion of Paris, i.e., its petit-bourgeois subjectivity. To do this, we will necessarily focus on the movements of Mathieu, who of all the characters most personifies subjectivity and who spends the most time in the streets.[8] What might be termed Mathieu's ambulatory world begins with his apartment at 12 rue Huyghens in the 14th Arrondissement and radiates outward from there. In spite of the incongruous nature of the *real* rue Huyghens, one can see that the street is excellently positioned geographically for Sartre's narrative purpose. It is quite close to the Dôme, which Mathieu frequents regularly; it is near the Luxembourg Gardens and the Sorbonne student area along the boulevard Saint-Michel, where Mathieu goes to meet with Boris and Ivich; it is very near Sarah and Gomez on the rue Delambre; and, of course, it is not far from the rue Vercingétorix, where Mathieu goes four times weekly to make love to Marcelle. It is in this area that Mathieu has his encounter with the Spanish Civil War anarchist at the outset of the novel—"halfway down the rue Vercingétorix"—and it is in this general area that he goes to see the abortionist woman, pays a visit to Sarah, and meets with Ivich.

In addition to circling about in this Left Bank region that constitutes his immediate milieu, Mathieu makes excursions to the Right Bank—to visit the art exhibit with Ivich, to see his brother Jacques, to see Daniel, and to go to a credit union for government officials. Indeed, as one might expect, all his attempts at borrowing money for the abortion are on the Right Bank. After a thoroughly frustrating conversation with his brother Jacques, in his home-office in a "squat building in the rue Réaumur" (p. 108), Mathieu walks down the street to a "cheap café at the corner of rue Montorgueil" to call Marcelle and inform her of his unsuccessful efforts in raising the money. Mathieu is at this point acutely aware of the sordidness and the absurdity of the situation. Leaving the café, he suddenly stops at the edge of the sidewalk as it occurs to him for the first time that Marcelle might want the child. Then, buying an *Excelsior* at the newspaper kiosk, he becomes momentarily aware of the outside world: " 'Aerial bombardment of Valencia,' Mathieu read, and looked up with a vague sense of irritation: the rue Réaumur, a street of blackened copper" (pp. 122–123).

He tries to feel genuine anger and he can't; it is too abstract: "It's no use, the moment will not come. I am in Paris, in my own particular environment. Jacques behind his desk saying: 'No,' Daniel laughing derisively, Marcelle in the pink room, and Ivich whom I kissed this morning. . . . Everyone has his own world, mine is a hospital containing a pregnant Marcelle, and a Jew who asks a fee of four thousand francs. There are other worlds" (p. 124). His mind then goes to Gomez, who "had seized his moment and had gone," and to the anarchist who had come up to him the day before: "He had not gone; 'he must be wandering about the streets, like me. But if he picks up a newspaper and reads: "Bombardment of Valencia," he will not need to put pressure on himself, he would suffer *there*, in the ruined town' " (p. 125). This is what Mathieu cannot do; he cannot suffer *there*; he cannot get out of his own little world, which is the world of Paris, of his particular situation, and of his subjective consciousness.

That night Mathieu is sitting in the Sumatra nightclub. He is momentarily alone at the table, as Boris is dancing with a tall blonde who interests him and Ivich is dancing with Lola, and he starts to ruminate on his enclosed existence: "I've yawned, I've read, I've made love. And all that *left its mark!* Every movement of mine evoked, beyond itself, and in the future, something that insistently waited and matured. And those waiting-points—they are *myself*, I am waiting for myself in the squares and at the crossroads, in the great hall of the *mairie* of the Fourteenth District . . ." (p. 209). Then he proceeds to circumscribe his world:

> "In the center there's my apartment with myself inside it, and my green leather armchair; outside there's the rue de la Gaîté, one-way only, because I always walk down it, the avenue du Maine and all Paris encircling me, north in front, south behind, the Panthéon on my right hand, the Eiffel Tower on my left, the Clingnancourt Gate opposite, and halfway down the rue Vercingétorix a small, pink, satined lair, Marcelle's room, my wife's room, and Marcelle inside it, naked, and awaiting me. And then all around Paris lies France, furrowed with one-way roads, and then the seas dyed blue or black, the Mediterranean blue, the North Sea black, the Channel coffee-colored, and then the foreign lands, Germany, Italy—Spain white, because I did not go and fight there—and all the round cities, at fixed distances from my room, Timbuktu, Toronto, Kazan, Nizhnii Novgorod, immutable as frontier points." (pp. 209–210)

Here sketched out in its entirety is the map of Mathieu's world. Like the ancient maps drawn by European cartographers, what is known is drawn in detail at the map's center and what is relatively unknown is sketched in around the circumference. Thus, at the very center is Mathieu himself in his green leather armchair; then there is the apartment on rue Huyghens, and spiraling out, the surrounding streets that Mathieu frequents so much — the rue de la Gaîté, the avenue du Maine, the rue Vercingétorix. The rue de la Gaîté is "one-way only" because Mathieu only walks "down it." Literally, this may mean that whenever Mathieu is in the rue de la Gaîté it is because he is on his way to visit Marcelle, "halfway down the rue Vercingétorix," but when Sartre goes on to speak of the "one-way roads" with which all of France is "furrowed," we realize that there must be more to it than this. One pictures the Paris streets radiating out, like spokes of a wheel, and becoming the *roads* of France. The movement is always one-way: *out*. And indeed, to follow the rue de la Gaîté into the rue Vercingétorix and then to continue down the rue Vercingétorix is to move *out*, toward the periphery of Paris. What is most significant about this picture conjured by Mathieu is the way it flings us in a dizzy spiral outside Paris, outside of France, outside of Europe — beyond the seas to the "frontier points" of the world. In doing this, Sartre is giving us a momentary glimpse of what is to come in *The Reprieve*, where suddenly under the threatening shadow of World War II, Mathieu and his friends find themselves thrust out of their individual, personal selves and into the broader outside world where everyone becomes greatly affected by external circumstances.

But before we actually explode into that vaster world of *The Reprieve*, we get some final looks at the Mathieu of the *Age of Reason* as he gets more and more entangled in his subjective situation. Now Mathieu's place is becoming more frantic; he no longer is able to walk about leisurely but has to hurry here and there by taxi or bus.[9] While Boris and Ivich wait in the Dôme, thinking that Lola is dead, he takes a taxi down the boulevard Raspail and through the "narrow gulley" of the rue du Bac to Lola's hotel, and then back again. Later, after his frustrating experience with the bureaucracy of the credit union, Mathieu walks to the boulevard de Sebastopol, enters a café to make a phone call to Sarah, and catches a bus back to Denfert-Rochereau. The bus ride, which seems to take a slightly circuitous route delineated for us by an old woman's coughing — "she coughed at the corner of the rue aux Ours and the boulevard de Sébastopol, she coughed along the rue Réaumur, she coughed in the rue Montorgueil, she coughed on the Pont-Neuf, above the grey, calm waters" (p. 275) — occasions one of Mathieu's frequent speculations concerning his freedom. He and all the other passengers, he feels, are being carried along by destiny; he watches "the heavy, dark buildings of the rue des Saints-Pères leap up one by one into the sky," and he feels he is watching "his life go past" (p. 275). But then the bus brakes suddenly to a stop and ". . . all his freedom had come back on him once more . . . he was free, free in every way, free to behave like a fool or a machine, free to accept, free to refuse, free to equivocate; to marry, to give up the game, to drag this dead weight about with him for years to come" (p. 275). This awareness of freedom, however, is in no sense exhilarating, for Mathieu realizes he is alone, "enveloped in this monstrous silence, free and alone, without assistance and without excuse, condemned to decide without support from any quarter, condemned forever to be free" (pp. 275–276).

In spite of this existential revelation, Mathieu is as lost as he ever was, probably more so, as he continues to be buffeted about by events. He leaves the bus, walks down the rue Froidevaux, and arrives at his apartment building, only to learn through an express message from Ivich, that she has flunked her exams. He then travels back and forth by taxi looking for Ivich—first to her hostel, then to Boris' hotel, then from the quays down the boulevard Saint-Michel, checking the Biarritz, the Source—until finally, as the taxi turns around the Medicis fountain, about to head for Vavin square, he sees Ivich's friend Renata, who reveals that Ivich has gone to the Tarantula on rue Monsieur-le-Prince (pp. 278–279).[10] He has the taxi wait while he rescues Ivich and then takes her to his apartment. There, events continue to close in on Mathieu. Sarah arrives to let him know that the Jewish doctor won't undertake the abortion without cash payment; Mathieu forlornly informs Ivich that Marcelle is pregnant, and he intends to marry her; and the scene ends with Ivich livid with rage, and Mathieu angrily walking out into the streets.

This time the description of Mathieu's walk—the last one that he will take in this novel—is strangely surrealistic. Whereas previously Mathieu has always had a realistic awareness of his whereabouts, even when he was most preoccupied with other matters, his perceptions now become impressionistic. He hears a song emanating from the Three Musketeers café while walking along "a long, straight street"—a street which, significantly, is nameless. Greatly depressed, contemplating the "little malevolent consciousness" in the green room behind him and the "motionless woman" waiting in the pink room ahead of him, he falls to the pavement as he is almost run over by a car. He feels an impulse to cry but then begins to laugh at the absurdity of his situation: "To think I used to take myself seriously" (p. 295). He starts off again but has the feeling that it is not really *he*, that what walks along the streets is no more than a body: "The body turned to the right and plunged into a luminous maze at the far end of a noisome, cleft, between iceblocks streaked by intermittent flashes. Dark masses creaked as they crawled past. At the level of the eyes swung a line of flurry flowers. Between these flowers, in the depths of the crevasses, glided a transparency that contemplated itself with frozen fury" (p. 296). The description is not so much of a Paris street as of Mathieu's own state of mind. Suddenly he decides that he will steal the money that he knows is in Lola's trunk, and in that instant he is jolted out of this surrealistic world of the "luminous maze" and of "iceblocks" and "furry flowers" and back into reality: "The world resumed its shape—a noisy, bustling world, of cars and people and shop windows." He realizes that as a matter of fact he is in the middle of the rue du Départ (p. 296). However, as Sartre informs us, it is "no longer the same world, nor quite the same Mathieu" (p. 296).

One is tempted to see this as an instance of losing oneself in order to find oneself, but such is not the case. Mathieu has hardly found himself just because he decides it is better to steal than to marry. At the end of the novel, when he watches Daniel walking off, pausing "at the corner of the rue Huyghens and the rue Froidevaux" to look at the sky,[11] and he hears the "gusts" of music coming from the avenue du Maine, he realizes that he is still very much alone and "no freer than before" (p. 342). The truth is that he has been lost all along. Even as he always knew the names of those streets he traversed and always knew where, in the immediate physical sense, they were leading him, he was lost in a web of fundamentally aimless meanderings that always brought him back to his aloneness and his lack of freedom and always ended, as he puts it himself, in nothing.

Just how much Mathieu, as well as those around him, is lost in the subjectivity of Paris does not become fully apparent until the second novel, *The Reprieve*. *The Reprieve*, of course, is the epic of the trilogy. Using techniques of simultaneity and rapidly shifting points of view among a multiplicity of characters, Sartre expands his horizon to include the whole of France as well as parts of Europe and North Africa. As is the Parisian custom, most of the characters of *The Age of Reason* have abandoned Paris and gone to the provinces for the summer. Mathieu is staying with Jacques and Odette at their villa at Juan les Pins on the Riviera; Ivich has returned to her parents in Laon; Boris is with Lola, who has a singing engagement in Biarritz; Sarah has gone to Marseilles to meet Gomez; and Daniel and his pregnant wife Marcelle are off "honeymooning" in the country. Only Brunet, of the major characters, is still in Paris.

We come upon Brunet early in one of only two scenes in *The Reprieve* set in the streets of Paris. He is walking along the rue Royale, between the Madeleine and the Concorde, when he encounters Maurice and Zézette. The contrast between this street scene and those that we have witnessed in *The Age of Reason* is striking in one significant respect: Maurice and Zézette belong to the working class. They are strolling along the rue Royale looking in shop windows, and Maurice feels bored and out of place. When Zézette who clearly has petit-bourgeois tendencies points out Maxim's, Maurice thinks angrily about how the "bourgeois swilled champagne" there while workers were fighting and dying in the First World War (pp. 7–8). The rue Royale, to him at least, is "bourgeois country": ". . . this street didn't lead anywhere; it had no direction; some people were making their way towards the boulevards, others down to the Seine, and others stood with their noses glued to shop windows — isolated eddies, but no co-ordinated movements; a man felt isolated" (p. 8). And Maurice finds himself contrasting this in his mind's eye with a street that is much more familiar to him, the avenue de Saint-Ouen: "When he left his lodging in the morning, guys would pass him, whistling, with satchels on their backs, bent over the handlebars of their bicycles. He used to feel happy; some stopped at Saint-Denis, and others went on farther; everybody was going in the same direction, the workers were on their way" (p.

8). The avenue de Saint-Ouen is in the northern part of Paris. It runs north
to the porte de Saint-Ouen in the direction of the community of Saint-
Ouen in the Paris outskirts. Saint-Denis is even farther to the north; so it is
clear that the movement of the workers as they go off to work in the
morning is *out*, away from the center of Paris. These are streets and
sections that are never alluded to in *The Age of Reason*;[12] they are the
outskirts of Paris, its factories and its working-class neighborhoods. The
contrast is striking. We now begin to see that in retrospect the world of
The Age of Reason is precisely the bourgeois world that Maurice describes — streets that don't lead anywhere, people going in all different
directions, "isolated eddies," "no co-ordinated movements." As he says, "A
man felt isolated," and we recall that Mathieu, too, has been isolated.
When Maurice and Zézette run into Brunet, their comrade and leader,
Maurice suddenly feels much less alienated as he calls to mind the workers
of Saint-Ouen and the other working-class communities: "Maurice looked
at Brunet and burst into a hearty laugh; he was snapping out of it; he
could see all the fellows around him, at Saint-Ouen, Ivry, Montreuil, in
Paris itself — at Belleville, Montrouge, and La Villette, squaring their
shoulders and preparing for the fray" (p. 11). As they talk together,
however, Maurice begins to feel alienated even from Brunet: "Brunet had
strong peasant's hands, a powerful jaw, and purposeful eyes, but he was
wearing a collar and tie and a flannel suit, and seemed at ease in middle-
class surroundings" (p. 12).

And Brunet himself, leaving them and continuing down the rue
Royale toward Concorde and the Seine, senses his own alienation from the
working-class movement. He looks about him at the street and the shops,
and he has a vision of the pending war:

> . . . it was there, in the depths of that luminous haze, inscribed for all
> to see on the walls of that frail city; it was a palpable explosion that had
> split the rue Royale. People passed and did not see it, but Brunet saw it.
> Brunet had thought: "The sky will fall on our heads." The city was in
> the act of falling; he had seen the houses as they really were — in
> imminent collapse. Above that elegant shop were tons of stone, and each
> stone, interlocking with the rest, had been falling steadily for fifty years
> past; a couple more pounds and the collapse would start again. (p. 15)

He thinks of the two-thousand-pound bombs possessed by the Germans; he
envisions the city destroyed, lying in ruins, occupied by soldiers setting up
encampments, and he shudders with the realization that he loved Paris.
Although he has just advised Maurice and Zézette that the working classes
must not be afraid of war, he finds himself wishing vehemently that war
did not exist. And as he gazes "avidly at the great arched gateways,
Driscoll's glittering shop window, the royal-blue hangings of the Brasserie
Weber," Brunet thinks ashamedly, "I am too fond of Paris" (p. 16). In the
context of the war that looms like an ominous black cloud over the entire

action of *The Reprieve*, Paris is a kind of island of peace—a peace that is already dissolving, that Brunet imagines already in decay. Sartre has now placed Paris in both a class context and an historical context. The Paris so loved by Mathieu, by Boris and Ivich, even by Brunet—the great inner city with all its buildings and trees, its varied and colorful shops and cafés, its curving river and intricate patterns of narrow streets and broad boulevards—is now clearly seen as a bourgeois, isolated Paris of the past, a Paris that in a sense never existed, except in the minds of Mathieu and his friends.

In the trilogy Mathieu returns to Paris just one more time—when he is called up from the reserves and must get things in order at his apartment before reporting for duty at Nancy. This is toward the end of *The Reprieve* and is the only other section of the second novel that is set in the Paris streets. Of course, the Paris that Mathieu finds is no longer the same. He arrives at his apartment late at night, "twenty-two thirty o'clock," to be precise (p. 262), and at "twenty-three thirty o'clock" we see him out on

> A dead street, immersed in shadow; at rare intervals a street light. A nondescript street, edged with tall, nameless mausoleums. All the shutters closed, not a single glint of light. It was once the rue Delambre. Mathieu had crossed the rue Cels, the rue Froidevaux, walked along the avenue de Maine and even the rue de la Gaîté: they were alike: still warm, already unrecognizable, already streets of war. Something had perished. Paris was no more than a vast street-cemetery. (pp. 267–268)

"No more than a vast street-cemetery." The street names, except for the rue Cels, are familiar to us, but all the life has been lost. He goes into the Dôme "because the Dôme happened to be there" and orders a brandy, but even the Dôme is no longer the same: "In July the Dôme had no precise confines, it overflowed through the windows and the revolving door into the street, and spread over the road. . . . But now the outer darkness surged against the windows, and the Dôme was reduced to what it was: a collection of tables, benches, glasses, dry and unresponsive, denuded of that diffused flow which shadowed them by night" (p. 268). Indeed, the Dôme is a microcosm of Paris, "denuded of that diffused glow," "reduced to what it was." There are particularly no lights; Paris is so dark that she has "lost her pink cotton ceiling." Mathieu is actually able to see the night sky, "a dark vaporous pall of sky overhanging the city" (p. 269). There is one patch of light, the boulevard Raspail, but saying this name aloud to himself—"Paris, boulevard Raspail"—Mathieu realizes that even the familiar *names* of the streets are dead, that they, too, have been "mobilized" (p. 269).

Once again, in a passage rather similar to the one in *The Age of Reason* where Mathieu conjures the map in which the Paris streets become one-way roads radiating out into France and the surrounding world, he now imagines that all those former street names, "those delicious names," are printed on an army map:

Nothing was left of the boulevard Raspail. Roads they were, just roads, speeding south to north, west to east, just numbered roads; paved for a mile or two here and there, set between sidewalks and houses, and named, rue, avenue, and boulevard. But they were still segments of the same road. Mathieu, facing towards the Belgian frontier, was walking along a section of the Route Départementale which ran out of Route Nationale No. 14. He turned into the long, straight highway that formed a continuation of the Ouest railway, once the rue de Rennes. (pp. 269–270)

Just roads after all. All those chestnut trees, those buildings with balconies and elegant façades, those sidewalk cafés, those "delicious names" dating from previous centuries — they are all constructs, all a mystification of the fact that these are just roads that for maybe a mile or two happen to be paved or cobblestoned and called rue, avenue, or boulevard. If they are "roads of freedom" it is only in the subjective, individualistic sense of a freedom *from* the world; it is not the more genuine freedom of engaging *in* the world. Perhaps when these roads become demystified of the veneer, the illusions, and the bourgeois isolation of Paris, they will become genuine roads of freedom, and Mathieu, as he follows them out into the countryside as a common foot soldier in the army will himself possibly acquire some of that freedom. Now, however, Mathieu is turning down what *was once* the rue de Rennes with a long night still ahead of him, and he is about to get a taste of freedom which is more existentially authentic than anything he has experienced before, but he is still not engaged.

Just before midnight he orders a beer on the terrace of the Café des Deux-Magots and contemplates the Church of Saint-Germain-des-Prés, which now looks like a village church, "a handsome new church, white against the black sky" (p. 270). Gazing at the church, which he feels is somehow eternal even though "a tiny black speck in the sky could blow it to powder," and feeling the death of Paris, he realizes that something in him has died, too: "It had all happened painlessly. There had once been a kindly, rather diffident man who was fond of Paris and enjoyed walking in its streets. That man was dead" (p. 271). A woman crosses in front of him in a hurry, and Mathieu thinks, "I was like her once — a hive of schemes. Her life is *my* life; beneath that look, under the indifferent sky, all lives are equivalent. The darkness swallowed her up as she pattered into the rue Bonaparte; human lives melted into the shadows, clacking heels were silent" (pp. 271–272). Continuing to dwell upon the church of Saint-Germain-des-Prés and the absoluteness of its stones, he suddenly says, "I am free." And what has been a feeling of joy changes, "on the spot, to a crushing sense of anguish" (p. 272). All of Mathieu's former illusions, schemes, and preoccupations have slipped from him like a discarded snake skin, and he is left with a pure, naked consciousness confronting the universe. At first the feeling is one of joy and release, but the anguish comes with the realization of what it really means to be utterly free. One asks oneself, "Free to do what?" and there is no answer.

When we next see Mathieu, he has stopped on the Pont Neuf over the Seine. "Liberty," he thinks, "I sought it far away; it was so near that I couldn't touch it, that I can't touch it; it is, in fact, myself" (p. 280). Reaching out and sliding his hands over the stone parapet, which is "wrinkled and furrowed, like a petrified sponge," he realizes that he is nothing; he is "outside the world, outside the past, outside myself: freedom is exile, and I am condemned to be free" (p. 281). A moment later, thinking he must "risk that freedom," he leans out over the Seine, and, Hamlet-like, contemplates suicide: "Why not? He had no special reason for letting himself drop, nor any reason for not doing so." But he suddenly decides "it would merely be a trial," and he walks on, "gliding over the crest of a dead star." The poetic phrase serves to remind us that Paris is dead, but beyond that that Mathieu is really not in the context of Paris at all but in the context of the universe. We no longer have a kindly diffident fellow who likes to walk the streets of Paris but an existential being who "glides" over the planet earth making such choices as whether it is better to live or die.

It is at this point that we have the coincidental meeting between Mathieu and a woman who is a stranger to him, Irène. She has followed Philippe out of the cabaret and into the rue Pigalle where he is hurrying down toward the Trinité Church (p. 276), then on to the "boulevards" Haussman, Montmartre, etc. where he starts calling out "Down with war" to passers-by (p. 276), then "into the darkness of rue Richelieu" (p. 277), and finally running along the rue Montmartre until he enters "a square, opposite the dark, gaping entrance of a clamorous alleyway that smelt of cabbage and raw meat" (p. 283). Here, at what is undoubtedly Les Halles, Philippe starts shouting his refrain — "Down with war" — until people begin to beat him and Irène jumps in, struggling with his attackers and crying, "Bum, dirty bum! He's just a kid, you leave him alone!" (p. 284). Mathieu, walking down from Pont Neuf, hears this cry, sees the struggle, feels it is no concern of his, and then suddenly decides it is and intervenes, pretending to be a policeman. The incident is significant in that it involves an action on Mathieu's part, an action which temporarily salvages Philippe and, more importantly, brings Mathieu and Irène together for a one-night stand. Mathieu feels "a sudden impulse to walk down the rue Montorgueil" but goes off with Irène when she urges him to help her control the raving Philippe in the taxi.

Why is it that the new, existential Mathieu, who considers Paris a "vast street-cemetery," would want so "to have another look at the rue Montorgueil"? Has he slipped partially back into his former self, the "rather diffident man who was fond of Paris and enjoyed walking in its streets"? Does he still want to recapture the Paris that was? Perhaps so, for the rue Montorgueil, which runs into what used to be les Halles, is a lively and colorful street.[13] It is probable that his desire to walk in the rue Montorgueil represents a vestige of his old self, a vestige that perhaps he can purge from his system once and for all in one last farewell walk before leaving in the morning to go to war. "Where would you be at this moment if you hadn't met me?" Irène asks him. And when he replies "In the rue Montorgueil," she asks, "What would you be doing there?" "Walking around," he says. But then he realizes that "he no longer wanted to walk along the rue Montorgueil: the rue Montorgueil was there, traversing that room: all the roads of France passed through it, all its herbage grew there" (p. 292). Now that he is with Irène, he has lost the need for that last Paris walk. Irène herself, looking to him "like a Breton woman" (p. 292) and living in a section of Paris that is unknown to him (p. 288), somehow represents all of France. Quite the opposite of Ivich, who is at this very moment fleeing Laon to be with Mathieu and to see the city again. Indeed it seems to Mathieu that passing through Iréne's room are "all the roads of France."

Moreover, just as this night with Irène helps to bring Mathieu out of his geographic isolation—his Paris-centrism, as it were—so does it call attention to his petit-bourgeois isolation. When he alludes to Philippe being unhappy, Irène scoffs and brings him quickly down to earth: "People are unhappy," she says, "when they are cold or ill or hungry. The rest is all imagination." She acknowledges that she is quite willing to help Philippe out and prevent him from making a fool of himself, but she doesn't want Mathieu pitying him because she knows what suffering is all about and is quite put out by bourgeois who pretend to be unhappy. She then asks Mathieu, "But you are bourgeois, aren't you?" Mathieu feels that she "sees" him, that he is caught in her look: "And for her, I *am*; a particle suspended in a look, a bourgeois. It is *true* that I am a bourgeois. And yet he never managed to feel that he was" (p. 293). Sartre is doing two things here. He is showing how for Mathieu Irène represents the Other. First he "sees" her; then she "sees" him. They are alternately caught—momentarily reduced to an *en-soi*—in each other's look. Then, a moment later when he takes her arm, she leans against him and the look is "dimmed." It is one of those rare moments (at least for Sartre) when two people are able to transcend the perpetual tug-of-war between one look and the other. But beyond this Sartre is showing that even though it may be existentially false to say Mathieu *is* a bourgeois—in the sense that a table *is* a table—it is socially, politically, and economically *true*. Regardless of how he may think of himself, he is a bourgeois, or at least a petit-bourgeois. Indeed it is part of the bourgeois isolation and subjectivity *not* to think of oneself in a class context.

Our last look at Paris before it falls to the Germany army is a nostalgic one, and appropriately it is through the eyes of Ivich, who has come to Paris to be with Mathieu the very night/morning that he is sleeping with a total stranger, Irène. Ivich of course is convinced that Paris will be destroyed, and she has determined that she will be destroyed with it. Arriving at the Gare de l'Est at six in the morning, she pauses at the outer gate and stands "in pious contemplation of the boulevard de Strasbourg, feasting her eyes on it and gradually visualizing her memories of the trees, the shuttered shops, the motor-buses and the car tracks, the cafés now just opening, and the smoky air of early morning" (p. 302). She tells herself that "even if they dropped their bombs in the next two minutes, or in thirty seconds," they could not take away these memories. But there are the many things that she must revisit before "they" come — the Flea Market, the Catacombs, Ménilmontant — and the other places such as the Musée Grévin, which she has not yet seen. She is like the tourist who only has a week to "do" Paris, not because she has to go on to Rome, however, but because Paris will cease to exist. "Everything will be burned — women, children, and old people, and I shall perish in the flames." Stepping on to "a real Parisian sidewalk," she hails a taxi, giving the driver rather circuitous directions to get to Mathieu's apartment: "go along the boulevard Saint-Michel, the rue Auguste-Comte, the rue Vavin, the rue Delambre, and then by the rue de la Gaîté, and the avenue du Maine" (p. 303). As they drive along, she thinks, "What a lovely day! . . . This afternoon we'll go to the rue des Rosiers and the Île Saint-Louis." But she does not know that Mathieu is leaving to report for duty later that morning, that she will not even be able to see him off, for at this very moment he is arranging with Irène to meet at seven at the Dôme.

The latter two, Mathieu and Irène, take a taxi from the Dôme to the Gare de l'Est. Speeding by les Halles they think of the incident the night before with Philippe: "So that's over," comments Irène, watching les Halles recede through the small window in the back of the cab (p. 809). Les Halles, which ironically has since been destroyed by the French ruling class, is Mathieu's last view of Paris. And it is Irène who is his last memory: "One night — yes, but you will be my sole memory of Paris" (p. 310). No reflection on the times with Marcelle, Ivich, Boris, Daniel, Brunet — merely the memory of the stranger whom he feels he has known for ten years, Irène. Mathieu has already abandoned the old world of Paris and all that it represents to enter the new world of France, Europe, the war, and class-consciousness.

The final look, indeed the only look, we have of Paris in the third novel of the trilogy, *Troubled Sleep*, is after Paris has fallen, and, appropriately once again, it is through the eyes of Daniel. Everyone else has left. Mathieu is in the army, about to make a hero of himself; Brunet is a warrant officer, about to let himself become captured so he can organize prisoners; Gomez is in New York and Sarah has joined the mass exodus from Paris with their son Pablo; Odette and Jacques, too, are fleeing the former bourgeois security of Paris; Boris is in Marseille recuperating from a hernia operation, about to make his decision, with Lola's blessing, to join the Free French in England; Ivich, having offered herself to a man she despises ("anyway, I shan't die a virgin"), has been forced into pregnancy, marriage, and a miscarriage and is living a lonely and miserable life in the country; Marcelle, too, is living in the country, "pupping at Dax" as Daniel puts it. Only Daniel, the sado-masochist, the "Archangel," remains to preside over the fall of Paris. When we first see him, he is walking down the boulevard Saint Germain to rue Danton, then down the latter to the place Saint-André-des-Arts. The dominant motif of this scene is that of emptiness. Nobody is there; it is a perpetual Sunday: "The tiny square of Saint-André-des-Arts lay abandoned in the sunlight, lifeless; black night reigned in the heart of noon" (p. 77). Daniel takes an iron chair from the terrace of the closed Brasserie Alsacienne, where he once lunched with Mathieu, and sits down at the edge of the sidewalk to contemplate the square and the Seine beyond it. He looks "at the empty bridge, at the padlocked book-boxes on the quay, at the clock face that had no hands," and he thinks, "they should have smashed all this up a bit . . . a few bombs, just to make us realize what was what" (p. 78). Of course, Paris is not totally devoid of people; Daniel sees "shadows" slipping by here and there. It is "peopled by little scraps of time" that spring fleetingly to life, "to be almost immediately absorbed again into this radiance of eternity" (p. 78). He gets up and walks across to look at the "green bronze dragon" on the Saint-Michel fountain, and he begins to sense his freedom: "There is nothing now that I can't do": "He could take down his trousers beneath the glassy stare of all these darkened windows, pull up a paving-stone, and heave it through the plate glass of the Brasserie, he could shout: 'Long live Germany!' and nothing would happen" (p. 78). For Paris, being empty, is now devoid of all those bourgeois values that have hemmed Daniel in, have labeled him a homosexual and forced him into bad faith, refusing to accept his own homosexuality; for after all, Daniel is bourgeois, too. Now that world of secure bourgeois complacency is shattered, Daniel is "filled with a sense of vast and pointless freedom" (pp. 78–79). He watches a "procession" of women and children and old men walk slowly by; he pauses "at the near end of the Pont Saint-Michel," leaning on the stone parapet, and turns with disgust back up the boulevard Saint-Michel, which now seems "like a stranded whale, belly upwards" (p. 79). Alternating between boredom and despair at this point, Daniel sees a French poster that ironically proclaims, "We shall win because we are stronger," and he begins to exult in delight as he thinks: "They're running, they're running, they've never stopped running." They, who have been putting him "on trial" for twenty years, who have had spies "even beneath his bed" and have turned every passer-by into "a witness for the prosecution or a judge or both," they are running, and the only one left is he, Daniel, the one they had condemned: "I, the Criminal, reign over their city" (p. 80).

Then he suddenly becomes aware that a convoy of the German army is coming toward him down the boulevard Saint-Michel: "They were standing upright, images grave and chaste, fifteen or twenty of them together in long camouflaged trucks, moving slowly toward the Seine, effortlessly gliding, standing stiffly, the inexpressive glances of their eyes resting momentarily on him" (p. 80). For Daniel they are the "angels." With their blond hair, their sun-tanned faces with eyes "like glacier lakes," their narrow waists and long thighs, they are to him creatures of beauty; they are the avenging conquerers to whom David surrenders willingly and "with confidence." He feels himself to be the only survivor, the only ordinary mortal, and they are "the angels of hate and fury" come to be the "new judges," the "new law." A handsome young Nazi standing on the back of a tank smiles at Daniel and throws him a pack of cigarettes, and Daniel is ecstatic: "Just like butter—they are going through Paris like a knife through butter" (p. 81). For him the "Reign of Evil" has begun, and it gives him great joy. When we next see Daniel, it is the following day, and once again he has been walking. "What else to do in a dead city but walk?" (p. 117). The city is a desert; he envisions it as a Roman ruin to be visited in ages hence. "He must walk, walk without ceasing over the surface of this cooling planet" (p. 118). The language is reminiscent of Mathieu's "gliding over the crest of a dead star," and indeed Daniel's walks through this vacant city bear some similarity to Mathieu's walk on his last night in Paris. The difference is that for Mathieu it is a dead city that he is now abandoning for a new world, whereas for Daniel it is a newly acquired realm, a Hades, over which he is obliged to rule in company with the forces of Evil that have conquered it.[14]

In political terms what has happened to Paris is that a bourgeois democracy has been replaced by fascism. Unquestionably, fascism represents a "reign of evil," and yet there is an authenticity to Paris at this moment that it did not possess before its fall. Now that it is dead and empty it is devoid of the cobwebs of mystification that had been spread over it. For the truth of the matter is that a bourgeois democracy *needs* mystification to maintain the class relationships that exist under capitalism. It needs its people to think of themselves as isolated individuals rather than as a part of society and of history. Fascism, on the other hand, can rely on naked force; there is little need for mystification. To be sure, the Paris that we see in *Troubled Sleep* has not yet become engulfed by fascism; it is in a kind of limbo between one rule and another. But we know from accounts of the days of the Occupation that many Frenchmen, Sartre among them, found that they were able to achieve an authenticity through the resistance that they never had before.[15] Indeed, from what Simone de Beauvoir has told us, we know that Sartre's projected fourth novel, *The Last Chance*, was to have depicted the Paris of the Occupation and the theme of freedom through resistance, i.e., through commitment.[16] However, no matter how one might have wished to read this sequel, it is no doubt for the best that it was never written, for as Sartre himself has said it would have been too neat. It would have implied that freedom is something you *find* as if arriving, at last, at some mountain peak. In reality it does not strike one in a sudden epiphany, as with Sartre's Orestes in *The Flies*, but is something discovered, lost again, and rediscovered, as with Mathieu. Indeed it is a process rather than a goal — an unending road extending out from the center. Hence the appropriateness of the phase "roads *of* freedom" and hence the value in leaving the narrative open-ended.

The Paris that we do have in the trilogy is primarily the Paris that existed before the fall. It is the Paris of the summer and fall of 1938, and this Paris, as we have seen, represents, above all, subjectivity. As Sartre has said,

> During the deceitful calm of the years of 37–38, there were people who could still hold the illusion, in certain *milieux*, of having an individual history completely partitioned off, completely watertight. That is why I chose to relate *The Age of Reason* as is ordinarily done, in showing only the relations of a few individuals. But with the days of September, 1938, the partitions collapsed. The individual, without ceasing to be a monad, felt himself engaged in a role that was overtaking him.[17]

The *milieux*, in this case, are the streets of Paris. Sartre is using them in all their beauty, all their color and variety, and, indeed, all their aimlessness, to depict the subjectivity of consciousness that prevailed in those years. Revisiting those streets today, one perceives that they have changed very little. They are just as real as in Sartre's portrayal of them. Just as real and just as illusory. Paris did not get burned; it is still standing in all its glory as a cultural symbol of the Western world, but one cannot help feeling that once again the walls are going to collapse — not the walls of the buildings along the boulevard Saint Germain or the rue de Réaumur but those watertight partitions of which Sartre speaks. Once again we are going to find ourselves engaged in roles that overtake us.

Notes

1. It is now called the avenue du Général Leclerc, after one of France's few military heroes of World War II. One can see that the street signs on the corners of the buildings have been altered; indeed, at one corner, the authorities apparently neglected to remove the old "d'Orléans" sign, for it is still on the wall.

2. Unfortunately, les Halles is no more; in its place (at the time of this writing, 1974) is a gigantic crater with angular cranes looming above it and steam shoves working on its floor. The French authorities have decided to build a modern plaza and cultural center à la Rockefeller.

3. The café on this corner today is called the Select Latin. Since Sartre does not as a rule alter the names of cafés. I would guess that the name has been changed since 1945.

4. All quoted passages from the three novels of *Roads to Freedom* are from the Bantam English editions.

5. All of one side of the street is taken up with the buildings of the Lycée Paul Bert. On the other side, where #12 would be, there is a municipal gymnasium (#10) next to an office

building, Éditions Albin Michel (#22). The large black letters on the face of the lycée—
"DÉFENSE D'AFFICHER LOI DU 29 JUILLET 1881"—testify that this particular building at least has
been around for a long time.

6. The rue de la Gaîté is very near; it is in fact a kind of extension of Marcelle's own rue
Vercingétorix and as the name suggests has today an array of stores, cafés, erotic theatres, sex
shops, etc.

7. On this corner today is a rather fancy men's clothing store called 100000 Chemises.
The Garbure Bookstore is probably patterned on the Gilbert Bookstore, which is one block
away down the boulevard Saint-Michel and is very much as Sartre describes: a door opening
onto each street and six long tables in front laden mainly with second-hand books.

8. Of course Mathieu's last name is Delarue—"of the street."

9. We never see Mathieu, or any of the others for that matter, take the metro anywhere,
though it is sometimes mentioned, as when Boris is reassured by the knowledge that a metro
line runs beneath the rue Denfert-Rochereau (p. 157).

10. The Tarantula is described as being a dance-hall "under a gramophone-record
shop." Interestingly enough, there is today a Tarantula record and music shop in the
immediate vicinity (on boulevard Saint-Michel).

11. Actually, the rue Huyghens and the rue Froidevaux do not intersect. Unless
something has changed drastically in the last twenty years, this is a lapse on Sartre's part.

12. One exception would be the passing reference to Vitry when Daniel is contemplating the advantages of the part of the Seine he has chosen for drowning his cats: "The water of
the Seine was particularly dark and dirty at that spot, being covered with greenish patches of
oil from the Vitry factories" (*The Age of Reason*, p. 93).

13. Today the narrow sidewalks of the rue Montorgueil are lined with café-bars,
bakeries, meat markets, *charcuteries*, flower shops, street vegetable stands, and the like.
During the day people hurry back and forth, and the narrow street is jammed with trucks
stopping to deliver their produce. At one or two in the morning Mathieu might be able to see
trucks bringing their goods in from the provinces to be sold along the street and in the once
famous market place of Les Halles.

14. Sartre rings many changes on the Daniel-devil motif. In *The Age of Reason* he is
spoken of as the Archangel, and it is implicit here that he is none other than the fallen
Archangel, Lucifer. Later, when he makes a kind of Faustian pact with Philippe in order to
seduce him it is clear that he is Mephistopheles as well. There is no doubt that all this
represents an important sub-theme in Sartre's trilogy, and it is worth noting that his original
working title was *Lucifer* (cf. Michel Contat and Michel Rybalka, *Les Ecrits de Sartre*, p.
114).

15. Cf. Sartre's well known declaration: "Never were we freer than under the
Occupation" ("Paris sous l'occupation," *Situations, III*).

16. For a résumé of the projected story line of *The Last Chance*, see Beauvoir, *Force of
Circumstance*, pp. 194–196. Sartre did actually write the beginning, which he published in
two parts in *Les Temps modernes* (cf. Contat and Rybalka, pp. 219–220).

17. Contat and Rybalka, p. 113 (my translation).

Politics and the Private Self in
Sartre's *Les Chemins de la liberté*   S. Beynon John*

To move from the world of *La Nausée* and the short stories to that of
Sartre's unfinished tetralogy, *Les Chemins de la liberté* (1945–49), is to
pass from an almost morbidly private to a public realm where the
characteristic and recurring Sartrian myth-makers are no longer insulated
from the larger interests of society. The novel sequence ceases to exploit
politics as mere violent background, which is what happens in "Le Mur,"
or as a kind of laboratory model of the psychology of fascism, which seems
to me what occurs in "L'Enfance d'un chef." On the contrary, the novels
reflect the view once expressed by Thomas Mann: "In our time, the destiny
of man presents its meaning in political terms." In *Les Chemins* we are
dealing with a work which bears on the nerve of contemporary politics
and in which an acutely personal experience of the life of our times has
been disciplined and subdued to a larger ironic awareness of the movement of history, though there are moments when the force of private
feeling disturbs the ironic balance.

All creeds emerged from *La Nausée* as equally irrelevant to the
scandal of contingency, but in *Les Chemins* allegiance to Communism
emerges as a serious and dominant theme. Indeed, what chiefly makes the
novel sequence distinct from Sartre's previous fiction and unifies its
separate volumes is its way of connecting men with the world of politics
and of conjuring up that world as the natural, and perhaps inevitable,
arena of human choice. This aspect of the novels is the one I should like to
concentrate on, though it must also be seen as inseparable from the
general movement of the novels, which is to do with freedom and the
illusion of freedom working themselves out in a variety of contexts among
characters who are self-deluding and in flight from the full implications of
personal responsibility. In effect, one of Sartre's most distinctive achieve-
ments is to relate the private microcosm, with its play of evasion and moral
ambiguity, to the political macrocosm with its strains and conflicts. The
author's alertness to the change and detail of the external world is never
divorced from his acute feeling for the motions of the individual consciousness. The political character of the novel sequence becomes progressively
more explicit as the narrative proceeds and this general movement also
represents a change in scale. We leave the small, self-absorbed world of
Parisian friends and lovers in *L'Age de raison* for the broader canvas of
European politics and the threat of war in *Le Sursis* and the brutal impact
of military defeat in *La Mort dans l'âme*.[1] Sartre's invented world is
juxtaposed to actual historical events and personages so that we are driven
to judge of some part of the truth of the fictional experience by an appeal

*From *Australian Journal of French Studies* 19, no. 2 (May–August 1982): 185–203.
Reprinted with permission.

to life outside the novels. To put it another way, our sense of the quality of the moral insight and formal order we encounter in the novels cannot quite be divorced from our feelings about the adequacy of the fiction as a picture of European political life between 1938 and 1940. Judged in this way, I would have thought that *Le Sursis* and *La Mort dans l'âme* fail to render the full complexity of the political events which inspired them, though they are uncannily sensitive to the mood of bafflement, anxiety and confusion which prevailed in Europe at the time of Munich.

The actual dates on which the separate volumes in the sequence were composed suggest the outside pressures which helped to shape the general sense of the tetralogy. In the summer of 1938, as Simone de Beauvoir records,[2] Sartre first intimated that he had an idea for a new novel sequence. So we are dealing with a work conceived in the wake of the Austrian *Anschluss* of March 1938 and in the climate of violent propaganda designed by the Nazis to prepare the way for the break-up of Czechoslovakia in September of the same year. The dominant theme of the new novel sequence was to be freedom and its general title *Lucifer*. The first volume was to be called *La Révolte*, the second *Le Serment*, and an epigraph was to suggest the nature of the central problem: ["The misfortune is that we are free"]. On 2 November 1939, while Europe was still adjusting to the tensions of the phoney war, Sartre dispatched a hundred pages of the manuscript of volume one to Simone de Beauvoir. The first draft of the completed first volume was finished by May 1940 and rehandled between 1941, when he was released from a prisoner of war camp, and 1945 when its definitive version appeared under the title of *L'Age de raison*. A fragment of the text (Brunet's invitation to Mathieu to join the Communist Party) was published in August 1943 in *Domaine français*, a special number of the periodical *Messages* appearing in Geneva, and another (Daniel's attempt to drown his cats) in the same month at Lyons in the review *L'Arbalète*. So a novel originally conceived in the pre-war months of appeasement and bitter disillusion was modified and reshaped under the impact of military defeat, foreign occupation and clandestine resistance. The second volume, as Simone de Beauvoir recalls in *La Force de l'âge* (p. 556), was written by July 1943 and its opening pages, under the title "23 septembre 1938" (the date of Hitler's Godesberg memorandum on Czechoslovakia), appeared in an issue of the periodical *Les Lettres françaises* in November 1944, prior to publication of the novel in its entirety in 1945 when it too was given a new title, *Le Sursis*. Both new titles seem to me to suggest more ironic detachment than the rather melodramatic originals and perhaps point to the author's growing concern with distancing his material. The general title of the novel-cycle reflects the central importance which the idea of freedom is given in the fiction, though the form and texture of the novels cannot be said to *configure* the idea of freedom in quite the astonishingly apt way in which the form and texture of *La Nausée* embody the notion of contingency.

To judge from a reference in *La Force de l'âge* (p. 387) the third volume of the cycle, as envisaged by Sartre in late August 1939, was to turn on a dramatic reversal of roles in which the Communist Brunet, alienated by the Nazi-Soviet non-aggression pact of 23 August 1939, was to quit the Party and seek Mathieu Delarue's help. It is significant that this reversal, which looks dangerously like an attempt to show a chastened and fictionalised Paul Nizan appealing to a lucid and fictionalised Sartre, does not actually figure in *La Mort dans l'âme* (1949), the third volume of the cycle, which was written between 1947 and 1948 and serialised in the pages of *Les Temps Modernes* between December 1948 and June 1949. The roots of this volume clearly lie in Sartre's own experience, as is partly confirmed by the two fragments of his wartime diary that have been published.[3] These offer a vivid and direct account of Sartre's own involvement in the French military defeat, an account that is particularly good at rendering the ghostly emptiness of the small provincial town, all dust, silence and sunlight, where the French troops are holed up. It is true that with the brutal death of Schneider/Vicarios in "Drôle d'amitié," the one fragment of the abandoned fourth volume that has found its way into print,[4] Brunet reaches a crisis of disillusionment with the Communist Party over the issue of Nazi-Soviet relations in 1940. But the irony in this situation is not dramatically reinforced for us by showing him appealing to Mathieu (who does not, in fact, appear in this fragment).

A reversal of Mathieu and Brunet's situations does take place in the scheme Sartre originally planned for the abortive fourth volume but, according to Simone de Beauvoir's notes and recollections,[5] this reversal in no sense suggests Brunet's abandonment of the Party in favour of Mathieu's own brand of politics. Brunet's predicament is painful enough in this context but his crisis of faith is not contrasted for effect with Mathieu's lucidity. Sartre's original plot for this volume appears to have provided for the recapture of Brunet who then determines to establish contact with the Party outside the prisoner of war camp. To this end he enlists the help of the camp escapes-organiser who turns out, by a coincidence which strains credulity, to be Mathieu. He has missed death on the church-tower in that scene, heavy with intimations of a final catastrophe, which concludes the first part of *La Mort dans l'âme*.

In Simone de Beauvoir's version of this projected outline for the fourth volume, Mathieu epitomizes the break with his old and uncommitted way of life by participating in the execution of a camp spy. Brunet escapes and reaches Paris only to find that, with the entry of the USSR into the war, the French Communist Party's previous policy toward Nazi Germany now lies in ruins. He helps to rehabilitate Schneider/Vicarios' reputation and resumes his activities as a party functionary in the Resistance, but his experiences have undermined his faith in the Party. Ironically he discovers his own freedom and subjectivity at the very moment Mathieu chooses to move away from subjectivity to commitment.

The latter joins the ranks of the Resistance, embraces the collective discipline of clandestine struggle and commits himself fully to a cause. He eventually dies under torture—"heroic because he has made himself a hero"—to quote Simone de Beauvoir's account. This looks pretty extraordinary stuff, but that some form of positive and voluntaristic ending was part of Sartre's original intentions for the tetralogy may be judged from a remark he made in an interview with Claudine Chonez as early as 1938: ["*La Nausée* has been accused of being overly pessimistic. But let's wait until the end. In my next novel, which will be a sequel, the hero will right the machine. One will see existence rehabilitated, and my hero acting and enjoying the taste of action"].[6]

Philippe, Daniel's last homosexual conquest, also joins the Resistance as a gesture of resentment against the masterful Daniel and as a way of proving he is not a coward. He is killed in an affray at some café and Daniel, distraught with grief and anger, uses one of Philippe's handgrenades to blow up a meeting of important German officials to which he has access as a prominent collaborator. Sarah, a refugee in Marseilles, throws herself and her small son Pablo out of the window in order to avoid arrest by the Germans; Boris is parachuted into the anonymity of the *maquis*.

If I have laboured the matter of the dates at which the novels of the cycle were composed and the plots projected and discarded, it is not simply to emphasize the strong and persistent intertraffic which occurs between Sartre's real-life experience of politics and specific elements of plotting and characterisation which are a feature of the novels themselves, but also to indicate how Sartre's own struggle, in the world of post-war politics, to divest himself of subjective and simplistic explanations leads him to abandon aspects of the novel he had planned. The rather eccentric segment of Parisian society which Sartre introduces to us in *L'Age de raison*, and with which he himself was familiar, is surely quite deliberately stylised so as to inflate the tedium, triviality and aimlessness of private life on the eve of the Second World War. It is a picture of that society seen *after* the deluge, its shallowness rendered grossly culpable by the knowledge we, as readers, share with the author of the historical catastrophe which is to overwhelm what the characters themselves assume to be a normal and permanent way of life.

Similarly, parts of the political argument of *La Mort dans l'âme* and "Drôle d'amitié," especially in their relation to Brunet, seem to me to reflect the frustrations and divisions typical of French domestic politics immediately after the Liberation and, more narrowly, Sartre's own estrangement from the French Communist Party between 1947 and 1948. The real world infects the imaginary life of the novel. One result is that Sartre's outraged personal feelings about the campaign of slander mounted by the French Communist Party against himself and the memory of his old friend, Paul Nizan, who had defected from the Party on the issue of the Nazi-Soviet Pact, fill certain pages of "Drôle d'amitié" with a very special urgency and rancour. For instance, Vicario's defence of himself against the lies and fabrications of the Party has an intensity that does not relate quite naturally to the gentle and rather mysterious figure the author has created. I suspect that here Sartre's own voice comes dangerously close to drowning the autonomous voice of the character. In the same way, the viciousness with which Chalais, the Party's hatchet man, is portrayed and the glee with which the author displays the hollowness of Brunet's relationships with his Communist comrades, both tend to overreach the ironic detachment required in this part of the narrative if the human inadequacy of political bureaucrats of the Left is to be exposed without also exposing the author's intrusive judgement.

So far as the abandoned fourth volume, *La Dernière chance*, is concerned, its character (to judge from Simone de Beauvoir's summary) is almost wholly sensational. Its structure reflects a schematic irony which serves in a crude way to diminish both Daniel, the symbolic representative of the incipient fascism of French capitalism; Philippe, the confused and egotistical rebel against the bourgeois family; and even Brunet, the militant Communist, who is left in a state of political schizophrenia. Only a reformed Mathieu, symbolising the fusion of the liberal mind and the collectivist ethos, rises to the level of events. The world of the Resistance is viewed in somewhat Wagnerian terms as the end of an epoch and, in its edifying distribution of rewards and punishments, seems to me to fulfil a private fantasy rather than to embody the imaginative realisation of the great and meaningful themes of freedom and commitment which had animated the volumes preceding *La Dernière chance*. The "resurrection" of Mathieu is perhaps the most profoundly significant feature of this outline. It points without ambiguity to Sartre's need (at least, at this stage of his life) to show the socialist intellectual if not actually triumphing over the Communist Party, at least as offering a valid alternative to it. In this sense, the dialogue between Communism and the uncommitted intellectual of the Left has to be artificially revived in the person of Mathieu, even though this runs counter to the effects actually produced by the skill and energy of the writing in that scene of *La Mort dans l'âme* in which Mathieu appears to share the death of his comrades on the church-tower.

In the light of this plan for *La Dernière chance*, the abandonment of the tetralogy, which is confirmed by the failure to publish any sequel to the episode in "Drôle d'amitié," reflects Sartre's awareness that the relatively simple conflicts of loyalty and principle he associated with the Resistance, however skilfully and imaginatively conveyed in retrospect, were likely to offer too facile and schematic a picture of authentic political involvement to the French reading public of 1949, disenchanted as it was with the peace, conscious of its own divisions and of the complex, shifting and ambiguous character of politics in postwar Europe.[7] In the last resort, of course, we must judge *Les Chemins* in its incomplete state and this very incompleteness reinforces its ambiguities. The final impact of *Les Chemins*, in the form in which we now read it, remains negative and ironic in all that concerns personal relations and political choices (or so I shall argue in what follows). The ironies are rooted in an acute awareness of the ways in which men deceive themselves and mask or deny the reality of their freedom, and in an equally strong sense of how the meaning of their actions can be distorted or even nullified by historical events and processes from which they cannot escape. Hence Sartre's own description of *L'Age de raison* and *Le Sursis* as constituting "an inventory of false, mutilated and incomplete freedoms."[8]

At one level, this ironic sense is present in the nature of Mathieu's predicament in *L'Age de raison*. It is that of a humane, decent, self-doubting intellectual whose moral and philosophic scruples are lavished on a comically conceived private crisis at a time when great public issues are at stake: the fate of republicanism in Spain, the clash of Communist and Fascist ideologies. I say "comically conceived" because Mathieu's fumbling and ineffectual attempts to solve it, like the ease with which he can be deflected from dealing with it, are sources of comedy and even farce. At another level, the irony is embodied in the dramatic reversal of fortunes undergone by Mathieu and Brunet by the time the tetralogy breaks off. With what are apparently his last shots from the church tower the hesitant and isolated intellectual involves himself in violence and, however dubious and subjective his motives, vividly affirms his solidarity with others. On the other hand, the loyal party functionary, heartbroken by the ruthless liquidation of Vicarios, is left alone and despairing in the night of the prisoner of war camp. The contrast between the vertical tower in the full light of morning and the barbed-wire cage of the darkened camp emphasizes graphically Mathieu's involvement and affirmation of self (however mistaken these may be from an objective point of view) and Brunet's humiliation and effacement.

As elaborated in the unfinished version of the tetralogy the respective fates of Mathieu and Brunet illuminate symbolically the political direction of the work. The relation between Mathieu's private life as a slightly raffish school-master and the world of political conflict around him as initially established early in the narrative, in that encounter between him and the drunken beggar which opens *L'Age de raison*. Mathieu is making his way dutifully to the flat where Marcelle, his mistress of seven years standing, expects his regular visit when he is accosted by a beggar smelling of drink. Mathieu gives him money and then protects him from harrassment by an officious young policeman. In return, the man insists on giving him a postcard with a Madrid stamp on it. He fingers it reverently before handing it over and expresses maudlin remorse for not having gone to Madrid himself. As he moves off, Mathieu registers irritation:

[Mathieu walked away with a vague sense of regret. There had been a time in his life when he used to wander through the streets, hang around in bars, when he would have accepted anyone's invitation. That was all over now. That kind of thing never produced anything. It was amusing. Yes! He had wanted to go and fight in Spain. Mathieu hastened his step, he thought with irritation: "In any case we had nothing to say to each other." . . . He remembered the guy's face and the expression he had assumed in order to examine the stamp: a funny passionate look. Mathieu examined the stamp in his turn without stopping his walk, then he put the postcard in his pocket. A train whistled and Mathieu thought: "I am old."] (p. 10)

This passage is revealing. The author/narrator is discreetly effaced here but his presence is sensed in the devices he uses to signal to us the significance of this encounter. The "vague regret" which he attributes to Mathieu is carefully planted to suggest Mathieu's residual nostalgia for his old, carefree, unattached days and, more particularly, to hint at the resentment he now feels for the life of habit and obligation he shares with Marcelle, a resentment that will loom larger and more explicit as the plot develops. Similarly, Mathieu's "irritation," as reported by the narrator, is deliberately linked with his private reflection that he has "nothing to say" to the beggar precisely so as to throw doubt on the truthfulness of that remark and to imply that Mathieu and the beggar share a sense of guilt and remorse about the Spanish Civil War. Indeed, each of Mathieu's reactions in this episode emphasizes how ambiguous is the quality of his moral response, how uncertain his sense of personal involvement. He cannot side with respectable society (in the shape of the policeman) against the beggar, but his casual charity, like the ease with which he deflects the policeman, merely serve to show how much a part of that society he is and how "superior" to the object of his attentions. His subsequent refusal to join the beggar in a drink confirms his social embarrassment. In juxtaposing Mathieu's reference to his ageing to the whistle of a passing train, with its evocation of a world in which others are on the move to new destinations, the narrator skilfully marks the break from a war-torn Madrid, briefly conjured up by the postcard, to a Paris which frames Mathieu's own settled routine. Here, in his unexpected meeting with the beggar, Mathieu's listlessly regular life is abruptly exposed to another, more intense and painful world coloured by failure, guilt and suffering. The theme of the Spanish Civil War, introduced so suddenly and obliquely, recurs like a leit-motiv throughout the novel, a perpetual (though discreet and hidden) threat to the private relationships with which it is chiefly concerned and a perpetual (though indirect) reproach to the narrowness and complacency of those relationships. The Civil War in Spain distracts Mathieu from his worries about whether his salary, the symbol of his bourgeois security, will last out until the end of the month; recurs in conversation with his solid and assured Communist friend, Brunet: wells up in self-recrimination in the Sumatra night-club, and spoils the taste of the sherry he drinks with the homosexual Daniel.

By providing a specifically political dimension the novel-sequence as a whole expresses an enlargement of the scope of human action, at least in comparison with *La Nausée*. In spite of this, *L'Age de raison* itself never becomes a fully political novel but remains essentially the description of a world of individuals insulated from the life of politics. It offers a criticism of the pseudo-freedoms pursued by these individuals and, particularly in the case of Mathieu, a revelation of the disturbances which accompany the recognition of freedom, though the tone surrounding some of these disturbances is distinctly ironic. Significantly, most of these characters live in the margins of respectable society and their relationship with the workaday world of tasks and professional responsibilities is tenuous. Mathieu is a teacher on vacation, Marcelle a model of enforced idleness, Boris and Ivich students untouched by any strong sense of intellectual interests, Sarah a housewife never shown at her chores, Daniel apparently a stockbroker, though never seen at work at the Bourse. Certainly Lola works as a night-club singer but the exotic nature of the setting tends to place her apart from the life of office, shop or factory. In fact, the world of jobs and routine is purposely held at bay so that interest can focus on personal relationships, on inner, rather than social, experience. And these relations of dependence between individuals, the wary and often disaffected attitudes towards society, the habit of strenuous self-scrutiny, the preoccupation with time, all express a deep and painful uncertainty about the nature of the self and its relation to the world outside.

It is, of course, true that Mathieu's career of drift is contrasted with the energy of Gomez, the absent but unforgotten painter who is an officer in the International Brigade, and with the assurance of Brunet, the party activist, though descriptions of the latter ("a Prussian cast of face," "a great tower") are not unambiguously admiring. But though these two symbolise modes of political commitment, they are marginal to the action of the novel which is principally concerned with private individuals making and regretting decisions, displaying integrity, bad faith or confusion in their friendships and love-affairs among the distraction of bars, night-clubs and art galleries. At this stage one can say of Brunet and Gomez (whose abandoned canvas significantly provokes feelings of guilt in Mathieu) that they presage the violence that is to come and are the shadows of public causes falling across purely private dilemmas. In this sense, they make *L'Age de raison* a novel haunted by the absence of politics.

This feeling of politics as existing in a ghostly way at the edges of the narrative in *L'Age de raison* helps to create the sense of strain we experience when we turn to *Le Sursis*, every part of which imaginatively recreates the atmosphere of the Munich crisis of 1938 and is permeated with politics and the threat of war. This sense of strain springs from our awareness that the political content of *L'Age de raison* is too tenuous and latent to be thought of as the necessary prelude to the conflicts of *Le Sursis*. We cannot resist the impression that the second novel of the sequence does not derive naturally from the experience of the first but has had to be imposed on it.[9] Besides, Sartre's preference for rendering reality through the almost solipsistic consciousnesses of isolated individuals is difficult to reconcile with a narrative centred on major political events. There are strains involved in relating the contents of an individual consciousness to a political reality outside it. Actions and events tend to be seen in terms of their value to the private self in its struggle to define itself, and not in terms of the wisdom or utility of particular political choices. Even so, when compared with *L'Age de raison*, *Le Sursis* must be accounted a novel in which the balance between private and public activity has been radically altered and in which a quite new importance is granted to the impact of politics on individual lives. The imagined, and often caricatured, conduct of real-life ministers and diplomats in a variety of European cities combines with vividly rendered episodes of street violence in Czechoslovakia and scenes of mobilisation and evacuation of hospitals to create an atmosphere of feverish activity arising from political decisions. The claims of personal life collide with an anonymous external experience which brings individuals sharply up against the nature and limits of their own freedom. Characters keep their different styles of life but are drawn irresistibly into experiences which transcend their private needs and inclinations. As Sartre expresses it in the advertisement for the 1945 edition of the first two volumes of the cycle, the individual is ["a monad which leaks, which will never stop leaking, without ever sinking"].[10] The shifting chaos of individual lives is everywhere contained within a historical framework, sometimes allusively sketched in with a maximum of fictional invention, sometimes made explicit with almost documentary fidelity. Such is the transcription of Hitler's strident broadcast ultimatum to Dr. Benes which occupies several pages of the chapter entitled "Lundi, 26 septembre" and which reinforces the novel's public dimension while also reminding us of Sartre's debt to the fictional techniques of John Dos Passos, particularly the device of "Newsreels" — a combination of newspaper headlines, stock-market reports, official communiqués, etc. — which the American writer incorporates in novels like *1919*. But, as with Dos Passos, Sartre's use of documentary elements remains an essentially fictive procedure intended to communicate something of the movement and texture of society. *Le Sursis* is still a metaphor about existential choice exercised in a concrete historical situation, not some kind of sociological explanation of why the French were to be defeated in June 1940.

So the idea of politics, of a realm in which man is seen in relation to public obligations and responsibilities, emerges very strongly from the pages of *Le Sursis*. It is embodied in the intertraffic between authority, speaking through the medium of official communiqués and mobilisation orders, and the surprised individual shaken out of the torpor and routine of his normal life. But it is only in *La Mort dans l'âme* and "Drôle d'amitié" that politics is presented to us as the collective drama of a nation. This is already reflected in the defeated French soldiers, inhabitants of a "paradise of despair," who roam innocently through the luminous summer landscape in the first part of *La Mort dans l'âme*. Caught in the unreal hiatus between defeat and capture, they carry bunches of flowers and appear to Mathieu to be "angels sauntering at their ease." For a moment they affirm what is precious about private life before private life itself comes to an end, an end brilliantly conveyed in the second part of the novel by the trail of confetti from torn-up personal letters scattered behind them by the French troops as they move across the countryside into captivity: ["The whole road is a long, soiled love-letter"]. The same sense of collective experience is suggested by the animal patience of the captured masses of soldiers. The plight of individuals is effaced before that of the community and the social dimensions of the catastrophe are fully established. That is why we cease to encounter individuals of much variety and interest in the barracks. Brunet is surrounded by social stereotypes who, with the exception of Schneider and the young printer who subsequently throws himself off the train, fail to engage us imaginatively. The poverty of their mental and emotional lives tends to epitomize the degree to which the "inner" life has become irrelevant. Here, as elsewhere in *La Mort dans l'âme*, private relationships—Ivich's botched marriage, the collapse of Odette's love for Jacques, Boris' break with the stricken Lola—dwindle to nothing and are lost in the turmoil of public events: refugees streaming south, the dazed defeat of the French army, the entry of the Germans into Paris.

So in its second and third volumes, as in the fragment we possess of the abandoned fourth, *Les Chemins de la liberté* affirms itself conspicuously as a political novel. This is something different from a social novel which I take to be one in which the novelist affords us fresh insight into the way in which the experience of individuals is shaped by their social medium. Sartre's skill lies rather in communicating the distance between the vivid life of consciousness, always so brilliantly in focus, and the confused movement of social and political events, always shifting and blurred. In *Les Chemins* we gain small sense of individuals as exhibiting styles of life that spring from concrete economic and social conditions, but a strong sense of discrete minds of varying degree of lucidity and sophistication worrying away at the problems of personal freedom and political involvement. The specifically political strain is, perhaps, too narrowly and technically conceived in the intense and elaborate discussions about the policies of the French Communist Party which characterise parts of the second section of *La Mort dans l'âme* and parts of "Drôle d'amitié." On the other hand, the almost theological acrimony of the debate between Schneider and Brunet or between Brunet and the inflexible Chalais is imaginatively consistent with the desperation felt by these men as events confront them with a cruel test of their political faith and loyalty.

Nowhere in the abandoned tetralogy do we learn unambiguously what sort of commitment in politics is proper for a person living in good faith, though we learn a lot from the fates of Mathieu, Gomez and Brunet about what does *not* constitute authentic commitment. Certainly freedom is not to be equated with Mathieu's irresponsibility or Daniel's slavery as he veers between self-indulgence and expiation. It is yet to be discovered beyond the bankruptcy of these modes of behaviour. The motives and acts of these four characters, in particular, reinforce for us a sense of the fundamental difficulty and complexity of the moral life and, more especially, of the problems involved in connecting private and public choices. As the sequence proceeds, there is a greater sense of honesty and lucidity, a sharper awareness of the risks of living in a changing world, but if we concentrate on Mathieu, Gomez and Brunet in their public or political roles, we are struck by the ultimately unpersuasive character of all their modes of commitment. None of them embodies a fully satisfying style of life. The failure of *L'Etre et le néant* to transcend a kind of social stalemate is here transposed, in a fictive way, into the field of politics.

If we look closely at Mathieu's one outstanding act of involvement in a public cause (his last stand on the church-tower), we need to say at the outset that it is rendered by a vivid and effective narrative of action. Indeed, in making Mathieu the sole survivor of a particularly bloody encounter, the Sartre who envisaged him as resurrected in the projected fourth volume positively invites us to deny the imaginative power of the scene itself and to suspend disbelief about Mathieu's death simply so that he can take up again a particular argument about valid commitment. Mathieu's actions on the tower are primarily seen in personal terms as a revenge on a botched life, on his own inadequacy and indecisiveness, and as an act of destruction that will make up for all the hesitations and frustrations of his past: [". . . One bullet for Lola who I didn't dare to rob, one for Marcelle who I should have jilted, one for Odette who I didn't want to screw . . ."] (p. 193). Though this is recognizably the voice of Mathieu, the recalcitrant schoolmaster and haunter of bars, it is not the idiom of a man responding to philosophic imperatives. Something of these is, however, present in the language with which the author/narrator surrounds Mathieu's act of wild destruction in which military necessities are temporarily eclipsed: ["He was firing on mankind, on Virtue, on the World: Liberty is Terror. . . . He fired. He was pure, he was omnipotent, he was free"] (p. 193). Here the narrator identifies the act with the concept of "Terror" borrowed from Hegel[11] and though this probably makes Mathieu the only French soldier in the campaign to go down fighting in a blaze of metaphysical notions taken from a German philosopher, it is certainly consistent with the rather cerebral philosophy teacher we have got to know in the course of the novel-cycle.

In avoiding the use of direct speech at this point, the author/narrator emphasizes the distance between himself and his creature, mockingly granting to Mathieu a language that both parodies his normal philosophic self-consciousness and establishes its incongruity in the brutal context in which he finds himself. Such self-dramatizing rhetoric at such a moment effectively punctures any sense we might have that Mathieu's act represents a serious commitment worthy of his sophistication and good will. The whole notion of freedom is here equated with destruction, self-destruction and delusions of omnipotence. The inflated language attributed to Mathieu, like his tendency to see himself as the centre of a falling world are consistent with his earlier thoughts (pp. 174–5) as he takes up his position on the church-tower and prepares for the German attack:

> [I decide that death was the secret meaning of my life, that I have lived in order to die. I die in order to witness that it is impossible to live; my eyes will extinguish the world and will close it for ever.
>
> The earth shrugged its inverted face towards this dying man, the capsized sky flowed across him with all its stars: but Mathieu watched these useless gifts without deigning to gather them in.]

The first paragraph reads like the last spasm of a solipsistic mind; in the second, the lyrical expansion of the language, with its poetic image of almost regal disdain, seems to me to produce a portentous effect and to render Mathieu for us as a self-absorbed actor in some cosmic spectacle. We are coaxed by the emphases of the language, by the stylistic tone of these crucial passages into viewing this heroism as suspect because excessively self-regarding. It is surely significant that of all the snipers left behind to fight this rear-guard action on the tower, Mathieu alone is shown as choosing a rifle carelessly and at random (p. 155) while Pinette makes a deliberate choice, like a workman who knows that the job requires good tools. Equally significant is the fact that we are given access to only one mind, Mathieu's, a mind which expresses itself with a kind of apocalyptic relish that is very much at variance with the plain speech of his comrades. We are being invited to judge this supreme act of violence on Mathieu's part as not very different from the sort of futile romantic gesture which he has performed in the past. One thinks of the incident in the night-club (in *L'Age de raison*) when he drove the knife into the palm of his hand, an incident he significantly recalls (p. 173) during his last vigil on the tower. In fact, we are encouraged to interpret this act on the tower as emblematic of those "false, mutilated and incomplete freedoms" to which Sartre has referred elsewhere. Both these scenes seem contrived in order to establish Mathieu's violence not as an exemplary act reflecting an authentic choice, but as the rather theatrical expression of the tensions and frustrations of a self-deceiving bourgeois intellectual who has yet to find a valid form of commitment in the larger world.

Yet when all this is said, the pages devoted to Mathieu's last stand (especially pp. 292–3) have their ambiguities. Certain moments in the rapid narrative seem curiously at variance with the ironic spirit which I have argued is central to this episode. It is true that Pinette chooses his rifle more carefully than Mathieu, but, in the end, it is Pinette who is demoralized and paralysed with fear while Mathieu, finding himself alone among the blood and rubble, stands up recklessly and fires a defiant last burst in a spirit that is oddly close to regimental pride: [". . . it will not be said that we didn't hold out for 15 minutes"] (p. 193). If it is true that Mathieu's own irate, self-accusing outburst about the women in his life tends to undermine the seriousness of the act in which he is engaged, and even if one admits the discreet authorial mockery at the expense of his endless philosophising, the ironic possibilities of these moments are at least contained and subdued by the respect and fellow-feeling we have for Mathieu, injured by a beam from the roof that falls in on him and still spattered with the blood from Chasseriau's decapitated body. I am not sure it is possible to accommodate both impulses (the ironic and the affirmative) within this episode without damaging one of them. However, this may simply be the novelist's device for warning us against writing off even those characters whom he persistently surrounds with irony. No matter how trivial or inadequate his motives, Mathieu does, at least, break with a dead past and stand alongside other men in a common, if doomed, enterprise. He may not be an "authentic" man but his essential decency shines through.

If we turn to Gomez, the first thing that has to be said is that he is discredited for us in purely human terms because of the harsh indifference he displays towards the loyal, patient and long-suffering Sarah. And it is precisely this lack of human sympathy which lies at the root of our misgivings about the quality of his *political* commitment. Through Mathieu's eyes we are given a view of Gomez which sharply reduces the admiration we have been willing to grant him as a brave man devoted to the Spanish republican cause. Here the crucial scene is that of the dinner which Mathieu shares with Gomez in *Le Sursis*. It is framed between two episodes involving that self-deceiving mythomaniac, Philippe. The final moment of the scene with Gomez in the restaurant shows him, confident of his military glamour, picking up an attractive actress who is sitting at a nearby table and leading her on to the dance floor. This moment merges with a scene in which the play-acting Philippe is shown dancing with the coloured prostitute, Flossie (p. 223). In this way, we seem to pass imperceptibly from one kind of actor to another. The meal is lavish. Gomez, newly promoted to general, takes it and the actress quite naturally as his due. Mathieu has his reservations about the Spaniard ["Mathieu didn't think that much of Gomez"]) but is prone to feel inadequate in his presence. He is given to hectic bouts of self-reproach but, because of the comic exaggeration of the language he uses, we rather tend to discount these, sensing their false and theatrical character: ["If I eat, a hundred dead Spaniards leap at my throat. I have not paid"] (p. 219). In fact, Mathieu's zealous self-reproach simply serves to emphasize his own good nature and decency when contrasted with Gomez's hardness, egoism and vanity. We share in Mathieu's shock at the callousness with which Gomez refers to his dead comrades in Spain; and, like Mathieu, we are alienated by the streak of sheer adventurer which Gomez reveals in his appetite for the spoils of war, whether these take the form of gold braid or fifteen year old girls. "Mars and Venus," says Gomez lightly as he shows Mathieu the snapshot of his little Spanish conquest, but the tone suggests he is only half-joking, and that half-joke condemns him. He is brave but the antithesis of Brunet's party activist; an adventurer who embraces causes because they nurture his ego and resolve his personal conflicts. There is nothing in him of disinterested commitment; he is a performer who has found a congenial stage for his activities and who pursues action for its own sake: [" 'Mathieu,' he said in a deep slow voice, 'war is beautiful.' His face was glowing. Mathieu tried to disengage himself but Gomez gripped his arm forcefully and went on: 'I love war . . .' "] (p. 222).

Significantly, the last appearance Gomez makes in the novel-sequence (the opening pages of La Mort dans l'âme) shows him in exile in New York, suffering from the humid heat and remote from the events that rack his native continent. He is no longer the dashing lady-killer dining out with Mathieu in Le Sursis. We meet him in a mood of despair in which he has lost his faith in politics as a valid and meaningful activity, and his confidence in his own possibilities as a painter or even an art-critic. He is advised to keep quiet about having been a general in Spain and, bitterly contrasting all that past glory with his worn trousers and sweat-stained shirt, reveals his wounded vanity at being seen by the pretty girl at the bus-stop as a "dago" down on his luck (p. 12). The abrupt shift in the narrative from this exiled and shabby figure, touting for work and humiliated in a foreign land, to Sarah, bearing the brunt of war as she seeks with fierce maternal desperation to protect her child in the great flood of refugees, emphasizes in the sharpest way the change in Gomez's stature and his virtual displacement in the novel-cycle.

It is tempting to suppose that when we pass from Mathieu to Brunet, we are moving from a world of petty introspection and moral inertia into a world of constructive work and meaningful commitment; from the solitude of the self-doubting intellectual to the fraternal warmth of the party activist. In fact, we gradually become aware that there is no real fraternal warmth or consolation in Brunet's life. Though, in L'Age de raison, he is sketched in sympathetically and described in terms of the open air, the calm of the sea and the solid reality of manual work, Brunet is revealed to be just as much the product of a bourgeois upbringing as

Mathieu. Indeed, at one level, the writing in both *Le Sursis* and *La Mort dans l'âme* seems intended to break down the idealised image of Brunet which we initially get from Mathieu. It is not simply that Brunet cannot manage to stifle his distaste for the vulgarity of the working-class Zézette, with her red hands, cheap scent and over-powdered face, but that, like Mathieu, he is constantly reproaching himself with harbouring these "class" reactions. When, in *Le Sursis* (p. 19), he murmurs: ["Intellectual. Bourgeois. Separated forever"], his fit of self-pity undermines him in our eyes, obliges us to see him in a very different light from Mathieu's rather fatuous hero-worship, and confirms the distance between him and the workers who form the backbone of the party. This is reinforced when Zézette's Maurice, a staunch proletarian member of the party, privately expresses irritation with Brunet for parrotting the editorial platitudes of *L'Humanité* (p. 17) instead of talking to them in a direct and human way. Brunet's evangelical manner of looking at the workers (["To love them. To love them all, men and women, each and everyone, without distinction"]) simply emphasizes the gulf between his ideological position and his human feeling. His self-reproach is couched in the language of desperation, not the language of fraternity. Brunet's membership of the Communist Party is shown to be as incapable of securing for him the blessings of fraternity as Mathieu's endless cogitation about the true nature of freedom.

Mathieu may fumble for fraternity but Brunet too readily assumes it to be an automatic function of party membership, though his actual behaviour shows at every turn how lacking in human content is this form of political brotherhood. Brunet certainly embodies the stoic virtues but he also displays unfeeling bureaucratic zeal. He thinks of men as material for the party to work on. In his eyes, the soldier Moûlu, trudging into captivity in *La Mort dans l'âme*, is simply poor raw material: ["That one's a petty bourgeois too, just like the other, but more stupid. It won't be easy to work on that"] (p. 202). This tendency to use men as nothing but disciplined instruments has ugly undercurrents, as when Brunet looks down the straggling line of French prisoners: [". . . pity this bunch isn't surrounded by five hundred soldiers, bayonet at the ready, pricking the thighs of the stragglers and smashing a rifle butt into the talkers . . ."] (pp. 203–4). It is not Schneider alone who reproves Brunet's unfeeling laughter when a French prisoner of war is publicly slapped by a German guard, but the human sympathy in each of us who reads the novel. We experience the same reaction when Brunet's authoritarian contempt for human frailty takes the form of forcibly preventing the corporal from scrambling for a slice of bread. We share Schneider's opinion that it is hard to help people when you have no feeling for them. Certainly Brunet is concerned for his comrades but chiefly in the sense of saving them from doctrinal error. He cares for them only insofar as they are already of the Party or can be used for its ends. The rest he sees as "children shouting in the timeless afternoon," and he is shocked to discover that, after they have eaten, his fellow-prisoners are transformed from a cowed mob into something like a carnival crowd. In his eyes, the camp takes on the air of a beach, a fairground, a place of pleasure — and he cannot forgive the French troops for it. For Brunet defeat is the necessary ordeal through which France must pass on the road to a new Communist society. An ultimate optimism about the advent of that society permits him to bear with the ignominy of defeat and the hard life of the transit camp, but he can be sustained in this atttude only so long as the Party is shown to be right and he himself can feel guided, supplanted by its superior wisdom and by the prospect of the inevitable success of its policies. Once Schneider/Vicarios can insinuate into Brunet's mind the notion of a purely opportunistic Soviet Union, willing to sacrifice France and the French Communist Party to its own interests, Brunet is dismayed and disarmed.

It is left to the second section of *La Mort dans l'âme* and to "Drôle d'amitié" to supply the fictional images which will convince us that Brunet's commitment to the Communist Party is no more a form of personal salvation, no more a way of living "authenticity" in the world, than Mathieu's quest of absolute freedom or Gomez's cult of action. It is the crowning irony of Brunet's political career that, as he slaves away in the barracks, and later, in the prisoner of war camp, to rescue the Party from the wreckage of defeat and to animate its few survivors with a new purpose, he has already been overtaken by events. While he believes he is following the party line in fostering resistance, he is, in fact, acting contrary to the French Communist Party's new policy of sympathetic neutrality to the German occupier.

Communism, in the sense of total political commitment of a naive and unquestioning kind, is subjected to critical scrutiny in the person of Brunet both because it holds out an illusory notion of infallible and unchanging truth (significantly, Brunet likens Marxism to the natural laws of the physical universe) and because it fails to respond adequately to the human claims that are made on it by men in deprivation and despair. The Communist Party is principally condemned not for being mistaken or inconsistent in its analysis of political change, but for driving men of good will to despair.[12] The emergence of Brunet as a pivotal figure in the second part of *La Mort dans l'âme*, and again in the pages of "Drôle d'amitié," is necessary if the argument about the merits of political commitment is to be fully articulated in imaginative terms. The worker, Maurice, is too peripheral a figure to have much significance in this moral scheme, and what we know of him is scarcely encouraging. One has only to recall his brutal reactions to silly Philippe's pathetic pleas in the hotel room or his simple-minded mouthing of party slogans.

By contrast, Schneider/Vicarios is Brunet's necessary complement, the voice of inwardness, of that "subjectivity" Brunet has learned to suspect and despise in the service of the Party. Vicarios is both enigmatic and appealing; appealing, in part, *because* he is an enigma and because we are granted only scattered glimpses of his past history and quality. We are never allowed to know him well enough to be able to give him, with complete confidence, the stature of an authentic Sartrian hero, though he gains immeasurably in our eyes from the manner of his death, from the way in which he is sacrificed to a cause that uses men cynically and pretends to infallibility. As the Latin root of his name implies, he carries vicariously the burden of the Party's errors and is killed so that no voice can dispute the Party's claim to embody the truth. It is Brunet's final distinction to recognize this and, at the point at which we leave him, crouched over the body of Vicarios in "Drôle d'amitié," he stands on the brink of what is arguably an "authentic" moral life, though this remains unrealised in the fiction Sartre has actually published. The precise nature of this authentic life is at least suggested by Brunet's refusal either to surrender to the claims of the wholly private self or to continue to accept the total validity of the Communist view of the world: ["No victory of men will be able to efface this absolute of suffering: — it's the Party who has killed him. Even if the u.s.s.r. wins, men are alone"] (p. 1039). Here, in the nightmarish moment when Vicarios is shot dead in the glare of the camp searchlights, Brunet also stumbles on another truth, that the love men bear each other transcends ideology. Paradoxically, it is at the culmination of his personal crisis of belief, the moment when he renounces the Party and declares his solidarity with fallible and suffering men, that Brunet really comes alive for us. And that very aliveness is a criticism of the sterility of the political creed by which he has previously lived. If pasasges of *La Mort dans l'âme* already suggest the unreality of Brunet's personal relations with other men, "Drôle d'amitié" spells out the disintegration of fraternity as embodied in the Communist Party. In *La Mort dans l'âme* Brunet learns from the fate of the young printer who leaps to his death from the train that there are party members who do not find the Party enough to live by. In "Drôle d'amitié" he learns what Schneider/Vicarios already knows, namely that the solitude of the militant cut off from the party is terrible and complete.[13] Like Vicarios, Brunet discovers in bitterness and anguish that if the Party gives life, it also takes it away.

Vicarios is *murdered* for political reasons, and this sets his death apart from the other kinds of, largely private, violence diffused throughout the novel-cycle. These range from the latent violence contained in Daniel's abortive attempts to drown his cats or castrate himself to the overt violence suffered by Gros-Louis when he is beaten up by petty crooks or Philippe when he is man-handled by the mob of conscripts at the railway station. It is this personal and almost random violence which is communicated to us with the greatest immediacy and vividness. There can be no question about how strongly we feel implicated in the sense of humiliation and outrage experienced by the paralysed Charles as he is clumsily bundled into the cattle-truck, in *Le Sursis*, or the raging desire to dominate by force which is expressed in the ugly wrestling-match between Daniel and his homosexual pickup, in *L'Age de raison*. But political violence, the violence inseparable from radical changes in society — a central preoccupation of Sartre's theatre — is almost never raised, in the novel-sequence, to the same level of expressiveness as private acts of violence. For example, in *La Mort dans l'âme*, what chiefly distinguishes Sartre's treatment of even so portentous a public event as the collapse of the French army in June 1940 is not the concrete realisation of violence as the very stuff of political breakdown, but the marvellous skill in conveying how the significance of this violence is blurred and diminished to the level of private dreams as the defeated French soldiers make their individual adjustments to it. It is true that the delaying action fought out on the church tower has the power to recall us to the fury of war, but it is so uniquely centred on Mathieu's introspection that it impresses us chiefly as the lurid enactment of a personal caprice. Only in the brutal death of Vicarios in "Drôle d'amitié" does one see spelt out, in a fully expressive way, the connection between public and private selves, force and ideology, violence and history. At that point in the novel-cycle political violence emerges as a significant theme, though in view of Sartre's subsequent abandonment of the tetralogy, it emerges too late to justify one in speaking of it as a potent and animating idea in *Les Chemins de la liberté*.

Notes

1. All references will be to *L'Age de raison* and *Le Sursis* (Paris, Gallimard, 1945), and to *La Mort dans l'âme* (Paris, Gallimard, 1949).

2. *La Force de l'âge*, Paris, Gallimard, 1960, p. 337.

3. "La Mort dans l'âme, pages de journal," reproduced in Michel Contat & Michel Rybalka, *Les Ecrits de Sartre*, Paris, Gallimard, 1970, pp. 638–49. These excerpts, dated 10 and 11 June 1940, originally appeared in Brussels in December 1942 as part of *Exercice du silence*, a special number of the review *Messages*.

4. In *Les Temps modernes*, 49, November 1949, pp. 769–806, and 50, December 1949, pp. 1009–39.

5. *La Force des choses*, Paris, Gallimard, 1963, pp. 213–4. This is confirmed by what Sartre himself told Robert Champigny, *Stages on Sartre's Way*, Bloomington, Indiana University Press, 1959, p. 194, note 3.

6. "A qui les lauriers des Goncourt, Fémina, Renaudot, Inter-allié?," *Marianne*, 7 December 1938.

7. A view supported by Sartre's comment to Kenneth Tynan: "To write a novel whose hero dies in the Resistance would be much too easy," *The Observer*, 25 June 1961.

8. Christian Grisoli, "Entretien avec Jean-Paul Sartre," *Paru*, 13, December 1945, p. 7.

9. Catharine Savage, *Malraux, Sartre and Aragon as Political Novelists*, Gainesville, University of Florida Press, 1965, p. 29.

10. Reprinted in Contat & Rybalka, *Les Ecrits de Sartre*, p. 113.

11. As Sartre confirms in his interview with Christian Grisoli (loc. cit.) when he argues that Mathieu embodies that absence of attachments which Hegel defines as the freedom of terror and which Sartre himself interprets as a kind of anti-freedom.

12. Cf. Sartre's preface to Juan Hermanos' *La Fin de l'espoir*: ["Died in despair: can

you still understand what these words mean? It's nothing to die: but to die in shame, in hatred, in horror, regretting have been born? That is the radical Evil and don't think that any victory will ever efface it"] Reprinted in *Situations VI*, Paris, Gallimard, 1964, p. 78.

13. Sartre deals discursively with this issue in his prefatory essay to Roger Stéphane's *Portrait de l'aventurier*, reprinted in *Situations VI*, pp. 7–22.

Sartre Resartus:
A Reading of *Les Mots*   Jane P. Tompkins*

The criticism of *Les Mots* which appeared following its publication in 1963–64 ranges from more or less off-the-cuff reviews to essays that place this work in the context of Sartre's philosophy. Three of the more comprehensive essays argue cogently that Sartre's autobiography reverses his earlier notion of the self as radically free, and demonstrates instead that man is a creature of social circumstance, the prisoner of his background and upbringing.[1] ["I was fleeing," proclaims Sartre, "external forces shaped my flight and made me"].[2] But while it appears to be true that *Les Mots* is a turning point in Sartre's theory of the self, it will never do to take him literally as a source of truth about his own life. Sartre's book has not yet been read as autobiography, that is, as a testament to his individuality (which he denies), and as evidence of the kind of person he is, of his characteristic values and behavior. The key to an autobiography lies in the stylistic and substantive choices an author makes as the historian of his past, and not in his theory of the self, or of *himself*—though that he has such theories is revealing. Sartre tells us in his last sentence that he is a man among men, ["who is worth them all and whom anyone is worth"] (213). That may be so, but his conduct as the author of this history proves quite the opposite. Philosophically, Sartre may have arrived at a new egalitarian notion of his relation to humanity; empirically, he acts as if he were at once the best and the worst of men.

One's natural inclination to identify with the protagonist of an autobiography is thwarted by Sartre's satiric attack upon himself. He writes about his past only in order to debunk it, and the manner of his exposé is sharp and deadly. He dissects his forbears in a few deft strokes, launches a sustained attack on the maternal grandparents who raised him, and endlessly castigates himself. In effect, Sartre reduces his readers to the position of helpless onlookers at a trial in which he, as prosecuting attorney and judge, had all the information and all the power, while the defendants, with whom the reader secretly sympathizes, have no advocate and cannot speak on their own behalf. The brilliant arguments which

*From the *Romanic Review* 76, no. 1 (January 1980):47–56. Reprinted with permission.

prove the grossness of the young Sartre's delusions, serve to establish his intellectual prowess in the present. His readiness to convict himself of crimes which to ordinary people seem quite venial, implies a present standard of conduct higher and more rigorous than that of other mortals. Intellectually and morally I can either look down on him in scorn or up at him in admiration; never can I regard him as a person like myself.

By placing himself simultaneously below and above his readers, Sartre effectively excludes them from sharing in the process of self-discovery. I may envy the ruthless virtuosity of the author or pity the vicissitudes of his youth, but nowhere do I find a reflection of my own middling condition. The only way to arrive at an estimate of Sartre which corresponds to one's experience of what people, in general, are like, is to see what the case he makes against himself implies about its author. For though the elaborate scheme Sartre imposes on his past distances readers from the reality of his childhood, it allows them to see his mind at work, forcing experience into the patterns which his present needs dictate.

Stripped of its convolutions, Sartre's theory consists of a series of stages which follow each other in a logical sequence. The series starts at zero. Having no father and no property to inherit, Sartre felt he was an "unwonted presence" in the world, surrounded by people whose existences seemed necessary and justified. In the case of their "depth" and "impenetrability," Sartre writes, ["I was *nothing:* an ineffaceable transparency"] (73). His identity was formed in response to the cues he received from others; this was the first stage of his imposture. ["My truth, my character, and my name were in the hands of the adults. . . . I was a child, that monster which they fabricate with their regrets"] (66). The projection of other people's expectations, Sartre learned to satisfy the adults around him by exhibiting his virtue, his precocity, his affection. Regarded by his mother and grandmother as a ["gift from heaven"], Sartre subordinated his real preferences to the requirements of his role. He would play up to his grandfather's fondness for dramatic outbursts by performing with him a series of masquerades calculated to reinforce the family belief that he was the light of his grandfather's old age.

But the secret conviction that he had no true function, no place, deprived his gestures of reality. He began to suspect that the adults, too, were faking. And so in order to escape from the round of empty rituals he retreated into a private fantasy life. In this second stage of his imposture, Sartre modelled himself after the heroes and heroines he had read about in books that he liked—Pardaillan, Griselda, Michael Strogoff. He pictured himself rescuing young maidens from burning buildings, slaying the enemies of virtue single-handed. These fantasies became the material for the "novels" he began to write, and gradually, his ideal of heroism shifted: the hero of the sword became a hero of the pen. ["I transformed Corneille into Pardaillan. . . . An imaginary child, I became a real paladin whose exploits would be real books. I was required!"] (141). But writing of itself did not provide a justification for being. Lacking a political or ideological struggle in the service of which to wield his pen, Sartre conceived of his literary vocation as a religious calling. ["My brothers, I decided, were asking me, quite simply, to devote my pen to their redemption. . . . And I, too, would restrain the species at the edge of the abyss by my mystic offering, by my work; discreetly the soldier gave way to the priest . . ."] (149). Seeking to evade the charades of his public routine, Sartre fulfilled their prophecy in private. Champion of the distressed as soldier, spiritual intercessor as saint, he performed, in his imagination, deeds worthy of the glory with which he was falsely credited by his family.

The dreams of glory compensated Sartre not only for the insecurity he felt as an object of adulation at home, but also for humiliation suffered outside the family circle. Despite his grandiose fantasies, Sartre lacked the confidence to put himself forward among his peers, preferring the security of an imagined victory to the risks of an actual defeat.[3] Even after he has gone to school and made friends, he continues to use his imagination as a resource against potential disaster. Finally, he parlays the notion of literary sainthood into a vision of himself as an immortal author. ["I had stepped back before the risks of an open, free existence with no guarantee from providence . . ."] (164–65). ["I had chosen to be reassured; . . . I had killed myself in advance because the deceased alone can enjoy immortality"] (164). He will outwit death by killing himself in advance; he will transform his vulnerable body into an indestructible book.[4] Reborn as leather and cardboard, glue and parchment, no one will be able to forget or ignore him, at last he will *be.*

The progression Sartre traces from "nobody" to family savior, to epic hero, to writer-martyr, to celebrated dead author forms the conceptual backbone of his memoirs. Each incident he recalls fits into the design. We have no way of knowing whether his boyhood consisted entirely of efforts to please, or if he dreamt of anything besides *beaux gestes* and posthumous fame. All of the evidence goes to prove that his life was a series of impostures. It remains to be seen what this theory implies about the man who created it. For though Sartre's schema stands between us and his childhood self, it hands him over to us in the present, as it were, stark naked.

The fact that Sartre has completely enclosed his past in a theory emphasizes his need to make experience conform to a pattern that is intellectually comprehensible. Never does he recall a favorite scene, a lost playmate, an old toy simply out of nostalgia; each reminiscence carries its conceptual payload.

[My grandfather would be snoozing, wrapped up in his plaid; beneath his bushy mustache I would perceive the pink nudity of his lips, it was unbearable. Fortunately his glasses would slip off and I would bound to pick them up. He would awaken, hoist me into his arms, and we would play our great love-scene. That was no longer what I had wanted. What

had I wanted? . . . I was a false child. . . . I could feel my actions
changing into gestures. Comedy hid the world and men from me. I only
saw roles and costumes. Serving by my buffoonery the undertakings of
the adults, how could I ever have taken their cares seriously? . . . A
stranger to the needs, the hopes and the pleasures of the species, I would
coldly squander myself in order to seduce it; it was my public, the
footlights separated me from it, and threw me into a proud exile which
rapidly turned to anguish.] (67–68)

The plaid blanket, the bushy moustache, and pink lips appear
fleetingly only to lend body to the idea Sartre is at pains to illustrate. At
the center of interest we find, not Sartre's grandfather, nor the child who
readjusted the glasses with false solicitude, but a paradigm of the
inauthentic self: exile, anguish, unreality. ["Comedy hid the world and
men from me. I only saw roles and costumes"]. Whatever Sartre saw when
he took part in this scene, he now sees material for exegesis. He cannot let
memory speak for itself, slyly juxtaposing events so that the pattern will
seem to emerge of its own accord, as Nabokov does in his autobiography.
Sartre's past needs a master, someone to extract meanings and make
overarching connections; it must be explained. If the explanation convicts
him of fraud, if it drains his experience of substance and leaves him with a
heap of cast-off skins, that is a small price to pay for an elegant theory.
The "words" of the title refer not simply to Sartre's youthful immersion in
reading and writing but to his conception of reality; ["the big Larousse"],
he says, ["took the place of everything for me"].

[Men and beasts were there *in person* . . . outside the house one
encountered vague sketches which more or less approached these arche-
types without attaining their perfection. At the Zoo the monkeys were
less monkeys, in the Jardin du Luxembourg, the men were less men. A
born Platonist, I went from knowledge to its object. I found more reality
in the idea than in the thing. . . . It was in books that I encountered the
universe, assimilated, classified, labeled, thought. . . . Whence came
that idealism which it has taken me thirty years to get rid of.] (38–9)

But the evidence of his autobiography demonstrates that Sartre has yet to
jilt Platonic forms in favor of experience. In the guise, this time, of a
theory of "impostures," their reality remains more forceful than the
experiences which they purport to explain.

Besides supplying the framework for a theory, the notion that he was
a play-actor serves Sartre in several other ways. It establishes him as a
person shrewd enough to see through his own disguises, and therefore as a
reliable guide to his own past. His willingness to cast the first stone at
himself disarms potential critics. Through the role-playing metaphor he
can disavow his former self and thus demonstrate that he has "progressed."
But even more essential to Sartre than the notion that he is more honest
now than he used to be, is the need to make his story exciting. Finding the
reality of his past insufficiently striking—he led a sheltered life, was

neither poor nor ill-treated — he finds grounds for pity and alarm in the idea that he had been deprived of *reality*. What could be worse than to have had no self at all? While Sartre relinquishes in the end the idea that he has progressed, admitting that his claim to have shaken off his impostures is mistaken, it never occurs to him that his theory of imposture itself might be revoked. He clings to the image of himself as an unmasked actor, as he writes, just as, in the past, he clung to the images of Pardaillan and Corneille.

The usefulness of role-playing as a vehicle for his story becomes apparent when one scrutinizes the verbal style of *Les Mots*. Sartre is not content with the well-worn term "rôle," he is a "fraud," a "false major character," who participates in "scenes" and *"tableaux vivants."* ["A faithless, lawless, stupified vermin with neither reason nor purpose, I used to escape into the family comedy, turning, running, flying from imposture to imposture"] (75). An ordinary child, unsure of his identity, may exaggerate the gestures that bring adult approbation. Not Sartre. In him the instinct to please becomes a monstrous charade, and the process of finding a place for himself within the family unit is transformed into the desperate wanderings of a derelict. A description of his grandfather, from whom Sartre claims to have learned the impersonator's art, exhibits the same tendency towards exaggeration and caricature. ["Everything was a pretext for him to suspend his gestures, to freeze himself into a fine attitude, to petrify himself. He used to adore these fleeting moments of eternity in which he became his own statue"] (16).

The hyperbolic impulse, for which Sartre castigates his boyhood self so harshly, is everywhere manifest in the language of the mature autobiographer. While explaining the origins of his epic cast of mind, he speaks in the very tones which he condemns: ["No matter; I am marked. If, in a century of iron, I have committed the mad mistake of taking life for an epic poem it's because I am a grandson of the Defeat. A convinced materialist, my epic idealism will compensate until the day of my death for an affront which I have not borne, for a shame which I have not suffered, the loss of two provinces which were returned to us a long time ago"] (96). Where another man might have confessed to a bad habit, Sartre commits a ["mad mistake"]. He deplores his heroic frame of mind in heroic accents (["grandson of the Defeat," "century of iron," "until the day of my death"]). Aware that his epic idealism is obsolete, he nevertheless cannot rid himself of the idiom. One might conclude, from the hyperbolic language of *Les Mots*, that Sartre's theory about himself is absolutely correct, that he was and is an incorrigible poseur. But it is impossible to tell, based on the evidence of the autobiography, what Sartre's childhood was really like. As one reviewer put it, "among all these intricately placed, pivoting mirrors . . . the bloody business of childhood has managed to get left out."[5] But we can be sure that Sartre saw himself as a dramatic figure when he wrote this book. The metaphor of role-playing allows him to magnify the vicissitudes of his past, transforming the story of an only child growing up in a middle-class family into the drama of a soul victimized by illusions. Like his grandfather before him, Sartre revels in the opportunity to make philosophic points and assume tragic attitudes: theory and drama combine to galvanize the abject actual.

This fusion of the didactic and histrionic elements of Sartre's personality occurs regularly in epigrammatic statements which serve as capstones to passages of speculation. These sentences, the hallmark of Sartre's style, epitomize his mode of perceiving reality and of projecting his vision before the world. Grounding himself in the material supplied by specific recollections, as in the reminiscence about his grandfather's glasses, Sartre launches a theory into the air and tops the performance off with an epigram calculated to startle and amaze: ["I would parade before children not yet born who resembled me exactly, I would draw tears from myself in invoking those that I would cause them to shed. I saw my death through their eyes. It had taken place, it was my truth. I became my own obituary"] (71). ["I became my own obituary," "I became quite posthumous," "I became a military dictator," "I was born in a river of blood," "clandestine, I was real."] At the close of declamatory passages, like the finale in a display of fireworks, these aphorisms light up the whole page. Nearly all commentators on *Les Mots* have noted their prominence, favorably or unfavorably.

At the simplest level, these expressions are a manifestation of Sartre's wit. When he delivers a particularly preposterous line — ["I became a military dictator"] — one cannot take him altogether seriously. His exaggerations involve clowning as well as self-reproach, and are a game he enjoys playing, not for masochistic reasons but for the glee that accompanies skillful satire. These sentences also provide a kind of emphatic punctuation for his ideas and mark moments of fulfillment and release. But while their function is partly humorous and partly aesthetic, Sartre's impulse to underline and condense his thought in paradoxical language seems connected to his notion of the truth — and of himself. Statements such as ["all children are mirrors of death"] and ["my truth ran the great risk of remaining until the end the alternation of my lies"] juxtapose ideas which are normally antipodal. Substantively, the statements are not difficult to accept because the context has rendered them plausible, but their form is paradoxical in that the identification of childhood and death, truth and lies, runs contrary to our expectations. Sartre likes to express the pith of his argument in a perverse and contrary form and seems unsatisfied until he has formulated an idea in a sentence that wears a look of incongruity and surprise. When he makes a statement like ["I became quite posthumous"], he is attacking not only his former illusion and the self that entertained it, but generally accepted beliefs about what is possible and reasonable. He dares us to believe him, and dares us not to believe him at the same time.

Near the end of *Les Mots*, Sartre promises to write another book which will explain ["by what reason I was led to think systematically against myself to the point of measuring the evidence for an idea by the displeasure it caused me"] (210). And elsewhere he remarks that when he has written books against himself, that means ["against all"] (136). In effect, Sartre is striking back at the audience he formerly played up to. Since his own beliefs have turned out to be false, the complacencies of others must be shaken as well. The angel-child and inveterate pleaser of others had become, in adulthood, an *enfant terrible*, unable to resist the chance to violate his readers' common sense. So that the truth of an idea comes to be measured, perhaps, not only by the displeasure it causes him, but by the extent to which it shocks his audience by seeming to defy received opinion.

At the very end of his autobiography Sartre steps back from the role he has played as his own prosecutor and announces that he has succeeded in making his case. ["The retrospective illusion is in pieces; . . . I believe I have taken it the whole way. I see clearly, I am disabused . . ."] (210–11). But on the next page he admits that he has not been able to root out the play-actor's instinct entirely. ["Moreover, this old building in ruins, my imposture, is also my character. One may overcome a neurosis, one never is cured of oneself. Worn down, effaced, humiliated, cornered, ignored, all the traits of the child have remained with the fifty year-old"] (211–12). The autobiography, which was a retraction of Sartre's past, repudiates itself in the end. But Sartre is one jump ahead of us. Well aware of this need to denounce yesterday's self in favor of today's, he has already warned the reader not to rely on him: ["I became a traitor and I have remained one. In vain have I been wholehearted in my enterprises, in vain have I given myself without reservation to work, to anger, to friendships, in a second I will deny myself. . . . From lack of loving myself sufficiently I have fled before. . . . Adolescence, maturity, or even the year which has just gone, will always be the Ancien Régime: the New One is announced in the present moment, but it is never instituted. Tomorrow there will be free shaves."] Just as each stage of his imposture provided the impetus for a new disguise, so each realization of the truth about himself leads Sartre to a further realization which cancels and supercedes the old. The interpretation of his past offered in the autobiography must also go by the board.

Another way of describing this process of imposture and self-repudiation is to call it bad faith, a concept Sartre had developed many years before in *L'Etre et le Néant*. Bad faith, he says, is a condition in which ["I can maintain behavior concerning my own anguish, in particular, behavior of flight. . . . Thus, let us flee anguish by trying to grasp ourselves *from outside* as if we were *other*, or as if we were *a thing*"].[6] This account of bad faith recalls the way Sartre, as a child, used glamorous conceptions of his destiny to escape an anguished awareness of his unjustified existence, ["turning, running, flying, from imposture to imposture"]. The long process of self-accusation which he carries out in *Les Mots*, moreover, resembles closely ["the bad faith [whose] goal is to put itself out of reach"] (106). The person in bad faith says to himself: ["I am in a space where no reproach can reach me since what I truly *am* is my transcendence; I flee, I escape, I leave my rags in the hands of the fault-finder"] (96). This is precisely what Sartre seems to do in *Les Mots*, both in rejecting his past as a series of impostures (["my rags"]), and in admitting that the attempt to cast off his impostures has failed. Nor is it of any use to him to admit, in addition, that he is a person who continually repudiates yesterday's credo in favor of today's; the very admission is a further act of bad faith, since it likewise disarms his critics in advance. But Sartre does not rest his case after making these admissions. After indulging, momentarily, in a gesture of helplessness (["Go and recognize yourselves in that. For my part, I do not recognize myself"]), he does one more about-face, and, in the final sentence, offers a new description of himself, totally at odds with everything that has preceded it. This description, which he cannot retract because it is the last, is the only point at which he makes himself vulnerable to the reader, the only place where he puts himself on a level with us. ["If I put impossible Salvation back on the shelf of the theatrical property-shop, what remains? A whole man, made of all men and who is worth them all and whom anyone is worth"] (213).

Now, finally, we may say to ourselves, Sartre has learned to accept himself with equanimity. He sees himself, commonsensically, as a man among men, neither better nor worse than ourselves. The new description represents a break with the self-recriminations of the past; Sartre offers himself up to the reader without apologies. His position is no longer that of a person in bad faith because he has not tried to put himself beyond reach.

But the sentence which saves him, in the nick of time, from the cycle of impostures is not so much a solution to the problem of flight as a way of ending his book. If we have learned anything at all about Sartre from reading this autobiography, we are bound to suspect him of having adopted a new disguise. The wise old man who places himself above no one, but acknowledges his worth with a forthrightness that is touching, is the same person who declared his childhood a fraud, announced that he had outgrown it, admitted that he had not, and confessed that he is still playing ["loser takes all . . . so that everything will be given back to me a hundredfold"] (212). The quick turnabouts Sartre makes in the last few pages seem an accelerated version of the succession of impostures he has previously described. In the light of his authorial behavior, the theory of imposture comes to seem less outlandish a description of the author than the prudent generality he leaves us with.

What *is* left? If we set the last sentence aside, by his own account the author's past self is an exploded fiction and his present self consists of its shattered remains. Sartre's original feeling that he was a "nothing, an ineffaceable transparency" is mitigated only by the ineffaceable remnants of his delusions. We are left with the tattered garment in our hands; the real Sartre has escaped again. Remaining undefined, he remains forever full of possibility—a nothing which may still become an everything. But this is only true in theory. In actuality, the autobiography having been written, the self which emerges from the text is as vivid and sharply defined as the self which it brings to bay is empty and phantasmagoric. In the process of searching for a self, a self has been revealed—not to the autobiographer but to his readers. It comprises those habits of mind and temperament which Sartre consistently displays as he reviews his past, and whose profile has gradually come into focus. As Sartre says in the introduction of *L'Etre et le Néant*: ["Appearance does not hide essence, it reveals it: it *is* essence. The essence of an existent is no longer a virtue embedded in the hollow of this existent, it is the manifest law that presides over the succession of its appearances, it is the principle of the series"].

The self which Sartre manifests in *Les Mots*, in the succession of its appearances, is devoted to abstractions and to heroic attitudes more than to particular experiences. Sartre has exchanged the fabric of sensation and event for a montage of exciting ideas. Flamboyant, playful, iconoclastic, he emerges from his self-portrait an idealist and actor in spite of himself. Superb entertainer, relentless moralist, he can recognize his love of show and damn it, but his theatrical denunciation only confirms the rejected trait. This paradox lies at the center of his book. "I was *nothing*," proclaims Sartre at the top of his lungs, but the egotistical style of his assertion denies what its content affirms.

Notes

1. Bernard Elevitch, "Jean-Paul Sartre: From the Roof of the World," *Massachusetts Review*, VI (Aug., 1964–Aug., 1965), 367–78; Joseph Fell, "Sartre's *The Words*: An Existential Self-Analysis," *Psychoanalytic Review*, LV (Spring, 1968), 426–41; Philip Thody, "Sartre's Autobiography: Existential Psychoanalysis or Self-Denial?" *Southern Review*, V (Autumn, 1969), 1030–44.

2. Jean-Paul Sartre, *Les Mots*, (Paris: Gallimard, 1964), p. 207. Page numbers for future citations will be given in parentheses in text.

3. On numerous occasions he went with his mother to the Luxembourg gardens where other children were playing. Leaning against a tree, he would yearn for an invitation to join in their games: [". . . I would have accepted the meanest tasks, I put my pride in not soliciting them. . . . She would take my hand and we would go off again, we went from tree to tree and from group to group, always imploring, always excluded. At dusk I would be back on my perch on those high places where the spirit whispered, my dreams: I would take revenge for my mortifications by six childish words and the massacre of a hundred mercenaries"] (111).

4. ["My vocation changed everything: the sword-thrusts fly away, the writings remain. I discovered that the Giver, in literature, can transform himself into his own Gift, that is to say into a pure object. . . . I could pour my babbling, my conscience, into characters of bronze, replace the noises of my life by ineffaceable inscriptions, my flesh by a style, the soft spirals of time by eternity . . ."] (160–61).

5. Conor Cruise O'Brien, "A Vocation," *The New Statesman*, LXVIII, October 9, 1964, p. 538.

6. Jean-Paul Sartre, *L'Etre et le Néant* (Paris: Gallimard, 1949), pp. 78, 81. Page numbers for future citations will be given in the text.

The Play's the Thing: Three Essays on Sartre's Theater

Sartre's *Kean*: The Drama of Consciousness

C. R. Bukala*

Emerging from within all of Sartre's writings are men and women who illustrate his concern from his earliest years with the various stages of personal commitment. *The Flies* and *No Exit* are discussed more than any of his other plays in regard to "meaning and validity" in the human situation. Both serve as excellent introductions to his "dramatic philosophy," a term which refers not only to the philosophy within his plays but also to the dramatic structure within all of his other writings.[1] Most of Sartre's plays are either variations or further developments of themes already considered in other writings; one such play is *Kean*, an adaptation of a play first presented by Alexander Dumas in 1836. This essay will consider the meaning of consciousness and its implications in the person of the famous actor, Edmund Kean. Our presentation will be divided into three parts: (1) The meaning of dramatic philosophy; (2) The meaning of consciousness; and (3) The consciousness of meaning.

The Meaning of Dramatic Philosophy

In all of his writings, regardless of genre, Sartre's interest centers upon man as an actor. He is concerned with man's acting ability in the play-situation as well as in life-situations. A distinction is made not only to indicate the different elements surrounding the human performance on and off stage but also to suggest that play-acting can also take place within concrete life-situations. A dramatic structure, constituted by the dialectic of dialogue and human activity, pervades all his writings, not only his numerous plays.

Sartre insists that all men and women play roles, either freely assumed or forced upon them by others. If freely assumed, the individual's freedom is assured in his role; if forced upon him, he either reacts to become free or denies that he is free and thus practices "bad faith." The roles in real life do not differ from those played on stage. Both have an

*From *Review of Existential Psychology and Psychiatry* 13, no. 1 (1974):57–69. Reprinted with permission.

audience which, seldom of itself, requires an understanding of the meaning of a particular activity. To the contrary, the true meaning of a human act, distinguished from an apparent meaning, follows only as a result of communication with the actor. For it is within the actor that meaning exists, and it is only through him and by him that it can be conveyed or communicated to others. All of Sartre's writings are meant to enable the reader to acquire the meanings of specific human activities, thus affirming these within the world of one's own possibilities. Speaking of the activity which takes place on stage, but allowing an extension to life-situations, he remarks:

> Action, in the true sense of the word, is that of the character; there are no images in the theatre but the image of the act, and if one seeks the definition of theatre one must ask what an act is, because the theatre can represent nothing but the act. Sculpture represents the form of the body, the theatre the act of this body. Consequently, what we want to recover when we go to the theatre is evidently ourselves, but ourselves not as we are, more or less poor, more or less proud of our youth and our beauty; rather to recover ourselves as we act, as we work, as we meet difficulties, as we are men who have rules for these actions.[2]

Sartre's emphasis on the activity of the characters follows from his description of existentialism as a philosophy which tells man "that the only hope is in his acting."[3] This is the significance of action within the dramatic setting either on or off stage:

> Dramatic action is the narration of action, is the staging of an action, one or several, of a few individuals or of a whole group—some people find themselves at the point of wanting something and try to realize this desire. It makes no difference whether they succeed or fail; what is clear is that they must realize an attempt on the stage and this is what we demand to see.[4]

The attempt on or off stage to realize this desire is important. This attempt, however, involves an individual in the tension of a dialectic with others. Interestingly, the dialectic is experienced even when we find the actor alone, for within his own consciousness he dialogues with himself for a greater realization of himself as one who is condemned to be free. His freedom is realized in what he chooses for himself as a result of this dialectic. The human dialectic is constituted ultimately of those individuals who are passionately involved in the human condition.

As a prisoner in Germany in 1940 Sartre wrote, staged, and acted in a Christmas play along with his fellow-prisoners. Christian in appearance only, this drama, *Bariona*,[5] was addressed to prisoners regarding their common concern as prisoners. Philip Thody describes Bariona as "Sartre's first committed hero, and the only character in the whole of his work to centre his actions and speeches round an appeal for joy."[6] As he spoke to his fellow-prisoners Sartre was impressed by their remarkable silence and attention and concluded then that theatre ought to be a great collective and religious event.[7] The play thus became a religious rite for Sartre and enabled the audience to relate to it through its common experiences and concerns. If the theatre is to regain its former value, says Sartre, it must become a rite which awakens the audience to the critical issues of its time and avoids the trap of that pure participation which eliminates important roles. Sartre's theatre actually involves the audience—just as his other writings involve his readers—as participants in situations which ultimately enable it to understand itself. The drama of the human condition experienced by the audience is what is portrayed on stage. The stage merely mirrors to the audience what it already experiences or will soon experience. Thus, there is a continuity between life on and off stage.

The drama that interests Sartre is a "theatre of situation" as distinguished from a "theatre of characters." He sees in the former a return to a theatrical tradition and a break from the so-called psychological theatre which emphasizes inner feelings and the development of character. Sartre's intention is to rid the stage of long analyses of specific characters. He is more interested in the meaning of the dramatic dialectic of the human situation in which these characters find themselves. "As a successor to the theatre of characters," he says, "we want a theatre of situations."[8] For man is ultimately "nothing but his situation."[9]

The *dramatis personae* of all of Sartre's writings are distinguished by their particular choices of dialogue and action in given situations, instead of by their peculiar psychological characterizations. This, however, does not mean that character traits of an individual have no part in the actor's choice of action. In the same way, the men and women of the drama are situated in ways which help explain and decide the action of the situation. Individual roles in intersubjective settings enable each character to know himself through the activity of an other individual. Robert Champigny remarks that "character does not come into the play as a certain object to be gradually revealed. The character will have to interpret what he 'is' from what the other characters tell him he is. His being is perpetually in question."[10] An unavoidable dialectic with others, as well as with oneself, is involved in this questioning.

One such situation is the human condition of the famous English actor, Edmund Kean. Although it includes elements of comedy, it would be a mistake to classify this play as comedy without qualification. The serious elements within the drama are what we are concerned with in this essay. Edmund Kean is the glory of his nation as an actor on the stage of Drury Lane. He performs for audiences who thirst for illusion. However, Kean is rejected as a man by those who applaud him as an actor on stage. As a man among men Kean is an individual of illegitimate birth and of low social class. Society refuses to resolve the dialectic between "Kean the actor" and "Kean the man."

Kean pretends a love affair with Elena, the Countess of Koefeld, and has the Prince of Wales competing with him as his shadow. While involved in this masquerade off stage, he is pursued by Anna Danby who truly loves him. She, in turn, is pursued by Lord Neville, who becomes one of many of Kean's antagonists. Conflicts among the *dramatis personae* result when the relationships become entangled. The reasons for the entangled relationships are many: confusion in role-playing, a reckless spirit of adventure, confusion between play-acting and life-acting, jealousy, emulation of others and a forgetfulness of oneself, social taboos which condemn individuals and then ostracize them, and bad faith. It is this entanglement which explains Sartre's famous phrase, "Hell is — other people!"[11] "I mean that if relations with others are twisted, damaged," says Sartre, "then the others are hell. Why? Because the others are really the factor which is most important in ourselves for knowledge of ourselves."[12] In the end, this entanglement forces Kean to break with his Shakespearean role at a benefit performance in order to condemn the audience. He leaves his former admirers and goes into forced exile in New York with Anna Danby, whom he marries. This climactic event causes everyone to reconsider their roles, the masks they have assumed for their own performances, and the various stages in the dialectic of dialogue and human activity which have led to the present situation.

The Meaning of Consciousness

In an early writing Sartre described existentialism as "a doctrine which makes human life possible and, in addition, declares that every truth implies a human setting and a human subjectivity."[13] It is the opposite of quietism because it holds that "There is no reality except in action. . . . Man is nothing else than his plan; he exists only to the extent that he fulfills himself; he is therefore nothing else than the ensemble of his acts, nothing else than his life."[14]

Sartre's phenomenological ontology centers around a dualism: "Being-for-itself" and "Being-in-itself." Viewed as a method, phenomenology is interested, according to Sartre, in a dramatic description of this dualism in the various moments of its manifestations. Whereas the "Being-for-itself" refers specifically to the Sartrean man and is interchangeable with human consciousness, subjectivity, and freedom, the "Being-in-itself" refers to all things other than man or human consciousness. Moreover, the being of the "being-in-itself" is complete according to its own individuality as something other than human consciousness; but the being of the "being-for-itself" is never complete, for it is never established but is rather continually sought. Human consciousness, to use Husserl's basic thesis, is always consciousness of something. Human consciousness suggests, therefore, a constant projection toward that which fulfills it at least for a time.

"All consciousness," says Sartre, "is positional in that it transcends itself in order to reach an object, and it exhausts itself in this same positing."[15] Consciousness calls forth the presence of an object through an act of positing and thus creates itself by positing that of which consciousness is conscious. There is also a reflective consciousness that is concerned with the reflected-on consciousness. "In the act of reflecting," says Sartre, "I pass judgment on the consciousness reflected-on; I am ashamed of it, I am proud of it, I will it, I deny it, etc. The immediate consciousness which I have of perceiving does not permit me either to judge or to will or to be ashamed."[16] The difference between the positional consciousness and the reflective consciousness is that the former is incapable of judging itself because it is concerned with the object outside of itself, whereas the latter has the ability to turn back upon itself.

Consciousness and freedom are, according to Sartre, one and the same thing. He posits freedom as logically prior to thought, as the essence of the Cartesian "cogito." When we speak in this essay of the "consciousness of an actor," we do not intend a distinction between the two terms, for the actor is his consciousness, and consciousness is the actor. This is man's basic role as an actor: To be an individual who creates and then identifies with that creation because that creation is his own person. The Sartrean man is thus a creator who himself is in need of creation. Sartre formulates the following thesis: "Transcendental consciousness is an impersonal spontaneity. It determines its existence at each instant, without our being able to conceive anything *before* it. Thus each instant of our conscious life reveals to us a creation *ex nihilo*. Not a new arrangement, but a new existence."[17]

Consciousness separates from its own peculiar past in projecting itself toward that which it is not. "Freedom is the human being," says Sartre, "putting his past out of play by secreting his own nothingness."[18] The Sartrean man appears in the world faceless, without characteristics and attributes which could be used in his definition or description of himself; he is a nothingness. The nothingness of human consciousness is explained by the existential reality that man is what he is not and not what he is. Consciousness continually encounters nothingness or is involved in "nihilation" because it flees from its own existence in order to remake and redefine itself. Thus, man is nothing, and, says Sartre, "Freedom in its foundation coincides with the nothingness which is at the heart of man. Human reality is free because it is not enough. It is free because it is perpetually wrenched away from itself and because it has been separated by a nothingness from what it is and from what it will be."[19] In the beginning the Sartrean man is nothing; only after he has made his appearance in the world will he become through his own activity what he wishes to become: "Only afterwards will he [man] be something, and he himself will have made what he will be. Thus, there is no human nature, since there is no God to conceive it. Not only is man what he conceives himself to be, but he is only what he wills himself to be after this thrust toward existence."[20] The Sartrean man becomes a man only by escaping from the reality of God. The simultaneous existence of both God and man is impossible. For if God exists, man is nothing by comparison to Him. But if the existence of God is denied, then a whole world of possibilities opens up before him. The mistake of Zeus, as Orestes describes it in *The Flies*, was that he created man free.[21] Freedom now turns against his giver and manifests itself in anguish in regard to all the possibilities, as its own possibilities, that are now open to man.

The meaning of consciousness as it refers to Edmund Kean the actor and the man is explicated by his activity and dialogue with other actors in play and life situations. Hailed as the pride of the nation for his extraordinary talents on stage, Kean performs a ritual in his dressing room before each performance in preparation for his offering of himself to his audience. He chooses carefully one role from among others, and the mask to accompany this role. His life off stage has been influenced by his life on stage. His most ardent admirers express their concern:

ELENA: Kean? Is there such a man as Kean? The creature I saw last night was the Prince of Denmark in person. . . .

AMY: Yes — as he was Romeo the night before, and the Thane of Glamis the night before that. . . .[22]

Elena, the Countess of Koefeld, is a special admirer, or at least she pretends to be. She reveals first a love for Kean the man and then an infatuation for Kean the actor of the stage. Who he makes himself to be — for this is his special talent — is more attractive to Elena and others than who he is in real life. Kean the actor can make the audience forget their own lives and become involved in the lives of the great Shakespearean characters whom he portrays on stage. Everyone, thus, seems to be involved in a masquerade and every person wears his own mask in the excitement of the drama.

Elena and her friend, Amy, object to Kean's masquerading off stage. He is described as a man who "leaves his kingly robes in the theatre and frequents the lowest taverns dressed as a common sailor."[23] If freedom is identified with his consciousness, and if it is for Kean to determine how he will express his freedom, the question of what he does on as well as off stage concerns ultimately only Kean. Elena masquerades in life-situations first as the wife of a noble lord, and then as a woman who pretends a love-affair with the famous actor. Elena is not in love with Kean the man but with Kean the actor whom audiences applaud. "The thought of ruining her reputation for the love of Kean excites her imagination; she encourages him just enough to keep the fantasy alive without, in fact, compromising herself. Elena wants Kean in the same way he wants her: as a trophy."[24]

The Prince of Wales also objects in his own peculiar way to Kean's masquerades. His is an interesting objection precisely because he is competing with Kean in those matters which most make Kean the topic of conversation and gossip. It will be a lie, a spontaneous but yet effective masquerade, which will separate the two men not only geographically but also psychologically from each other at the end of the drama.

Anna Danby is a wealthy heiress who recognizes the masquerade surrounding Kean and enters it only to lead him out of it. She asks Kean to help her become an actress. However, she is already play-acting when she makes this request, for her true desire is to become his wife. She knows Kean better than he knows her. "She has seen Kean's limitations in the theatre — under the influence of alcohol he tends to slip from one role into another — and her keen observations there, as elsewhere, indicate that in pursuing him she knows what she is after. She also knows what she is offering: a chance to play a human role with someone who will respect her because she loves him."[25]

Within Kean's consciousness, as he continues his masquerade on and off stage, are two facts which exist as obstacles to his acceptance by society: He is of illegitimate birth and of a low social class. In the consciousness of his freedom he realizes that these are the specific ways in which he has been condemned as a free individual. Because of these two facts, rejecting specific rules, taboos, and set styles of behavior, he strives to be accepted as a man as well as a great actor of the stage. It is in this frame of mind that Kean realizes his nothingness, subjectivity, and freedom in a specific situation. It is in this situation that he is forced to create himself anew against the demands of his world.

The Consciousness of Meaning

What Kean has done, and who Kean has become, suggest several important questions regarding the consciousness of meaning: Who is Edmund Kean? Who does Kean think he is? Who would Kean want to be? The consciousness of meaning rests on the answers to these questions. The answers are explained according to the *plan* — if there is a plan — that Kean has determined for himself. In his early writings Sartre describes man as "nothing else than his plan; he exists only to the extent that he fulfills himself he is therefore nothing else then the ensemble of his acts, nothing else than his life."[26]

Sartre's emphasis on human activity follows specifically from his existentialist axiom, "existence precedes essence." Man first exists, then only later defines himself. Every activity, whatever its specific nature — intellectual, verbal, physical — refers back to the individual to be included in his definition. *What an individual does is who he becomes.* A man comes into the world faceless, an actor without any masks. In the beginning he is nothing; only after he has made his appearance will he become someone with specifications which will enable him to stand out in a crowd. J. S. R. Goodlad remarks that "Sartre argues that we invent values — that there is no sense in life *a priori*. Life is nothing until it is lived. The individual must make sense of life by choosing what he will do and how he will live. This whole approach to existence, to 'reality,' is an approach from inside — an approach from the point of view of the 'actor' as opposed to that of the observer from without."[27]

The concept of God is crucial in Sartre's philosophy of the actor. In his first major philosophical work he states its importance:

> Imperfect being surpasses itself toward perfect being: the being which is the foundation only of its nothingness surpasses itself toward the being which is the foundation of its being. But the being toward which human reality surpasses itself is not a transcendent God; it is at the heart of all reality; it is only human reality itself as totality.[28]

The Sartrean man experiences various tensions from within and from without as he proceeds to realize his freedom. He realizes self-deification as an illusion which he is unwilling to discard: All of reality ultimately is described as a passion that seeks to lose itself, and man is "forlorn, because neither within him nor without does he find anything to cling to. He can't start making excuses for himself."[29] "Thus the passion of man is the reverse of that of Christ, for man loses himself as man in order that God may be born. But the idea of God is contradictory and we lose ourselves in vain. Man is a useless passion."[30] Sartre says:

> There is in every human heart such a hunger for the absolute, that people have often confused eternity, which would be a timeless absolute, with immortality which is only a perpetual delay of execution and a long series of vicissitudes. I understand this desire for the absolute very well. I desire it also. But need we go so far afield to look for it? It is there all around us, under our feet and in our gestures. We make absolutes. . . .[31]

This is the stance of Kean, who already is the acknowledged master of the stage; but he now strives also to become an equal among other men. The Sartrean man, Kean, takes the place of God in this philosophical perspective and projects himself continually towards the future. It is only through his projections into the future that meaning is found. These projections ultimately provide meaning for his validity as a man. For human meaning is not something that is found outside of man but is something created within him.

Kean exists for his audience through their look; they scrutinize his portrayals of Shakespearean characters and then objectify him through their applause. He has been play-acting most of his life, and his roles on stage have been confused with his roles off stage. The impression given half-way through the drama is that Kean is either unable or unwilling to distinguish between his roles on and off stage. Taking Sartre's axiom, "existence precedes essence," as a point of departure, it could be said that once Kean appears on the stage to become the great actor who wins the applause of the entire nation he never leaves the stage but rather extends it wherever his feet take him. If this is the case, the consciousness of meaning, as it refers to Kean, invalidates the great emotion he gives expression to as he smears make-up on his face and exhorts his audience to "Behold the man."[32]

A confusion in role-playing is evident. Although Kean may have appeared on stage to become the glory of the nation, and although he may have confused his roles on and off stage, it seems as though he expresses, after recognizing this confusion, a desire for things to be other than what they are at present. Kean's emotional response to the distractions from the audience during the benefit performance is more than a mere transition to a new role and character. He expresses real, not pretend emotion. He is not play-acting when he breaks with the Shakespearean role of Othello. He has in the past continually taken himself for someone else. Now he stands in agony on the stage as Kean the man.

Kean's great ability as an actor on the stage of Drury Lane has been attributed to his talent to forget himself in order to become someone else, in one instance Hamlet, then Lear, Macbeth, or Othello. His forgetting of himself as a man suggests the nothingness which Sartre speaks of as situated at the very center of his being. The nothingness within each man is a personal problem which each as an individual must solve for himself. The solution, however, involves a personal risk and can intensify the experience of nothingness. This is what Kean seems to have suffered in his own life: He has satisfied the nothingness within him by becoming an actor but in doing so he has forgotten his basic needs as a man. His forgetfulness has cost him his identity. Who he is, what he has become, is accounted to his own free activity. He shoulders the responsibility for this activity. He tries to react to his forgetfulness by imposing the blame for this "monstrosity," a term he uses to describe himself, on the audience which has continually acknowledged his greatness through their applause. They have never, however, proclaimed his greatness off stage.

Kean attempts to realize himself as a man in the fifth act of the play. Up to this point, Elena has flirted with Kean in a pretended love-affair; Anna Danby has pursued Kean with a true love for him; the Prince of Wales has followed closely behind Kean, as his shadow, to establish his own meaning and validity. The problem which results is that Kean is acclaimed a great actor, but is not accepted by society as a man. This is the answer to the first question: "Who is Edmund Kean?" Edmund Kean is a great English actor, the glory of his nation. The second question: "Who does Kean think he is?" Kean thinks, in fact knows, that he is a great actor, and the applause of the audience confirms this. The third question: "Who would Kean want to be?" He would like to be able to continue to entertain his audiences as an actor, but would also like to be accepted as an ordinary man of feeling, fear, loneliness, laughter, and love, a man among other men.

The disturbance from the audience during his benefit performance in *Othello* is occasioned by the fact that Kean, despite Elena's objections and jealousy, allows Anna Danby to play Desdemona. Suspecting that he has created a threatening situation, Kean beseeches Elena to be tolerant and not to carry on with the Prince of Wales during the performance. His suspicions are well founded.

In the past Kean has followed the strict rules of the theatre and pledged his allegiance to its institution. But his performances suggest an animal confined in a cage to entertain audiences interested not in who he is but only in what he does. Recognizing his enslavement, he rebels. His use of the phrases "murderous faces" and "real aspects"[33] suggests that the once friendly audiences, now challenged, have become vicious. His parting words are autobiographical and show that he is becoming conscious of his meaning in their presence:

> . . . Good night, ladies—good night, sweet ladies. Romeo, Lear, and Macbeth make their adieus. I must rejoin them, and give them your regards. I must return to the imaginary world where my real fury awaits me. Tonight, kind ladies, I shall be Othello, in my own house, sold out, house full, and commit my murders in my own fashion. Of course, if you had really moved me. . . . But we must not ask too much, must we? By the way, I was wrong just now to mention Kean. Kean, the actor, died very young. [Laughter.] Be quiet, murderers, it was you who killed him. It was you who took an infant and turned him into a monster. [The audience is silent.] That's right. Silence—a silence of death. Why were you booing just now? There was nobody on stage. No one. Or perhaps an actor playing the part of Kean playing the part of Othello. Listen—I am going to tell you something. I am not alive—I only pretend.[34]

These words parallel those of Sartre himself in his autobiography. He describes the world of his youth as one of imaginary heroes in various situations in which he also had roles to play. He was an imaginary child, sustained by and through his imagination,[35] distanced from reality, as was Kean, through his various roles. The audience's consciousness of Kean is only of Hamlet, Lear, Macbeth, or Othello, never of the reality behind Kean's many masks.

James M. Edie remarks that "Sartre takes the final step of showing that in real life, no less than in theatrical experience, persons are alienated from themselves, i.e., from their roles, their essences, their very emotion, and all learned behaviours."[36] The consequences of this confusion and misunderstanding must now be faced. As far as society is concerned, some individuals have assumed the role of master, while others have had the role of slave forced upon them, or in bad faith have willingly assumed that role. Kean has been a slave throughout most of his acting career.

Sartre's philosophy of intersubjectivity is constitutive of various problems and difficulties. Every human consciousness is always a consciousness of something which ultimately refers to or constitutes the essence of man. Man is basically a "freedom-in-situation" which demands realization through specific activity. He is free only in a situation to which he gives meaning through his various acts. "The situation is the whole subject (he is nothing but his situation). . . . The situation is the subject illuminating things by his very surpassing, if you like; it is things referring to the subject his own image. It is the total facticity, the absolute contingency of the world, of my birth, of my place, of my past, of my environment, of the fact of my fellowman — and it is my freedom without limits as that which causes there to be for me a facticity."[37] Sartre points to a paradoxical aspect of the situation: "I, by whom meanings come to things, I find myself engaged in an *already meaningful* world which reflects to me meanings which I have not put into it."[38] The Sartrean man thus necessarily encounters meanings in his world which others have placed in it; he is forced to react to these, either to affirm them or to negate them, as he searches for his own meaning. The existence of an other in his world can frustrate his efforts to realize himself as a "freedom-in-situation," since the other is also a "freedom-in-situation."

Man's consciousness is always conscious of itself as an actor who assumes various roles, whose activity ultimately bears on the creation of his own self. Bad faith is possible because "consciousness conceals in its being a permanent risk of bad faith. The origin of this risk is the fact that the nature of consciousness simultaneously is to be what it is not and not to be what it is."[39] Sartre says that "the one who practices bad faith is hiding a displeasing truth or presenting as truth a displeasing untruth. Bad faith then has in appearance the structure of falsehood. Only what changes everything is the fact that in bad faith it is from myself that I am hiding the truth."[40] It is the result of an original project of human consciousness. Moreover, bad faith is not practiced indiscriminately, but has a definite goal: ". . . to put oneself out of reach; it is an escape."[41] Through bad faith the Sartrean man seeks to escape the responsibility which accompanies his freedom.

This is the situation in which Edmund Kean finds himself. He is conscious of himself as a great actor; he has confused his roles and thus forgotten himself as a man. His forgetfulness approaches the realm of untruth or the lie, and the life he leads thereafter is a life lived in "bad faith." Bad faith does not come from the outside, although it might be occasioned in a situation in which another individual is present. Rollo May offers an interesting remark: "Sartre's concept of 'bad faith' and 'good faith' is also an illustration [of the difficulty of knowing oneself] — the dilemma of honesty with one's self lying in the fact that there is always some element of self-distortion in our acts and beliefs. The man who thinks he is in 'good faith' is at the point in 'bad faith,' and the only way to be in 'good faith' is to know that you are in bad faith, i.e., to know that there is some element of distortion and illusion in your perception."[42] "By the lie," says Sartre, "consciousness affirms that it exists by nature as *hidden from the Other*; it utilizes for its own profit the ontological duality of myself and myself in the eyes of the Other."[43]

An actual denial of the freedom of human consciousness becomes understandable if we imagine an individual's aversion to greater responsibility in his life. This aversion is understood in Sartre's description of anguish: "The man who involves himself and who realizes that he is not only the person he chooses to be, but also a lawmaker who is, at the same time, choosing all mankind as well as himself, can not help escape the feeling of his total and deep responsibility."[44] The true existentialist hero shoulders the responsibility for his committed acts and does not lie either to himself or to others regarding their authorship.

The dialectic of encounter in intersubjectivity situates at least two individuals in stances from which they project into their own futures and become entangled in each others' desires and hopes. This has been Kean's continuing experience. The elements of his world are constituted of a delicate fabric; the appearance of an other carries a threat to, if not an actual disintegration of that world. When Kean is *seen by* the audience he is grasped as an object in a world not of his own choosing. As an object in a foreign world he becomes alienated from the world and the world from him. All that can be said at this point is that Kean is "somebody." His own world of possibilities, hopes, and desires has been superseded by that of an other. He has become a slave in the Hegelian sense. Speaking of this condition, Sartre says that "I am a slave to the degree that my being is dependent at the center of a freedom which is not mine and which is the very condition of my being. In so far as I am the object of values which come to qualify me without my being able to act on this qualification or even know it, I am enslaved."[45] This is what Kean has experienced at the hands of those who continue to applaud his performances. Their applause is as threatening as their look: "I grasp the Other's look at the very center of my act as the solidification and alienation of my own possibilities. In fear or in anxious or prudent anticipation, I perceive that these possibilities which I am and which are the condition of my transcendence are given also to another, given as about to be transcended in turn by his own possibilities. The Other as a look is only that—my transcendence transcended."[46] Kean's only salvation is to do to "society as the Other" what society is doing to him, namely, to electrify society with his look and thus objectify it. To be a subject means ultimately to realize one's freedom to such an extent that one can overwhelm an other. The demand placed on Kean, if he is to survive, is that he must look at the look of the other and cause its disintegration, so that only powerless eyes are left behind. He can then establish his own subjectivity on the remains of the other's freedom, precisely what he does when he breaks away from "the theatre as a vast fabric of deception and lies."

In conclusion, we ask once more, "Who is Edmund Kean?" But now we hesitate to answer the question. For every man must ultimately answer for himself the question regarding his identity. Kean's realization of self demands that he experience the "center" of himself as freedom and creativity. But to do this he must bracket out of experience all his fears, conflicts, and misunderstandings, as well as his hopes, desires, and needs, so to produce a somewhat mystical experience of his own existence. Moreover, this question will never be answered satisfactorily even by Kean, because, as an existentialist subject, he is continually creating himself, his meaning and validity through specific activity and thus will never complete the creation of his own person. He is continually "the giver and the gift" to himself. This constitutes the drama of human consciousness.

Notes

1. C. R. Bukala, S.J., "Sartre's Dramatic Philosophical Quest," *Thought. A Review of Culture and Idea*, XLVIII (Spring, 1973), 79–106.

2. Jean-Paul Sartre, "Beyond Bourgeois Theatre," *The Tulane Drama Review*, V (March, 1961), 4–5.

3. Jean-Paul Sartre, *Existentialism*. Trans. Bernard Frechtman (New York: Philosophical Library, 1947), 42.

4. "Beyond Bourgeois Theatre," 6–7.

5. Jean-Paul Sartre, *Bariona*, in *The Writings of Jean-Paul Sartre. Vol. II: Selected Prose*. Edit. Michel Contat and Michel Rybalka. Trans. Richard C. McCleary (Evanston, Illinois: Northwestern University Press, 1974).

6. Philip Thody, *Sartre, A Biographical Introduction* (London: Studio Vista, 1971), 61.

7. Jean-Paul Sartre, "Forgers of Myths. The Young Playwrights of France," *Theatre Arts*, XXX (1946), 330.

8. *Ibid.*, 326.

9. Jean-Paul Sartre, *Being and Nothingness: An Essay on Phenomenological Ontology*. Trans. Hazel E. Barnes (New York: Philosophical Library, 1956), 549.

10. Robert Champigny, *Stages on Sartre's Way, 1938–1952* (Bloomington, Indiana: Indiana University Press, 1959), 129.

11. Jean-Paul Sartre, *No Exit and Three Other Plays* (New York: Alfred A. Knopf, 1946), 47.

12. Jean-Paul Sartre, in *Le Figaro Littéraire* (Jan. 7–13, 1968).

13. *Existentialism*, 12.

14. *Ibid.*, 37–38.

15. *Being and Nothingness*, li.

16. *Ibid.*, liii.

17. Jean-Paul Sartre. *The Transcendence of the Ego. An Existentialist Theory of Consciousness*. Trans. Forrest Williams and Robert Kirkpatrick (New York: The Noonday Press, 1965), 98–99.

18. *Being and Nothingness*, 28.

19. *Ibid.*, 440.

20. *Existentialism*, 18.

21. Jean-Paul Sartre, *The Flies*, in *No Exit and Three Other Plays* (New York: Alfred A. Knopf, 1946), 120.

22. Jean-Paul Sartre, *Kean*, in *The Devil and the Good Lord and Two Other Plays, Nekrassov and Kean*. Trans. Kitty Black (New York: Alfred A. Knopf, 1960), 155.

23. *Kean*, 195.

24. Dorothy McCall, *The Theatre of Jean-Paul Sartre* (New York: Columbia University Press, 1971), 103.

25. Joseph H. McMahon, *Human Being. The World of Jean-Paul Sartre* (Chicago: The University of Chicago Press, 1971), 187.

26. *Existentialism*, 37–38.

27. J. S. R. Goodlad. *A Sociology of Popular Drama* (London: Heinemann Educational Books, 1971), 32.

28. *Being and Nothingness*, 89.

29. *Existentialism*, 27.

30. *Being and Nothingness*, 615.

31. Jean-Paul Sartre, "We Write for Our Time," *Virginia Quarterly Review*, XXIII (1947), 237.

32. *Kean*, 251.

33. *Ibid.*, 250–251.

34. *Ibid.*, 251.

35. Jean-Paul Sartre, *The Words*. Trans. Bernard Frechtman (New York: George Braziller, 1964), 113.

36. James M. Edie, "The Problem of Enactment," *Journal of Aesthetics and Art Criticism*, XXIX (Spring, 1971), 113.

37. *Being and Nothingness*, 549.

38. *Ibid.*, 510.

39. *Ibid.*, 70

40. *Ibid.*, 49.

41. *Ibid.*, 65.

42. Rollo May, *Love and Will* (New York: Dell, 1969), 157–158.

43. *Being and Nothingness*, 49.

44. *Existentialism*, 22.

45. *Being and Nothingness*, 267.

46. *Ibid.*, 263.

Sartre's *Kean* and Self-Portrait Catharine Savage Brosman*

In 1953, the same year that he began *Les Mots*, and just one year after publishing his massive study on Jean Genet, Jean-Paul Sartre composed *Kean*, one of his two dramatic adaptations (excluding film scripts). The premiere took place on 14 November 1953 at the Théâtre Sarah-Bernhardt; the play was a great stage success. It is a reading in five acts of *Kean ou Désordre et génie* (1836), written by Alexandre Dumas père and included in his complete works, but based on a text composed by Frédéric de Courcy and Théaulon de Saint Lambert for Frédérick Lemaître, the renowned actor, who had met the actor Edmund Kean and,

*From the *French Review* 55, Special Issue, no. 7 (Summer 1982):109–22. Reprinted with permission.

after the latter's death, wanted to play him on the stage.[1] Thus it is at several removes from the biographical reality it would purport to portray; Sartre's Kean is, as he termed him, a myth, the "patron des acteurs" (C&R, p. 268), reflecting the author's interest in self-mythification. It was Pierre Brasseur who proposed that Sartre adapt for him the Dumas text. The latter, who had been interested in Kean for some time, was inspired to accept the suggestion, he said, because he had heard laughter at *Hernani*, which he liked, along with the Romantic theatre in general.[2] The play, which abounds in melodramatic situations, does indeed bear some resemblance to the Victor Hugo masterpiece. Sartre considered the subject to be timeless because it dealt with self-identity and allowed a great actor of each generation to take his bearings and test himself, as it were (C&R,p. 268). My purpose is not, however, to study the play as a virtuoso piece for a great performer but rather as an oblique self-portrait, closely associated with the author's autobiographical undertaking. In particular, it illustrates three themes which mark *Les Mots* (1964) and other major works of the period, all three fundamental in Sartre's psyche and catalogue of personal myths, and related to the questions of appearance versus reality, identity, authenticity, and social alienation, which he treats elsewhere. These themes—the major theme of imposture or playacting, the minor ones of treachery and bastardy—and their expression in Kean and *Les Mots* can profitably be examined in terms of both the ontology of the 30s and 40s and the Marxist analyses of the 50s and 60s.[3]

Although Sartre stated that all he wanted to do was to give the play the "petit coup de pouce" that would modernize it enough to make it suitable for the contemporary stage (*Figaro*, p. 10), the changes are considerable and bear a characteristic Sartrean stamp.[4] They include tightening of the plot by reducing the cast and sub-plots, increased banter, great concentration on the two heroines, an entirely different characterization of Anna Damby, and a new interpretation given to Kean and his dilemmas. The emphasis on society reveals Sartre the social commentator as well as Sartre the psychologist, and points to the Marxist social analyses, already adumbrated in *Saint Genet, comédien et martyr*, which would be elaborated only a few years later. Sparkling with humor and psychological insight, the play shows again how its author, sometimes heavyhanded, could rival Giraudoux and Anouilh in Gallic wit, as in the maxim, ["There's no one more punctual than a woman one doesn't love"].[5]

The play is built around four overlapping amorous triangles, which reflect on each other:[6] Kean, the great actor, admired but socially scorned for his illegitimate birth, the Danish ambassador, and Eléna, his wife; Kean, Eléna, and the Prince of Wales, who, as his companion in pleasure, has also been his rival and chooses clothes and women because Kean likes them (a peculiar sexual form of the other as mediator to the self, or the dependence of the for-itself for its reality on the for-others); Kean, Eléna, and Anna Damby, a merchant's daughter, who takes a fancy to the actor

and wants to become both an actress and his wife; and Kean, Anna, and
Lord Mewill, her fiancé, who is furious that Anna should have jilted him.
The dynamics of their multiple relationships are not all pertinent to the
present analysis, nor are the probings into masculine and feminine ways of
loving and the nuances of class relationships, as Sartre saw them, in early
nineteenth-century England. It is useful, however, to quote at the outset
Kean's suggestive remark, of both social and ontological import, that he,
the prince, and Anna are alike, all victims, all reflections: he was born too
low, the prince too high, and Anna a woman. ["You enjoy your beauty
through the eyes of others and . . . I discover my genius in their applause;
as for him, he's a flower; in order for him to feel himself a prince, we have
to breathe him in"] (p. 199). All are alienated from the dominant society;
none can easily achieve authenticity.

Within this social context, Sartre explores the ambiguous relationships between actor and role and man and actor, in this privileged case of
["an actor whose role is to incarnate his own stage-character"] (C&R,
p. 268). These aspects of the more general relationship between self and
self and the distance between subjective and objective images introduce
the major Sartrean theme of imposture, which he had already considered
at length as the phenomenological problem of appearance versus reality.
The theme can be expressed as a question of the identity of the self, one of
the most characteristic of modern themes.[7] Who is Kean? That depends on
who is answering the question. To most of London, he is Hamlet, Romeo,
or Othello; that is why Anna is first attracted to him, why Eléna thinks she
is in love with him. The latter asks, ["Is there a Kean? The man I saw
yesterday was Hamlet in person"] (p. 14). He is also, socially speaking, an
outcast, because he is not well born: his is an extreme case, since he is a
bastard, as well as an actor. As Franck Laraque writes, he is ["living
inside-out"] through his ambiguous profession, whereas society ["declares
it lives right-side out"].[8] In the first act he distinguishes between the
actor—to whom flattering invitations are sent—and the man, noting that
his profession is to live by ["false situations"] (pp. 24, 30). Both views are
condescending, in the Romantic tradition that makes the audience at once
applaud the buffoon and scorn him, misunderstanding his genius; they are
also anguishing and objectifying, as is any judgment of the other. ["You're
ripping me to pieces with your admiration and your contempt!"] (p. 69).
To the prince, Kean is a charming companion, to whom many boudoirs
open; the prince is not unaware that Kean takes pleasure in spiting the
aristocrats by seducing their wives as well as by dominating them with his
talent, thus excluding *them*, whereas elsewhere he is excluded. To Kean
himself, he is a subject, a project, felt and lived from the inside, ["the true
Kean that I alone knew"] (p. 55), carrying with him the past of his humble
beginnings, which he validates in a sense by his success but which he feels
in some way he has betrayed by catering to those who despise him and to
whom, in the true Romantic vein, he feels superior. He is also, for himself,

an actor and a pariah, since others see him thus; their judgment has been internalized. He thus reveals simultaneously lack of self-image and megalomania. As elsewhere in Sartre's works, the for-itself and the for-others are conflicting, the latter tainting and objectifying the former since it is its mediator. Even the luxury he has lived with for ten years, being purchased on credit, is ["others' luxury"] (p. 43). He thinks with nostalgia of the old group of actors who would take him back, if he wished — and the time when his poverty was a *genuine* one, whereas now he is surrounded by furniture he does not own and flowers which, because he has not really paid for them, are an optical illusion. Yet ["it pleases me to reign over mirages"] (p. 45) — he lives now on such illusion, which can be multiplied indefinitely.

In addition, Kean is the roles he has played; that is, he no longer distinguishes between private and stage selves, chiefly because the public will not allow it, for social reasons. ["I'm a false prince, a false minister, a false general. Apart from that nothing. Ah! Yes: a national glory. But on the condition that I don't decide to exist for real"]. Using the contrast of weight and lightness which often serves in Sartre's imagery to indicate the reality of human beings, he says he would prefer to ["weigh with my own weight upon the world"] and perform acts rather than gestures (pp. 64–65). He even reaches the point of acting himself — that is, conforming to an image he has previously created, which he and others expect to see in him. ["Fear nought, it's only Kean, the actor, playing the role of Kean"] (p. 69). He epitomizes one type of player which Sartre has described. In contrast to the ordinary actor who, when he has finished work, goes back to being just another man again, he is the sort who ["plays himself at every second. It's a marvellous gift and a curse, at the same time: and he's the real victim of it, never knowing who he truly is, whether he's playing or not playing. . . . [He] even plays his own life, no longer recognizes himself, no longer knows who he is. And who, in the end, is no one"] (C&R, p. 270). Acting is not self-expression but self-creation, in an almost dialectical movement of reconciled contraries, but which has no permanence. ["One doesn't act to earn one's living. One acts in order to lie, to lie to oneself, to be what one cannot be and because one has had enough of being what one is. One acts in order not to know oneself and because one knows oneself too well. . . . One acts because one loves the truth and because one hates it. One acts because one would go mad if one didn't act. Act! Do I know when I'm acting? Is there ever a moment when I stop acting?"] (p. 81). He recognizes that even his love for Eléna is illusionism. When he tries to cast off his actor's personality, and be simply Kean (whatever that may mean), it is socially impossible: Eléna, who like so many previous mistresses is in love with the actor, or rather with his roles, accepts his suit only if it is expressed dramatically, the prince finds him amusing only because he is an actor, and Lord Mewill can applaud him but never fight him in a duel.

In short, Kean the impostor cannot locate his true self. ["I am nothing, my chick, I play at being what I am"] (p. 75). Having expressed all passions, he chooses every day which one he wants to assume, and thus chooses what he shall be. C. R. Bukala has observed that Kean's "forgetting of himself as a man suggests the nothingness which Sartre speaks of as situated at the very center of his being."[9] Indeed, it is because man is nothingness, consciousness being always occupied by its object, and thus is not what he is and is what he is not, that role-playing is possible; it springs from the aspiration to *be* as the in-itself is, absolutely and with total identity, which aspiration is a negative result of human freedom. As Sartre had argued in one of his earliest and most interesting philosophic texts, there is no transcendent ego, no contents of the self.[10] Moreover, man is always temporally as well as ontologically distant from himself, projected ahead to what Valéry termed the ["ever future hollow"]. All emotion, as Sartre showed, is behavior, a free choice (and a "magical" one which aims at simplifying the world); we are not identical to our emotion but rather adopt it as a reaction, that is, play it.[11] ["We actors, when a misfortune happens to us, we have to mime the emotion in order to feel it"] (p. 179). The emotions Kean displays are no more nor less genuine because they are those of a character. In fact, he suggests that life is a poor copy of art. ["I wonder if true feelings aren't just feelings badly acted"], that is, where they dominate rather than being under control (p. 31). ["Do I hate women or do I play at hating them? Am I playing at making you feel frightened and disgusted, or do I want, very really and very wickedly, to make you pay for the others?"] (p. 81). As Robert J. Nelson writes, "Kean's esthetic (if he may be said to have one at all) contains no idea of experiencing all the passions which are to be shown on the stage, for the actor, having no real self to expose to experience, has no real passions to present" (p. 101). Furthermore, man is always non-positionally conscious of his choice of behavior: there is no such thing as an unconscious consciousness, or consciousness being an obstacle to itself. Thus, to find any authenticity at all is a difficult, perhaps contradictory enterprise which the actor illustrates most clearly, but which is shared by all, and to which, Sartre later asserted, only a totally changed society can offer a solution.

In short, everyone on the world's stage is indeed a player, the professional actor merely carrying his role to a higher degree. Readers will recall countless memorable instances of role-playing in Sartrean works. In *Kean*, the prince plays at being a prince, Kean at being an actor, Eléna at being in love (and she is the best, he says). Like *Nekrassov*, it is a ballet of imposture and illusions. Sartre commented that his personages are struggling with shadows which are their own characters (C&R, p. 270). Only Anna Damby, he added, achieves some authenticity. Leaving her social circle and the expectations others have about her, she chooses Kean; she announces her purposes honestly, is aware of the role she is playing when she first comes to him, and uses it for a purpose which transcends it. Even when employing familiar feminine stratagems to make herself loved, she at least acknowledges them, so that her public and private selves are much closer to being identical. It is appropriate that she should win out by getting what she wants, as she puts it, taking the banished Kean to New York, away from the audiences who loved only Kean-playing-Othello. Perhaps there both Kean, who had forsworn the theatre after his outburst of act IV, and Anna can act again.[12] This ending does not solve all the problems associated with the multiple, illusory, and alienated selves, but it is suggestive, for instance, of the influence that a more democratic society could have in fostering authenticity. Kean has accused his idle aristocratic audiences of not respecting the work of others (p. 163), whereas American society (however much Sartre may criticize it elsewhere) is founded first of all on work. When Anna lies to the prince to make him think Kean still loves Eléna, so that he may continue to find her interesting, illusion again assumes its proper place in a society based on illusion (hereditary privilege), opposed to the genuine love of Kean and Anna, which needs no such lie.

In the fourth act, which is built around the play within a play, Sartre replaced, at Brasseur's request, the scene from *Romeo and Juliet* in the Dumas text with the final scenes of *Othello*.[13] They have the advantage of making Kean attempt to reproduce on stage the emotions he is truly feeling, or extend to the "real world" the dramatic illusion. The closer connection between the stage scene and Kean's own drama is developed effectively, as the real jealousy he feels when he realizes the prince of Wales is courting Eléna also and will be in her box prohibits him from playing Othello successfully. As he had said, ["I have all the gifts. The nuisance is that they are imaginary. Let a false prince steal a false mistress from me this evening and you will see if I know how to shout. But when the real Prince of Wales comes and says to my face, 'You have confided in a woman, and yesterday that woman and I have flouted you,' then rage leaves me helpless and makes me stutter"] (p. 58). Sartre's interpretation recalls Diderot's well-known thesis in *Le Paradoxe sur le comédien* that a player is more effective if he is emotionally removed from his role. Provoked by Eléna's flirtations with the prince and the latter's loud comments, he ruins his career by interrupting the scene and addressing first the prince, then other spectators, even stuttering. Declaring his emancipation from his role, and baring his schizophrenic multiplicity, he taunts the nobles, especially their most illustrious member, the prince, and suggests their fundamental misunderstanding in taking the stage for illusion (on which they feed) and themselves for real, whereas they are greater impostors yet, the true hypocrites who lie to themselves. They feed on the imaginary grandeur of being descended from Plantagenets and fear true reality. Instead of chicken blood, he would like to make human blood flow. ["You came here each evening and you threw bouquets on the stage crying 'Bravo.' I ended up believing that you loved me. But tell me: *who* were you applauding? Huh? Othello? Impossible: he's a bloodthirsty madman. So it must be Kean"]. He rubs off his makeup: ["All the same it's curious, you only like what is false"] (pp. 165–66). The spectators are in bad faith; they have the *esprit de sérieux* like the bourgeois in *La Nausée* and the alienating society of *Saint Genet*. They have created the actor so that he can amuse them and his obvious imposture will hide their own; he is a sacrificial monster.[14] ["What am I but what you have made of me? . . . You and all the others. Lord! So serious men need illusion. . . . They take a child and change him into an optical illusion. An optical illusion, a phantasmagoria, that's what they've done with Kean"] (p. 64). In his final outburst he accuses them—not Othello—of murder: ["Kean died in his infancy. Shut up, you murderers, it was you who killed him. It was you who took a child and turned him into a monster!"] (p. 166).

He had earlier felt that only in the presence of *real* people—those who do not have social prerogatives, whom Sartre elsewhere calls *prolétaires*—did he have a sense of his potential real self. For his former actor friends, ["I am a man, d'you understand, and they believe it so strongly that they will end up by persuading me of it"] (p. 99). This explains how in act V he can seriously renounce his career and propose taking up the identity of "Monsieur Edmond, [jeweller]." Moreover, he has committed an irreparable act, or what he hopes is one, by insulting the prince. Like Sartre in *Les Mots*, and characters such as Hugo in *Les Mains sales* and Goetz in *Le Diable et le Bon Dieu*, other plays where the stage motif is featured, he meditates on the motivation and reality of his own actions. At one moment his outburst seems to him just another gesture: jealous of Eléna, his Desdemona, he took himself for Othello. ["I was peopled with gestures"] (p. 177). As Goetz asks, ["And so, then, everything was lies and playacting? I've committed no acts, only gestures"].[15] But by its consequences—a prison sentence—it is an act, which he espouses, even if he was committing only a "suicide pour rire" and it was the *public* who loaded the pistol (p. 178). ["If they put me in prison it's because they consider me a man. . . . Prison, believe me, that'll be real"] (pp. 175, 183).[16]

This major theme of imposture conveys the author's primary self-expression in the play. The parallels are numerous between Kean and Poulou in *Les Mots*, surrounded by the ["the faded theatricality of the Schweitzers"] and by ["virtuous playactors"], especially his buffoon grandfather, who, like Victor Hugo, took himself for Victor Hugo, writes Sartre, if not God the Father.[17] As Kean observes, ["When a man is false, everything around him is false"] (p. 176). The reader will recall the childish histrion inventing scenes and dialogues, assuming the identity of romantic heroes, living out adventures under the table in his grandfather's study: ["I would throw myself recklessly into the imaginary and more than once I thought of letting myself be engulfed entirely by it"] (*Les Mots*, p. 121). This was in order to cover, as well as possible, the void he felt in himself, in a world where his behavior was dictated by the others—the adults—who made him conform to their view of a model child. ["I was born to fill the great need that I had of myself"] (*Les Mots*, p. 90). That is to say that he sought objectification or being through the approval of an audience, the for-others, and then release in private fantastic reveries, played out for himself. He has noted elsewhere that children in general are actors, attempting to work on their parents by their antics, as does Lucien Fleurier in "L'Enfance d'un chef." Speaking of Genet at the age of ten, Sartre contrasts him with ["We [who] were only busy playing the servile buffoon to please"] (*S. par lui-même*, p. 72). Jean-Paul's earliest experiences were satisfying, since playacting and falsehood were all he knew. But he later came to fear that his lack of justification and the great transparency he felt were also those of adults (*Les Mots*, p. 73). He then suspect that, since they too were perhaps actors, there was no *real* reality beyond playacting which could give it its guarantee, no audience, but only other actors. Using the same distinction between acts and gestures which he had already attributed to Goetz and Kean, he writes, ["I was an imposter. How can one playact without knowing that one is acting? . . . I was a false child, I was holding a false salad basket; I could feel my actions changing into gestures. Comedy hid the world and men from me. I only saw roles and costumes"] (*Les Mots*, pp. 67–69). Yet behind the imposture of the adults there was nonetheless something he could not reach, the genuine concerns of whispered family conferences of those whose "acting" really counted, when the "petit chéri" was sent out of the room. ["They had persuaded me that we were created to play-act with each other. I accepted the play-acting, but I insisted on being the main character. Now . . . I perceived that I had a 'false leading-role,' with a text, lots of stage-presence, but no scene 'for me'; in a word, I was giving the grown-ups their cues"] (*Les Mots*, p. 69).

To offset this realization that, while others ultimately had being, his masks merely covered an empty for-itself, and the consequent feeling of contingency and inferiority, he attempted to cultivate a sense of necessity and superiority (like Kean's Romantic pride), a sense bestowed by the ostensible family beliefs (that he was a gift from heaven, his grandfather's greatest joy), but undermined by the falsehood on which these beliefs rested, as well as by the existence of an autonomous and indifferent world. As he put it, he wished that at every gathering at which he was not present there would be someone missing—Jean-Paul—whose absence, far from being accessory, was the most imposing fact of the situation (*Les Mots*, p. 74). The boy's predilection for heights, never outgrown, is representative of this sense of superiority, which may be associated with the lack of superego which Sartre ascribes to the absence of acquaintance with his father, his moral bastardy (*Les Mots*, pp. 11, 47). It is likewise related to his conviction that he would become a great writer, a conviction both sincere and a sham (*Les Mots*, pp. 172–73). After his dramatic and even "cinematic" experiences, in which he tried to *realize* by acting a mental image — an eminently romantic project — he could no longer hide his imposture from himself. Speaking like the self-aware Kean, he states, ["I pretended to be an actor pretending to be a hero"] (*Les Mots*, p. 117).

He then adopted the stratagem of transferring his images into words, an activity which remained integral to him for something like four decades: ["The imposture was the same but . . . I took words to be the quintessence of things"] (ibid.). Unlike his playacting, this new imposture, which allowed for a distance between self and self (the writer and his hero), gave him a new autonomy with respect to adults because the writing self bore a type of authenticity, which might be compared to Kean's realization that he is acting (unlike the audience, which does not recognize its imposture), and his conscious and creative adoption of the passions suited to that role. Noticing his nothingness, he nevertheless managed at a second stage to find his being: ["I was almost nothing, at the very most an activity with no content; but no more was necessary. I was escaping from the play-acting; I was not yet working, but already I was no longer playing. The liar found his truth in the elaboration of his lies. I was born from writing: before it there was merely a game of mirrors; from my first novel I knew that a child had entered the Hall of Mirrors. Writing, I existed, I escaped from the grown-ups"] (*Les Mots*, p. 127). This "child," who is an authentic being, can be contrasted to the monster which society makes of Genet and Kean, before each learns to divest himself of the alienated self. Unfortunately, in the young Sartre's life the adults contributed to this early authenticity a new element of imposture by their lip-service recognition of his talent, as an ornament and a "destiny," that is, their version of the myth of the writer, by which he could however never presume to live, since, as they emphasized, it had so many disadvantages. Thus labeling it and him, and giving him a mandate to write because he would thus fulfill his supposed destiny, they removed the freedom he had gained and made of him too something of the monster which he identified with Genet and Kean, what has been called the ["writer-messiah of a dechristianized bourgeoisie"].[18] He wrote that he lived in the unreal, both "prince et cordonnier," that is, future genius writer on the one hand and pitiful boy duping himself on the other (*Les Mots*, p. 173). In time, as he adds, this mandate became his character, an ingenious solution to the problem of alienation, which he later had to unlearn.

Sartre documented his playacting as a child in order to demolish it, as well as the teleological view of his (and any) destiny, the myth of literature, and its promise of salvation, that is, his profoundly neurotic false departure which lasted, he repeatedly emphasized, until the early 1950s. He wished also to illustrate the lie of bourgeois family life, since Charles Schweitzer's roles were no more genuine than Poulou's, just overlaid with an additional layer of unconsciousness. He wanted to show (somewhat paradoxically, of course) that without the "impossible Salut," he was just an ordinary project — ["A whole man, made of all men and who is worth them all and whom anyone is worth"] (*Les Mots*, p. 213) — much as Kean, wanting to leave the stage, says ["I will be able to be anyone"] (p. 180). His approach to the theme of imposture in *Les Mots* is thus critical in the first instance, as he denounces his own role-playing and that of an entire society, indeed, of the whole of bourgeois France and the Occident, the image of which in his mind was derived first of all from his family. ["The radical *imposture* of the actor sends us back, in fact, to the contradictions of our society"], writes Jeanson (*Sartre*, p. 172). Yet the corresponding portrait of the actor in *Kean* is nevertheless sympathetic, as is that of Poulou himself to a considerable degree. In this connection it will be remembered that as a university student Sartre acted in student-produced reviews, and that he was an excellent mimic (C&R, p. 23). His interest in the production of his own plays included concern for the techniques of acting, and his attention to the drama as a cultural manifestation, as well as an artistic genre, is amply documented. More-over, he continued to write for the theatre well after he had abandoned the novel, apparently seeing no contradiction between it and his evolving political views. His critique of role-playing, then, pervasive as it may be, is not without an element of fascination and comprehension, as is to be expected because it is self-criticism. In fact, Sartre's whole approach to existence may be seen as close to that of an actor, who must *put on* being or essence, rather than having it already given; his criticism of the Schweitzer milieu would then refer to the content of the playacting, and its unconsciousness, rather than the acting itself, which is inevitable, at least in a society the basis of which is alienation.

One can in fact be both "comédien" and "martyr," like Genet. Sartre's developing social orientation of the 1950s made him see that this universal role-playing in order to create a being for oneself, as he had analyzed it in *L'Etre et le néant*, was not done in a vacuum but rather was also a response of an original freedom to the pressures of an unjust, but self-righteous, society: the for-itself which adopts a mask is conditioned by the mask around it, and may indeed, through its playacting, develop a very creative response. Similarly, as it has been observed, Sartre's denunciation of literature in *Les Mots* came in the form of a highly literary autobiography, and in the years following the denunciation he produced works of considerable literary value. It must then be seen as qualified; as Sartre later saw, in an alienated society the person must be alienated also, and in this desperate situation the actor, like Kean, reasserts his freedom despite his roles; he defines himself as Camus wrote, by his "comédies" as well as by his sincere impulses.[19]

Similarly, Sartre's interest in the allied figure of the traitor, illustrated variously by such imaginary figures as Philippe and Daniel in *Le Sursis*, Goetz and Heinrich in *Le Diable et le Bon Dieu*, and his portrait of Genet and analysis of the character of collaborators, as well as by Kean, has a positive aspect, closely allied to his own self-understanding. This obsessive theme has been insufficiently recognized, as John M. Hoberman has recently noted.[20] Jeanson, one of the few who have approached it, has analyzed the basic identity of the bastard and the traitor (S. par lui-même, pp. 57, 89 ff.). In Kean's case, he "betrays" the conventions under which society has allowed him to operate, thus society itself, which he dares to show up in the fourth act as an illusion and an imposture. As Hernani is an outlaw, Kean is an actor; he is, notes Laraque, a revolutionary (p. 204), criticizing hereditary privileges due to birth and the idleness of the aristocracy. ["I raged against the nobles; since their blood didn't flow in my veins, I wanted to make it flow out of theirs"] (p. 206). As an actor Kean is king on the stage. Though playing for an audience, he is not phenomenologically dependent upon them; rather, they derive their justification from his identity with his role. Moreover, by pointing out his own role, and thus undermining the security of the audience, forcing it to make a response other than the aesthetic one, he turns himself into the other — the judge, the accuser — rather than allowing society to continue to be his. He points out that the prince too is a creature of illusion, a reflection, like himself, in others' eyes, but the prince has no counterbalancing stage existence and would give anything to be Kean (p. 199). Yet Kean remains the imposter par excellence, whence the irony of this judgment.

Sartre similarly considers himself a traitor. ["I became a traitor and I have remained one. In vain do I put myself entirely into whatever I undertake, or give myself wholeheartedly to work, to friendship, in a minute I will deny myself, I know it, I wish it and I betray myself already — in the midst of my passion — by the foreboding of my future treason"] (Les Mots, p. 198). He betrays himself partly through the momentum of his project, always ahead of himself, projected beyond today to tomorrow, with the past having no claim on him. This is symbolized by Sartre's personal unwillingness to save money — capitalize or collect a patrimony — and even to keep his books and other such possessions, which, as Simone de Beauvoir noted, he usually gave away — much as Kean refuses to save what little cash remains and instead gives it to a street musician in a grand gesture, not wishing to be possessed by money.[21] Most of all Sartre is a traitor to his family and his class — by his political ideas — to his early readership, which his later works denounce, and additionally to a certain deep self, by a movement of self-opposition and denial which is not unknown among other writers, especially of Protestant background. ["I am doubly a traitor — a traitor in the conflict between the generations and a traitor in the class-struggle. The generation of 1945 thinks that I have betrayed it because it was taught to know me through Huis clos and La Nausée, works written at a time when I hadn't yet realized the Marxist implications of my ideas"] (quoted in Sartre, p. 231). His interest in André Gorz, whose volume Le Traître he prefaced in

1958, is another instance of acknowledgement of the profound fascination which moral treason exercises on him.

Similarly, in one sense Sartre espouses morally the bastardy which, after *Saint Genet*, both *Kean* and *Les Mots* illustrate. Though he was born legitimate, his father's early death and his consequent upbringing by his mother and grandparents gave him the sense of being fatherless, a circumstance which, it is well known, he viewed as an advantage, since the basic paternal role, which is to exercise authority over the freedom of the child, is corrupt (*Les Mots*, p. 11). This attitude recalls Gide's contention that the bastard, freed from the obligation to fulfill an image and carry on a family destiny, is able to invent his values, and ultimately himself; he alone is authentic. However, Sartre puts greater stress on the social pressures exercised on the illegitimate child and on a kind of schizophrenia induced within him by the fact that to others he is flawed from birth, whereas, like everyone else, to himself he is an absolute, perfect freedom. His status is thus originally false; society receives him only to exclude him; he is born an impostor. This is the case with Kean. As one can judge from such works as *La Nausée* and *Les Mots*, this feeling of being unjustified is the *original* feeling, not confined to illegitimate children; but in their case, nothing counteracts it. As a result of this social judgment, the other becomes internalized, and the theme of illegitimacy rejoins those of imposture and treachery, since the bastard, not knowing which self is real, the inner project and freedom or the internalized other, plays himself and feels untrue to himself.

Bastardy is also, however, something of an advantage in the Sartrean context, as the previous remarks indicate. Kean asserts to Lord Mewill that his own name is rising, whereas the lord merely "descends" from his ancestors, who are psychologically speaking an immense superego. Sartre later agreed that all intellectuals were bastards, in the positive sense.[22] Observing this connection, Jeanson points out that both are forced to see what other men succeed in dissimulating, and that, conversely, lucidity makes one a bastard, stripping away the false justifications and *raisons d'être* which give to the "just" their prerogatives, and making consciousness separate from action (*S. par lui-même*, p. 57). The problem is to explain why some intellectuals become cognizant of this status and others do not; Sartre has been unable to shed light on this, as in the case of Raymond Queneau, for instance, who has remained a bourgeois writer, except by referring to the data that analysis might produce upon examination of his childhood (Verstraeten, pp. 4, 44). In Genet's case it is partly thanks to pederasty; in Sartre's own, there is no clear answer.

If Kean is an impostor, fabricated by a flawed society against which he turns in self-defense, and who therefore as artist depends upon an erroneous, vicious circumstance, the question can be raised concerning what the position of theatre would be in an authentic, unalienated society, the sort whose coming Sartre imagines in *Critique de la raison dialectique* and other late writings. In *Qu'est-ce que la littérature?* he affirmed that the contemporary artist — at least the novelist and dramatist — could function effectively and authentically by presenting a critical literature intended for his own time, according to techniques which suit changing circumstances. In *Saint Genet*, it is writing, including poetry, which is one of the forms in which Genet's self-creative genius asserts itself against society. In later writings on the theatre he emphasized the critical function of plays such as *Les Séquestrés d'Altona*, yet suggested that he no longer believed literature and theatre could change things, that is, overcome the alienation and falsehood of the entire society to which they are directed.[23] Art, like ethics (as he suggested in *Saint Genet*),[24] would seem to be impossible. Only in a new society, based on radically different modes of production which would eliminate scarcity, would the position of the writer and artist no longer be adversarial and critical. What this would produce has to be left to the imagination. Until such a revolution takes place, the artist and actor remain in a false position and work, even if creativity, through falsity itself.

Sartre's severe self-portrait in *Les Mots*, like his more sympathetic one of Kean, must thus be understood as a self-accusation in the first instance only; his mirrors reflect back on society and the autobiographical enterprise is a social one. Reminding us of Sartre's great predecessor Rousseau, it concludes that corrupt individuals are produced by corrupt institutions. We are all, he would say, playactors, traitors, and bastards, but in *Kean*, the mirror is held up to our slavery, and our freedom.

Notes

1. See Michel Contat and Michel Rybalka, *Les Ecrits de Sartre* (Paris: Gallimard, 1970), pp. 266–71 (hereafter cited in the text as C&R), and Jean-Paul Sartre, *Un Théâtre de situations*, ed. Michel Contat and Michel Rybalka (Paris: Gallimard, 1973), pp. 282–91, for Sartre's program notes, extracts from his published comments on the play, and other aspects of the play's history. See also Douglas Munro, *Alexandre Dumas père: A Bibliography of Works Translated into English to 1910* (New York: Garland, 1978), p. 18, for Dumas's statement on the play, and Robert Lorris, *Sartre dramaturge* (Paris: Nizet, 1975), p. 290.

2. *Le Figaro*, 4 Nov. 1953, p. 10.

3. Francis Jeanson notes that the impostor, traitor, and bastard are all related and that they all three stand for the intellectual, i.e., Sartre himself. These are thus not only themes but personal projections and problems, which Sartre posed especially in his theatre in the 1950s. In this perspective, his drama, all of which can be likened to *Kean*, would represent a sort of catharsis of the self, if one may apply this non-Sartrean psychological concept. See Jeanson's *Sartre dans sa vie* (Paris: Seuil, 1973), pp. 211–12, (hereafter cited in the text as *Sartre*), and his *Sartre par lui-même* (Paris: Seuil, 1967), p. 94 (hereafter cited in the text as *S. par lui-même*).

4. For comparisons between the Dumas and Sartre texts, see Robert J. Nelson, "Sartre: The Play as Lie," in his *Play Within a Play* (New Haven: Yale University Press, 1958), pp. 100–14.

5. Jean-Paul Sartre, *Kean* (Paris: Gallimard, 1954), p. 39 (hereafter cited in the text).

6. The personal relationships have been described elsewhere as being in the *Andromaque* pattern (Lorris, p. 305), but the image of triangles seems somewhat better.

7. It is worthwhile noting that Sartre seems indebted to Hegel for certain ideas on the self. See Douglas Collins, *Sartre as Biographer* (Cambridge: Harvard University Press, 1980), p. 85.

8. Franck Laraque, *La Révolte dans le théâtre de Sartre* (Paris: J.-P. Delarge, 1976), p. 199.

9. C. R. Bukala, "Sartre's *Kean*: The Drama of Consciousness," *Review of Existential Psychology and Psychiatry*, 13 (1974), 65.

10. Jean-Paul Sartre, *La Transcendance de l'ego* (Paris: Vrin, 1965 [originally published in 1937]).

11. Jean-Paul Sartre, *Esquisse d'une théorie des émotions* (Paris: Hermann, 1939). One is repeatedly reminded in this connection of Gide's earlier theories (set forth especially by Edouard in *Les-Faux-Monnayeurs*) of the self as variable, influenceable almost to the point of non-existence, and in which imaginary emotion is identical to emotion, so that the very notion of sincerity is meaningless.

12. Nelson (pp. 107–08) finds the ending flawed to the degree that it suggests that Kean will resume acting in America; according to his view, Kean realizes in the play that he prefers being "M. Edmond, bijoutier," and having *that* reality, to the nonreality of the actor. This is strongly suggested in act V but is not quite consistent with the implication that all "reality" is as unreal as the stage. Of course another intepretation of the final remark by Salomon, the prompter, is that he is alluding to the playacting at the basis of the love relationship between Kean and Anna: ["As soon as you both start play-acting, you'll need a prompter!"] (p. 216).

13. Dorothy McCall, *The Theatre of Jean-Paul Sartre* (New York: Columbia University Press, 1969), p. 99.

14. Collins (p. 99 ff.) has stressed Genet's "derealizing" project and his refuge into the imaginary.

15. Jean-Paul Sartre, *Le Diable et le Bon Dieu* (Paris: Gallimard, 1951), p. 262.

16. It is worth recalling that Sartre attributes to his own prison experience in Germany in 1940–41 the discovery of fraternity, the collectivity, and commitment—that is, the *real* in political terms. See his *Situations, IV* (Paris: Gallimard, 1964), p. 349, and Simone de Beauvoir, *La Force des choses* (Paris: Gallimard, 1963), p. 16.

17. Jean-Paul Sartre, *Les Mots* (Paris: Gallimard, 1964), pp. 5, 15 (hereafter cited in the text).

18. Marc Bensimon, "D'un mythe à l'autre: essai sur *Les Mots* de J.-P. Sartre," *Revue des Sciences Humaines*, no. 119 (July 1965), 416.

19. Albert Camus, *Le Mythe de Sisyphe*, Collection Soleil (Paris: Gallimard, c. 1942), p. 25. Camus's analysis later in this volume of the actor as one representative of the absurd man bears considerable resemblance to Sartre's portrait of Kean.

20. Unpublished paper delivered at the Fourth International Colloquium, Centre Interuniversitaire d'Etudes Européennes, Montreal, March 1981.

21. Such gestures and such divesting of money and other signs of value—the very values which the Schweitzers carefully protected—are, it would seem, characteristic of those given to multiple selves. I am thinking of Gide's well-documented prodigality (combined with avarice), and, in fiction, of Clappique's grand gesture of giving away nearly $100 at the beginning of Malraux's *La Condition humaine*. Genet's reaction to bourgeois valuation of property is different: recognize it negatively (by theft) rather than deny it.

22. In an interview with Sartre by Pierre Verstraeten, entitled "Jean-Paul Sartre: 'Je ne suis plus réaliste,' " in *Gulliver*, no. 1 (Nov. 1972), 40. It will be remembered that Orestes'

father is dead and that Hugo in *Les Mains sales* tries to deny his father. Goetz also is a bastard.

23. Oreste F. Pucciani, "An Interview with Jean-Paul Sartre," *Tulane Drama Review*, 5, 3 (March 1961), 12–13.

24. Jean-Paul Sartre, *Saint Genet, comédien et martyr* (Paris: Gallimard, 1952), p. 177. (Vol. I of Jean Genet's (*OEuvres complètes*.)

Les Séquestrés d'Altona:
Sartre's Black Tragedy
Jeremy N. J. Palmer*

Les Séquestrés d'Altona is no doubt Sartre's least accessible play; for while it is unmistakably stamped with the hall-marks of its author, it does not seem to say what we expect. Numerous lines in the text contain echoes of Sartre's philosophical and political essays and, as with the other plays, we attempt to use these references in order to understand the play. However, we find ourselves involved in a mass of contradictions, for the concepts embodied in so many commentaries on Sartre's fiction, and relevant to the earlier plays, seem meaningless in relationship to the overall impression we have of *Les Séquestrés d'Altona*.

The apparent irrelevance of the usual framework of exegesis is interesting in itself, for it suggests that *Les Séquestrés d'Altona* represents a radical departure from Sartre's previous writings. On the other hand, we are immediately aware that in certain respects the play is typical of Sartre's work in the theatre—the careful isolation of the characters, as if under laboratory conditions; the lack of concern with the trivia of everyday life; the depth of penetration of the dialogue into the consciousness of the characters—and we know that these formal traits are closely related to Sartre's theory of the theatre: the theatre is to reproduce situations which typify our civilization and to induce in the audience the willingness to change those aspects of the world and themselves which need changing.

Sartre's earlier plays were all concerned, fundamentally, with the states of bad faith and authenticity; and just as in clinical psycho-analysis a turning-point is reached when the patient is brought to recognize and admit his abnormal state, so in Sartre's theatre, once a character has recognized that he is in bad faith, he is well on the path to freedom and authenticity. Here, perhaps, is the fundamental difference between the earlier plays and *Les Séquestrés d'Altona*: in the latter, the characters are all perfectly aware that they are in bad faith, and they consciously choose to remain so. This is the explanation of the exegetical paradoxes referred to above: the characters are "playing at existentialism," they are using Sartre's

*From *French Studies* 24, no. 2 (April 1970):150–62. Reprinted with permission.

concepts as the basis of a series of games which they play with themselves and each other, and it is only when we examine how the characters use these concepts that they begin to have any meaning in relationship to the play as a whole.

Bad faith consists in the substitution of a persona for personality; it results in the refusal to examine one's reasons for acting in a certain way. Here we are at the heart of the motivation of the characters of *Les Séquestrés d'Altona*: in Leni's words: ["principles disappear, habits remain"].[1] The characters are quite aware that the reasons they profess for their actions are deprived of meaning, but rather than build a new set, they prefer to admit their lack of meaning and live their lives as lucid witnesses of their failure; in fact they *refuse*, consciously and with determination, to change their attitudes to life. To use Leni's words once more: ["Here, you know, we play at loser takes all."].[2]

This refusal is in fact seen at its clearest in Leni. In Act II, sc. I she tries to make Frantz face up to his past:

[LENI: Oh witness for the defense, bear witness before yourself! You will be invulnerable if you dare to declare: "I have done what I have wanted and I want what I have done."

FRANTZ: (*Suddenly stone-faced, he seems cold, hateful, and menacing. In a hard, mistrusting voice.*) What have I done, Leni?][3]

She fails — apparently — because she is the weaker personality, but the ensuing conversation is revealing:

[LENI: This evening, I will bring you your dinner.

FRANTZ: No use. I won't open up.

LENI: That's your business. Mine is to bring it to you.][4]

The juxtaposition is significant. Leni merely wants to act out her chosen role, she has no interest in effecting any chance in the situation. In fact, in so far as she gives way before Frantz's attack, she is conniving at her own defeat, she is actively avoiding success.

The reason for her choice of failure lies in her attitude towards her family. The Gerlach family represents a way of life, a code: the frequent references to what a Gerlach does and does not attest this. Her attitude is summarized by her incestuous relationship with Frantz. Incest may be considered as the action which, more than any other, incarnates the essence of the unnatural crime, for it is the negation of all that the family, which is traditionally the incarnation of the natural order, stands for.[5] On the level of the code which the family represents, her incest is paralleled by her refusal to take seriously the standards by which the family lives.[6] And yet Leni in fact lives according to the code: she does not adopt Johanna's moral attitude towards any of the events which led up to Frantz's self-sequestration, and she is just as shocked as Werner by Gerlach's suggestion that Johanna would have been the ideal wife for Frantz. Similarly, the idea of setting fire to the house may appeal to her, but it is only a childhood dream, not a serious intention. Leni is tied to the house: this is why she takes the oath her father demands from her and Werner without protest, reminding him for form's sake that an oath means nothing to her; her father, of course, is completely unconcerned by her flippant attitude, for he realizes that it is for form's sake only. Leni's rebellion takes the form of sarcastic rodomontades and cruel reminders to her father of his separation from Frantz. However, the paradox of her rebelliousness and her objective dependence on the code is in point of fact easily explicable:

> [LENI: Do you know what makes me invulnerable? I am happy.
>
> FATHER: You? What can you know of happiness?
>
> LENI: What about you? What do you know of it?
>
> FATHER: I can see you. If it has given you those eyes it is the most refined of tortures.
>
> LENI: (*Almost distraught*) Of course! The most refined, the most refined! I am turning! If I were to stop I would go to pieces. That's happiness, mad happiness.][7]

Leni has chosen to be a rebel, but she has added the rider: an unsuccessful rebel. Now, as Sartre frequently comments in his essay on Jean Genet, failure has only to be desired in order to be transmuted into success. The happiness to which she refers here is that which Sartre analyses in his discussion of Genet's "impossible nullités":

> [This is what Genet calls "impossible nullity." Everything is impossible: the wicked person *cannot be*, but neither can he evaporate into nothingness. All the efforts he makes to be his being bring him back to this pure *conscious nonbeing* which is consciousness; but if he returns to this nonbeing in order to annihilate himself in it, he exists for himself in full light, in a pitiless transparency. To the vanishing of his Ego corresponds the blinding eruption of his subjectivity. Thus, for Genet, the general scheme of his projects must remain a generalized *loser-takes-all*. The impossibility of living is precisely his life-spring, the impossibility of Evil is the triumph of the bad principle; the failure, willed and pursued without pause, in his least important activities as in his total destiny, becomes his victory; he is the being who makes himself exist by his will to be impossible.][8]

Here then is the explanation of her attitude toward Frantz's games of guilt and witness: she attacks his imaginary world in order that he shall defend it, for only thus can she be sure that he will not leave it of his own accord, and only if he maintains his self-sequestration can she use him as a weapon against her father in her nominal rebellion against all that the family stands for. Leni's interest is thus to maintain the fragile *status quo* which Gerlach's manipulation of Johanna threatens.

Werner, too, opts for the *status quo*, and in full knowledge of the implications of his choice: the game of ["loser takes all"]. Unfortunately the brevity necessary to an article precludes a full analysis of the detail of Sartre's vision of the man, and the statement that the essence of Werner's character, his "projet fondamental," is bitterness, is no doubt over-schematic. However, it can hardly be denied that this element in his personality is of decisive importance; Johanna's astute comment on his reaction to being told of her relationship with Frantz is sufficient indication of this:

[JOHANNA: He's staying here out of jealousy. . . . He will send me to you every day, including Sundays. He will martyr himself, in the shipyards, in his great ministerial office. And in the evening, I will pay.][9]

The significance for Werner of Johanna's relationship to Frantz is that it is the final indignity. However, the jealousy which Johanna notes is not primarily sexual, for the emotion survives discovery that Johanna's prefer-ence for Frantz has been given no physical expression (indeed her prefer-ence is hardly a sexual emotion). On the contrary, that Johanna's preference is the final indignity depends less on Werner's relationship to his wife than on the relationship of the two brothers to each other and to their father.

Werner is highly respectful towards the family hierarchy; he obeys his father—to the extent of abandoning his successful legal practice and returning to immure himself in the family business and the family mansion—not because he sees any gain involved, but because, in his own words, "C'est le père."[10] He wants nothing better than to please his father—this is clear from his behaviour during the family counsel in Act I—but he is constantly thwarted in his attempts to win a place in his father's heart by the love and esteem in which the latter holds Frantz. In his legal practice and his marriage Werner had achieved a degree of independence from the vicious triangle of his relationship with his brother and his father, and now this independence is lost. But it would be false to ascribe his bitterness to a sense of inextricable involvement in an unpleas-ant situation, for, as Johanna repeatedly points out to him, he has ample opportunity to free himself. Quite the contrary is true: he surrenders in order to have a reason for his bitterness. That is to say, he is in fact in a position to free himself, but "pretends" that he is not. Bitterness, to use Sartre's terminology, is a "choix de l'échec": just as Leni chooses to be an unsuccessful rebel, so Werner chooses to fail in his search for independence by directing all his energies towards a goal he knows to be unattainable, his father's love and esteem. He lives as a witness to his own failure.

Just as Leni and Werner choose to be failures, so does Johanna. Her ambition was to incarnate the essence of beauty, to achieve that state of being which is "en-soi-pour-soi," the "ens causa sui" which is for Sartre the common factor uniting all the forms of bad faith.[11] Naturally—since the aim is self-contradictory, in Sartrian terms — she failed and is fully aware of it:

> [FRANTZ: You used to spy on yourself, huh? You were seeking to surprise yourself? (*Johanna nods*) Did you ever catch yourself?
>
> JOHANNA: Of course not! (*She looks at herself in the mirror uncompromisingly.*) *That's* what I saw. (*She points to her reflection. Pause.*) I used to go into the local theaters. When the star Johanna Thies appeared against the backdrop, I would hear a little murmur. They were moved, each one by the emotion of the other. I would watch. . . .
>
> FRANTZ: And then?
>
> JOHANNA: And then nothing. I've never seen what they saw.][12]

Like Werner, she makes herself a martyr, and plays out her chosen rôle. Her marriage is a sham. As Leni astutely remarks, "Il y a des mariages qui sont des enterrements":[13] Johanna's wedding was the funeral of her quintessential beauty. However, she needs an audience for her martyrdom — no performance is complete without one — and the audience she has chosen is Werner. When Werner accedes to his father's request she is in danger of losing her audience, and to retain him she strikes a bargain with his father: she delivers a message to Frantz, Werner is released from his promise. What she neglects to take into account is the potential fascination of the "world" Frantz has created for himself in the upstairs room he occupies, and it is upon this fascination that Gerlach has based his strategy.[14] Gerlach, of course, calculated correctly, for in Frantz's world it is possible for Johanna to achieve her original ambition, to exist as the incarnation of beauty, and the possibility is tempting. Frantz offers himself as her accomplice, and she immediately grasps the sense of his proposition: ["It's a deal: 'Enter into my madness, I will enter yours' "].[15] Yet her attitude to the world she and Frantz create in the sealed room upstairs is ambiguous, and it is only the calculated destruction by Gerlach (in Act III) of her delicately poised relationship with Werner that ensures her return to Frantz in Act IV. The reasons for her doubt and for her eventual rejection of Frantz at the end of Act IV are ultimately the same: ["A traitor. Inspired. Convincing. He speaks, one listens. And then, all of a sudden, he catches sight of himself in the mirror; across his chest this one word is inscribed: treason, That's the nightmare waiting for me each day in your son's bedroom"].[16] The reference to Sartre's preface to Gorz's *Le Traître* is plain.[17] In Sartre's analysis the traitor is a man who sees very clearly that absolute norms of conduct, human rights, the highest values of post-Renaissance Europe in fact, are no more than fictions. But the traitor is also aware that other people act as if these entities had real value; therefore he copies them, and it is by being a "counterfeit man" that he is a traitor, for he makes himself so typically a product of the civilization in which he lives that it is quite obvious that it is all only appearance; the hollowness of his persona reveals to those who come into contact with him the hollowness of what they considered their personalities. Frantz is a traitor because he is such a perfect counterfeit of a defeated patriot; Johanna sees revealed in his imitation of a shattered titan the theatricality of her own imitation of a rejected star. Thus she too is prevented from finding the stability she sought in the hallucinatory dialectic of ["loser takes all"].

The curious chess-like manipulations to which the younger generation of the household are subjected are of course planned by Gerlach — this much is self-evident. What is less apparent, however, is his motive. Clearly he wants to see his eldest son before he dies, but one should not assume that his motive is merely the normal human desire for reconciliation: the nature of the conflict between them, and its eventual solution, preclude this interpretation.

The driving force in Gerlach's life has been a belief in the rectitude of capitalist power: he collaborated with the Nazi Government because he saw that it was playing his game for him, strengthening the power of German big business, and disregarded all normal objections to the nature of Nazi power (the concentration camps, etc.) as youthful idealism. Frantz, as we shall see, attempts to escape from this world, to create a world for himself based upon independent action: for Gerlach, despite appearances, is a victim of the system he so ardently upholds: ["It's been a long time since I've made any decisions. I just sign the mail. Next year it'll be you who signs it. . . . And me? What am I? A hat on a masthead. (*In a sad, gentle, almost senile tone.*) The greatest enterprise in Europe. . . . It's a whole organization, isn't it, a whole organization . . ."].[18] The capitalist is alienated by his own system. Sartre, following Marx, has commented upon this in *Critique de la Raison Dialectique*:[19]

> [. . . capital is opposed to society. . . . And yet it is a social power. The contradiction is explained by the fact that it has become *object*. But this object, which is not "the social mean" but "the antisocial reality," is only maintained as such to the extent that it is supported and guided by the real and active power of *the capitalist* (who, in his turn, is entirely possessed by the alienated objectification of his own power, for it is this which is the object of other transcendances [*dépassements*] by other capitalists). These relationships are molecular because *there are only* individuals and the singular relationships (opposition, alliance, dependency, etc.) which they have with each other; but they are not mechanical because *in no case* is it a question of the clash of simple inertias. In the very unity of his enterprise each one transcends the other and incorporates him as means (and vice versa), each couple of unificatory relationships is in its turn transcended by the enterprise of a third party.][20]

In other words, Gerlach is a victim of the serialization which Sartre sees as typifying the fate of the individual in capitalist society, and Frantz is trying to escape this fate. If he succeeds, Gerlach's basic premise and ultimate justification — that escape is impossible — will fall to the ground; therefore, when the interview eventually takes place, Gerlach's concern is to prove to Frantz that his actions never had the independence he claims: ["In order to act, you took the greatest of risks and, you see, [the Enterprise] transformed all your actions into gestures. Your torment ended up pushing you into crime and even in crime the Enterprise quashes you; it grows fat on your defeat"].[21] Their suicide pact marks Frantz's surrender; it is the final desperate gesture of heroic defiance. ["I am tired of everything, my son, except [winning]; one never wins. I'm trying to save the stake"].[22] The argument is clear. The stake is the justifiability of the capitalist way of life and the justification is that there are no viable alternatives. Frantz admits that his alternative was not even really an alternative at all, let alone a viable one, and Gerlach has achieved his aim; not victory, for in capitalism no one ever wins, but the possibility of choosing the manner of his defeat. In their death he and his son achieve apotheosis.

But in what sense can one say that Frantz's self-sequestration represents an attempt at autonomy? On the face of it, his retirement reflects the terrible guilt he suffers as a result of the torture he inflicted during the war, and his elaborate pretenses seem intended to conceal or mitigate his responsibility. Equally, it would seem to make theatrical sense to see the key to his character rather in his speeches to the crabs, especially as there are clear references here to certain of Sartre's statements in *Critique de la Raison Dialectique*:

> [But I will tell you the secret of this multiple perforation: the century would have been good had man not been marked down by his cruel, immemorial enemy, by the carnivorous species that had sworn his defeat, by the hairless, malignant beast, by man. . . . The beast was hiding. All of a sudden we caught its glance in the intimate eyes of our fellow creatures; so we struck: legitimate self-defense. I surprised the beast. I struck. A man fell. In his dying eyes I saw the beast, still alive. Me. One and one make one: what a misunderstanding.][23]

Frantz's argument is, basically: ["we've been had"]; the world is such that violence is endemic, and here he is echoing, on the level of an intuitive insight, Sartre's theoretical analyses in *Critique de la Raison Dialectique* of the relationship between economic scarcity and violence:

> [However, at least up to this moment of our prehistory, scarcity, in whatever form, has dominated all *praxis*. Hence we must understand *at the same time* that man's inhumanity: (1) does not come from his nature; (2) far from excluding his humanity, can only be understood through it. *But* we must also understand that as long as the reign of scarcity continues, there will be *in each man and in all* an inert structure of inhumanity which is nothing other in sum than material negation to the extent that it has been interiorized . . . Nothing, in fact, neither the great beasts nor the microbes, can be more terrible for man

than an intelligent, cruel, carnivorous species that can understand and thwart human intelligence and whose end is precisely the destruction of man. This species is obviously our own as it is perceived in others by each man in the context of scarcity.][24]

Considering the widely divergent nature of these two works, the similarity in the passages quoted is striking, and whereas the vision of man as a carnivore has considerable impact in the theatre, certain of sentences in the pages of *Critique de la Raison Dialectique* referred to above strike a curiously emotive note, in much the same way as the more obviously quotable remarks from *L'Etre et le Néant* seem to owe their heritage more to the pronunciamentos of mysticism than to the traditionally dispassionate deductions of the philosopher. Clearly the vision of ["the man of scarcity"] is deeply rooted in Sartre's Weltanschauung.

In the twentieth century, "l'homme de la rareté" is capitalist man, and just as Marx attached great importance to the category of fetishism,[25] so Sartre analyses at great length in *Critique de la Raison Dialectique* the manner in which money mediates human relationships:

[The unity of the concerted accumulative process gave to the matter [i.e., gold] its passive unity as wealth and this material unity in turn unified the indiscriminate increase in frauds and imports. But, by the same token, it was the matter itself that became essential and the individuals, unknown and interchangeable, disappeared into inessentiality. It was the *flight of gold* that had to be stopped. And this flight *by means of the Other* became a spontaneous movement of matter *as Other*, i.e., as it was, in its very humanization, *Other than man*. But since it was Other by virtue of its inertia, its molecular structure and the reciprocal exteriority of its parts, i.e., *as matter*, it absorbed the recurrence and made of it a kind of spontaneous resistance of matter to the wishes and to the practices of men. This time it was the inertia itself which, *merged with alterity*, became the synthetic principle producing new forces. But these forces were negative. Gold took on a "life of its own" halfway between real praxis (whose unificatory power and negativity it absorbed) and the simple succession of physical phenomena (whose dispersion in exteriority it reaffirmed). The characteristics of this magic *life* . . . turned *praxis* inside-out and transformed ends into counter-ends. . . .][26]

It seems to me that this is the underlying theme of *Les Séquestrés d'Altona*: the reason why all the characters play the games that they play is that they are victims of the serialization that is the subject-matter of much of *Critique de la Raison Dialectique*.

There are of course other valid, internal reasons for interpreting the character of Frantz in this manner. To understand Frantz's self-sequestration on the basis of his guilt is clearly erroneous, for he ceased to have any communication with his family long before he tortured Russian prisoners. As his father realizes, he rejected his family at the moment of the murder of the Polish rabbi, who had escaped from the concentration camp built on the Gerlach estate, and whom Frantz had hidden in his room.

Gerlach realized that even his influence was insufficient to save Frantz from the consequences of his action unless the rabbi "disappeared." But rescuing was not what Frantz wanted: he wanted to perform an action, an action which he could really say was his own, an expression of his conscience, and, precisely, his father negated this—his action was transmuted into a gesture, for it had no effect; no effect, that is to say, other than precipitating the death of the rabbi.[27]

The question must be asked: why does Frantz feel guilty about the murder and the torture? For while it may be "only human" to be disgusted at these incidents, for Sartre there must be a reason why it is human. Frantz is disgusted because he was powerless to do anything else. Undoubtedly he had a conscience, but, as Gerlach says, this was probably due to his youth; the dominant desire was for power: ["Four good Germans will crush me on the ground and my own men will bleed the prisoners white. No! I will never fall into abject impotence. I swear it. Horror is still chained up. . . . I'll take them quickly: if anyone is to unchain it, it will be me. I shall claim the evil, I shall manifest my power by the uniqueness of an unforgettable act . . ."].[28]

The explanation is still far from complete. Frantz suggests the suicide pact only after his father has convinced him that he was in fact powerless to do anything else at Smolensk but use torture, just as he was powerless in everything else, whereas during his thirteen years of self-sequestration he has done nothing but try to convince himself that the responsibility for the torture was his; for if he was responsible, he must have been free to choose this course of action. All the games he plays with himself are designed to heighten the reality of his self-accusation; to say "I am responsible for this atrocity" is insufficient, for the assertion can be questioned; the way to avoid the questioning is to assume a pre-rational attitude to the events: he hides from a guilt which he presupposes, and by concentrating on the "guilt-as-some-thing-to-be-hidden from" he tries to avoid considering the "guilt-as-something-questionable." The game of phenomenological hide-and-seek is designed to increase the reality of the guilt he is trying to feel, which he needs to feel, for the guilt is the "proof" of the responsibility. Of course, it is impossible to play tricks like this on oneself successfully; at best, Frantz only partly convinces himself. As Gerlach says: ["For fourteen years you have been possessed by a suffering which you caused and which you don't feel"].[29]

We are now in a position to appreciate the true nature of the games Frantz plays. Allowances made for minor variations, there are two of these games: the game of "sensiblerie" and the game of "témoignage." Of the two, "sensiblerie" is the uppermost layer of the crust with which Frantz covers his impotence. The game consists in pretending that he did not torture the prisoners at Smolensk, for humanitarian reasons, and that he was wrong to refrain, for the result of humanitarianism was the ruin of Germany. This is the explanation of the flash-back sequence in the ruined village in Act IV.[30]

The vision of Germany lying in ruins about him is the link with the game of "témoignage." Here Frantz imagines the world in a thousand years' time, inhabited only by crabs, and he spends his time composing funeral orations for his century, excusing his contemporaries for the evil they have done.[31] His plea is that the nature of the historical process is such that evil was the only possible result of human activity. In pleading mitigating circumstances for the evil he is implying his own guilt; and guilt posits freedom.

Thus Frantz too is forced into a position where he has no choice but to resolve the insurmountable contradictions inherent in his situation by suicide. The other members of his generation, of course, do not commit suicide, but they might just as well: Leni takes Frantz's place in the upstairs room, and Johanna and Werner are left to the ruins of their sham marriage. The play ends in total catastrophe. The final vision is a vision of the apocalypse.

The vision is also specifically tragic: the characters are driven, like Racinian heroes, by their own inability to compromise with their desires; were the perception of the impossibility of attaining their ends accompanied by the will to cease striving for them, the dénouement would be quite different. But this will is lacking, and the characters revel in their "impotence": they are the lucid and triumphant witnesses of their own failure, and the playing out of their chosen rôles is the source of a bitter and paradoxical satisfaction. Like the Red Queen, they run even faster in order to get nowhere, and the degree of their retreat into lucid impotence is a measure of how black the play is. In *Huis Clos*, for example, the characters are certainly unable, or unwilling, to break out of the circle of bad faith, but Garcin's despairing "L'Enfer, c'est les Autres" is by no means the moment when perception breaks through passion into a triumphant epiphany: relationships with other people constitute hell only in so far as we are unwilling to live authentically, and Garcin's cry is a judgment on him, not the *mathema* of Greek tragedy; Sartre clearly intends that we should not follow his example. Similarly, in *Les Mains Sales*, although Sartre's personal position no doubt predisposed him to a sympathetic presentation of Hugo, it is not his intention that we should regard his young hero as justified in his refusal of compromise: Sartre is no Anouilh, and in his suicide Hugo reveals his own inadequacy.

In *Huis Clos* we have the sense that the characters have done wrong, but that they could have done otherwise, and in *Les Mains Sales* the figures of Hoederer and Jessica represent a hope for the future, for the rejection of them is Hugo's, not Sartre's or ours. In *Les Séquestrés d'Altona*, on the other hand, hope seems to be dead; the world of the play is rotten to the core, for the characters' cult of failure paralyses the springs of action, and the social system which is responsible for the tragedy will continue, the Gerlach mansion will continue to be inhabited. The implication of *Les Séquestrés d'Altona* is clear: as long as we live under a capitalist system, this is what life will be like; but the play presents no alternative, and we are left with nothing. As in *Morts sans Sépulture*, the characters' efforts are foredoomed, for they are seeking the wrong goal, but whereas in the earlier play the sense of bitterness because the catastrophe could have been avoided predominates, in *Les Séquestrés d'Altona* the action is informed by a sense of tragedy: all was foreseen, inevitable.

In an interview some years ago with Kenneth Tynan, Sartre discussed the play which would follow *Les Séquestrés d'Altona*. It was to be based on the Alcestis myth and was to 'imply the whole story of female emancipation.'[32] In point of fact, the play which he wrote, or rather adapted, was a version of Euripides's *Trojan Women*,[33] and the theme is Western imperialism. In either case, the subject-matter is rather different from that of his preceding plays. One might have anticipated this from a reading of *Les Séquestrés d'Altona*: here Sartre seems to have given his most coherent, and perhaps final, expression to his analyses of human fallibility. One imagines that anything he writes in the future will be a radical departure.

Notes

1. *Les Séquestrés d'Altona*, p. 15. (The edition of *Les Séquestrés d'Altona* referred to throughout is the original: Paris, Gallimard [1960]).

2. Id., p. 58.

3. Id., p. 92.

4. Id., p. 93.

5. Cf. Claude Vigée, *L'Été Indien*, Paris, Gallimard (1957), pp. 131–43. Also: Serge Doubrovsky, *Corneille et la Dialectique du Héros*, Paris, Gallimard (1965), pp. 151-2.

6. Cf. Act I, Scs. I and 2.

7. *Les Séquestrés d'Altona*, p. 65.

8. *Saint Genet*, Paris, Gallimard (1952), p. 175.

9. *Les Séquestrés d'Altona*, pp. 156-7.

10. *Les Séquestrés d'Altona*, p. 29.

11. Cf. *L'Etre et le Néant*, Paris, Gallimard (1943), pp. 133-4.

12. *Les Séquestrés d'Altona*, p. 118.

13. Id., p. 38.

14. The extent to which Gerlach's advance strategy is all-embracing seems open to question: it is perfectly possible that Johanna's reaction to meeting Frantz, and the equilibrium they achieve, are contrary to his original intentions and that in Act III he is either improvising or acting according to a revised plan. Suffice it to say that ultimately all works out as if his original plan took into account all possible contingencies. Perhaps, as in the case of Iago, the question is best left to the discretion of the individual actor and producer.

15. *Les Séquestrés d'Altona*, p. 119.

16. Id., p. 135.

17. André Gorz, *Le Traître*, Paris, Éditions du Seuil (1958).

18. *Les Séquestrés d'Altona*, pp. 22–3.

19. *Critique de la Raison Dialectique*, Paris, Gallimard (1960). For a fuller discussion of the relavance of this text to *Les Séquestrés d'Altona* cf. A. R. Manser, *Sartre, A Philosophic Study* (London, Athlone Press, 1966), pp. 208–9 and 242–4.

20. P. 101, cf, p. 224 for further remarks on the subject.

21. *Les Séquestrés d'Altona*, p. 215.

22. Id., p. 202.

23. Id., p. 222.

24. *Critique de la Raison Dialectique*, pp. 206–8.

25. Cf. e.g. *Capital*, vol. I, pp. 71–83, and vol. III, pp. 381–90 and 803–6 (London, Lawrence and Wishart, 1961–2).

26. *Critique de la Raison Dialectique*, p. 241; cf. "De la 'praxis' individuelle au practico-inerte," passim.

27. Cf. *Les Séquestrés d'Altona*, pp. 50–5.

28. Id., p. 206.

29. Id., p. 212.

30. Id., pp. 172 ff.

31. Cf. especially the closing speech of the play.

32. *The Observer*, 25 June 1961, p. 20.

33. *Les Troyennes*, Paris, Gallimard, Coll. T.N.P. (1965).

Selected Bibliography of Books in English on Jean-Paul Sartre

Bibliographies

Contat, Michel and Rybalka, Michel, *The Writings of Jean-Paul Sartre*. Translated by Richard C. McCleary. Evanston, Ill.: Northwestern University Press, 1973, The indispensable work of reference on Sartre's writings and their reception. The English version (with revisions and important additions) is the translation of *Les Écrits de Sartre: chronologie, bibliographie commentée* (Paris: Gallimard, 1970).

Lapointe, François H., and Lapointe, Claire. *Jean-Paul Sartre and His Critics: An International Bibliography (1938–1980)*. 2d ed. Bowling Green, Ohio: Bowling Green University, 1981. An annotated edition that contains more entries than any other bibliography available in English. It should be used with caution, however, since it also contains more errors than any other standard bibliography.

Wilcocks, Robert. *Jean-Paul Sartre: A Bibliography of International Criticism*. Preface by Michel Contat and Michel Rybalka. Edmonton: University of Alberta Press, 1975. Much recent and contemporary Sartre scholarship is not represented in this work. It does, however, contain complete references from the Fonds Rondel collection of the Bibliothèque de l'Arsenal and frequent quotes from and comments on the Paris reception of all of Sartre's plays.

General

Barnes, Hazel E. *Sartre*. Philadelphia: J. B. Lippincott, 1973.

Manser, Anthony R. *Sartre: A Philosophic Study*. London: Athlone Press, 1966.

Murdoch, Iris. *Sartre, Romantic Rationalist*. New Haven: Yale University Press, 1953

Thody, Philip. *Jean-Paul Sartre: A Literary and Political Study*. New York: Macmillan, 1960.

On Philosophy, Psychology, and Politics

Aronson, Ronald. *Sartre's Second Critique*. Chicago: University of Chicago Press, 1987.

Catalano, Joseph S. *A Commentary on Jean-Paul Sartre's "Being and Nothingness."* Chicago: University Press, 1980.

– – – *A Commentary on Jean-Paul Sartre's "Critique of Dialectical Reason."* Chicago: University of Chicago Press, 1987.

Davies, Howard. *Sartre and "Les Temps Modernes."* Cambridge: Cambridge University Press, 1987.

Desan, Wilfrid. *The Tragic Finale: An Essay on the Philosophy of Jean-Paul Sartre.* Cambridge, Mass.: Harvard University Press, 1954. Reprint. New York: Harper Torchbooks, 1960.

— — —. *The Marxism of Jean-Paul Sartre.* Gloucester, Mass.: Peter Smith, 1974.

Fell, Joseph P. *Emotion in the Thought of Sartre.* New York: Columbia University Press, 1965.

Flynn, Thomas. *Sartre and Marxist Existentialism: The Test Case of Collective Responsibility.* Chicago: University of Chicago Press, 1984.

Goldthorpe, Rhiannon. *Sartre: Literature and Theory.* Cambridge: Cambridge University Press, 1984. Although on *La Nausée* and four of Sartre's plays, this book concentrates on aspects of and consequences of Sartre's philosophy.

On Criticism and Aesthetic Theories

Barnes, Hazel E. *Sartre and Flaubert.* Chicago: University of Chicago Press, 1981.

Champigny, Robert. *Stages on Sartre's Way.* Bloomington: Indiana University Press, 1959.

Collins, Douglas. *Sartre as Biographer.* (Cambridge (Mass.): Harvard University Press, 1980.

Jameson, Fredric. *Sartre: The Origins of a Style.* New Haven: Yale University Press, 1961.

LaCapra, Dominick. *A Preface to Sartre.* Ithaca: Cornell University Press, 1978.

Suhl, Benjamin. *Jean-Paul Sartre: The Philosopher as Literary Critic.* New York: Columbia University Press, 1970.

On Fiction

Bauer, George H. *Sartre and the Artist.* Chicago: University of Chicago Press, 1969. Includes an important study of all of Sartre's major essays in aesthetics.

On Theater

Goldthorpe, Rhiannon. *Sartre: Literature and Theory.* Cambridge: Cambridge University Press, 1984. Examines *Les Mouches, Huis clos, Les Mains sales,* and *Les Séquestrés d'Altona.*

McCall, Dorothy. *The Theater of Jean-Paul Sartre.* New York: Columbia University Press, 1969.

INDEX